White Rose Maths Edition

# Year 6C
## A Guide to Teaching for Mastery

Series Editor: Tony Staneff
Lead author: Josh Lury

# Contents

| | |
|---|---|
| Introduction to the author team | 4 |
| What is *Power Maths*? | 5 |
| What's different in the new edition? | 6 |
| Your *Power Maths* resources | 7 |
| The *Power Maths* teaching model | 10 |
| The *Power Maths* lesson sequence | 12 |
| Using the *Power Maths* Teacher Guide | 15 |
| *Power Maths* Year 6, yearly overview | 16 |
| Mindset: an introduction | 21 |
| The *Power Maths* characters | 22 |
| Mathematical language | 23 |
| The role of talk and discussion | 24 |
| Assessment strategies | 25 |
| Keeping the class together | 27 |
| Same-day intervention | 28 |
| The role of practice | 29 |
| Structures and representations | 30 |
| Variation helps visualisation | 31 |
| Practical aspects of *Power Maths* | 32 |
| Working with children below age-related expectation | 34 |
| Providing extra depth and challenge with *Power Maths* | 36 |
| Using *Power Maths* with mixed age classes | 38 |
| List of practical resources | 39 |
| Getting started with *Power Maths* | 41 |

## Unit 12 – Statistics — 42

| | |
|---|---|
| Interpret line graphs | 44 |
| Draw line graphs | 48 |
| Advanced bar charts | 52 |
| Understand and complete pie charts | 56 |
| Read and interpret pie charts | 60 |
| Pie charts and fractions (1) | 64 |
| Pie charts and fractions (2) | 68 |
| Pie charts and percentages | 72 |
| Introduction to the mean | 76 |
| Calculate the mean | 80 |
| Problem solving – mean | 84 |
| End of unit check | 88 |

## Unit 13 – Geometry – properties of shapes — 90

| | |
|---|---|
| Measure and classify angles | 92 |
| Vertically opposite angles | 96 |
| Angles in a triangle | 100 |
| Angles in a triangle – missing angles | 104 |
| Angles in a triangle – special cases | 108 |
| Angles in quadrilaterals | 112 |

| | |
|---|---|
| Angles in polygons | 116 |
| Circles | 120 |
| Parts of a circle | 124 |
| Draw shapes accurately | 128 |
| Nets of 3D shapes (1) | 132 |
| Nets of 3D shapes (2) | 136 |
| End of unit check | 140 |

## Unit 14 – Geometry – position and direction — 142

| | |
|---|---|
| The first quadrant | 144 |
| Read and plot points in four quadrants | 148 |
| Translations | 152 |
| Reflections | 156 |
| Solve problems with coordinates | 160 |
| End of unit check | 164 |

## Unit 15 – Problem solving — 166

| | |
|---|---|
| Problem solving – place value | 168 |
| Problem solving – negative numbers | 172 |
| Problem solving – addition and subtraction | 176 |
| Problem solving – four operations (1) | 180 |
| Problem solving – four operations (2) | 184 |
| Problem solving – fractions | 188 |
| Problem solving – decimals | 192 |
| Problem solving – percentages | 196 |
| Problem solving – ratio and proportion | 200 |
| Problem solving – time (1) | 204 |
| Problem solving – time (2) | 208 |
| Problem solving – position and direction | 212 |
| Problem solving – properties of shapes (1) | 216 |
| Problem solving – properties of shapes (2) | 220 |
| End of unit check | 224 |

# Introduction to the author team

*Power Maths* arises from the work of maths mastery experts who are committed to proving that, given the right mastery mindset and approach, **everyone can do maths**. Based on robust research and best practice from around the world, *Power Maths* was developed in partnership with a group of UK teachers to make sure that it not only meets our children's wide-ranging needs but also aligns with the National Curriculum in England.

## *Power Maths* – White Rose Maths edition

This edition of *Power Maths* has been developed and updated by:

### Tony Staneff, Series Editor and Author

Vice Principal at Trinity Academy, Halifax, Tony also leads a team of mastery experts who help schools across the UK to develop teaching for mastery via nationally recognised CPD courses, problem-solving and reasoning resources, schemes of work, assessment materials and other tools.

### Josh Lury, Lead Author

Josh is a specialist maths teacher, author and maths consultant with a passion for innovative and effective maths education.

The first edition of *Power Maths* was developed by a team of experienced authors, including:

- **Tony Staneff and Josh Lury**
- **Trinity Academy Halifax** (Michael Gosling CEO, Emily Fox, Kate Henshall, Rebecca Holland, Stephanie Kirk, Stephen Monaghan and Rachel Webster)
- **David Board, Belle Cottingham, Jonathan East, Tim Handley, Derek Huby, Neil Jarrett, Stephen Monaghan, Beth Smith, Tim Weal, Paul Wrangles** – skilled maths teachers and mastery experts
- **Cherri Moseley** – a maths author, former teacher and professional development provider
- **Professors Liu Jian and Zhang Dan**, Series Consultants and authors, and their team of mastery expert authors: **Wei Huinv, Huang Lihua, Zhu Dejiang, Zhu Yuhong, Hou Huiying, Yin Lili, Zhang Jing, Zhou Da and Liu Qimeng**

  Used by over 20 million children, Professor Liu Jian's textbook programme is one of the most popular in China. He and his author team are highly experienced in intelligent practice and in embedding key maths concepts using a C-P-A approach.

- **A group of 15 teachers and maths co-ordinators**

  We consulted our teacher group throughout the development of *Power Maths* to ensure we are meeting their real needs in the classroom.

# What is *Power Maths*?

Created especially for UK primary schools, and aligned with the new National Curriculum, *Power Maths* is a whole-class, textbook-based mastery resource that empowers every child to understand and succeed. *Power Maths* rejects the notion that some people simply 'can't do' maths. Instead, it develops growth mindsets and encourages hard work, practice and a willingness to see mistakes as learning tools.

Best practice consistently shows that mastery of small, cumulative steps builds a solid foundation of deep mathematical understanding. *Power Maths* combines interactive teaching tools, high-quality textbooks and continuing professional development (CPD) to help you equip children with a deep and long-lasting understanding. Based on extensive evidence, and developed in partnership with practising teachers, *Power Maths* ensures that it meets the needs of children in the UK.

## *Power Maths* and Mastery

*Power Maths* makes mastery practical and achievable by providing the structures, pathways, content, tools and support you need to make it happen in your classroom.

To develop mastery in maths, children must be enabled to acquire a deep understanding of maths concepts, structures and procedures, step by step. Complex mathematical concepts are built on simpler conceptual components and when children understand every step in the learning sequence, maths becomes transparent and makes logical sense. Interactive lessons establish deep understanding in small steps, as well as effortless fluency in key facts such as tables and number bonds. The whole class works on the same content and no child is left behind.

## *Power Maths*

- ⚡ Builds every concept in small, progressive steps
- ⚡ Is built with interactive, whole-class teaching in mind
- ⚡ Provides the tools you need to develop growth mindsets
- ⚡ Helps you check understanding and ensure that every child is keeping up
- ⚡ Establishes core elements such as intelligent practice and reflection

## The *Power Maths* approach

**Everyone can!**
Founded on the conviction that every child can achieve, *Power Maths* enables children to build number fluency, confidence and understanding, step by step.

**Child-centred learning**
Children master concepts one step at a time in lessons that embrace a concrete-pictorial-abstract (C-P-A) approach, avoid overload, build on prior learning and help them see patterns and connections. Same-day intervention ensures sustained progress.

**Continuing professional development**
Embedded teacher support and development offer every teacher the opportunity to continually improve their subject knowledge and manage whole-class teaching for mastery.

**Whole-class teaching**
An interactive, whole-class teaching model encourages thinking and precise mathematical language and allows children to deepen their understanding as far as they can.

# What's different in the new edition?

If you have previously used the first editions of *Power Maths*, you might be interested to know how this edition is different. All of the improvements described below are based on feedback from *Power Maths* customers.

## Changes to units and the progression

- The order of units has been slightly adjusted, creating closer alignment between adjacent year groups, which will be useful for mixed age teaching.

- The flow of lessons has been improved within units to optimise the pace of the progression and build in more recap where needed. For key topics, the sequence of lessons gives more opportunities to build up a solid base of understanding. Other units have fewer lessons than before, where appropriate, making it possible to fit in all the content.

- Overall, the lessons put more focus on the most essential content for that year, with less time given to non-statutory content.

- The progression of lessons matches the steps in the new White Rose Maths schemes of learning.

## Lesson resources

- There is a Quick recap for each lesson in the Teacher Guide, which offers an alternative lesson starter to the Power Up for cases where you feel it would be more beneficial to surface prerequisite learning than general number fluency.

- In the **Discover** and **Share** sections there is now more of a progression from 1 a) to 1 b). Whereas before, 1 b) was mainly designed as a separate question, now 1 a) leads directly into 1 b). This means that there is an improved whole-class flow, and also an opportunity to focus on the logic and skills in more detail. As a teacher, you will be using 1 a) to lead the class into the thinking, then 1 b) to mould that thinking into the core new learning of the lesson.

- In the **Share** section, for KS1 in particular, the number of different models and representations has been reduced, to support the clarity of thinking prompted by the flow from 1 a) into 1 b).

- More fluency questions have been built into the guided and independent practice.

- Pupil pages are as easy as possible for children to access independently. The pages are less full to provide greater focus on key ideas and instructions. Also, more freedom is offered around answer format, with fewer boxes scaffolding children's responses; squared paper backgrounds are used in the Practice Books where appropriate. Artwork has also been revisited to ensure the highest standards of accessibility.

## New components

480 Individual Practice Games are available in *ActiveLearn* for practising key facts and skills in Years 1 to 6. These are designed in an arcade style, to feel like fun games that children would choose to play outside school. They can be accessed via the Pupil World for homework or additional practice in school – and children can earn rewards. There are Support, Core and Extend levels to allocate, with Activity Reporting available for the teacher. There is a Quick Guide on *ActiveLearn* and you can use the Help area for support in setting up child accounts.

There is also a new set of lesson video resources on the Professional Development tile, designed for in-school training in 10- to 20-minute bursts. For each part of the *Power Maths* lesson sequence, there is a slide deck with embedded video, which will facilitate discussions about how you can take your *Power Maths* teaching to the next level.

# Your *Power Maths* resources

**Pupil Textbooks**

**Discover**, **Share** and **Think together** sections promote discussion and introduce mathematical ideas logically, so that children understand more easily.

Using a Concrete-Pictorial-Abstract approach, clear mathematical models help children to make connections and grasp concepts.

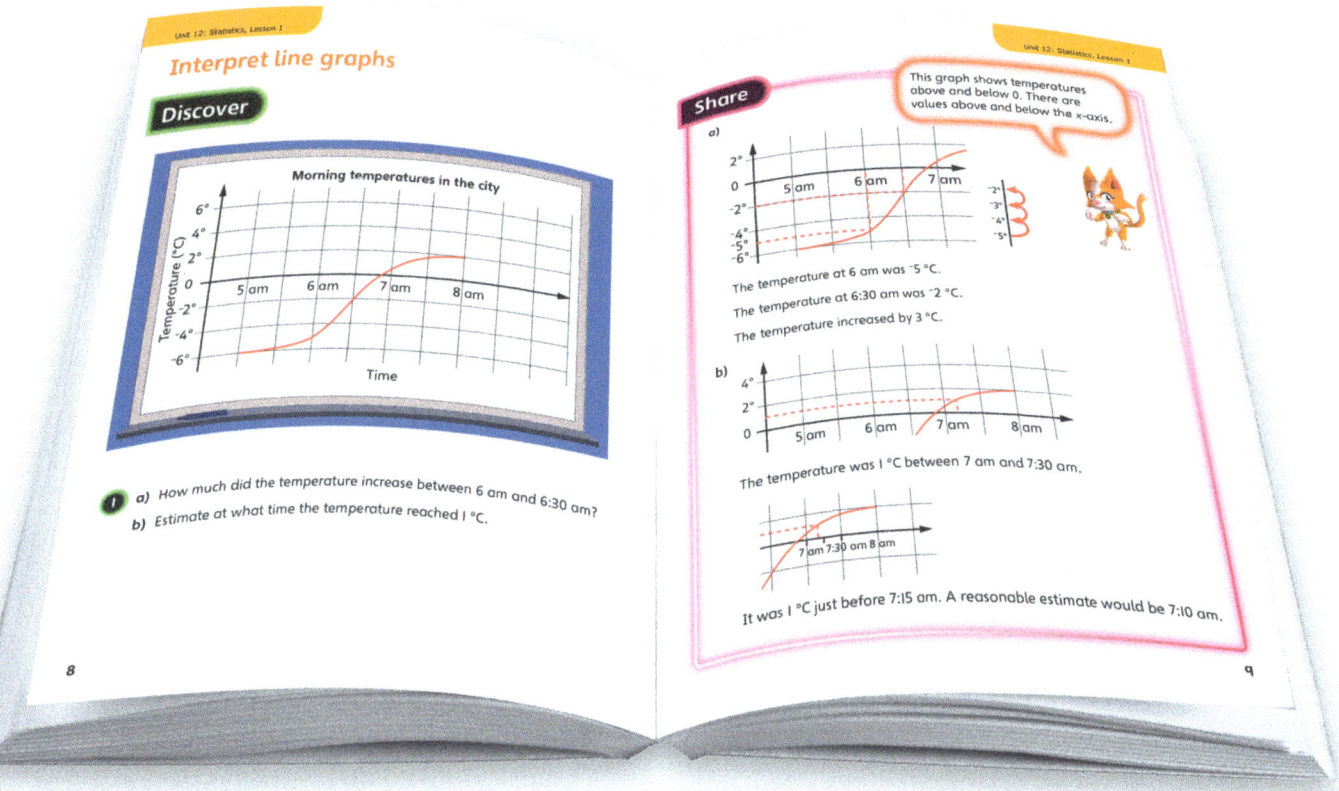

Appealing scenarios stimulate curiosity, helping children to identify the maths problem and discover patterns and relationships for themselves.

Friendly, supportive characters help children develop a growth mindset by prompting them to think, reason and reflect.

To help you teach for mastery, *Power Maths* comprises a variety of high-quality resources.

The coherent *Power Maths* lesson structure carries through into the vibrant, high-quality textbooks. Setting out the core learning objectives for each class, the lesson structure follows a carefully mapped journey through the curriculum and supports children on their journey to deeper understanding.

# Pupil Practice Books

The Practice Books offer just the right amount of intelligent practice for children to complete independently in the final section of each lesson.

Practice questions are finely tuned to move children forward in their thinking and to reveal misconceptions.

The practice questions are for everyone – each question varies one small element to move children on in their thinking.

Calculations are connected so that children think about the underlying concept.

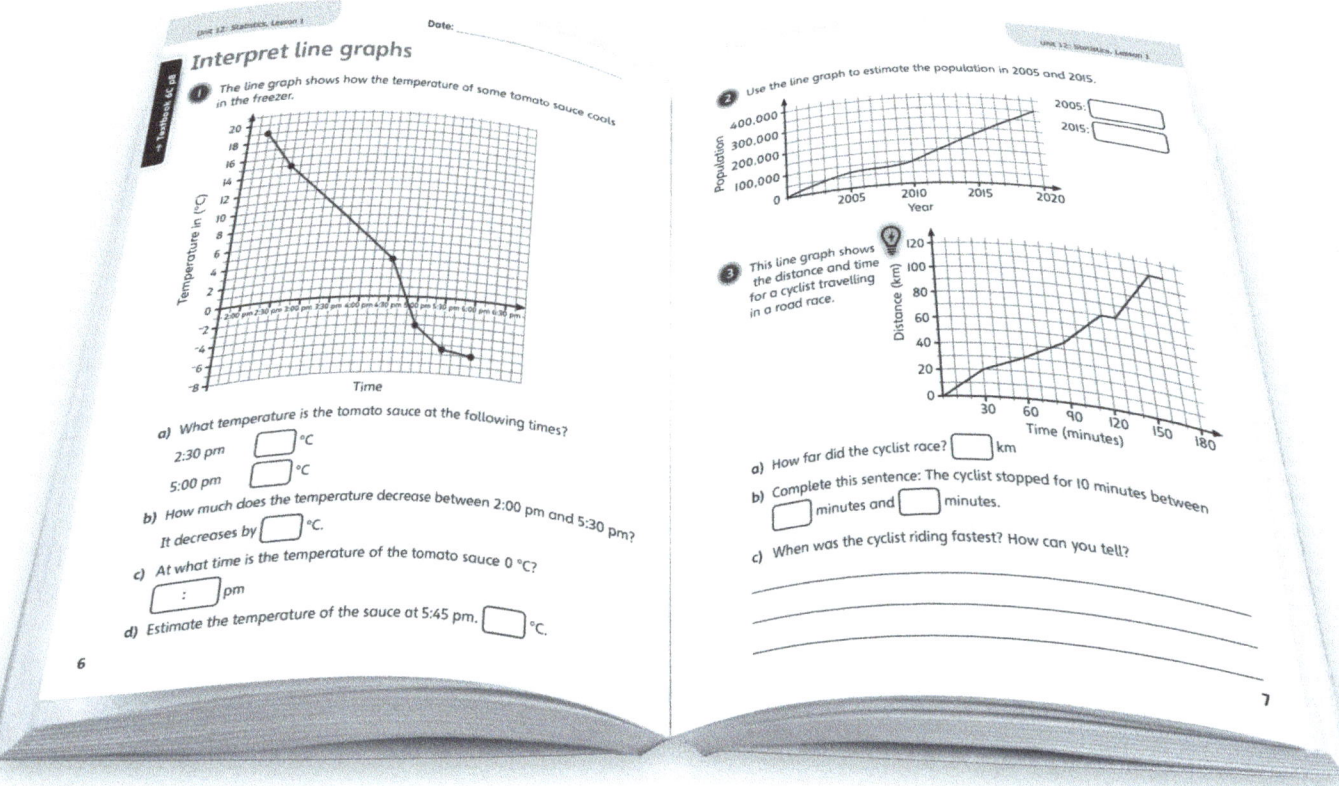

**Challenge** questions allow children to delve deeper into a concept.

**Think differently** questions encourage children to use reasoning as well as their mathematical knowledge to reach a solution.

**Reflect** questions reveal the depth of each child's understanding before they move on.

## Online subscription

The online subscription will give you access to additional resources and answers from the Textbook and Practice Book.

### eTextbooks

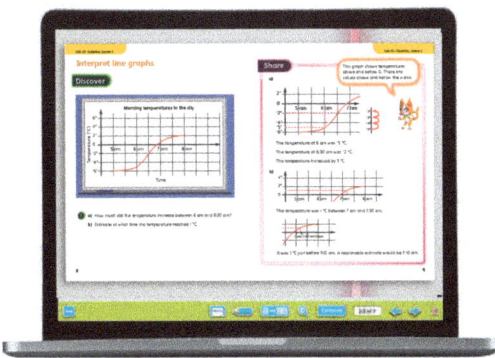

Digital versions of *Power Maths* Textbooks allow class groups to share and discuss questions, solutions and strategies. They allow you to project key structures and representations at the front of the class, to ensure all children are focusing on the same concept.

### Teaching tools

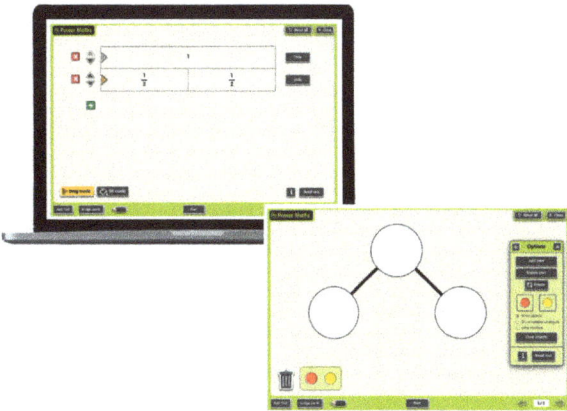

Here you will find interactive versions of key *Power Maths* structures and representations.

### Power Ups

Use this series of daily activities to promote and check number fluency.

### Online versions of Teacher Guide pages

PDF pages give support at both unit and lesson levels. You will also find help with key strategies and templates for tracking progress.

### Unit videos

Watch the professional development videos at the start of each unit to help you teach with confidence. The videos explore common misconceptions in the unit, and include intervention suggestions as well as suggestions on what to look out for when assessing mastery in your students.

### End of unit Strengthen and Deepen materials

The Strengthen activity at the end of every unit addresses a key misconception and can be used to support children who need it. The Deepen activities are designed to be low ceiling/high threshold and will challenge those children who can understand more deeply. These resources will help you ensure that every child understands and will help you keep the class moving forward together. These printable activities provide an optional resource bank for use after the assessment stage.

### Individual Practice Games

These enjoyable games can be used at home or at school to embed key number skills (see page 6).

### Professional Development videos and slides

These slides and videos of *Power Maths* lessons can be used for ongoing training in short bursts or to support new staff.

# The *Power Maths* teaching model

At the heart of *Power Maths* is a clearly structured teaching and learning process that helps you make certain that every child masters each maths concept securely and deeply. For each year group, the curriculum is broken down into core concepts, taught in units. A unit divides into smaller learning steps – lessons. Step by step, strong foundations of cumulative knowledge and understanding are built.

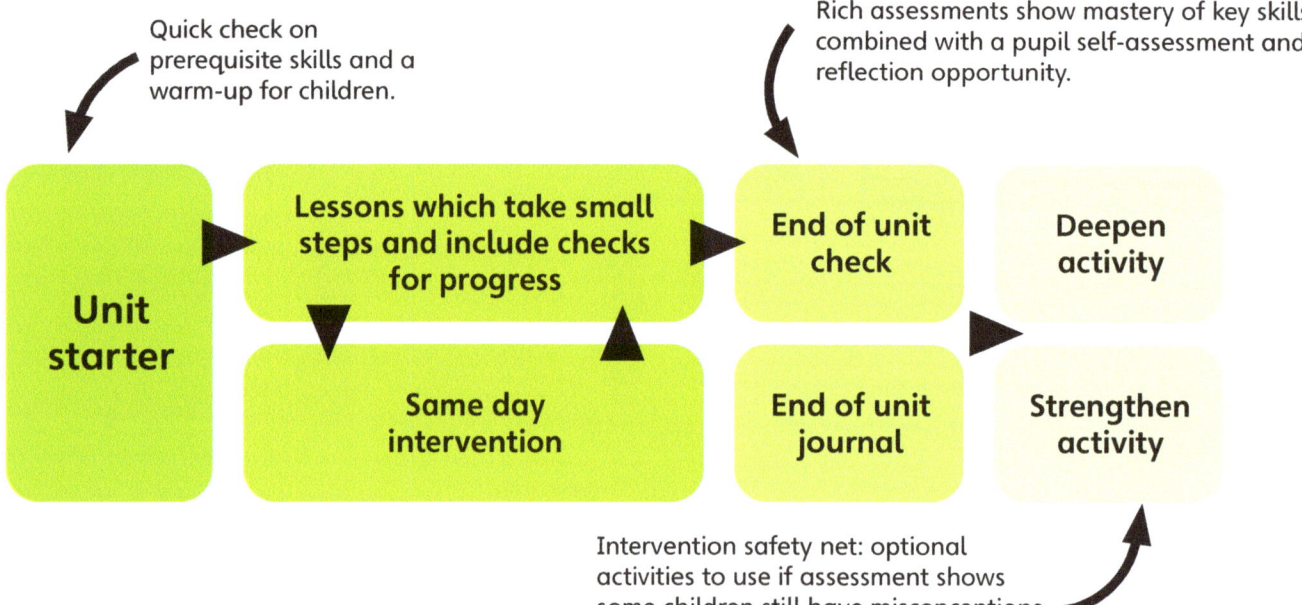

## Unit starter

Each unit begins with a unit starter, which introduces the learning context along with key mathematical vocabulary and structures and representations.

- The Textbooks include a check on readiness and a warm-up task for children to complete.
- Your Teacher Guide gives support right from the start on important structures and representations, mathematical language, common misconceptions and intervention strategies.
- Unit-specific videos develop your subject knowledge and insights so you feel confident and fully equipped to teach each new unit. These are available via the online subscription.

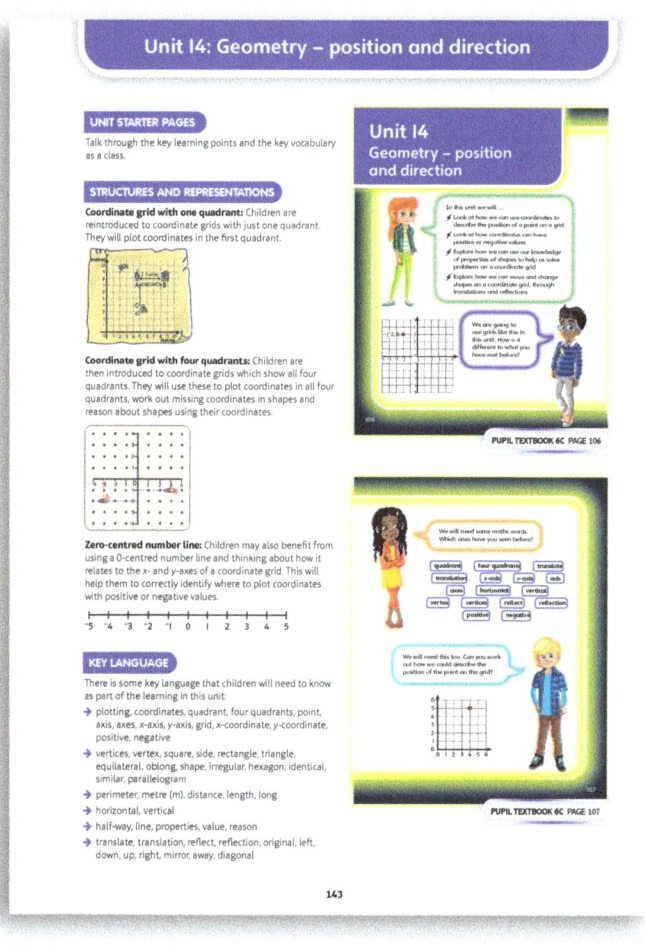

## Lesson

Once a unit has been introduced, it is time to start teaching the series of lessons.

- Each lesson is scaffolded with Textbook and Practice Book activities and begins with a Power Up activity (available via online subscription) or the Quick recap activity in the Teacher Guide (see page 15).
- *Power Maths* identifies lesson by lesson what concepts are to be taught.
- Your Teacher Guide offers lots of support for you to get the most from every child in every lesson. As well as highlighting key points, tricky areas and how to handle them, you will also find question prompts to check on understanding and clarification on why particular activities and questions are used.

## Same-day intervention

Same-day interventions are vital in order to keep the class progressing together. This can be during the lesson as well as afterwards (see page 28). Therefore, *Power Maths* provides plenty of support throughout the journey.

- Intervention is focused on keeping up now, not catching up later, so interventions should happen as soon as they are needed.
- Practice section questions are designed to bring misconceptions to the surface, allowing you to identify these easily as you circulate during independent practice time.
- Child-friendly assessment questions in the Teacher Guide help you identify easily which children need to strengthen their understanding.

## End of unit check and journal

For each unit, the End of unit check in the Textbook lets you see which children have mastered the key concepts, which children have not and where their misconceptions lie. The Practice Books also include an End of unit journal in which children can reflect on what they have learned. Each unit also offers Strengthen and Deepen activities, available via the online subscription.

> The Teacher Guide offers different ways of managing the End of unit assessments as well as giving support with handling misconceptions.

> The End of unit check presents multiple-choice questions. Children think about their answer, decide on a solution and explain their choice.

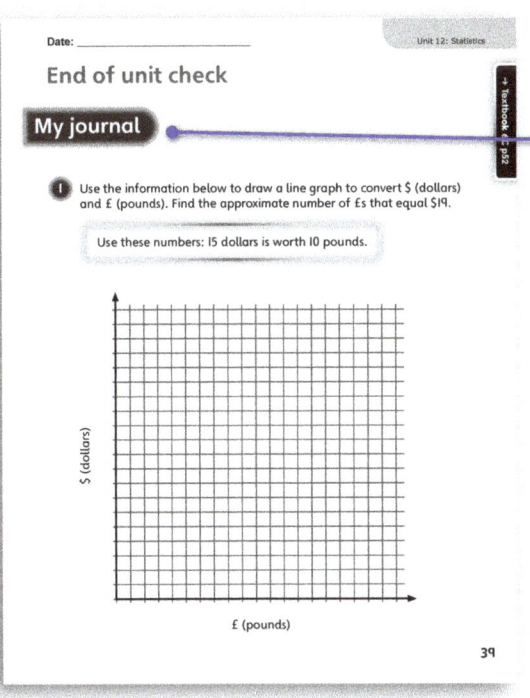

> The End of unit journal is an opportunity for children to test out their learning and reflect on how they feel about it. Tackling the 'journal' problem reveals whether a child understands the concept deeply enough to move on to the next unit.

> In KS2, the End of unit assessment will also include at least one SATs-style question.

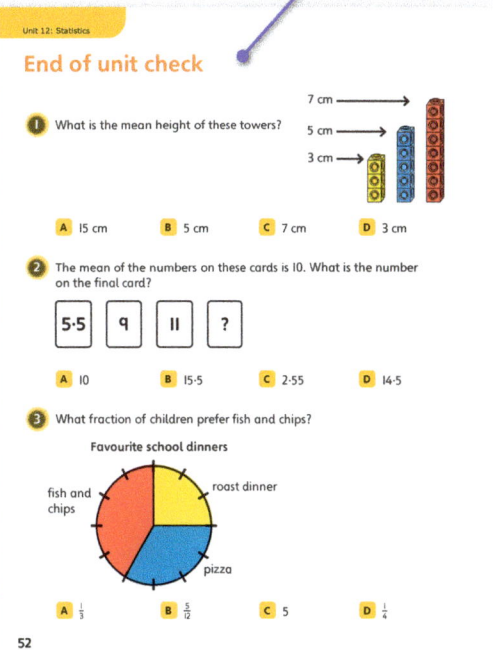

# The *Power Maths* lesson sequence

At the heart of *Power Maths* is a unique lesson sequence designed to empower children to understand core concepts and grow in confidence. Embracing the National Centre for Excellence in the Teaching of Mathematics' (NCETM's) definition of mastery, the sequence guides and shapes every *Power Maths* lesson you teach.

Flexibility is built into the *Power Maths* programme so there is no one-to-one mapping of lessons and concepts and you can pace your teaching according to your class. While some children will need to spend longer on a particular concept (through interventions or additional lessons), others will reach deeper levels of understanding. However, it is important that the class moves forward together through the termly schedules.

## Power Up  5 minutes

- Each lesson begins with a Power Up activity (available via the online subscription) which supports fluency in key number facts.

- The whole-class approach depends on fluency, so the Power Up is a powerful and essential activity.

- The Quick recap is an alternative starter, for when you think some or all children would benefit more from revisiting pre-requisite work (see page 15).

**TOP TIP**
If the class is struggling with the task, revisit it later and check understanding.

- Power Ups reinforce the two key things that are essential for success: times-tables and number bonds.

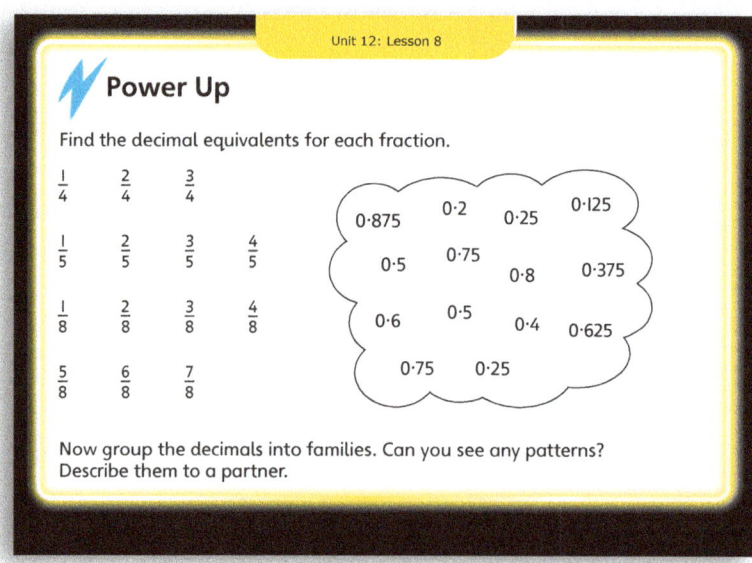

## Discover  10 minutes

- A practical, real-life problem arouses curiosity. Children find the maths through story telling.

- A real-life scenario is provided for the **Discover** section but feel free to build upon these with your own examples that are more relevant to your class, or get creative with the context.

**TOP TIP**
**Discover** works best when run at tables, in pairs with concrete objects.

- Question  a) tackles the key concept and question  b) digs a little deeper. Children have time to explore, play and discuss possible strategies.

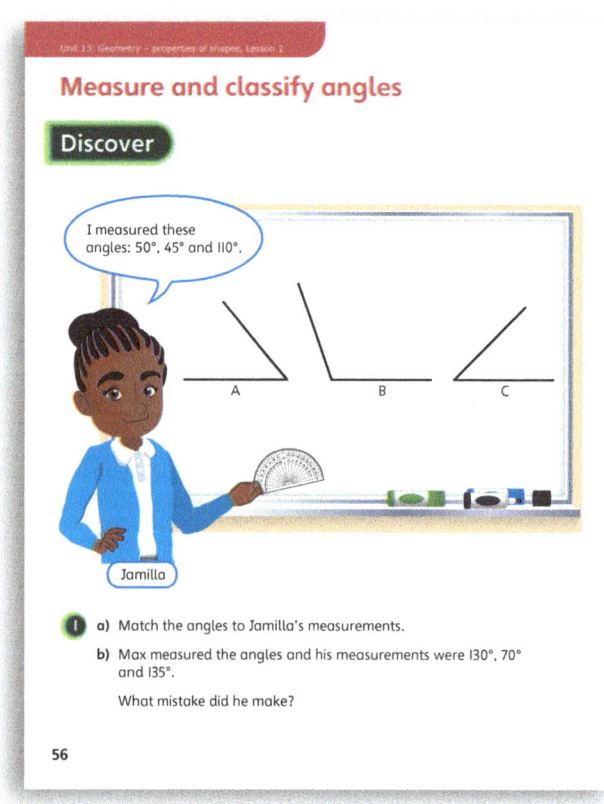

## Share  ⏱ 10 minutes

Teacher-led, this interactive section follows the **Discover** activity and highlights the variety of methods that can be used to solve a single problem.

**TOP TIP**
Pairs sharing a textbook is a great format for **Share**!

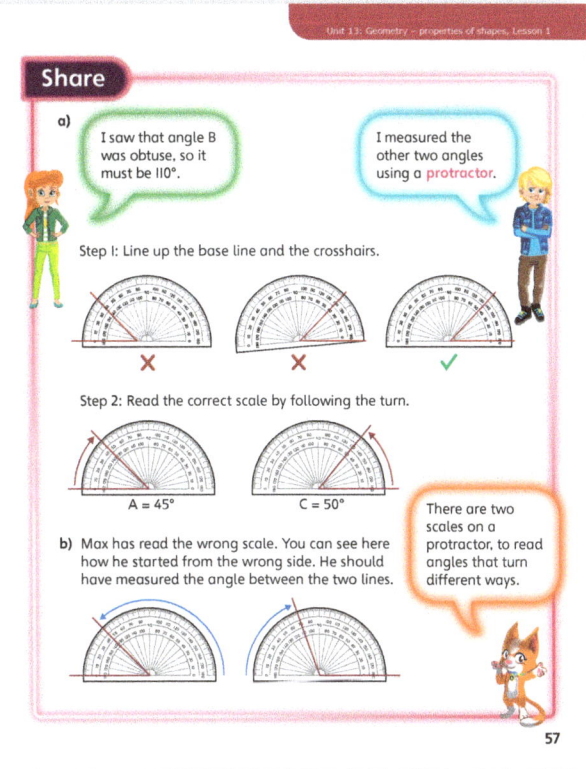

Your Teacher Guide gives target questions for children. The online toolkit provides interactive structures and representations to link concrete and pictorial to abstract concepts.

Bring children to the front to share and celebrate their solutions and strategies.

## Think together

⏱ 10 minutes

Children work in groups on the carpet or at tables, using their textbooks or eBooks.

**TOP TIP**
Make sure children have mini whiteboards or pads to write on if they are not at their tables.

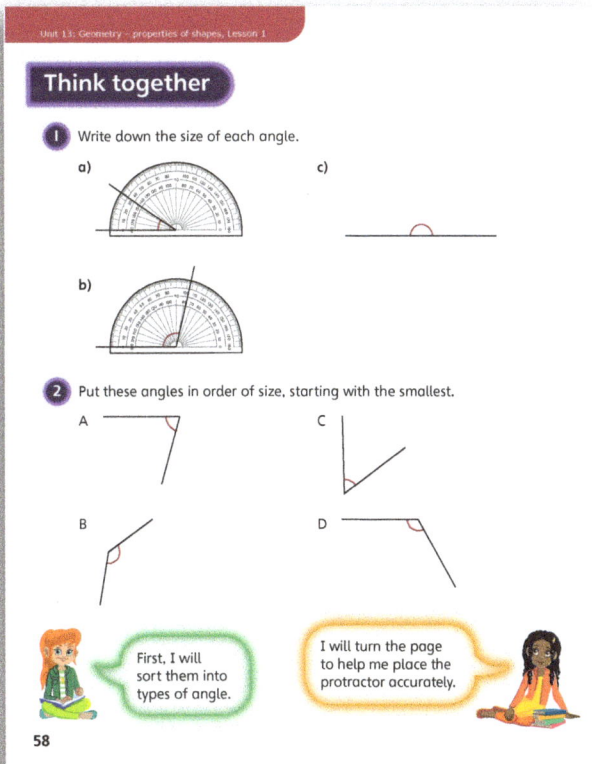

Using the Teacher Guide, model question ❶ for your class.

Question ❷ is less structured. Children will need to think together in their groups, then discuss their methods and solutions as a class.

In question ❸ children try working out the answer independently. The openness of the **Challenge** question helps to check depth of understanding.

# Practice ⏱ 15 minutes

Using their Practice Books, children work independently while you circulate and check on progress.

Questions follow small steps of progression to deepen learning.

**TOP TIP**
Some children could work separately with a teacher or assistant.

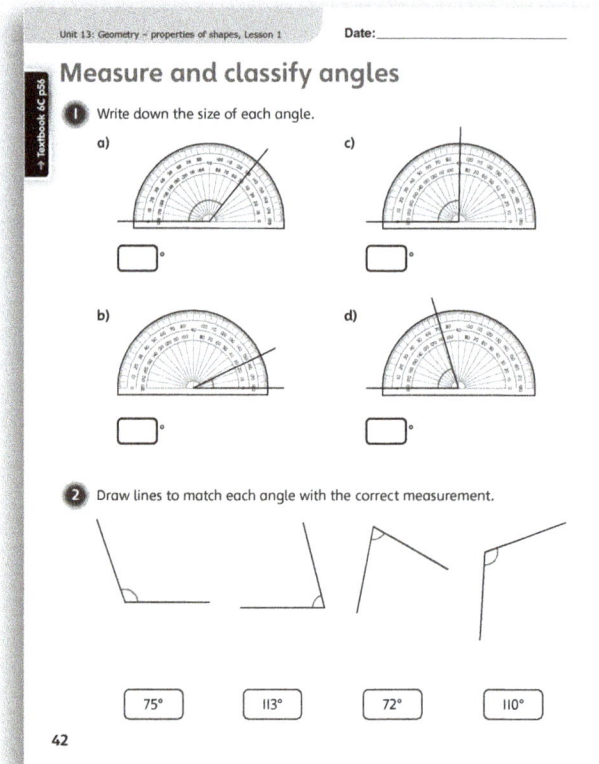

Are some children struggling? If so, work with them as a group, using mathematical structures and representations to support understanding as necessary.

There are no set routines: for real understanding, children need to think about the problem in different ways.

# Reflect ⏱ 5 minutes

'Spot the mistake' questions are great for checking misconceptions.

The **Reflect** section is your opportunity to check how deeply children understand the target concept.

The Practice Books use various approaches to check that children have fully understood each concept.

Looking like they understand is not enough! It is essential that children can show they have grasped the concept.

# Using the *Power Maths* Teacher Guide

Think of your Teacher Guides as *Power Maths* handbooks that will guide, support and inspire your day-to-day teaching. Clear and concise, and illustrated with helpful examples, your Teacher Guides will help you make the best possible use of every individual lesson. They also provide wrap-around professional development, enhancing your own subject knowledge and helping you to grow in confidence about moving your children forward together.

There is a Teacher Guide per year group for every term, with unit and lesson level guidance and support.

Never feel stuck! You will find ideas for introducing every unit and lesson and questions to encourage teacher reflection before and after each lesson.

Tips and advice on key elements such as C-P-A approaches, misconceptions, language, modelling growth mindsets and same day intervention.

Annotations for every Textbook and Practice Book page, providing prompts for key questions to ask to expose understanding and explanations as to why key questions have been chosen.

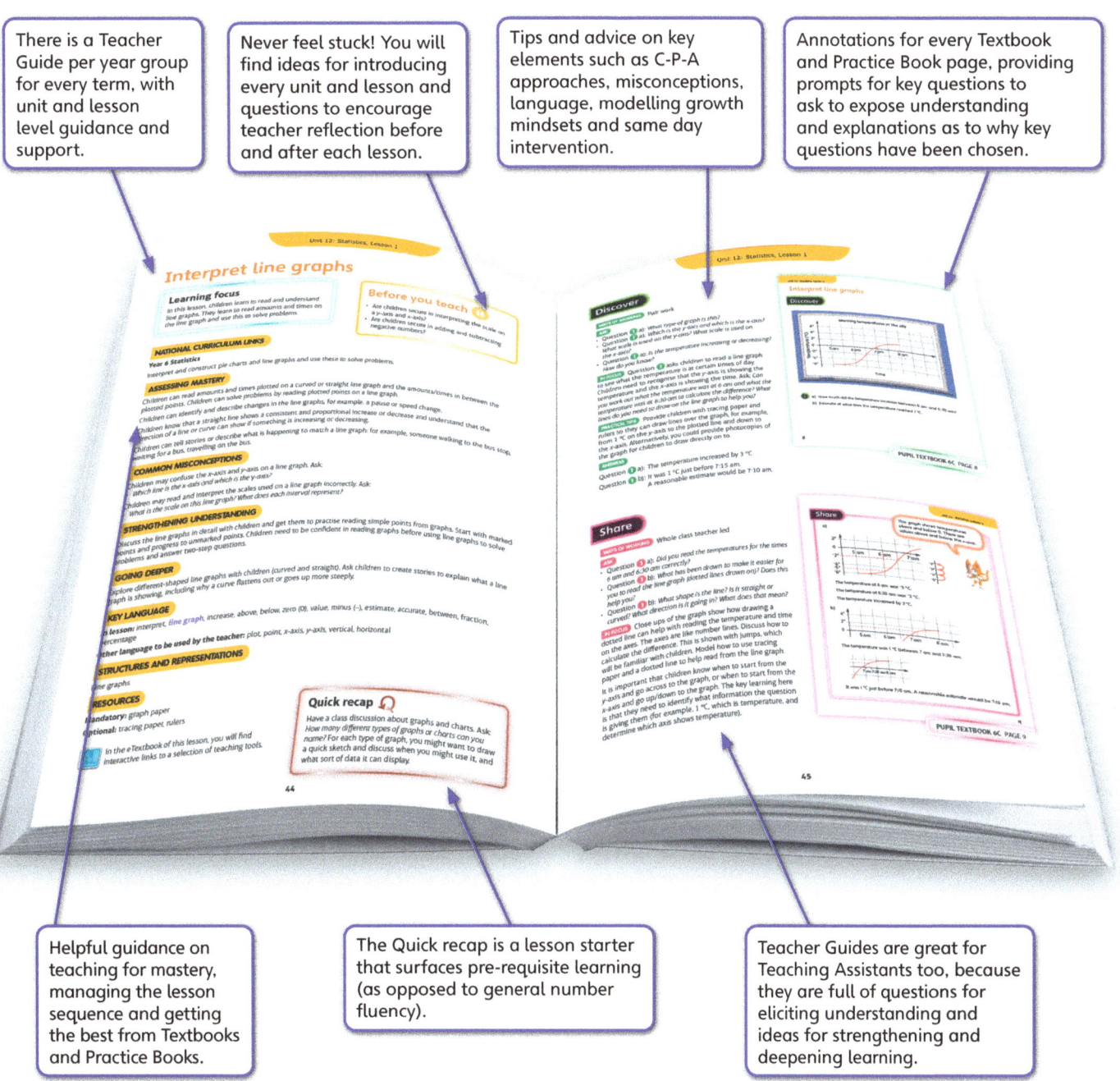

Helpful guidance on teaching for mastery, managing the lesson sequence and getting the best from Textbooks and Practice Books.

The Quick recap is a lesson starter that surfaces pre-requisite learning (as opposed to general number fluency).

Teacher Guides are great for Teaching Assistants too, because they are full of questions for eliciting understanding and ideas for strengthening and deepening learning.

At the end of each unit, your Teacher Guide helps you identify who has fully grasped the concept, who has not and how to move every child forward. This is covered later in the Assessment strategies section.

# Power Maths Year 6, yearly overview

| Textbook | Strand | Unit | | Number of lessons |
|---|---|---|---|---|
| Textbook A / Practice Workbook A (Term 1) | Number – number and place value | 1 | Place value within 10,000,000 | 8 |
| | Number – addition, subtraction, multiplication and division | 2 | Four operations (1) | 8 |
| | Number – addition, subtraction, multiplication and division | 3 | Four operations (2) | 12 |
| | Number - fractions | 4 | Fractions (1) | 9 |
| | Number - fractions | 5 | Fractions (2) | 9 |
| | Measurement | 6 | Measure – imperial and metric measures | 5 |
| Textbook B / Practice Workbook B (Term 2) | Ratio and proportion | 7 | Ratio and proportion | 9 |
| | Algebra | 8 | Algebra | 11 |
| | Number - fractions (including decimals and percentages) | 9 | Decimals | 9 |
| | Number - fractions (including decimals and percentages) | 10 | Percentages | 8 |
| | Measurement | 11 | Measure – perimeter, area and volume | 11 |
| Textbook C / Practice Workbook C (Term 3) | Statistics | 12 | Statistics | 11 |
| | Geometry – properties of shapes | 13 | Geometry – properties of shapes | 12 |
| | Geometry – position and direction | 14 | Geometry – position and direction | 5 |
| | Number – addition, subtraction, multiplication and division | 15 | Problem solving | 14 |

# Power Maths Year 6, Textbook 6C (Term 3) overview

| Strand | Unit | Unit title | Lesson number | Lesson title | NC Objective 1 | NC Objective 2 |
|---|---|---|---|---|---|---|
| Statistics | 12 | Statistics | 1 | Interpret line graphs | Interpret and construct pie charts and line graphs and use these to solve problems | |
| Statistics | 12 | Statistics | 2 | Draw line graphs | Interpret and construct pie charts and line graphs and use these to solve problems | |
| Statistics | 12 | Statistics | 3 | Advanced bar charts | Solve addition and subtraction multi-step problems in contexts, deciding which operations and methods to use and why | Use estimation to check answers to calculations and determine, in the context of a problem, an appropriate degree of accuracy. |
| Statistics | 12 | Statistics | 4 | Understand and complete pie charts | Interpret and construct pie charts and line graphs and use these to solve problems | |
| Statistics | 12 | Statistics | 5 | Read and interpret pie charts | Interpret and construct pie charts and line graphs and use these to solve problems | |
| Statistics | 12 | Statistics | 6 | Pie charts and fractions (1) | Interpret and construct pie charts and line graphs and use these to solve problems | |
| Statistics | 12 | Statistics | 7 | Pie charts and fractions (2) | Interpret and construct pie charts and line graphs and use these to solve problems | |
| Statistics | 12 | Statistics | 8 | Pie charts and percentages | Interpret and construct pie charts and line graphs and use these to solve problems | Pupils connect their work on angles, fractions and percentages to the interpretation of pie charts [non-stat] |
| Statistics | 12 | Statistics | 9 | Introduction to the mean | Calculate and interpret the mean as an average | |
| Statistics | 12 | Statistics | 10 | Calculate the mean | Calculate and interpret the mean as an average | |
| Statistics | 12 | Statistics | 11 | Problem solving – mean | Calculate and interpret the mean as an average | |
| Geometry – properties of shapes | 13 | Geometry – properties of shapes | 1 | Measure and classify angles | Recognise angles where they meet at a point, are on a straight line, or are vertically opposite, and find missing angles | |
| Geometry – properties of shapes | 13 | Geometry – properties of shapes | 2 | Vertically opposite angles | Recognise angles where they meet at a point, are on a straight line, or are vertically opposite, and find missing angles | |
| Geometry – properties of shapes | 13 | Geometry – properties of shapes | 3 | Angles in a triangle | Compare and classify geometric shapes based on their properties and sizes and find unknown angles in any triangles, quadrilaterals, and regular polygons | Draw 2D shapes using given dimensions and angles |

| Strand | Unit | Unit title | Lesson number | Lesson title | NC Objective 1 | NC Objective 2 |
|---|---|---|---|---|---|---|
| Geometry – properties of shapes | 13 | Geometry – properties of shapes | 4 | Angles in a triangle – missing angles | Compare and classify geometric shapes based on their properties and sizes and find unknown angles in any triangles, quadrilaterals, and regular polygons | |
| Geometry – properties of shapes | 13 | Geometry – properties of shapes | 5 | Angles in a triangle – special cases | Compare and classify geometric shapes based on their properties and sizes and find unknown angles in any triangles, quadrilaterals, and regular polygons | |
| Geometry – properties of shapes | 13 | Geometry – properties of shapes | 6 | Angles in quadrilaterals | Compare and classify geometric shapes based on their properties and sizes and find unknown angles in any triangles, quadrilaterals, and regular polygons | |
| Geometry – properties of shapes | 13 | Geometry – properties of shapes | 7 | Angles in polygons | Compare and classify geometric shapes based on their properties and sizes and find unknown angles in any triangles, quadrilaterals, and regular polygons | |
| Geometry – properties of shapes | 13 | Geometry – properties of shapes | 8 | Circles | Illustrate and name parts of circles, including radius, diameter and circumference and know that the diameter is twice the radius | |
| Geometry – properties of shapes | 13 | Geometry – properties of shapes | 9 | Parts of a circle | Illustrate and name parts of circles, including radius, diameter and circumference and know that the diameter is twice the radius | |
| Geometry – properties of shapes | 13 | Geometry – properties of shapes | 10 | Draw shapes accurately | Draw 2D shapes using given dimensions and angles | |
| Geometry – properties of shapes | 13 | Geometry – properties of shapes | 11 | Nets of 3D shapes (1) | Recognise, describe and build simple 3D shapes, including making nets | |
| Geometry – properties of shapes | 13 | Geometry – properties of shapes | 12 | Nets of 3D shapes (2) | Recognise, describe and build simple 3D shapes, including making nets | |
| Geometry – position and direction | 14 | Geometry – position and direction | 1 | The first quadrant | Describe positions on the full coordinate grid (all four quadrants) | |
| Geometry – position and direction | 14 | Geometry – position and direction | 2 | Read and plot points in four quadrants | Describe positions on the full coordinate grid (all four quadrants) | |
| Geometry – position and direction | 14 | Geometry – position and direction | 3 | Translations | Draw and translate simple shapes on the coordinate plane, and reflect them in the axes | |
| Geometry – position and direction | 14 | Geometry – position and direction | 4 | Reflections | Draw and translate simple shapes on the coordinate plane, and reflect them in the axes | |

| Strand | Unit | Unit title | Lesson number | Lesson title | NC Objective 1 | NC Objective 2 |
|---|---|---|---|---|---|---|
| Geometry – position and direction | 14 | Geometry – position and direction | 5 | Solve problems with coordinates | Describe positions on the full coordinate grid (all four quadrants) | Draw and translate simple shapes on the coordinate plane, and reflect them in the axes |
| Number – addition, subtraction, multiplication and division | 15 | Problem solving | 1 | Problem solving – place value | Solve number and practical problems that involve all of the above | |
| Number – addition, subtraction, multiplication and division | 15 | Problem solving | 2 | Problem solving – negative numbers | Solve number and practical problems that involve all of the above | |
| Number – addition, subtraction, multiplication and division | 15 | Problem solving | 3 | Problem solving – addition and subtraction | Use estimation to check answers to calculations and determine, in the context of a problem, an appropriate degree of accuracy | Solve addition and subtraction multi-step problems in contexts, deciding which operations and methods to use and why |
| Number – addition, subtraction, multiplication and division | 15 | Problem solving | 4 | Problem solving – four operations (1) | Solve problems involving addition, subtraction, multiplication and division | Use their knowledge of the order of operations to carry out calculations involving the four operations |
| Number – addition, subtraction, multiplication and division | 15 | Problem solving | 5 | Problem solving – four operations (2) | Solve problems involving addition, subtraction, multiplication and division | |
| Number – addition, subtraction, multiplication and division | 15 | Problem solving | 6 | Problem solving – fractions | Recall and use equivalences between simple fractions, decimals and percentages, including in different contexts | |
| Number – addition, subtraction, multiplication and division | 15 | Problem solving | 7 | Problem solving – decimals | Recall and use equivalences between simple fractions, decimals and percentages, including in different contexts | |
| Number – addition, subtraction, multiplication and division | 15 | Problem solving | 8 | Problem solving – percentages | Recall and use equivalences between simple fractions, decimals and percentages, including in different contexts | |
| Number – addition, subtraction, multiplication and division | 15 | Problem solving | 9 | Problem solving – ratio and proportion | Solve problems involving unequal sharing and grouping using knowledge of fractions and multiples | Solve problems involving the relative sizes of two quantities where missing values can be found by using integer multiplication and division facts |
| Number – addition, subtraction, multiplication and division | 15 | Problem solving | 10 | Problem solving – time (1) | Use, read, write and convert between standard units, converting measurements of length, mass, volume and time from a smaller unit of measure to a larger unit, and vice versa, using decimal notation to up to three decimal places | |

| Strand | Unit | Unit title | Lesson number | Lesson title | NC Objective 1 | NC Objective 2 |
|---|---|---|---|---|---|---|
| Number – addition, subtraction, multiplication and division | 15 | Problem solving | 11 | Problem solving – time (2) | Use, read, write and convert between standard units, converting measurements of length, mass, volume and time from a smaller unit of measure to a larger unit, and vice versa, using decimal notation to up to three decimal places | |
| Number – addition, subtraction, multiplication and division | 15 | Problem solving | 12 | Problem solving – position and direction | Describe positions on the full coordinate grid (all four quadrants) | |
| Number – addition, subtraction, multiplication and division | 15 | Problem solving | 13 | Problem solving – properties of shapes (1) | Recognise angles where they meet at a point, are on a straight line, or are vertically opposite, and find missing angles | Compare and classify geometric shapes based on their properties and sizes and find unknown angles in any triangles, quadrilaterals, and regular polygons |
| Number – addition, subtraction, multiplication and division | 15 | Problem solving | 14 | Problem solving – properties of shapes (2) | Recognise angles where they meet at a point, are on a straight line, or are vertically opposite, and find missing angles | Compare and classify geometric shapes based on their properties and sizes and find unknown angles in any triangles, quadrilaterals, and regular polygons |

# Mindset: an introduction

Global research and best practice deliver the same message: learning is greatly affected by what learners perceive they can or cannot do. What is more, it is also shaped by what their parents, carers and teachers perceive they can do. Mindset – the thinking that determines our beliefs and behaviours – therefore has a fundamental impact on teaching and learning.

## Everyone can!

*Power Maths* and mastery methods focus on the distinction between 'fixed' and 'growth' mindsets (Dweck, 2007).[1] Those with a fixed mindset believe that their basic qualities (for example, intelligence, talent and ability to learn) are pre-wired or fixed: 'If you have a talent for maths, you will succeed at it. If not, too bad!' By contrast, those with a growth mindset believe that hard work, effort and commitment drive success and that 'smart' is not something you are or are not, but something you become. In short, everyone can do maths!

## Key mindset strategies

A growth mindset needs to be actively nurtured and developed. *Power Maths* offers some key strategies for fostering healthy growth mindsets in your classroom.

### It is okay to get it wrong

Mistakes are valuable opportunities to re-think and understand more deeply. Learning is richer when children and teachers alike focus on spotting and sharing mistakes as well as solutions.

### Praise hard work

Praise is a great motivator, and by focusing on praising effort and learning rather than success, children will be more willing to try harder, take risks and persist for longer.

### Mind your language!

The language we use around learners has a profound effect on their mindsets. Make a habit of using growth phrases, such as, 'Everyone can!', 'Mistakes can help you learn' and 'Just try for a little longer'. The king of them all is one little word, 'yet'… I can't solve this…yet!' Encourage parents and carers to use the right language too.

### Build in opportunities for success

The step-by-small-step approach enables children to enjoy the experience of success. In addition, avoid ability grouping and encourage every child to answer questions and explain or demonstrate their methods to others.

[1] Dweck, C (2007) *The New Psychology of Success*, Ballantine Books: New York

# The *Power Maths* characters

The *Power Maths* characters model the traits of growth mindset learners and encourage resilience by prompting and questioning children as they work. Appearing frequently in the Textbooks and Practice Books, they are your allies in teaching and discussion, helping to model methods, alternatives and misconceptions, and to pose questions. They encourage and support your children, too: they are all hardworking, enthusiastic and unafraid of making and talking about mistakes.

## Meet the team!

**Creative Flo** is open-minded and sometimes indecisive. She likes to think differently and come up with a variety of methods or ideas.

**Determined Dexter** is resolute, resilient and systematic. He concentrates hard, always tries his best and he'll never give up – even though he doesn't always choose the most efficient methods!

'Let's try again.'
'Mistakes are cool!'
'Have I found all of the solutions?'

'Let's try it this way…'
'Can we do it differently?'
'I've got another way of doing this!'

'I'm going to try this!'
'I know how to do that!'
'Want to share my ideas?'

**Curious Ash** is eager, interested and inquisitive, and he loves solving puzzles and problems. Ash asks lots of questions but sometimes gets distracted.

'What if we tried this…?'
'I wonder…'
'Is there a pattern here?'

**Sparks the Cat**

Miaow!

**Brave Astrid** is confident, willing to take risks and unafraid of failure. She's never scared to jump straight into a problem or question, and although she often makes simple mistakes she's happy to talk them through with others.

# Mathematical language

Traditionally, we in the UK have tended to try simplifying mathematical language to make it easier for young children to understand. By contrast, evidence and experience show that by diluting the correct language, we actually mask concepts and meanings for children. We then wonder why they are confused by new and different terminology later down the line! *Power Maths* is not afraid of 'hard' words and avoids placing any barriers between children and their understanding of mathematical concepts. As a result, we need to be deliberate, precise and thorough in building every child's understanding of the language of maths. Throughout the Teacher Guides you will find support and guidance on how to deliver this, as well as individual explanations throughout the pupil Textbooks.

Use the following key strategies to build children's mathematical vocabulary, understanding and confidence.

**Precise and consistent**

Everyone in the classroom should use the correct mathematical terms in full, every time. For example, refer to 'equal parts', not 'parts'. Used consistently, precise maths language will be a familiar and non-threatening part of children's everyday experience.

**Full sentences**

Teachers and children alike need to use full sentences to explain or respond. When children use complete sentences, it both reveals their understanding and embeds their knowledge.

**Stem sentences**

These important sentences help children express mathematical concepts accurately, and are used throughout the *Power Maths* books. Encourage children to repeat them frequently, whether working independently or with others. Examples of stem sentences are:

'4 is a part, 5 is a part, 9 is the whole.'

'There are …. groups. There are …. in each group.'

**Key vocabulary**

The unit starters highlight essential vocabulary for every lesson. In the pupil books, characters flag new terminology and the Teacher Guide lists important mathematical language for every unit and lesson. New terms are never introduced without a clear explanation.

**Mathematical signs**

Mathematical signs are used early on so that children quickly become familiar with them and their meaning. Often, the *Power Maths* characters will highlight the connection between language and particular signs.

# The role of talk and discussion

When children learn to talk purposefully together about maths, barriers of fear and anxiety are broken down and they grow in confidence, skills and understanding. Building a healthy culture of 'maths talk' empowers their learning from day one.

Explanation and discussion are integral to the *Power Maths* structure, so by simply following the books your lessons will stimulate structured talk. The following key 'maths talk' strategies will help you strengthen that culture and ensure that every child is included.

### Sentences, not words

Encourage children to use full sentences when reasoning, explaining or discussing maths. This helps both speaker and listeners to clarify their own understanding. It also reveals whether or not the speaker truly understands, enabling you to address misconceptions as they arise.

### Working together

Working with others in pairs, groups or as a whole class is a great way to support maths talk and discussion. Use different group structures to add variety and challenge. For example, children could take timed turns for talking, work independently alongside a 'discussion buddy', or perhaps play different *Power Maths* character roles within their group.

### Think first – then talk

Provide clear opportunities within each lesson for children to think and reflect, so that their talk is purposeful, relevant and focused.

### Give every child a voice

Where the 'hands up' model allows only the more confident child to shine, *Power Maths* involves everyone. Make sure that no child dominates and that even the shyest child is encouraged to contribute – and praised when they do.

# Assessment strategies

Teaching for mastery demands that you are confident about what each child knows and where their misconceptions lie; therefore, practical and effective assessment is vitally important.

## Formative assessment within lessons

The **Think together** section will often reveal any confusions or insecurities; try ironing these out by doing the first **Think together** question as a class. For children who continue to struggle, you or your Teaching Assistant should provide support and enable them to move on.

▶

Performance in practice can be very revealing: check Practice Books and listen out both during and after practice to identify misconceptions.

▶

The **Reflect** section is designed to check on the all-important depth of understanding. Be sure to review how the children performed in this final stage before you teach the next lesson.

## End of unit check – Textbook

Each unit concludes with a summative check to help you assess quickly and clearly each child's understanding, fluency, reasoning and problem solving skills. Your Teacher Guide will suggest ideal ways of organising a given activity and offer advice and commentary on what children's responses mean. For example, 'What misconception does this reveal?'; 'How can you reinforce this particular concept?'

Assessment with young children should always be an enjoyable activity, so avoid one-to-one individual assessments, which they may find threatening or scary. If you prefer, the End of unit check can be carried out as a whole-class group using whiteboards and Practice Books.

## End of unit check – Practice Book

The Practice Book contains further opportunities for assessment, and can be completed by children independently whilst you are carrying out diagnostic assessment with small groups. Your Teacher Guide will advise you on what to do if children struggle to articulate an explanation – or perhaps encourage you to write down something they have explained well. It will also offer insights into children's answers and their implications for next learning steps. It is split into three main sections, outlined below.

My journal is designed to allow children to show their depth of understanding of the unit. It can also serve as a way of checking that children have grasped key mathematical vocabulary. The question children should answer is first presented in the Textbook in the Think! section. This provides an opportunity for you to discuss the question first as a class to ensure children have understood their task. Children should have some time to think about how they want to answer the question, and you could ask them to talk to a partner about their ideas. Then children should write their answer in their Practice Book, using the word bank provided to help them with vocabulary.

The **Power check** allows pupils to self-assess their level of confidence on the topic by colouring in different smiley faces. You may want to introduce the faces as follows:

Each unit ends with either a Power play or a Power puzzle. This is an activity, puzzle or game that allows children to use their new knowledge in a fun, informal way.

## Progress Tests

There are *Power Maths* Progress Tests for each half term and at the end of the year, including an Arithmetic test and Reasoning test in each case. You can enter results in the online markbook to track and analyse results and see the average for all schools' results. The tests use a 6-step scale to show results against age-related expectation.

## How to ask diagnostic questions

The diagnostic questions provided in children's Practice Books are carefully structured to identify both understanding and misconceptions (if children answer in a particular way, you will know why). The simple procedure below may be helpful:

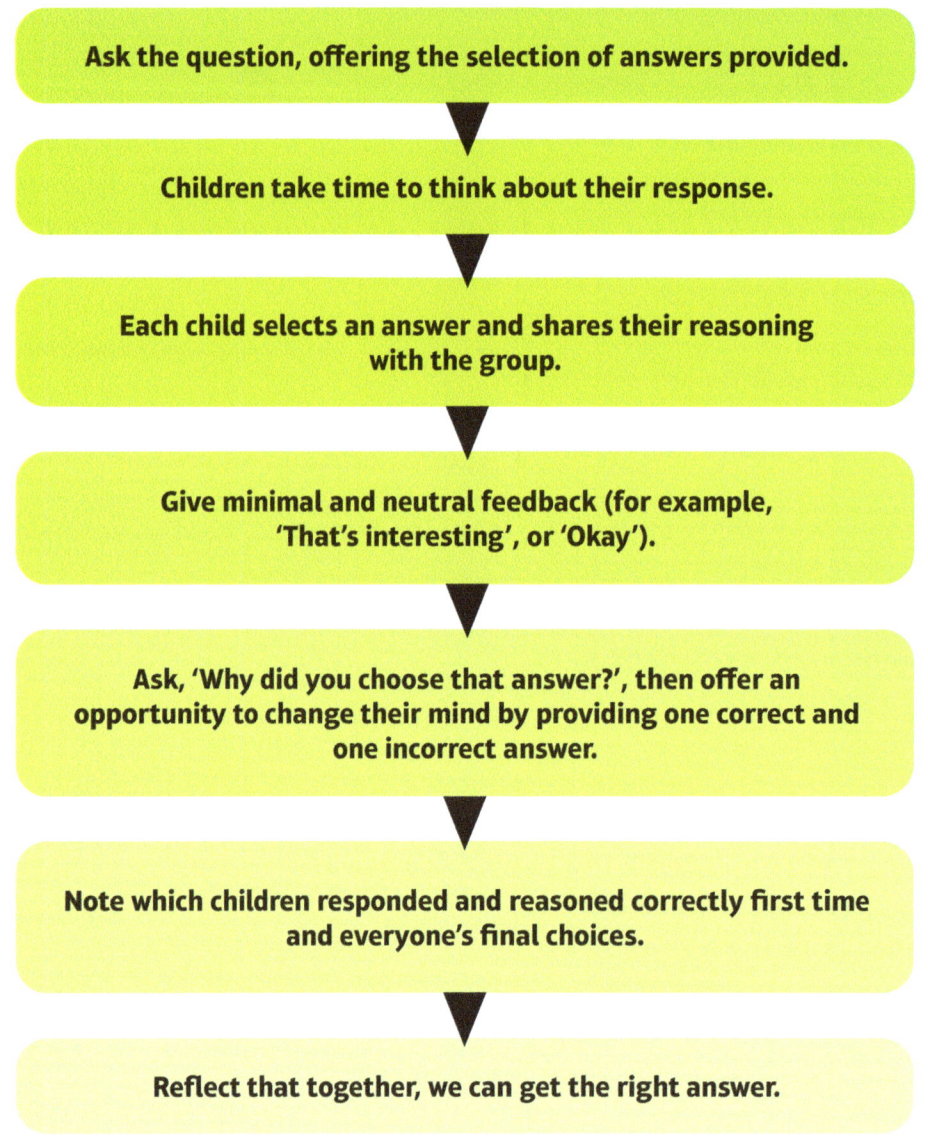

# Keeping the class together

Traditionally, children who learn quickly have been accelerated through the curriculum. As a consequence, their learning may be superficial and will lack the many benefits of enabling children to learn with and from each other.

By contrast, *Power Maths'* mastery approach values real understanding and richer, deeper learning above speed. It sees all children learning the same concept in small, cumulative steps, each finding and mastering challenge at their own level. Remember that when you teach for mastery, EVERYONE can do maths! Those who grasp a concept easily have time to explore and understand that concept at a deeper level. The whole class therefore moves through the curriculum at broadly the same pace via individual learning journeys.

For some teachers, the idea that a whole class can move forward together is revolutionary and challenging. However, the evidence of global good practice clearly shows that this approach drives engagement, confidence, motivation and success for all learners, and not just the high flyers. The strategies below will help you keep your class together on their maths journey.

### Mix it up

Do not stick to set groups at each table. Every child should be working on the same concept, and mixing up the groupings widens children's opportunities for exploring, discussing and sharing their understanding with others.

### Recycling questions

Reuse the Textbook and Practice Book questions with concrete materials to allow children to explore concepts and relationships and deepen their understanding. This strategy is especially useful for reinforcing learning in same-day interventions.

### Strengthen at every opportunity

The next lesson in a *Power Maths* sequence always revises and builds on the previous step to help embed learning. These activities provide golden opportunities for individual children to strengthen their learning with the support of Teaching Assistants.

### Prepare to be surprised!

Children may grasp a concept quickly or more slowly. The 'fast graspers' won't always be the same individuals, nor does the speed at which a child understands a concept predict their success in maths. Are they struggling or just working more slowly?

# Same-day intervention

Since maths competence depends on mastering concepts one by one in a logical progression, it is important that no gaps in understanding are ever left unfilled. Same-day interventions – either within or after a lesson – are a crucial safety net for any child who has not fully made the small step covered that day. In other words, intervention is always about keeping up, not catching up, so that every child has the skills and understanding they need to tackle the next lesson. That means presenting the same problems used in the lesson, with a variety of concrete materials to help children model their solutions.

We offer two intervention strategies below, but you should feel free to choose others if they work better for your class.

## Within-lesson intervention

The **Think together** activity will reveal those who are struggling, so when it is time for practice, bring these children together to work with you on the first practice questions. Observe these children carefully, ask questions, encourage them to use concrete models and check that they reach and can demonstrate their understanding.

## After-lesson intervention

You might like to use the **Think together** questions to recap the lesson with children who are working behind expectations during assembly time. Teaching Assistants could also work with these children at other convenient points in the school day. Some children may benefit from revisiting work from the same topic in the previous year group. Note also the suggestion for recycling questions from the Textbook and Practice Book with concrete materials on page 27.

# The role of practice

Practice plays a pivotal role in the *Power Maths* approach. It takes place in class groups, smaller groups, pairs, and independently, so that children always have the opportunities for thinking as well as the models and support they need to practise meaningfully and with understanding.

## Intelligent practice

In *Power Maths*, practice never equates to the simple repetition of a process. Instead we embrace the concept of intelligent practice, in which all children become fluent in maths through varied, frequent and thoughtful practice that deepens and embeds conceptual understanding in a logical, planned sequence. To see the difference, take a look at the following examples.

### Traditional practice

- Repetition can be rote – no need for a child to think hard about what they are doing
- Praise may be misplaced
- Does this prove understanding?

### Intelligent practice

- Varied methods – concrete, pictorial and abstract
- Equation expressed in different ways, requiring thought and understanding
- Constructive feedback

All practice questions are designed to move children on and reveal misconceptions.

Simple, logical steps build onto earlier learning.

C-P-A runs throughout – different ways of modelling and understanding the same concept.

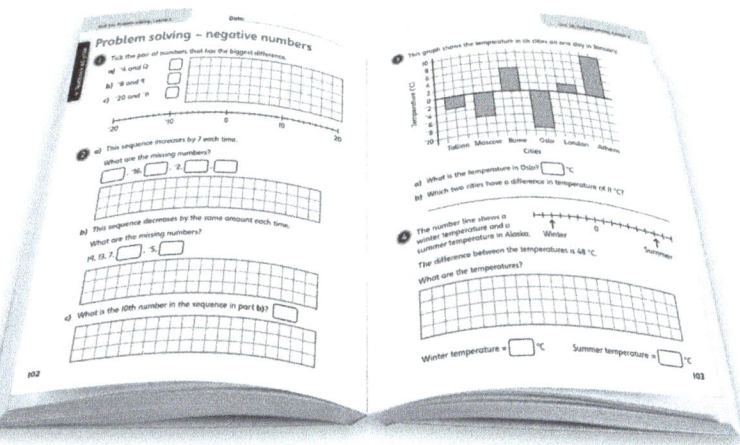

Conceptual variation – children work on different representations of the same maths concept.

Friendly characters offer support and encourage children to try different approaches.

## A carefully designed progression

The Practice Books provide just the right amount of intelligent practice for children to complete independently in the final sections of each lesson. It is really important that all children are exposed to the practice questions, and that children are not directed to complete different sections. That is because each question is different and has been designed to challenge children to think about the maths they are doing. The questions become more challenging so children grasping concepts more quickly will start to slow down as they progress. Meanwhile, you have the chance to circulate and spot any misconceptions before they become barriers to further learning.

## Homework and the role of parents and carers

While *Power Maths* does not prescribe any particular homework structure, we acknowledge the potential value of practice at home. For example, practising fluency in key facts, such as number bonds and times-tables, is an ideal homework task. You can share the Individual Practice Games for homework (see page 6), or parents and carers could work through uncompleted Practice Book questions with children at either primary stage.

However, it is important to recognise that many parents and carers may themselves lack confidence in maths, and few, if any, will be familiar with mastery methods. A Parents' and Carers' evening that helps them understand the basics of mindsets, mastery and mathematical language is a great way to ensure that children benefit from their homework. It could be a fun opportunity for children to teach their families that everyone can do maths!

# Structures and representations

Unlike most other subjects, maths comprises a wide array of abstract concepts – and that is why children and adults so often find it difficult. By taking a concrete-pictorial-abstract (C-P-A) approach, *Power Maths* allows children to tackle concepts in a tangible and more comfortable way.

**Non-linear stages**

## Concrete

Replacing the traditional approach of a teacher working through a problem in front of the class, the concrete stage introduces real objects that children can use to 'do' the maths – any familiar object that a child can manipulate and move to help bring the maths to life. It is important to appreciate, however, that children must always understand the link between models and the objects they represent. For example, children need to first understand that three cakes could be represented by three pretend cakes, and then by three counters or bricks. Frequent practice helps consolidate this essential insight. Although they can be used at any time, good concrete models are an essential first step in understanding.

## Pictorial

This stage uses pictorial representations of objects to let children 'see' what particular maths problems look like. It helps them make connections between the concrete and pictorial representations and the abstract maths concept. Children can also create or view a pictorial representation together, enabling discussion and comparisons. The *Power Maths* teaching tools are fantastic for this learning stage, and bar modelling is invaluable for problem solving throughout the primary curriculum.

## Abstract

Our ultimate goal is for children to understand abstract mathematical concepts, symbols and notation and of course, some children will reach this stage far more quickly than others. To work with abstract concepts, a child must be comfortable with the meaning of and relationships between concrete, pictorial and abstract models and representations. The C-P-A approach is not linear, and children may need different types of models at different times. However, when a child demonstrates with concrete models and pictorial representations that they have grasped a concept, we can be confident that they are ready to explore or model it with abstract symbols such as numbers and notation.

**Use at any time and with any age to support understanding**

# Variation helps visualisation

Children find it much easier to visualise and grasp concepts if they see them presented in a number of ways, so be prepared to offer and encourage many different representations.

For example, the number six could be represented in various ways:

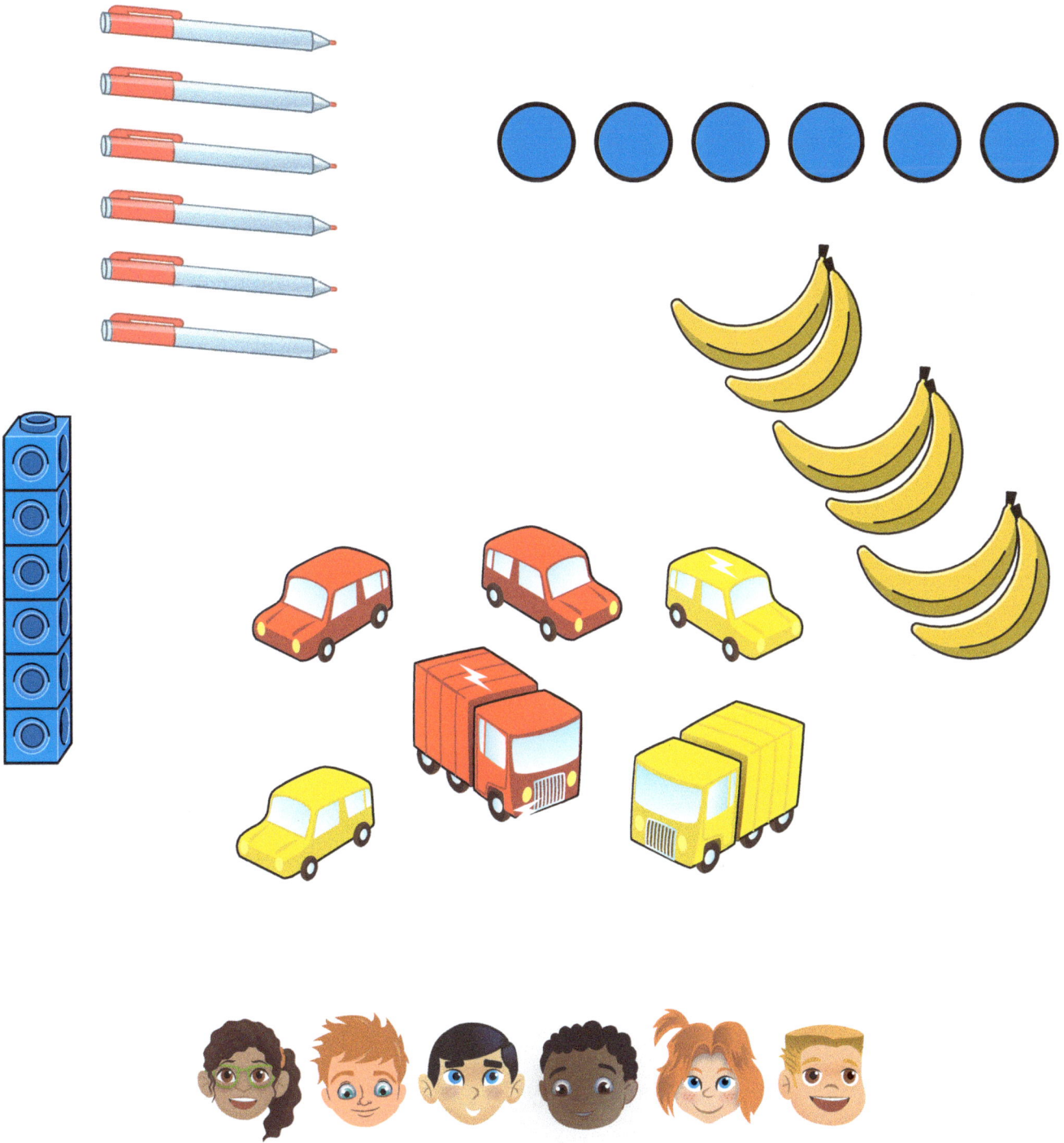

# Practical aspects of *Power Maths*

One of the key underlying elements of *Power Maths* is its practical approach, allowing you to make maths real and relevant to your children, no matter their age.

Manipulatives are essential resources for both key stages and *Power Maths* encourages teachers to use these at every opportunity, and to continue the Concrete-Pictorial-Abstract approach right through to Year 6.

The Textbooks and Teacher Guides include lots of opportunities for teaching in a practical way to show children what maths means in real life.

## Discover and Share

The **Discover** and **Share** sections of the Textbook give you scope to turn a real-life scenario into a practical and hands-on section of the lesson. Use these sections as inspiration to get active in the classroom. Where appropriate, use the **Discover** contexts as a springboard for your own examples that have particular resonance for your children – and allow them to get their hands dirty trying out the mathematics for themselves.

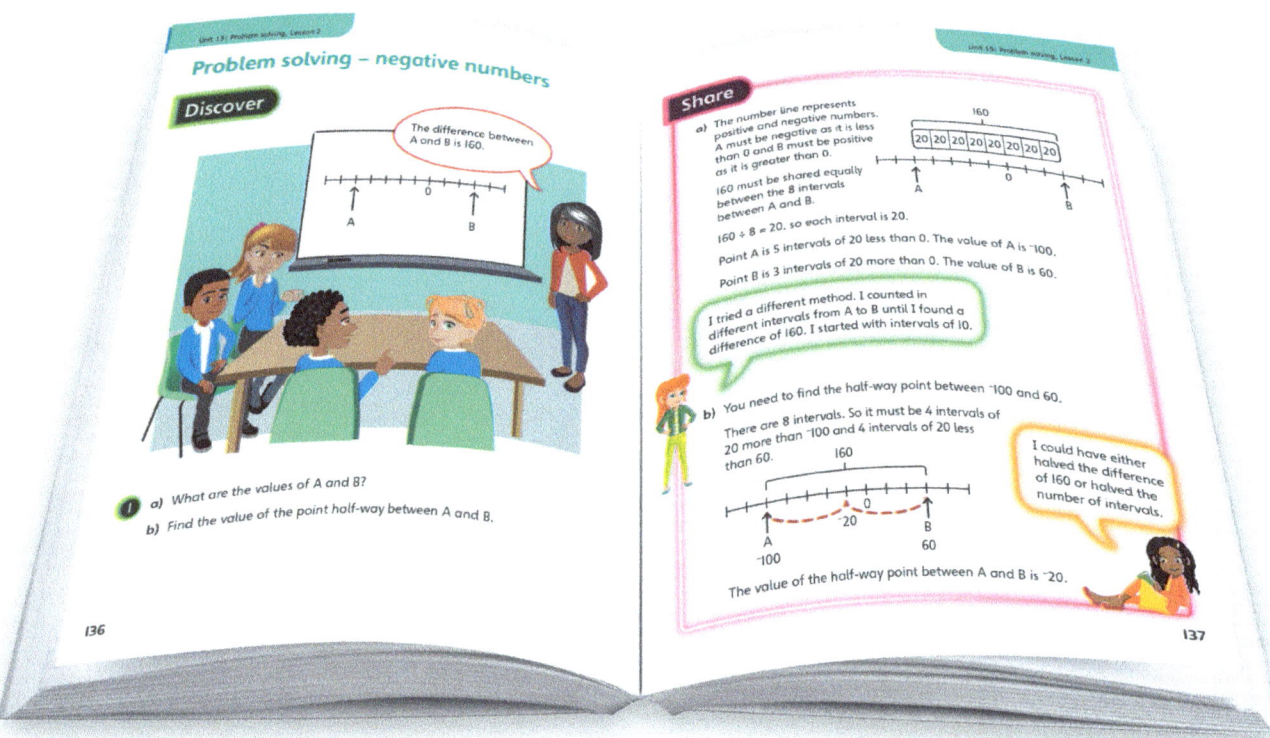

## Unit videos

Every term has one unit video which incorporates real-life classroom sequences.

These videos show you how the reasoning behind mathematics can be carried out in a practical manner by showing real children using various concrete and pictorial methods to come to the solution. You can see how using these practical models, such as part-whole and bar models, helps them to find and articulate their answer.

## Mastery tips

Mastery Experts give anecdotal advice on where they have used hands-on and real-life elements to inspire their children.

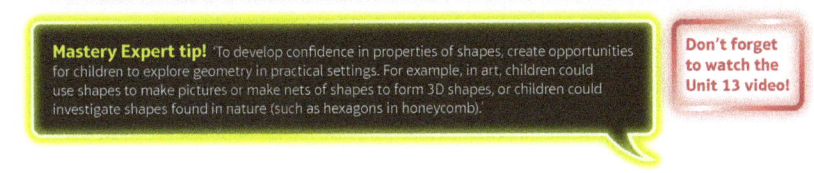

## Concrete-Pictorial-Abstract (C-P-A) approach

Each **Share** section uses various methods to explain an answer, helping children to access abstract concepts by using concrete tools, such as counters. Remember, this isn't a linear process, so even children who appear confident using the more abstract method can deepen their knowledge by exploring the concrete representations. Encourage children to use all three methods to really solidify their understanding of a concept.

Pictorial representation – drawing the problem in a logical way that helps children visualise the maths.

Concrete representation – using manipulatives to represent the problem. Encourage children to physically use resources to explore the maths.

Abstract representation – using words and calculations to represent the problem.

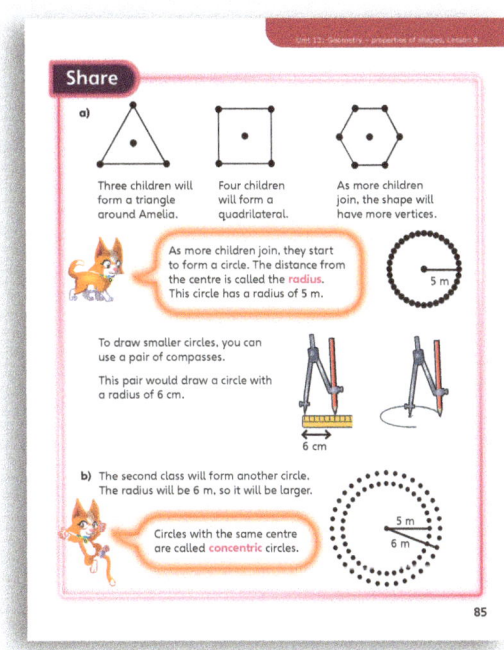

## Practical tips

Every lesson suggests how to draw out the practical side of the **Discover** context.

You'll find these in the **Discover** section of the Teacher Guide for each lesson.

> **PRACTICAL TIPS** Provide children with counters to explore the problem practically. Give them individual whiteboards and pens to draw representations.

## Resources

Every lesson lists the practical resources you will need or might want to use. There is also a summary of all of the resources used throughout the term on page 39 to help you be prepared.

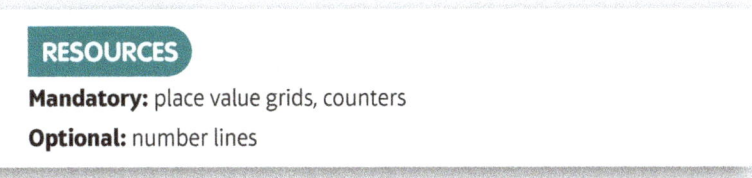

# Working with children below age-related expectation

This section offers advice on using *Power Maths* with children who are significantly behind age-related expectation. Teacher judgement will be crucial in terms of where and why children are struggling, and in choosing the right approach. The suggestions can of course be adapted for children with special educational needs, depending on the specific details of those needs.

## General approaches to support children who are struggling

**Keeping the pace manageable**
Remember, you have more teaching days than *Power Maths* lessons so you can cover a lesson over more than one day, and revisit key learning, to ensure all children are ready to move on. You can use the + and – buttons to adjust the time for each unit in the online planning. The NCETM's Ready-to-Progress criteria can be used to help determine what should be highest priority.

**Same-day intervention**
You could go over the Textbook pages or revisit the previous year's work if necessary (see Addressing gaps). Remember that same-day intervention can be within the lesson, as well as afterwards (see page 28). As children start their independent practice, you can work with those who found the first part of the lesson difficult, checking understanding using manipulatives.

**Fluency sessions**
Fit in as much practice as you can for number bonds and times-tables, etc., at other times of the day. If you can, plan a short 'maths meeting' for this in the afternoon. You might choose to use a Power Up you haven't used already.

**Addressing gaps**
Use material from the same topic in the previous year to consolidate or address gaps in learning, e.g. Textbook pages and Strengthen activities. The End of unit check will help gauge children's understanding.

**Pre-teaching**
Find a 5- to 10-minute slot before the lesson to work with the children you feel would benefit. The afternoon before the lesson can work well, because it gives children time to think in between. Recap previous work on the topic (addressing any gaps you're aware of) and do some fluency practice, targeting number facts etc. that will help children access the learning.

**Focusing on the key concepts**
If children are a long way behind, it can be helpful to take a step back and think about the key concepts for children to engage with, not just the fine detail of the objective for that year group (e.g. addition with a specific number of columns). Bearing that in mind, how could children advance their understanding of the topic?

## Providing extra support within the lesson

### Support in the Teacher Guide
First of all, use the Strengthen support in the Teacher Guide for guided and independent work in each lesson, and share this with Teaching Assistants, where relevant. As you read through the lesson content and corresponding Teacher Guide pages before the lesson, ask yourself what key idea or nugget of understanding is at the heart of the lesson. If children are struggling, this should help you decide what's essential for all children before they move on.

### Annotating pages
You can annotate questions to provide extra scaffolding or hints if you need to, but aim to build up children's ability to access questions independently wherever you can. Children tend to get used to the style of the *Power Maths* questions over time.

### Quick recap as lesson starter
The Quick recap for each lesson in the Teacher Guide is an alternative starter activity to the Power Up. You might choose to use this with some or all children if you feel they will need support accessing the main lesson.

### Consolidation questions
If you think some children would benefit from additional questions at the same level before moving on, write one or two similar questions on the board. (This shouldn't be at the expense of reasoning and problem-solving opportunities: take longer over the lesson if you need to.)

### Hard copy Textbooks
The Textbooks help children focus in more easily on the mathematical representations, read the text more comfortably, and revisit work from a previous lesson that you are building on, as well as giving children ownership of their learning journey. In main lessons, it can work well to use the e-Textbook for **Discover** and give out the books when discussing the methods in the **Share** section.

### Reading support
It's important that all children are exposed to problem solving and reasoning questions, which often involve reading. For whole-class work you can read questions together. For independent practice you could consider annotating pages to help children see what the question is asking, and stem sentences to help structure their answer. A general focus on specific mathematical language and vocabulary will help children access the questions. You could consider pairing weaker readers with stronger readers, or read questions as a group if those who need support are on the same table.

# Providing extra depth and challenge with *Power Maths*

Just as prescribed in the National Curriculum, the goal of *Power Maths* is never to accelerate through a topic but rather to gain a clear, deep and broad understanding. Here are some suggestions to help ensure all children are appropriately challenged as you work with the resources.

## Overall approaches

First of all, remember that the materials are designed to help you keep the class together, allowing all children to master a concept while those who grasp it quickly have time to explore it in more depth. Use the Deepen support in the Teacher Guide (see below) to challenge children who work through the questions quickly. Here are some questions and ideas to encourage breadth and depth during specific parts of the lesson, or at any time (where no part of the lesson sequence is specified):

- **Discover**: 'Can you demonstrate your solution another way?'
- **Share**: Make sure every child is encouraged to give answers and engage with the discussion, not just the most confident.
- **Think together**: 'Can you model your answers using concrete materials? Can you explain your solution to a partner?'
- Practice: Allow all children to work through the full set of questions, so that they benefit from the logical sequence.
- **Reflect**: 'Is there another way of working out the answer? And another way?'
  'Have you found all the solutions?'
  'Is that always true?'
  'What's different between this question and that question? And what's the same?'

Note that the **Challenge** questions are designed so that all children can access and attempt them, if they have worked through the steps leading up to them. There may be some children in a given lesson who don't manage to do the **Challenge**, but it is not supposed to be a distinct task for a subset of the class. When you look through the lesson materials before teaching, think about what each question is specifically asking, and compare this with the key learning point for the lesson. This will help you decide which questions you feel it's essential for all children to answer, before moving on. You can at least aim for all children to try the **Challenge**!

## Deepen activities and support

The Teacher Guide provides valuable support for each stage of the lesson. This includes Deepen tips for the guided and independent practice sections, which will help you provide extra stretch and challenge within your lesson, without having to organise additional tasks. If you have a Teaching Assistant, they can also make use of this advice. There are also suggestions for the lesson as a whole in the 'Going Deeper' section on the first page of the Teacher Guide section for that lesson. Every class is different, so you can always go a bit further in the direction indicated, if appropriate, and build on the suggestions given.

There is a Deepen activity for each unit. These are designed to follow on from the End of unit check, stretching children who have a firm understanding of the key learning from the unit. Children can work on them independently, which makes it easier for the teacher to facilitate the Strengthen activity for children who need extra support. Deepen activities could also be introduced earlier in the unit if the necessary work has been covered. The Deepen activities are on *ActiveLearn* on the Planning page for each unit, and also on the Resources page).

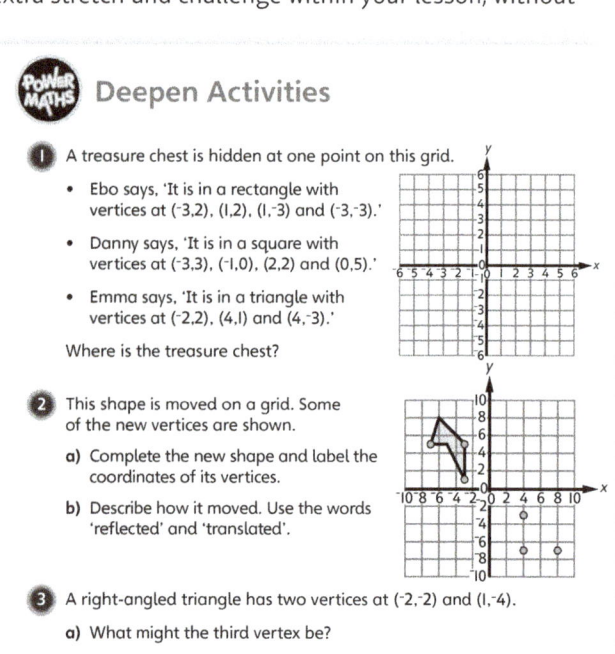

## Using the questions flexibly to provide extra challenge

Sometimes you may want to write an extra question on the board or provide this on paper. You can usually do this by tweaking the lesson materials. The questions are designed to form a carefully structured sequence that builds understanding step by step, but, with careful thought about the purpose of each question, you can use the materials flexibly where you need to. Sometimes you might feel that children would benefit from another similar question for consolidation before moving on to the next one, or you might feel that they would benefit from a harder example in the same style. It should be quick and easy to generate 'more of the same' type questions where this is the case.

When you see a question like this one (from Unit 2, Lesson 1), it's easy to make extra examples to do afterwards if you need them, maximising the number of exchanges if you want to make it tricky. You can also blot out more digits and ask children if this makes it easier or harder.

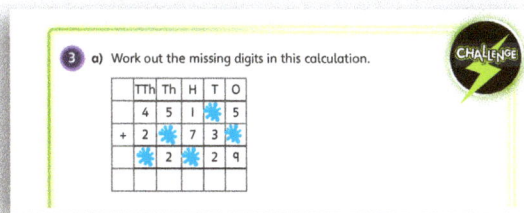

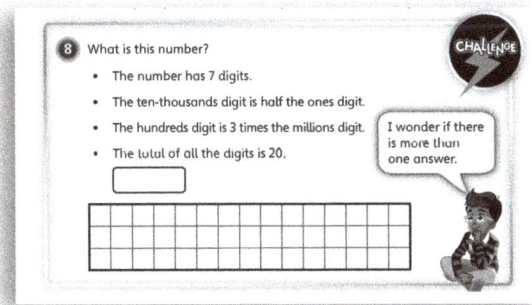

For this example (from Unit 1, Lesson 3), you could ask children to make up their own question(s) for a partner to solve, using 4 clues. (In fact, for any of these examples you could ask early finishers to create their own question for a partner.)

Here's an example (from Unit 4, Lesson 6) where the sum of two number cards is used in the question, but there are other combinations you could ask children to work out, for example, as an extra task at the end of the lesson.

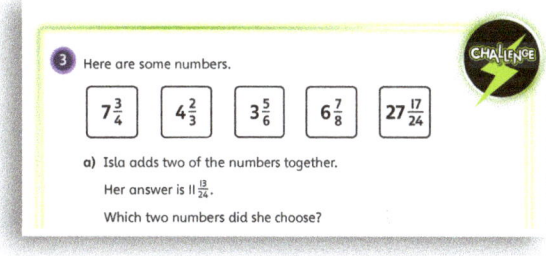

Besides creating additional questions, you should be able to find a question in the lesson that you can adapt into a game or open-ended investigation, if this helps to keep everyone engaged. It could simply be that, instead of answering 5 × 5 etc. on the page, they could build a robot with 5 lots of 5 cubes.

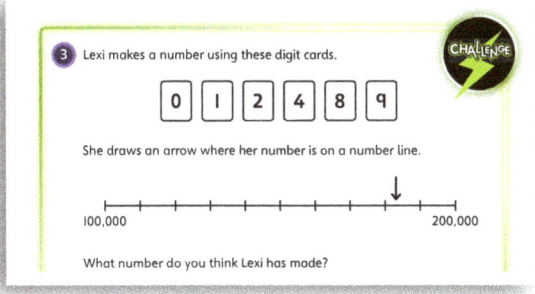

With a question like this (from Unit 1, Lesson 1), children could play a game where they have to guess their partner's mystery number, finding out each time if the guess is too high or too low.

See the bullets above for some general ideas that will help with 'opening out' questions in the books, e.g. 'Can you find all the solutions?' type questions.

## Other suggestions

Another way of stretching children is through mixed ability pairs, or via other opportunities for children to explain their understanding in their own way. This is a good way of encouraging children to go deeper into the learning, rather than, for instance, tackling questions that are computationally more challenging but conceptually equivalent in level.

# Using *Power Maths* with mixed age classes

## Overall approaches

There are many variables between schools that would make it inadvisable to recommend a one-size-fits-all approach to mixed age teaching with *Power Maths*. These include how year groups are merged, availability of Teaching Assistants, experience and preference of teaching staff, range in pupil attainment across years, classroom space and layout, level of flexibility around timetables, and overall organisational structure (whether the school is part of a trust).

Some schools will find it best to timetable separate maths lessons for the different year groups. Others will aim to teach the class together as much as possible using the mixed age planning support on *ActiveLearn* (see the lesson exemplars for ways of organising lessons with strong/medium/weak correlation between year groups). There will also be ways of adapting these general approaches. For example, offset lessons where Year A start their lesson with the teacher, while Year B work independently on the practice from the previous lesson, and then start the next lesson with the teacher while Year A work independently; or teachers may choose to base their provision around the lesson from one year group and tweak the content up/down for the other group.

## Key strategies for mixed age teaching

The mixed age teaching webinar on *ActiveLearn* provides advice on all aspects of mixed age teaching, including more detail on the ideas below.

**Developing independence over time**
Investing time in building up children's independence will pay off in the medium term.

**Clear rationale**
If someone asked, 'Why did you teach both Unit 3 and 4 in the same lesson/separate lessons?', what would your answer be?

**Designing a lesson**
1. Identify the core learning for each group
2. Identify any number skills necessary to access the core
3. Consider the flow of concepts and how one core leads to the other

**Challenging all children**
The questions are designed to build understanding step by step, but with careful thought about the purpose of each question you can tweak them to increase the challenge.

**Multiple years combined**
With more than two years together, teachers will inevitably need to use the resources flexibly if delivering a single lesson.

## Enjoy the positives!

Comparison deepens understanding and there will be lots of opportunities for children, as well as misconceptions to explore. There is also in-built pre-teaching and the chance to build up a concept from its foundations. For teachers there is double the material to draw on! Mixed age teachers require a strong understanding of the progression of ideas across year groups, which is highly valuable for all teachers. Also, it is necessary to engage deeply with the lesson to see how to use the materials flexibly – this is recommended for all teachers and will help you bring your lesson to life!

# List of practical resources

## Year 6C Mandatory resources

| Resource | Lesson |
|---|---|
| Hundredths grids | **Unit 11** Lessons 1, 7 |
| Metre ruler | **Unit 11** Lesson 4 |
| Multilink cubes | **Unit 11** Lesson 7 |
| Number cards | **Unit 11** Lesson 1 |
| Number lines (from 0 to 1) | **Unit 11** Lesson 7 |
| Paper (squared) | **Unit 16** Lesson 3 |
| Place value counters | **Unit 11** Lessons 2, 5 |
| Place value counters (1s and tenths, 0·1) | **Unit 11** Lesson 1 |
| Place value counters (blank) | **Unit 11** Lesson 7 |
| Place value equipment | **Unit 11** Lessons 3, 4 |
| Rulers | **Unit 15** Lessons 1, 2, 3, 4, 5 |
| Ten frames (blank) | **Unit 11** Lesson 1 |
| Weighing scales | **Unit 11** Lesson 5 |

# Year 6C Optional resources

| Resource | Lesson |
|---|---|
| 2D polygons (plastic or card) | **Unit 14** Lesson 6 |
| 2D shapes | **Unit 14** Lessons 1, 2, 3, 4, 5, 7, 8 |
| 24-hour clock times (examples from everyday life: computer clock, timetables, etc.) | **Unit 13** Lesson 4 |
| Axis grid (large) | **Unit 15** Lesson 6 |
| Calendars (or year planners) | **Unit 13** Lesson 5 |
| Cards for pair games (set: half with pictures of different shapes, half with names of different shapes) | **Unit 14** Lesson 6 |
| Chalk | **Unit 16** Lesson 4 |
| Chess board | **Unit 16** Lesson 6 |
| Clock faces | **Unit 14** Lesson 1 |
| Clocks (analogue) | **Unit 13** Lessons 3, 4, 5 |
| Clocks (digital) | **Unit 13** Lessons 3, 4, 5 |
| Coins (plastic) | **Unit 11** Lesson 4<br>**Unit 12** Lessons 1, 2, 3, 4, 5, 6 |
| Computer geometry package | **Unit 16** Lessons 2, 3, 4, 5, 6 |
| Counters | **Unit 15** Lesson 6 |
| Crayons | **Unit 12** Lesson 2 |
| Elastic bands | **Unit 14** Lesson 8 |
| Flashcards | **Unit 13** Lesson 5 |
| Geoboards (with elastic bands) | **Unit 14** Lessons 4, 8 |
| Geostrip kit | **Unit 14** Lesson 4 |
| Help envelopes | **Unit 15** Lesson 3 |
| Internet access | **Unit 16** Lesson 1 |
| Lolly sticks (or straws) | **Unit 14** Lesson 8 |
| Maps (simple) | **Unit 16** Lesson 1 |
| Mirrors | **Unit 14** Lessons 7, 8 |
| Multilink cubes | **Unit 15** Lessons 1, 2 |
| Number cards | **Unit 13** Lessons 3, 4, 5 |
| Number lines | **Unit 15** Lessons 3, 4, 5 |
| Paper (large pieces of) | **Unit 15** Lesson 6 |
| Paper (squared) | **Unit 15** Lessons 3, 4, 5<br>**Unit 16** Lessons 3, 4 |
| Paper squares | **Unit 14** Lessons 1, 6 |
| Part-whole model (large, laminated) | **Unit 11** Lesson 1 |
| Place value counters | **Unit 11** Lesson 6 |
| Place value grids | **Unit 11** Lesson 7<br>**Unit 12** Lesson 3 |
| Rulers | **Unit 14** Lessons 2, 5<br>**Unit 16** Lesson 3 |
| Set squares | **Unit 14** Lesson 2 |
| String (pieces of) | **Unit 13** Lesson 1 |
| Tape | **Unit 16** Lesson 4 |
| Timers or stopwatches (digital) | **Unit 13** Lesson 2 |
| Triangles (range of different) | **Unit 14** Lesson 3 |

# Getting started with *Power Maths*

As you prepare to put *Power Maths* into action, you might find the tips and advice below helpful.

### STEP 1: Train up!

A practical, up-front full day professional development course will give you and your team a brilliant head-start as you begin your *Power Maths* journey. You will learn more about the ethos, how it works and why.

### STEP 2: Check out the progression

Take a look at the yearly and termly overviews. Next take a look at the unit overview for the unit you are about to teach in your Teacher Guide, remembering that you can match your lessons and pacing to match your class.

### STEP 3: Explore the context

Take a little time to look at the context for this unit: what are the implications for the unit ahead? (Think about key language, common misunderstandings and intervention strategies, for example.) If you have the online subscription, don't forget to watch the corresponding unit video.

### STEP 4: Prepare for your first lesson

Familiarise yourself with the objectives, essential questions to ask and the resources you will need. The Teacher Guide offers tips, ideas and guidance on individual lessons to help you anticipate children's misconceptions and challenge those who are ready to think more deeply.

### STEP 5: Teach and reflect

Deliver your lesson — and enjoy!

Afterwards, reflect on how it went… Did you cover all five stages? Does the lesson need more time? How could you improve it? What percentage of your class do you think mastered the concept? How can you help those that didn't?

# Unit 12
## Statistics

> **Mastery Expert tip!** 'I found that this unit provided a great opportunity for cross-curricular links and real-life situations. Children can use data from science experiments such as growing plants and measuring shadows to draw and create line graphs. PE can provide the data for calculating the mean, for example, children can record the distances of a long jump and calculate the mean.'

**Don't forget to watch the Unit 12 video!**

## WHY THIS UNIT IS IMPORTANT

In this unit, children develop their ability to interpret and create line graphs and more advanced bar charts. Children learn what a pie chart is and how to interpret one, they compare tally charts and bar charts and learn when a pie chart is the best way to display data. Children learn what the mathematical mean is and how to calculate it and they consider when using the mean is particularly useful, for example, when comparing sets of data of different sizes.

## WHERE THIS UNIT FITS

→ Unit 11: Measure – perimeter, area and volume
→ **Unit 12: Statistics**
→ Unit 13: Geometry – properties of shapes

This unit builds on the skills children gained in Year 5 interpreting and using line graphs. They learn what the mathematical mean is and how to calculate it and are introduced to pie charts.

Before they start this unit, it is expected that children:
- can plot and interpret simple line graphs
- are confident with dividing 2- and 3-digit numbers by a 1-digit number
- understand that angles about a point add up to 360°
- can identify fractions of a circle when each part is the same size
- can do calculations with percentages.

## ASSESSING MASTERY

In this unit, children will learn to read and interpret pie charts, and will calculate fractions and percentages of data as a whole. At the end of the unit, children will show mastery if they can interpret and create line graphs and more advanced bar charts. Children who have mastered this unit can also calculate the mean of sets of data and can compare sets of data by calculating the mean. They should also be able to use the mean to identify missing data.

| COMMON MISCONCEPTIONS | STRENGTHENING UNDERSTANDING | GOING DEEPER |
|---|---|---|
| Some children may find the word 'mean' confusing as it is a homonym. | Explain that in maths 'mean' is the mathematical average. Ask: *What is the mean number of marshmallows on a stick?* | Challenge children to write a definition of the mathematical 'mean' or explain what the mean is and how to calculate it. |
| Children may mistake the number of sections in a pie chart as the fraction, for example, they may say that as there are 3 sections, each is $\frac{1}{3}$, even though they are not the same size. | Recap fractions of circles with children. Provide circles and ask children to shade $\frac{1}{2}, \frac{1}{4}, \frac{1}{3}, \frac{3}{4}$, etc. This will help them to visualise the fractions and to understand that a circle must be divided into equal parts in order to shade a fraction of it. | Discuss and compare different pie charts and how the angle at the centre determines the size of the sector. |
| Children may confuse the *x*-axis and *y*-axis when interpreting line graphs and may read/interpret the scales used incorrectly. | Discuss the line graphs in detail and practise reading simple points from the graph. Begin with marked points and progress to unmarked points. | Explore different-shaped line graphs – curved and straight.<br>Challenge children to create stories to explain what is happening in a line graph. |

# Unit 12: Statistics

## UNIT STARTER PAGES

Recap on percentages, fractions and angles, especially in circles. Children will need to be able to calculate and convert these to understand the work on pie charts.

## STRUCTURES AND REPRESENTATIONS

**Line graph:** This is used for continuous data. Values are plotted from a table and then joined by either straight lines, or a smooth curve.

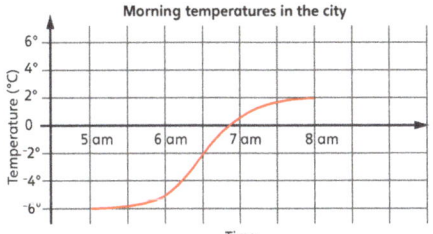

**Pie chart:** These can be used to show the size of different sectors of a population, as part of the whole.

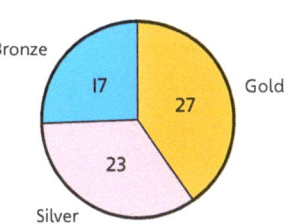

**Bar model:** These show how groups of different numbers can be made into equal-sized sections, showing the mean. They are also useful to demonstrate the whole, or total, represented in a pie chart, and how the sections represent different percentages or fractions of the whole.

## KEY LANGUAGE

Key language that children will need to know:
- average, mean, set, share
- line graph, axis/axes, estimate, accurate, interpret, increase, above, below, zero (0), value, x-axis, y-axis, minus (–), between, plot, point, vertical, horizontal, construct, convert/conversion, straight, equivalent, predict, curve
- tally chart, bar chart, pie chart, sector, whole, section, degree, angle, right angle
- fraction, percentage
- more, equal, even, size, total, share, great(er/est), calculate, divide, highest, compare, lowest, group, data, represent, balance, odd, different/difference, least, inverse, operation, advantages, disadvantages, largest, half, scale, quarter, frequency, smallest, part, same, more, category, results, exact

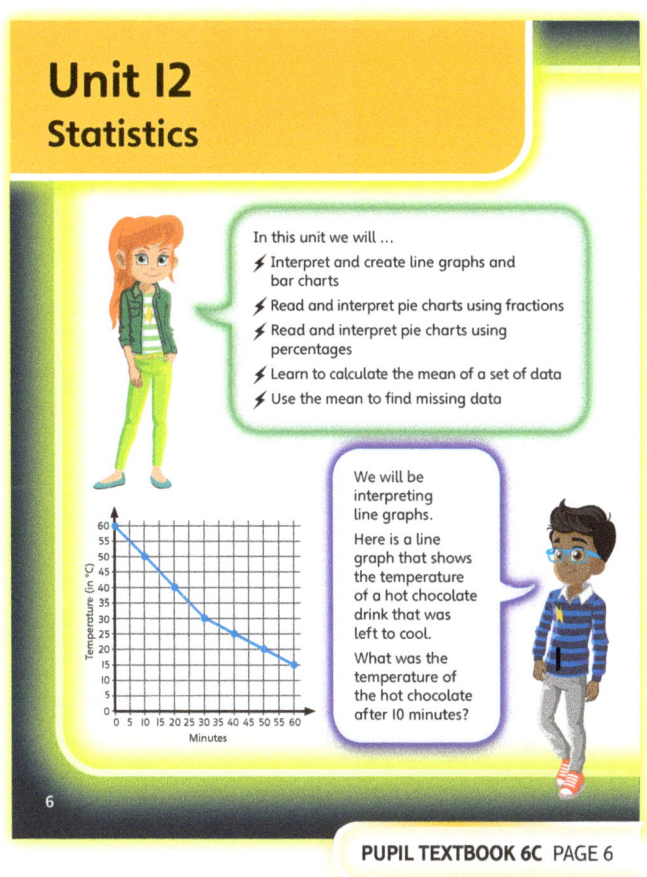

PUPIL TEXTBOOK 6C PAGE 6

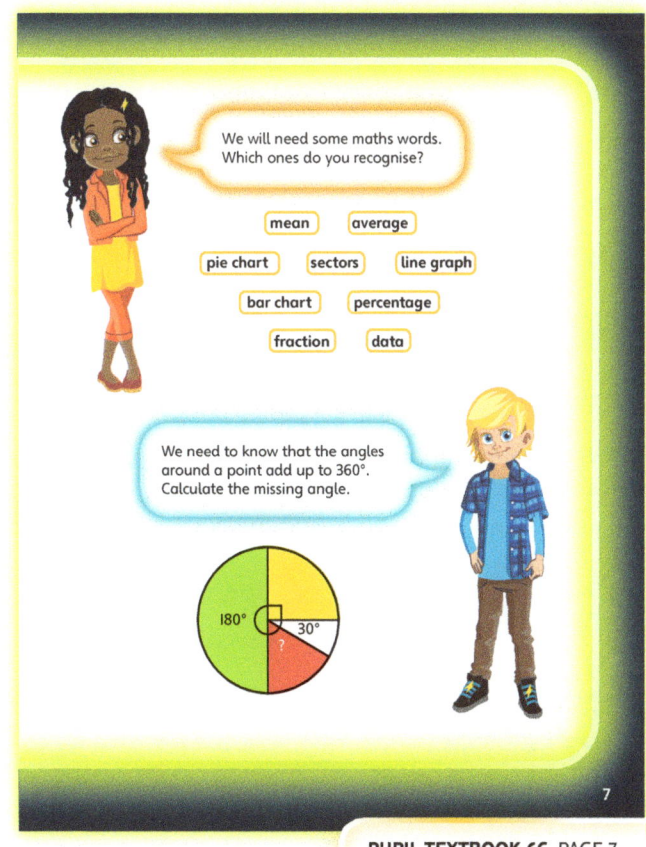

PUPIL TEXTBOOK 6C PAGE 7

Unit 12: Statistics, Lesson 1

# Interpret line graphs

## Learning focus

In this lesson, children learn to read and understand line graphs. They learn to read amounts and times on the line graph and use this to solve problems.

## Before you teach

- Are children secure in interpreting the scale on a *y*-axis and *x*-axis?
- Are children secure in adding and subtracting negative numbers?

### NATIONAL CURRICULUM LINKS

**Year 6 Statistics**

Interpret and construct pie charts and line graphs and use these to solve problems.

### ASSESSING MASTERY

Children can read amounts and times plotted on a curved or straight line graph and the amounts/times in between the plotted points. Children can solve problems by reading plotted points on a line graph.

Children can identify and describe changes in the line graphs, for example, a pause or speed change.

Children know that a straight line shows a consistent and proportional increase or decrease and understand that the direction of a line or curve can show if something is increasing or decreasing.

Children can tell stories or describe what is happening to match a line graph: for example, someone walking to the bus stop, waiting for a bus, travelling on the bus.

### COMMON MISCONCEPTIONS

Children may confuse the *x*-axis and *y*-axis on a line graph. Ask:
- *Which line is the* x*-axis and which is the* y*-axis?*

Children may read and interpret the scales used on a line graph incorrectly. Ask:
- *What is the scale on this line graph? What does each interval represent?*

### STRENGTHENING UNDERSTANDING

Discuss the line graphs in detail with children and get them to practise reading simple points from graphs. Start with marked points and progress to unmarked points. Children need to be confident in reading graphs before using line graphs to solve problems and answer two-step questions.

### GOING DEEPER

Explore different-shaped line graphs with children (curved and straight). Ask children to create stories to explain what a line graph is showing, including why a curve flattens out or goes up more steeply.

### KEY LANGUAGE

**In lesson:** interpret, **line graph**, increase, above, below, zero (0), value, minus (–), estimate, accurate, between, fraction, percentage

**Other language to be used by the teacher:** plot, point, *x*-axis, *y*-axis, vertical, horizontal

### STRUCTURES AND REPRESENTATIONS

Line graphs

### RESOURCES

**Mandatory:** graph paper

**Optional:** tracing paper, rulers

 In the eTextbook of this lesson, you will find interactive links to a selection of teaching tools.

## Quick recap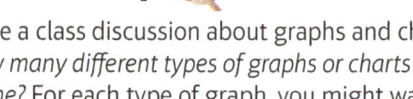

Have a class discussion about graphs and charts. Ask: *How many different types of graphs or charts can you name?* For each type of graph, you might want to draw a quick sketch and discuss when you might use it, and what sort of data it can display.

# Unit 12: Statistics, Lesson 1

## Discover

**WAYS OF WORKING** Pair work

**ASK**

- Question 1 a): *What type of graph is this?*
- Question 1 a): *Which is the y-axis and which is the x-axis? What scale is used on the y-axis? What scale is used on the x-axis?*
- Question 1 a): *Is the temperature increasing or decreasing? How do you know?*

**IN FOCUS** Question 1 asks children to read a line graph to see what the temperature is at certain times of day. Children need to recognise that the y-axis is showing the temperature and the x-axis is showing the time. Ask: *Can you work out what the temperature was at 6 am and what the temperature was at 6:30 am to calculate the difference? What lines do you need to draw on the line graph to help you?*

**PRACTICAL TIPS** Provide children with tracing paper and rulers so they can draw lines over the graph, for example, from 1 °C on the y-axis to the plotted line and down to the x-axis. Alternatively, you could provide photocopies of the graph for children to draw directly on to.

**ANSWERS**

Question 1 a): The temperature increased by 3 °C

Question 1 b): It was 1 °C just before 7:15 am. A reasonable estimate would be 7:10 am.

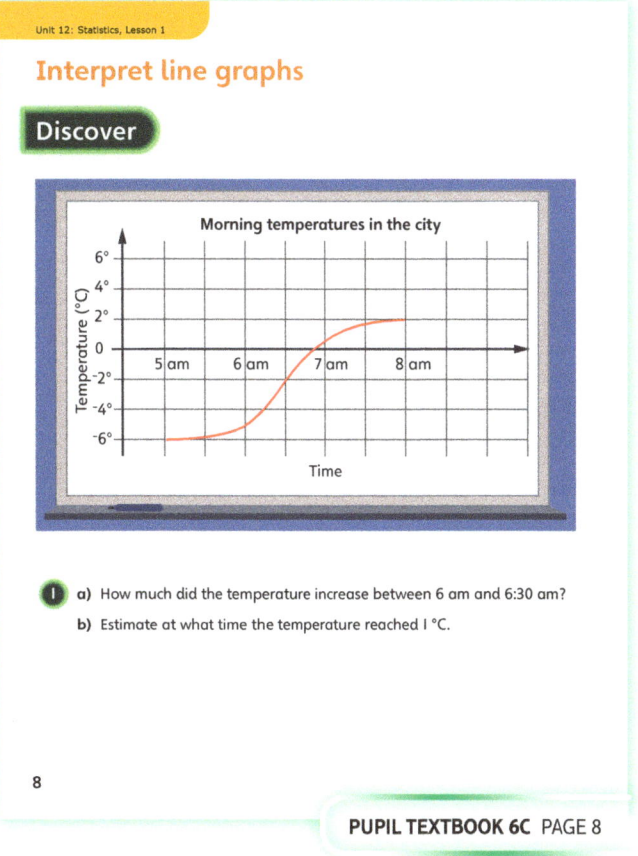

PUPIL TEXTBOOK 6C PAGE 8

## Share

**WAYS OF WORKING** Whole class teacher led

**ASK**

- Question 1 a): *Did you read the temperatures for the times 6 am and 6:30 am correctly?*
- Question 1 b): *What has been drawn to make it easier for you to read the line graph (dotted lines drawn on)? Does this help you?*
- Question 1 b): *What shape is the line? Is it straight or curved? What direction is it going in? What does that mean?*

**IN FOCUS** Close ups of the graph show how drawing a dotted line can help with reading the temperature and time on the axes. The axes are like number lines. Discuss how to calculate the difference. This is shown with jumps, which will be familiar with children. Model how to use tracing paper and a dotted line to help read from the line graph.

It is important that children know when to start from the y-axis and go across to the graph, or when to start from the x-axis and go up/down to the graph. The key learning here is that they need to identify what information the question is giving them (for example, 1 °C, which is temperature, and determine which axis shows temperature).

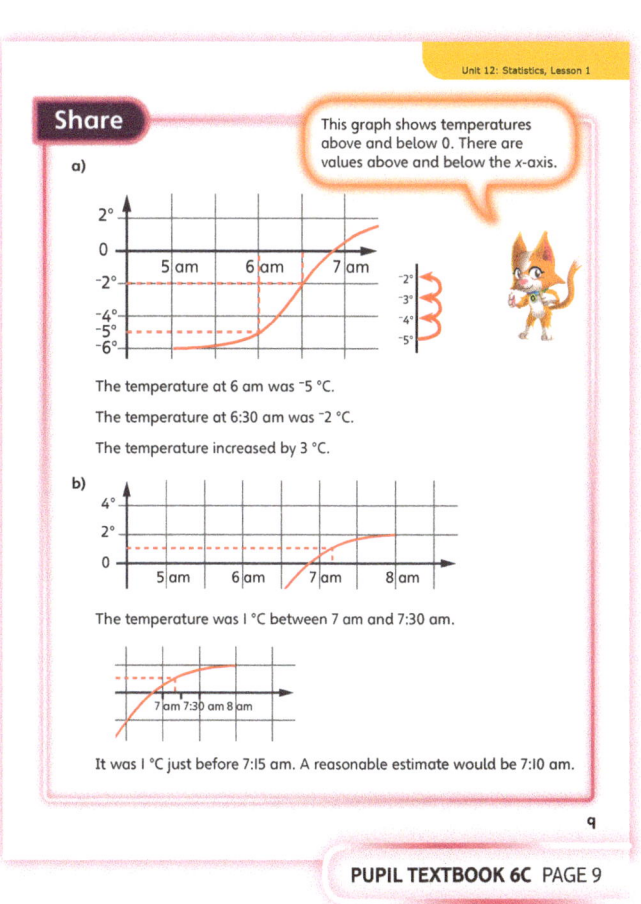

PUPIL TEXTBOOK 6C PAGE 9

# Think together

**WAYS OF WORKING** Whole class teacher led (I do, We do, You do)

**ASK**

- Question ❶: *What time did the balloon go above 500 m? What time did the balloon go below 500 m? Can you calculate the time in between?*
- Question ❷: *Could you use tracing paper and a ruler to help you find an unmarked point on the line graph?*
- Question ❸: *Can you describe the scale on the line graph? Why do you think it is flat in the middle?*

**IN FOCUS** For question ❶, children need to identify the time the balloon went above 500 m (this is a marked point) and the time the balloon came back down below the 500 m (this is an unmarked point), then calculate the time in between. To do this, they should identify 500 m on the y-axis and draw a horizontal line that cuts the graph in 2 places. From here, they can draw vertical lines down to find the times on the x-axis. To answer question ❷, children need to identify that 9 am is halfway between 6 am and 12 pm, both of which are marked on the x-axis. They then need to interpret the scale on the y-axis (1 square represents 0·5 °C). In question ❸, the challenge question, a line graph compares the time and distance travelled. Children need to interpret what is happening in the part of the graph in the middle where the distance remains the same (Ambika is in the shop/not walking/Ambika is resting/no distance has been covered during this time).

**STRENGTHEN** Discuss the line graphs in detail and practise reading simple points from the graph. Begin with marked points and progress to unmarked points. Children need to be confident in reading line graphs before using graphs to solve problems and answer two-step questions. Ensure they understand the process of drawing a horizontal/vertical line from one axis to the graph and then a vertical/horizontal line to the other axis.

**DEEPEN** Ask children to create further questions about the line graphs for a partner to answer. Ask them to create a story to show on a line graph. Ask: *Can you use the line graph to predict further data?*

**ASSESSMENT CHECKPOINT** Question ❶ assesses whether children can identify a point on a line graph and read its position on both axes.

In question ❷, children must estimate an unmarked point on a line graph. Check that they are able to read intervals on the axes correctly in order to estimate accurately.

**ANSWERS**

Question ❶: Approximately 2 hours 50 minutes. Accept any answers from 2 hours 45 minutes to 3 hours.

Question ❷: 
Day 1  Day 2  Day 3
38·7   37·75  37·1

Question ❸ a): Ambika takes 4 minutes. Children should be able to tell you that they know this because the line flattens out.
She stays 10 minutes.
The shop is 250 m from her home.

Question ❸ b): The vertical axis is labelled 'distance walked' not 'distance from home'.

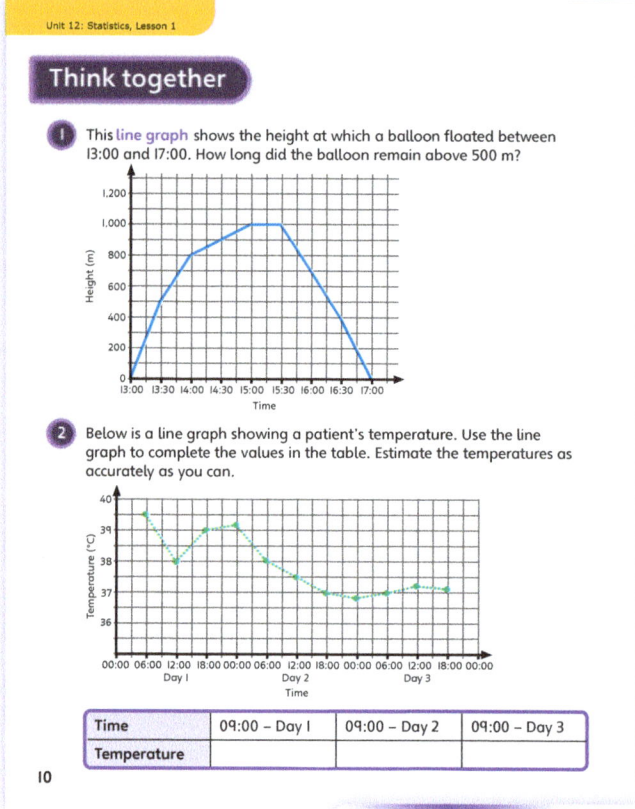

PUPIL TEXTBOOK 6C PAGE 10

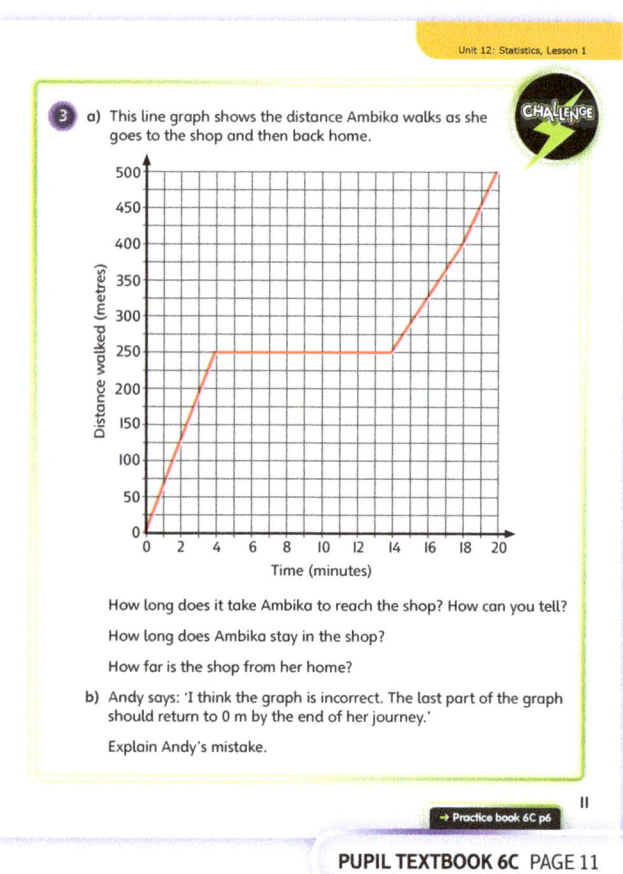

PUPIL TEXTBOOK 6C PAGE 11

# Unit 12: Statistics, Lesson 1

## Practice

**WAYS OF WORKING** Independent thinking

**IN FOCUS** In question 1 a), children read and estimate plotted points on a line graph and estimate times in between the plotted points. In question 1 b), they are asked to calculate the difference between two temperatures. Both require accurate reading of the x- and y-axis.

Question 2 asks children to estimate unmarked points on a line graph in order to identify a change in population. Before children read the scales on the graph, ask: *Do you think the population has increased or decreased between 2005 and 2015? How can you see this by looking at the graph?*

**STRENGTHEN** Discuss the line graphs in detail. Consider the shape and direction of the line: is it curved or straight, does it show a temperature increasing or decreasing? Support children to interpret the scales. Provide tracing paper for children to draw lines and estimate amounts in between plotted points.

**DEEPEN** Look at line graphs linked to cross-curricular topics such as plants growing over time or shadow lengths in science.

**THINK DIFFERENTLY** In question 3 a), children need to look for the highest point that the graph reaches. In parts b) and c), children will need to understand what the gradient or slope of the line tells them about the cyclist's speed at each point on the journey. When the line is horizontal, the cyclist has stopped. When the line is steepest, the cyclist is travelling fastest.

**ASSESSMENT CHECKPOINT** Use question 1 to check that children can read amounts and times plotted on a line graph and can read and estimate amounts and times in between plotted points.

Question 3 provides the opportunity to assess whether children can identify and describe changes in a line graph such as a change in speed.

**ANSWERS** Answers for the **Practice** part of the lesson can be found in the *Power Maths* online subscription.

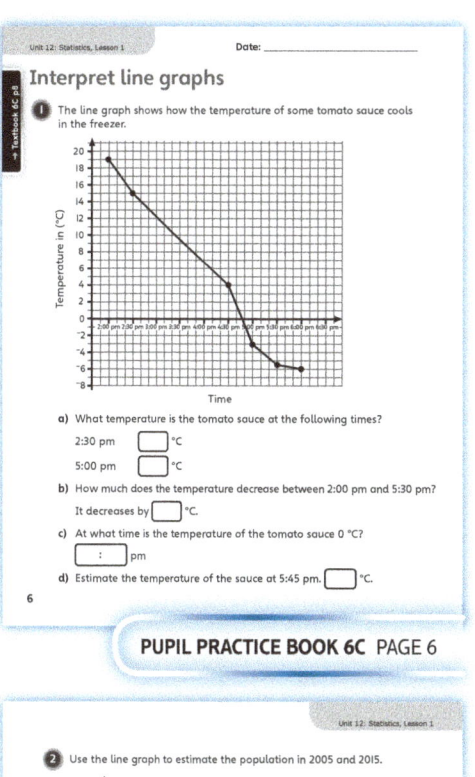

PUPIL PRACTICE BOOK 6C PAGE 6

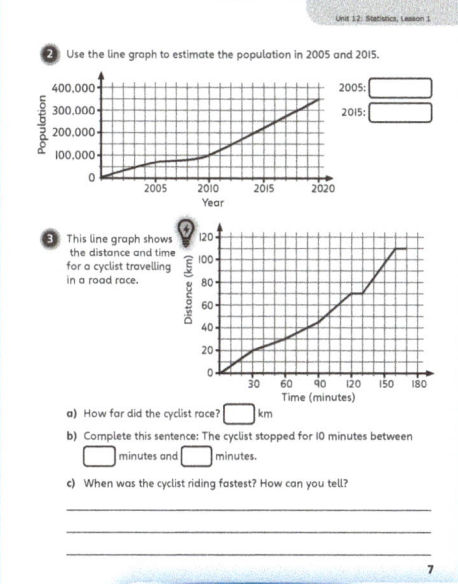

PUPIL PRACTICE BOOK 6C PAGE 7

## Reflect

**WAYS OF WORKING** Independent thinking

**IN FOCUS** Children are asked to give tips on reading a line graph accurately. Encourage them to imagine they are explaining to someone how to interpret line graphs. Ask them to consider the shape of the curve and pauses in the line as well as plotted points. Suggest that they use bullet points to list the tips they have.

**ASSESSMENT CHECKPOINT** Look for tips that include ways to avoid mistakes in reading scales and identifying missing points. This will prove that children have really understood the lesson and can interpret line graphs confidently.

**ANSWERS** Answers for the **Reflect** part of the lesson can be found in the *Power Maths* online subscription.

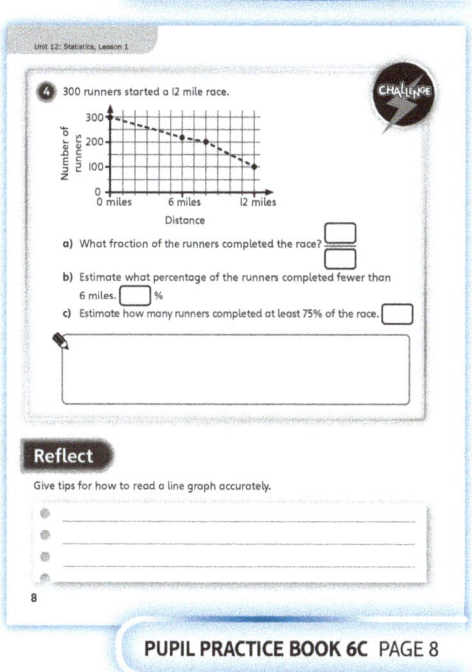

PUPIL PRACTICE BOOK 6C PAGE 8

## After the lesson

- Can children describe what the line graph shows?
- How many children can confidently read and estimate amounts and times from the line graph?
- Do children understand what the x-axis and y-axis are for?

Unit 12: Statistics, Lesson 2

# Draw line graphs

### Learning focus
In this lesson, children learn to create and plot more complex line graphs, building on skills from Year 5. They choose and draw an appropriate scale.

### Before you teach
- Are children secure in reading the scale on a *y*-axis and *x*-axis?
- Are children confident in interpreting tables of data?

#### NATIONAL CURRICULUM LINKS

**Year 6 Statistics**

Interpret and construct pie charts and line graphs and use these to solve problems.

#### ASSESSING MASTERY

Children can decide on an appropriate scale to use for the *y*-axis and *x*-axis. They can plot points accurately onto a graph and draw an accurate line linking the points they have plotted. Children can use the line graph to identify and plot missing data.

#### COMMON MISCONCEPTIONS

Children may find it difficult to decide on an appropriate scale. Encourage them to consider the smallest point and the greatest point and the difference between these. Ensure children use regular intervals that are easy to interpret: for example, 2s, 5s, 10s and hourly, half hourly, every 10 minutes, etc.

#### STRENGTHENING UNDERSTANDING

Provide children with the *x*-axis and *y*-axis completed. Discuss the intervals and why these are appropriate. Once children are secure in plotting points onto a graph, support them to draw their own. Provide step-by-step guidance. Ask: *What does the y-axis need to go up to? What does the x-axis need to go up to? How close are the points to plot? What regular intervals can we use?*

#### GOING DEEPER

Ask children to investigate conversion graphs. Ask: *Can you explain why they are in a straight line? Do all conversion line graphs have a straight line?*

#### KEY LANGUAGE

**In lesson:** construct, line graph, point, value, convert/conversion, straight line, equivalent, predict, scale, axis/axes

**Other language to be used by the teacher:** curve, plot, point, *x*-axis, *y*-axis, vertical, horizontal

#### STRUCTURES AND REPRESENTATIONS

Line graph

#### RESOURCES

**Mandatory:** graph paper

**Optional:** tracing paper, rulers

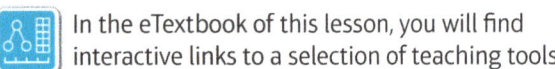

In the eTextbook of this lesson, you will find interactive links to a selection of teaching tools.

### Quick recap

Ask children to sketch an example of a simple line graph. Share examples and ask: *What information does your line graph show?*

# Discover

**WAYS OF WORKING** Pair work

**ASK**

- Question 1 a): *What are the points showing?*
- Question 1 a): *Where would the next points go?*
- Question 1 b): *Can you first draw a line through the points you have already plotted on the graph?*
- Question 1 b): *Which axis shows km? Can you find 44 km on this axis? What do you need to do to find this distance in miles?*

**IN FOCUS** This question introduces the use of a line graph to show a conversion. Encourage children to discuss and interpret the graph. Ask: *Do you recognise that the y-axis is showing the kilometres and the x-axis is showing the miles?* Discuss how children can use the data in the table to plot the next points and calculate how many kilometres there are in 20 miles.

**PRACTICAL TIPS** Provide children with tracing paper and rulers to plot the missing points on to the graph.

**ANSWERS**

Question 1 a): Children plot the known points and then draw a line to join them. They can then complete the table. The completed graph is shown in **Share**.

| Miles | Kilometres |
| --- | --- |
| 5 miles | 8 km |
| 10 miles | 16 km |
| 15 miles | 24 km |
| 20 miles | 32 km |
| 25 miles | 40 km |

Question 1 b): 44 km is half-way between 40 and 48 km.
27·5 miles is half-way between 25 and 30 miles.
So, 27·5 miles converts to 44 km.

# Share

**WAYS OF WORKING** Whole class teacher led

**ASK**

- Question 1 a): *Are the missing points plotted where you thought?*
- Question 1 a): *What did you need to do to complete the line graph?* (Plot points and connect the points with a line.)
- Question 1 b): *Did anyone notice the line was straight? What does this tell us?*

**IN FOCUS** Recap the questions together. Check the plotted points together. How many children worked these out? Discuss the straight line. Ask: *Can you recognise and explain whether this means the rate of change is consistent or proportional?*

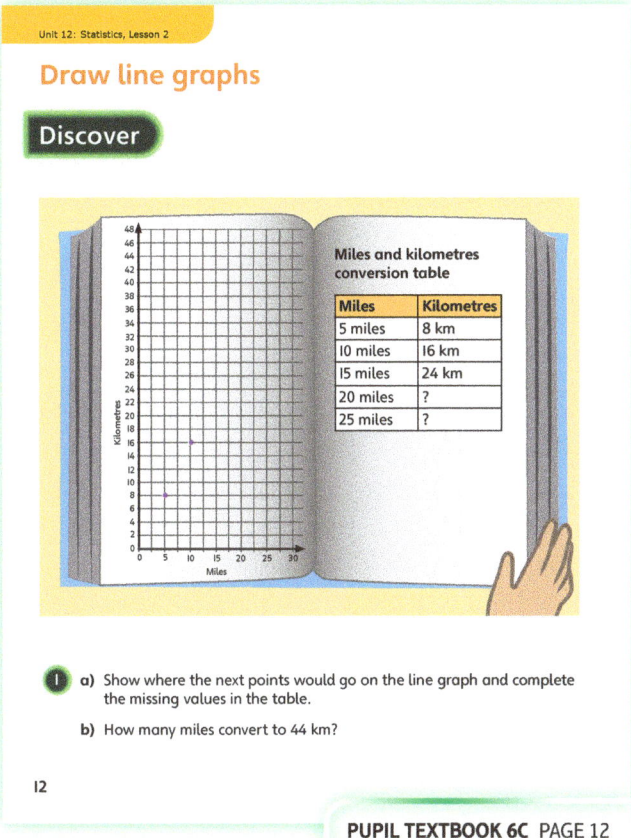

PUPIL TEXTBOOK 6C PAGE 12

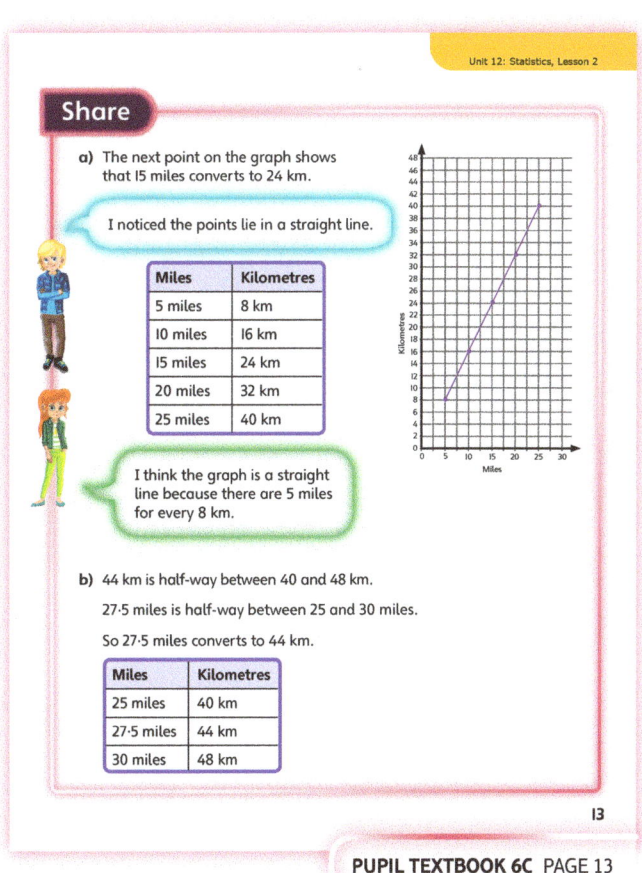

PUPIL TEXTBOOK 6C PAGE 13

# Think together

**WAYS OF WORKING** Whole class teacher led (I do, We do, You do)

**ASK**

- Question ②: *Where should you plot the point for 8 pm? How can you use the shape of the graph to help you estimate where that point should be plotted?*
- Question ③: *What scale would be appropriate to use and why? Can you explain why you need to start at zero on both axes?*
- Question ③: *How can you use the graph to find out other data?*

**IN FOCUS** For question ③, children have to draw a conversion line graph from data. Children should think about how they can use the graph specifically to find the conversions in part b), rather than calculate the conversions using data. Help children to identify which axis to start from for any given conversion. For example, if they are given a length in mm, they need to start from the *x*-axis, draw a vertical line to the graph, and then draw a horizontal line across to the *y*-axis.

**STRENGTHEN** Discuss the line graphs in detail and support children to identify what scale to use on the axes. Practise plotting points on to the graph and joining the dots with a line. Discuss what each graph shows.

**DEEPEN** Challenge children to draw a line graph to match a story of a journey, for example: Kate leaves the house at 4:30 pm and arrives at 6:00 pm. She walks 1 km to the train station. She waits 10 minutes for the train. The train journey is 100 km and takes 70 minutes.

**ASSESSMENT CHECKPOINT** Question ③ will show whether children can decide on an appropriate scale to use for the *y*-axis and *x*-axis.

All questions will show that children have understood the lessons on line graphs and are confident with identifying and plotting points, drawing appropriate horizontal and vertical lines on the graph, and reading off information.

**ANSWERS**

Question ①: 10 miles is equivalent to 16 kilometres.
20 kilometres is equivalent to 12·5 miles.
There are 1·6 kilometres in 1 mile.

Question ② a): The shadow was 10 m long between 8:45 and 9 am, approximately at 8:52 am.

Question ② b): Between 18 m and 20 m.

Question ③ a):

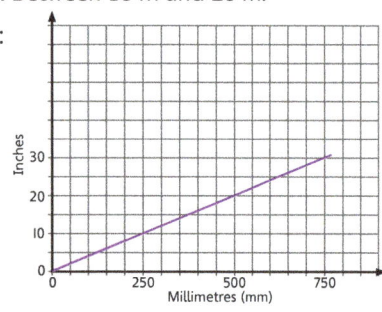

Question ③ b): 25 inches = 635 mm    1 m = 40 inches
800 mm = 31·5 inches    6 ft = 1·8 m
15 inches = 38 cm

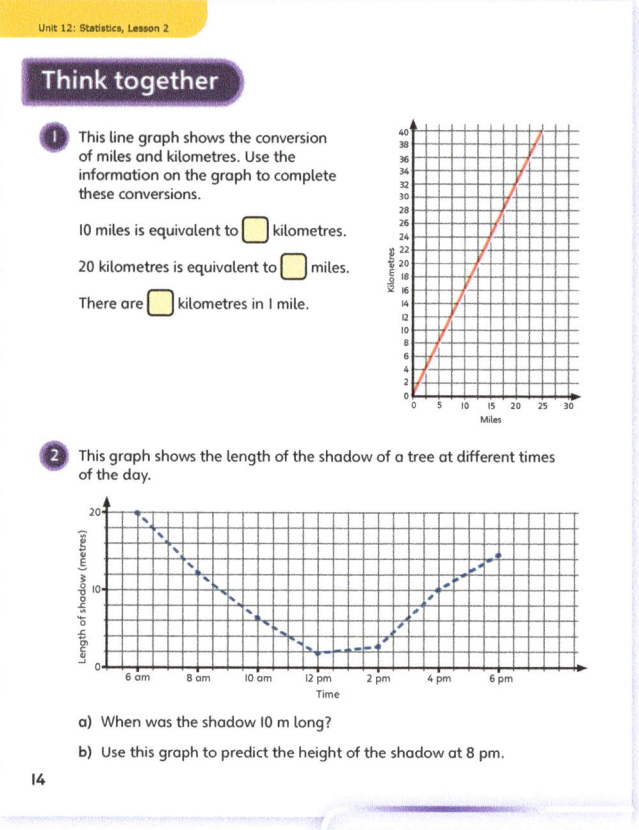

**PUPIL TEXTBOOK 6C** PAGE 14

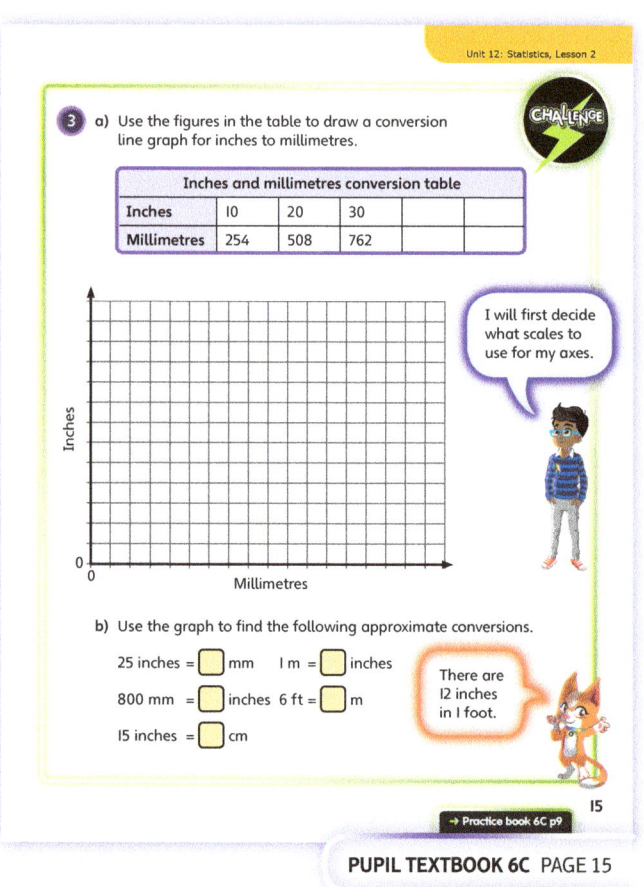

**PUPIL TEXTBOOK 6C** PAGE 15

# Unit 12: Statistics, Lesson 2

## Practice

**WAYS OF WORKING** Independent thinking

**IN FOCUS** Children use the data in tables to plot points onto line graphs. They need to use the graphs to identify other data. Ensure children use the graphs to read and identify unmarked points and add to the data listed in the table rather than calculating the further data.

**STRENGTHEN** Discuss the line graphs in detail and support children to identify the scale used on the axes. Discuss the shapes of each graph and what this tells you about the data. Look at the graph in question ❶ and ask: *Do you think a conversion graph will always be a straight line? Why?*

**DEEPEN** In question ❹, children need to draw a conversion line graph from an incomplete table. Children should think about how they can use the graph to complete both conversion tables, rather than calculating the conversions first and then plotting the graph.

**ASSESSMENT CHECKPOINT** All questions can be used to check that children can plot points accurately onto a graph, can draw an accurate line linking the points they have plotted and can use a line graph to identify and plot missing data.

**ANSWERS** Answers for the **Practice** part of the lesson can be found in the *Power Maths* online subscription.

## Reflect

**WAYS OF WORKING** Independent thinking

**IN FOCUS** Children need to explain how they would go about drawing a line graph to convert from metres to kilometres. Their explanation should include how to choose a scale for the axes as well as how to plot the points.

**ASSESSMENT CHECKPOINT** Writing an explanation of how to draw a line graph will show whether children are confident about constructing line graphs and whether there is anything they do not truly understand.

**ANSWERS** Answers for the **Reflect** part of the lesson can be found in the *Power Maths* online subscription.

> **After the lesson** ⏸
> - Can all children create a line graph accurately?
> - Are all children confident about using a line graph to identify data?

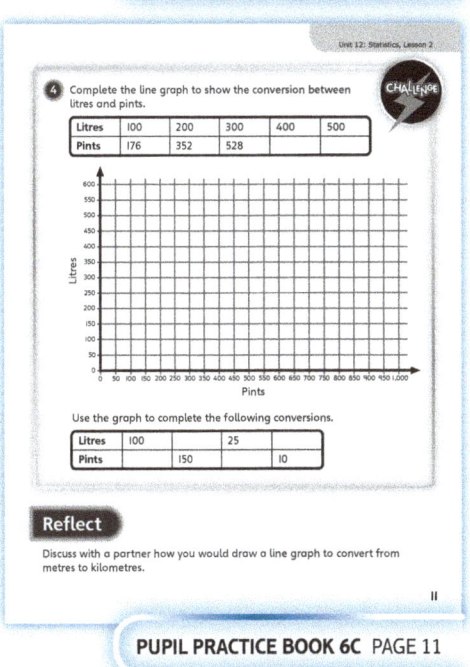

PUPIL PRACTICE BOOK 6C PAGE 9

PUPIL PRACTICE BOOK 6C PAGE 10

PUPIL PRACTICE BOOK 6C PAGE 11

Unit 12: Statistics, Lesson 3

# Advanced bar charts

### Learning focus
In this lesson, children will deepen their skills with interpreting bar charts by exploring more advanced examples.

### Before you teach
- Can children interpret simple bar charts?
- Can children read vertical scales accurately?

#### NATIONAL CURRICULUM LINKS

**Year 6 Number – Addition, subtraction, multiplication and division**

Solve addition and subtraction multi-step problems in contexts, deciding which operations and methods to use and why.

Use estimation to check answers to calculations and determine, in the context of a problem, an appropriate degree of accuracy.

#### ASSESSING MASTERY

Children can solve problems involving multi-step calculations by interpreting advanced bar charts where there are two bars for each category or one bar split into two parts.

#### COMMON MISCONCEPTIONS

Children may mis-read the vertical scales on bar charts. Ask:
- *What values can you read from the scale?*
- *How many intervals are here? What is the scale interval divided into?*

#### STRENGTHENING UNDERSTANDING

Encourage children to spend time discussing and interpreting each bar chart before thinking about how this information applies to the problem in the question.

#### GOING DEEPER

Challenge children to create their own bar charts for data that relates to their own interests, for example: sports scores or garden birds.

#### KEY LANGUAGE

**In lesson:** bar, scale, interval, **bar chart**

**Other language to be used by the teacher:** bar, height, taller, shorter, estimate, more, fewer, multi-step

#### STRUCTURES AND REPRESENTATIONS

Bar charts

#### RESOURCES

**Optional:** cubes in two colours, newspapers, spreadsheet software

 In the eTextbook of this lesson, you will find interactive links to a selection of teaching tools.

### Quick recap
Discuss the following vertical scales that can be used on graphs and charts:
0 to 1,000
0 to 100
0 to 2,000
Discuss which interval marks would usually be chosen for each scale and why.

# Discover

**WAYS OF WORKING** Pair work

**ASK**

- Question 1 a): *What type of chart is this?*
- Question 1 a): *What do you think the key means?*
- Question 1 b): *What do you need to look for to find which is the most popular club overall?*
- Question 1 b): *What do you need to look for to find out which club is most popular amongst children in Year 6?*

**IN FOCUS** Develop children's understanding by encouraging them to first spend time discussing everything they notice about the bar chart, before they start to answer the questions. Ask: *What is the scale on the vertical axis? What is each interval worth? What do the two colours mean? Why is each bar split in two? What information does this give us?*

In question 1 b), children begin to interpret the bar chart. Help them to see that the most popular club overall is the one with the tallest bar. However, the most popular club amongst children in Year 6 is the the one with the tallest yellow portion of the bar. This isn't necessarily the tallest bar overall!

**PRACTICAL TIPS** Children can use cubes in two colours to make cube towers that represent each bar. They can break their cube towers apart to compare and explore what each colour is worth and then recombine them to find the total.

**ANSWERS**

Question 1 a): Each bar is split to show the results for children in Year 5 and also for children in Year 6.

Question 1 b): Football is the most popular club overall. Basketball is the most popular choice for children in Year 6.

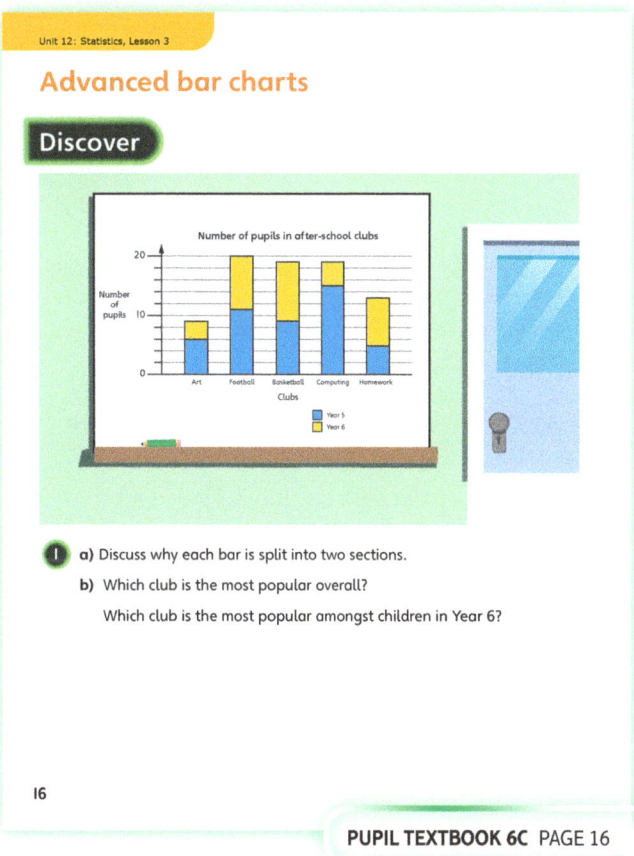

PUPIL TEXTBOOK 6C PAGE 16

# Share

**WAYS OF WORKING** Whole class teacher led

**ASK**

- Question 1 a): *What are the intervals on the vertical scale?*
- Question 1 b): *How do you know that football is the most popular club overall?*
- Question 1 b): *How did you work out the heights of the bars for Year 6 children only?*

**IN FOCUS** In question 1 b), explore different ways of finding the heights of the yellow bars. For example, if children are working with different coloured cubes, they may simply count the yellow cubes. This will help them understand that they need to focus only on yellow cubes for this part of the question. Alternatively, can they find the height of the yellow portions of each bar by finding the difference between the upper and lower limit of each yellow bar? Ask: *Which club was the most popular for Year 5 children? How many Year 5 children chose it? How many Year 6 children chose it? How did you work it out?*

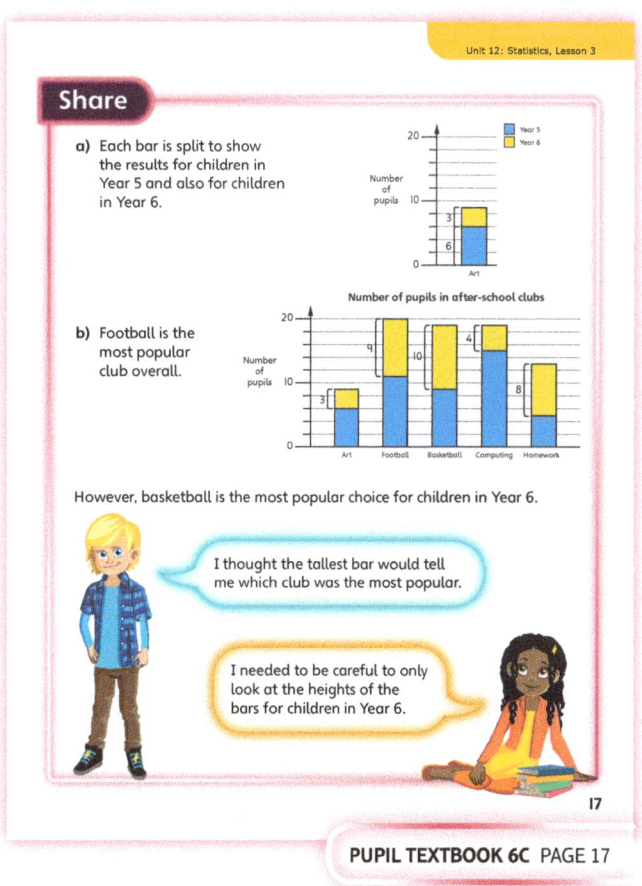

PUPIL TEXTBOOK 6C PAGE 17

# Think together

**WAYS OF WORKING** Whole class teacher led (I do, We do, You do)

**ASK**

- Question ❶: *What is the same and what is different about this chart and the chart on the Discover page? What are the intervals on the vertical scale?*
- Question ❷: *What do you notice about the categories on the horizontal axis?*
- Question ❸: *Have you ever seen a chart with horizontal bars before? Do you prefer working with horizontal bars or vertical bars?*

**IN FOCUS** The bar charts in questions ❶ and ❸ have two separate bars for each category. Look at the bar chart in question ❶ alongside the bar chart in the **Discover** section. Explore how the bar chart in question ❶ makes it easier to see the number of trees in each category for any given year because the bars are side-by-side; both start at zero so you do not have to calculate any differences to find the number of deciduous trees in a year. However, it is much harder to clearly see the total number of trees in this format. The bar chart in **Discover** shows totals for each category much more clearly. In question ❷, the bar chart shows grouped data, as each bar represents a range of numbers. Children will notice that the bar chart in question ❸ is presented horizontally, though they should realise that the type of information given and the skills required to interpret it are just the same as they would use with a vertical bar chart.

**STRENGTHEN** Remind children to spend time discussing and interpreting all the information they can find in a given bar chart before even reading the question and preparing to solve the problem.

**DEEPEN** Challenge children to create their own advanced bar charts for a data set of their choice. They can decide whether they would like to use a bar chart where each bar is split into two parts, or where there are two bars for each category, or where each bar shows grouped data. They write questions about the data in their bar chart for a partner to solve.

**ASSESSMENT CHECKPOINT** Question ❸ assesses whether children can consider and identify what information is or is not included in a given bar chart.

**ANSWERS**

Question ❶ a): 2013, 2018, 2023

Question ❶ b): 4,000 evergreens were planted in total.

Question ❶ c): Approximately 1,600 deciduous (just under half-way between 1,500 and 1,750).

Question ❷ a): 25 households have fewer than 11 pets.

Question ❷ b): 1 household has more than 16 pets.

Question ❸: Various responses are possible, for example:
A: What is the total screen time recorded for school A?
B: How does the graph show which year group has less screen time?
C: What is the total screen time recorded for school B? How much more screen time does Year 6 have than Year 2 in school C?

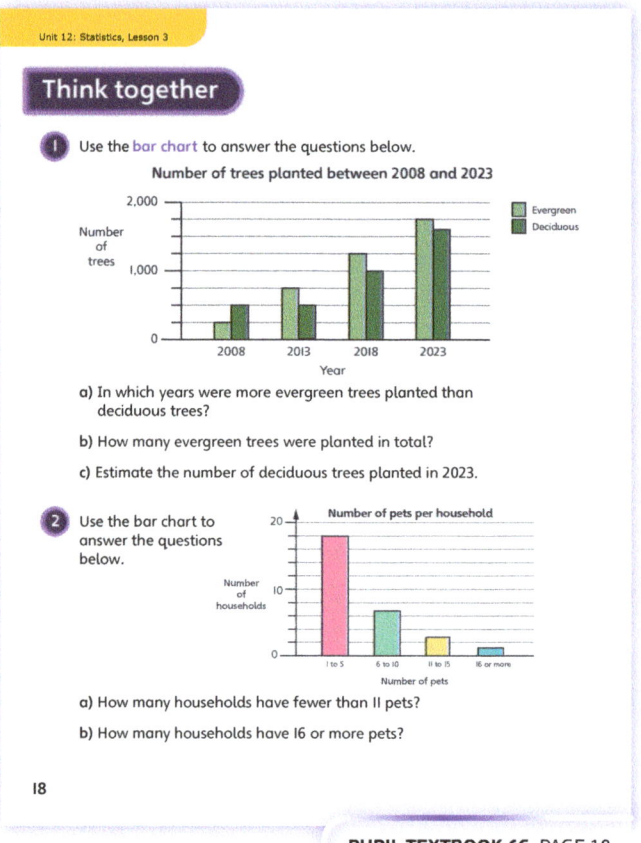

PUPIL TEXTBOOK 6C PAGE 18

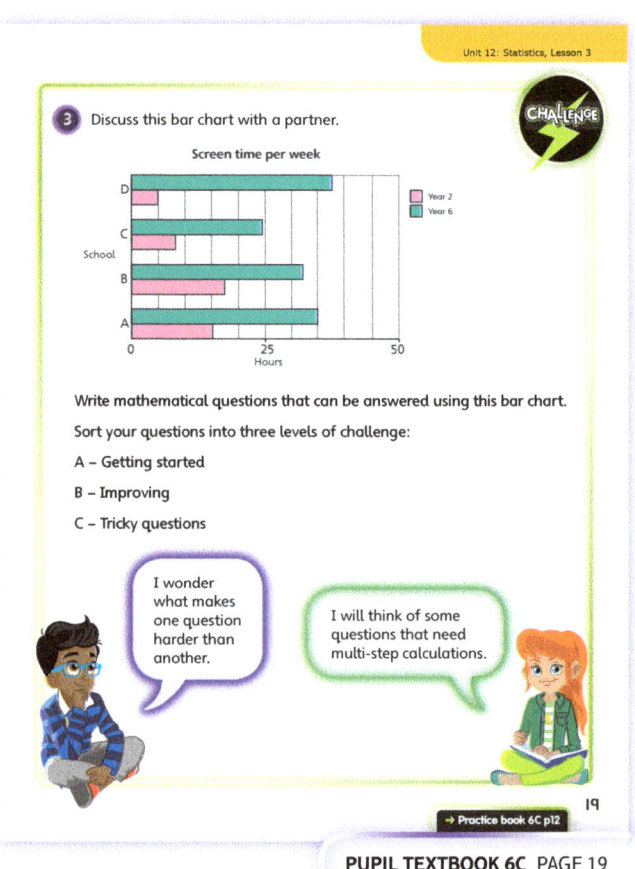

PUPIL TEXTBOOK 6C PAGE 19

# Unit 12: Statistics, Lesson 3

## Practice

**WAYS OF WORKING** Independent thinking

**IN FOCUS** Question ① presents children with an advanced bar chart that has two bars for each category and question ② has a bar chart where each bar represents grouped data. Children interpret and compare the bars to answer a series of problems. Check that children are reading the vertical scale accurately and understand what each interval represents. The bars on the chart in question ③ are each split into two parts. Children need to interpret this accurately in order to write questions about the information in the chart for others in the class to solve.

**STRENGTHEN** Strengthen children's understanding of what information can and cannot be captured in a more complex bar chart by asking increasingly difficult questions about the data in the chart, finishing with a question that cannot be answered by referring to the bar chart. For example, ask: *How many adults visited the cinema in week 1? How many adults and children visited the cinema altogether over 5 weeks? How old were the children that visited the cinema in week 3? Did the bar chart help you to answer that question? Why/why not?*

**DEEPEN** Ask children to look for bar charts in newspapers or other media. They can also use spreadsheet software to explore chart functions and create an advanced bar chart to represent a data set of their choice.

**ASSESSMENT CHECKPOINT** Use question ③ to assess whether children are able to understand the structure of an advanced bar chart and use it to derive related questions and answers.

**ANSWERS** Answers for the **Practice** part of the lesson can be found in the *Power Maths* online subscription.

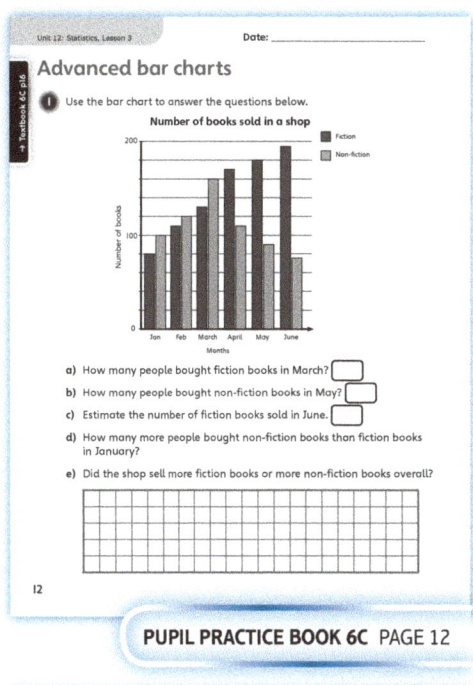

PUPIL PRACTICE BOOK 6C PAGE 12

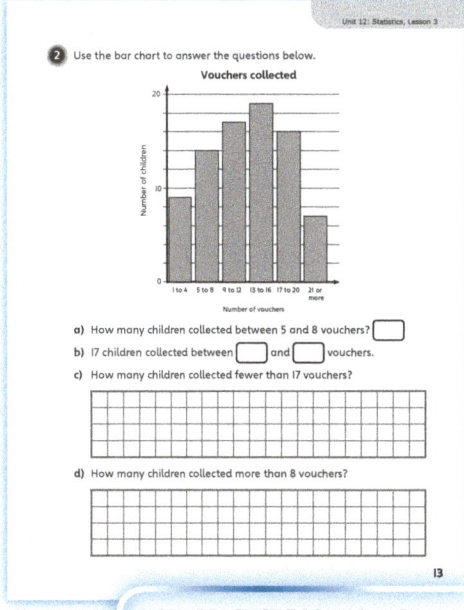

PUPIL PRACTICE BOOK 6C PAGE 13

## Reflect

**WAYS OF WORKING** Pair work

**IN FOCUS** The **Reflect** part of the lesson prompts children to think about the purpose of using different types of bar chart to present data. They can recap the three different bar charts that they encountered in the lesson (compound bars, side-by-side bars, and bars for grouped data) and describe how each of these is useful.

**ASSESSMENT CHECKPOINT** Assess whether children can discuss and justify the choices they will make when designing or selecting a type of advanced bar chart to present information.

**ANSWERS** Answers for the **Reflect** part of the lesson can be found in the *Power Maths* online subscription.

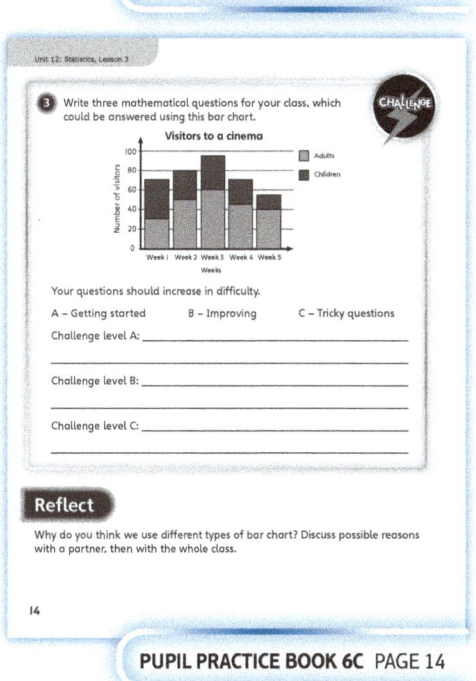

PUPIL PRACTICE BOOK 6C PAGE 14

## After the lesson

- Were children able to interpret the information presented in more complex bar charts?
- Did children identify sensible calculations that they could use to solve multi-step problems about data in advanced bar charts?

Unit 12: Statistics, Lesson 4

# Understand and complete pie charts

### Learning focus
In this lesson, children are introduced to pie charts. They compare pie charts to tally charts and bar charts. Children should begin to understand that pie charts show results as a whole split into parts.

### Before you teach
- Are children secure in identifying fractions of a circle such as $\frac{1}{2}, \frac{1}{4}, \frac{1}{3}$, etc.?
- Are children able to draw and use tally and bar charts accurately?

### NATIONAL CURRICULUM LINKS

**Year 6 Statistics**

Interpret and construct pie charts and line graphs and use these to solve problems.

### ASSESSING MASTERY

Children can recognise and name pie charts. They understand that the pie chart represents a set of data as a whole split into parts and the whole circle represents all the results together. Children can explain that a pie chart makes it easy to compare parts with a whole. They can suggest when a pie chart is more useful than other types of data representation such as tally charts or bar charts. Children can suggest types of questions that a pie chart is most suitable to answer.

### COMMON MISCONCEPTIONS

Some children may not recognise that a pie chart shows the same information as a tally and bar chart. Ask:
- *What is the pie chart showing? Does it show the same thing as a tally chart or a bar chart?*

Children may find it difficult to understand that a pie chart represents the whole. Ask:
- *Could you think of a pie chart like a cake or a pie? The pie chart represents the whole and a slice or sector is a part of the whole.*

### STRENGTHENING UNDERSTANDING

Provide children with circles and ask them to shade in fractions, for example, colour $\frac{1}{2}$ of the circle, colour $\frac{3}{4}$ of the circle and explain that the parts are fractions of the whole (the whole is the total number of people or data collected). Look at examples of pie charts representing data where half the children or a quarter of the children have chosen an activity or item. Ask: *Which activity or item did half the children choose? Which activity did a quarter of the children choose?*

### GOING DEEPER

Provide children with statements about different types of chart and ask them to identify which chart it is about (pie chart/ bar chart/tally chart). Ask: *Can you add any statements of your own?*
- You can draw the chart as you collect data.
- It is simple to draw this type of chart.
- You can calculate the numerical difference between parts easily.
- It is easy to compare the parts with the whole with this type of chart.
- It can be tricky to draw this type of chart precisely.

### KEY LANGUAGE

**In lesson:** **pie chart**, advantages, disadvantages, **sectors**, whole, represent, largest, section, half, **data**, tally chart, bar chart, compare, scale, quarter, total, frequency

**Other language to be used by the teacher:** smallest, percentage, fraction, part

### STRUCTURES AND REPRESENTATIONS

Pie charts, tally charts, bar charts

### RESOURCES

**Optional:** paper circles, counters, cubes

 In the eTextbook of this lesson, you will find interactive links to a selection of teaching tools.

### Quick recap
Ask children to draw a circle and split it into quarters. Then ask them to draw a circle and split it into eighths.

# Discover

**WAYS OF WORKING** Pair work

**ASK**

- Question 1 a): *What is each chart called? What does it show? Do all the charts show the same data?*
- Question 1 a): *Which were the most popular and the least popular activities? How do you know?*
- Question 1 a): *How many children were asked in total? What would half be?*
- Question 1 b): *What is similar or different about the charts?*
- Question 1 b): *Which chart do you prefer and why?*

**IN FOCUS** Question 1 gives children the opportunity to discuss the different ways of representing data. Ensure children understand that the different charts represent the same data. Encourage children to discuss what is the same or different about the charts and whether different charts can be better/easier to interpret in different situations or more suitable to answer certain questions. Ask children to consider how they could represent their comparisons of the different types of chart.

**PRACTICAL TIPS** Provide children with counters/cubes which they can group to represent the different votes.

**ANSWERS**

Question 1 a): The pie chart shows most clearly that no activity received half the votes.

Question 1 b): The completed table is shown in **Share**.

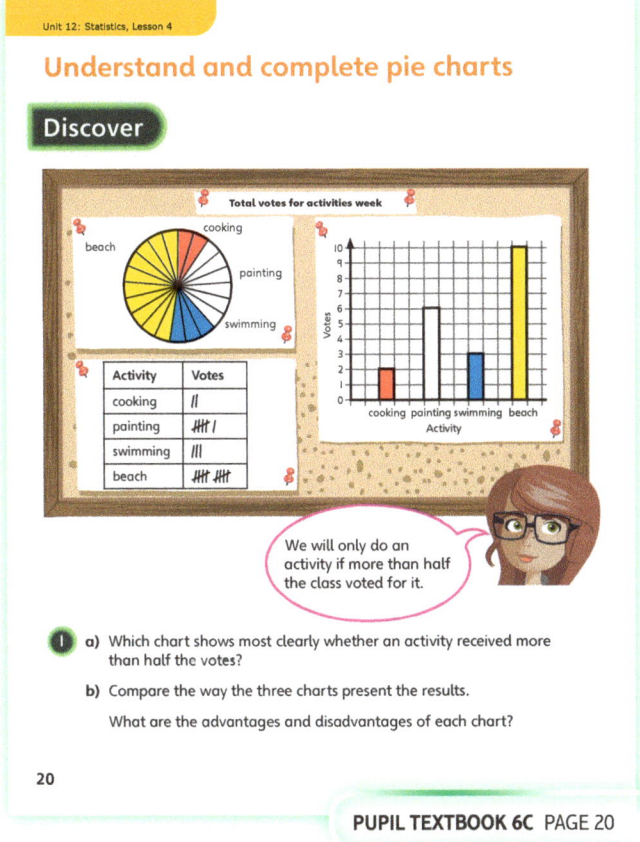

# Share

**WAYS OF WORKING** Whole class teacher led

**ASK**

- Question 1 b): *What is a pie chart? What are the advantages and disadvantages of a pie chart?*
- Question 1 b): *Do you agree with the advantages and disadvantages?*

**IN FOCUS** This is the first time children are formally introduced to pie charts. Ensure children understand that the circle represents all the results. Discuss the advantages and disadvantages of tally charts, bar charts and pie charts. Give example questions or situations and ask children to suggest which chart would be most suitable. Ask:

- *How many more children chose the beach than cooking?* (Bar chart)
- *Which is the least popular activity?* (Bar chart)
- *Which chart is the easiest to draw?* (Tally)
- *Which chart can I draw while collecting data?* (Tally)
- *Which chart shows if more or less than half chose the same activity?* (Pie chart)

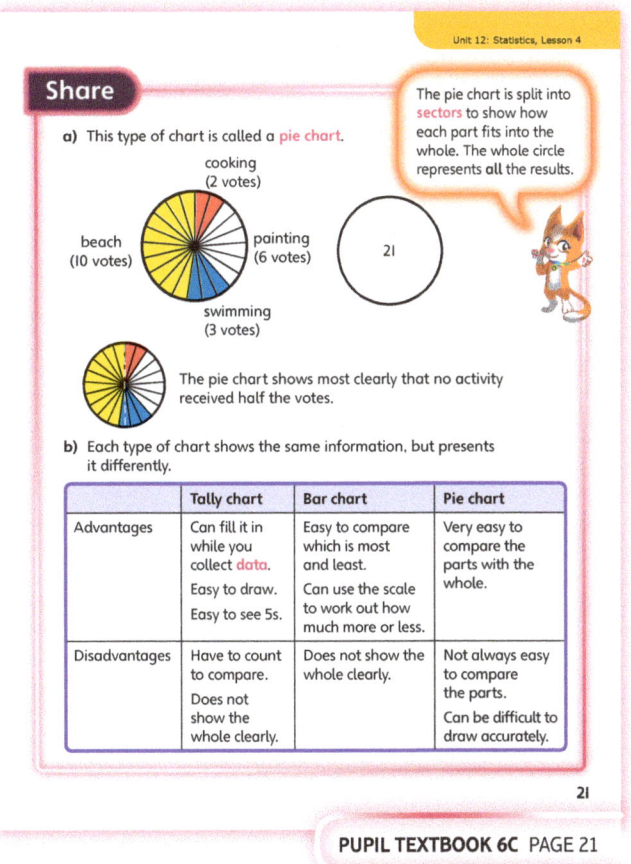

57

## Think together

**WAYS OF WORKING** Whole class teacher led (I do, We do, You do)

**ASK**
- Question ❶: *What do the different sections of the pie chart represent?*
- Question ❷: *How is a pie chart similar or different to a bar chart?*
- Question ❷: *Which chart is the best one to use for each question? Why?*

**IN FOCUS** In question ❶, children compare two different types of chart that represent the same data. Encourage them to explore the usefulness of pie charts. Elicit from children that pie charts show the whole and are particularly useful when comparing one category to all of the results as a whole.

Question ❸ focuses on children's ability to match a tally chart to a pie chart showing the same information. Discuss Ash's comment. Ask: *Can you explain why the charts match or don't match?*

**STRENGTHEN** For question ❷, help children understand what mathematical operation they need to do in order to answer each part of the question. For example, read part a) as a class and ask: *What do you need to do to find out how many more gold medals than silver medals were won? Is this an addition or a subtraction?* For part b), ask: *Look at the different sectors of the pie chart. Which one looks like it is almost a quarter? How can you check this using the numbers in the pie chart?*

**DEEPEN** Challenge children to draw a tally to match each pie chart in question ❸.

**ASSESSMENT CHECKPOINT** Use all the questions to check whether children understand that the circle of a pie chart represents all of the results and the sections represent the different categories. Ask: *Do you understand that the same data can be represented in different ways, and that different charts are more suited to answer different types of question?*

**ANSWERS**

Question ❶:

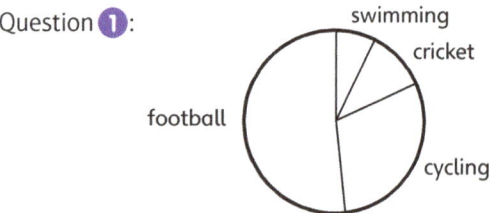

Question ❷ a): The team won 4 more gold medals than silver.

Question ❷ b): Bronze medals are about $\frac{1}{4}$ of the total medals.

Question ❷ c): 67 medals were won in total.

Question ❸: Pie chart C. The cat is just under half of the total number.

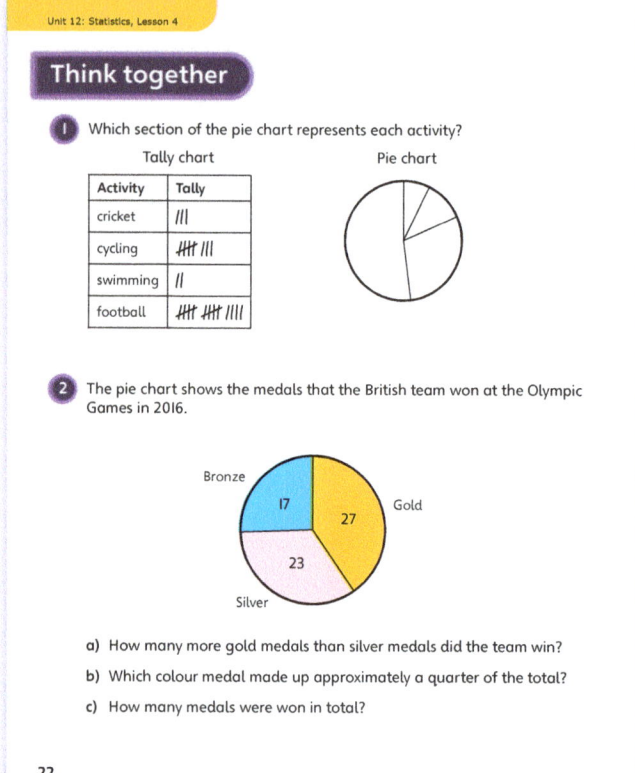

PUPIL TEXTBOOK 6C PAGE 22

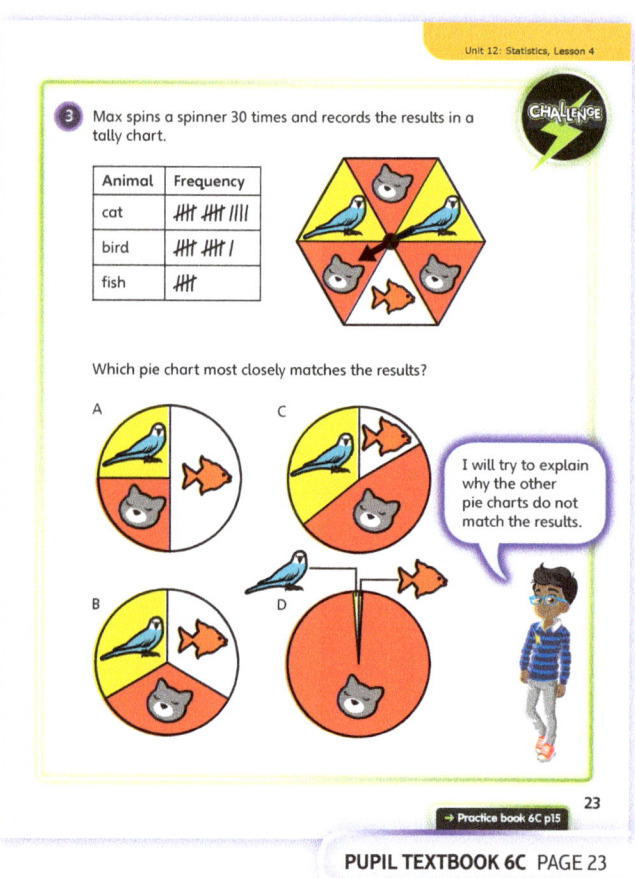

PUPIL TEXTBOOK 6C PAGE 23

# Unit 12: Statistics, Lesson 4

## Practice

**WAYS OF WORKING** Independent thinking

**IN FOCUS** In question ❶, children compare the information in three pie charts to work out which shows a fraction of more than half. This requires them to understand that parts of a pie chart represent fractions of a whole.

**STRENGTHEN** If children are finding it a challenge to recognise fractions in a pie chart, provide them with circles and ask them to shade in fractions, for example, colour $\frac{1}{2}$ of the circle, colour $\frac{3}{4}$ of the circle. Explain that the parts are fractions of the whole (the whole is the total number of (people/data collected).

**DEEPEN** Challenge children to draw a tally to match each pie chart in question ❶.

**THINK DIFFERENTLY** Question ❷ requires children to interpret the information shown on a pie chart in order to prove or disprove a statement. They should recognise that the category with the smallest section is the least popular.

**ASSESSMENT CHECKPOINT** Question ❹ assesses whether children can use the data in a tally chart to create a pie chart. Ensure children understand that the same data can be represented in different ways.

Question ❺ assesses whether children recognise that different charts are more appropriate for different types of question. They should be able to provide clear explanations as to why each one is better for different questions.

**ANSWERS** Answers for the **Practice** part of the lesson can be found in the *Power Maths* online subscription.

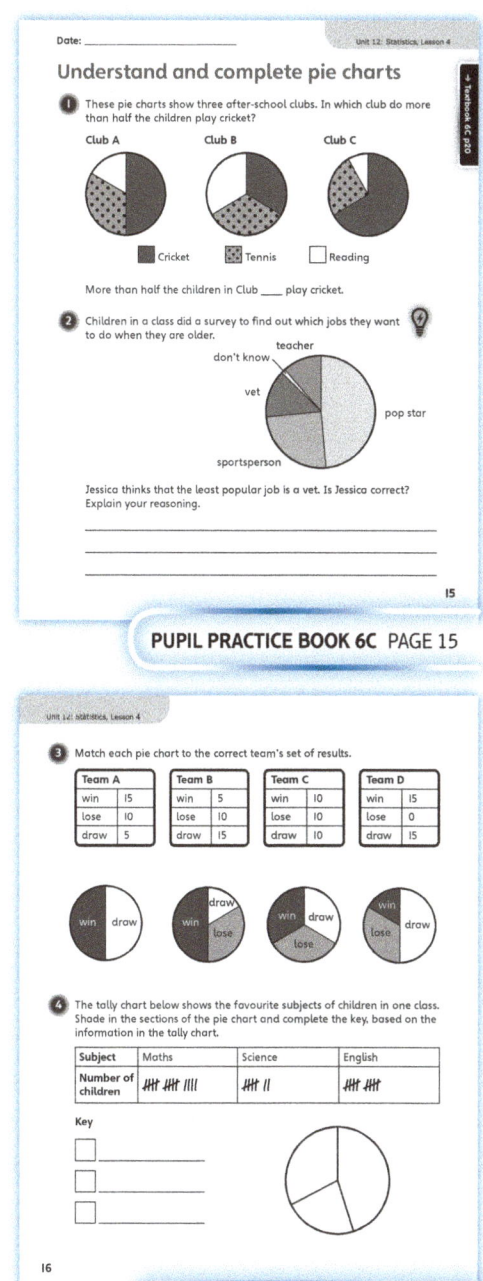

PUPIL PRACTICE BOOK 6C PAGE 15

PUPIL PRACTICE BOOK 6C PAGE 16

## Reflect

**WAYS OF WORKING** Independent thinking

**IN FOCUS** Children should identify that a pie chart is a circle that represents all the results, with each section showing a category of data. A bar chart shows each category of data as a separate bar. Children should recognise that bar charts are more useful to compare the categories, whereas a pie chart is particularly useful when comparing a category (as a fraction) to the results (as a whole).

**ASSESSMENT CHECKPOINT** Use this question to assess whether children recognise the differences and similarities between different types of chart and if they can suggest when a pie chart is most useful.

**ANSWERS** Answers for the **Reflect** part of the lesson can be found in the *Power Maths* online subscription.

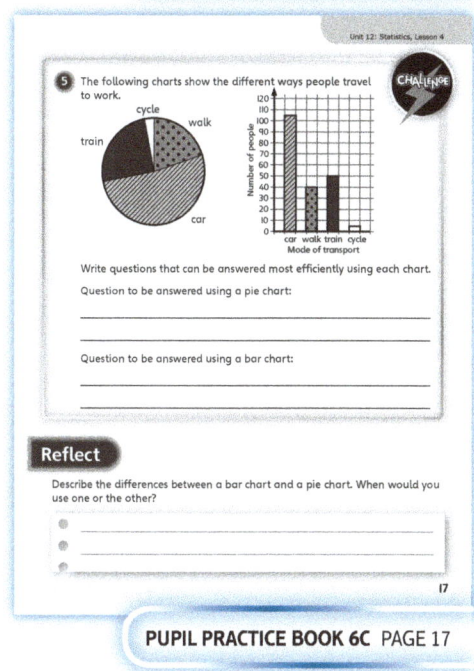

PUPIL PRACTICE BOOK 6C PAGE 17

## After the lesson

- What percentage of children are confident at matching different types of chart showing the same data?
- Are there any misconceptions you need to pick up on before next lesson?

59

Unit 12: Statistics, Lesson 5

# Read and interpret pie charts

**Learning focus**

In this lesson, children begin to read and interpret pie charts. Children can answer questions about pie charts.

**Before you teach**

- Are children secure in reading and interpreting tally charts?
- Are children able to use a key confidently?
- Do children understand that the circle of the pie chart represents all of the results as a whole?

### NATIONAL CURRICULUM LINKS

**Year 6 Statistics**

Interpret and construct pie charts and line graphs and use these to solve problems.

### ASSESSING MASTERY

Children can read and interpret pie charts using a key when provided. Children can use a pie chart to answer questions about a set of data. Children are able to complete a pie chart using data in a tally chart and a key by colouring in the appropriate sectors. Children are able to sketch simple pie charts to represent data by dividing the circle into equal parts to represent each person.

### COMMON MISCONCEPTIONS

When transferring information from a tally chart to a pie chart, children may not understand that they need to count up the total number of tallies and divide the circle into this number of equal-sized sectors. They may need help understanding that sectors which can be grouped together to represent one category should all be placed next to one another. Ask:
- What is the total of all the tallies in the tally chart? How many equal-sized sectors should I divide the pie chart into?
- Will it be easier to understand what fraction of the whole is represented by (for example, superheroes) if all the sectors for (superheroes) are next to each other or apart?

### STRENGTHENING UNDERSTANDING

Children may find it difficult to divide a circle into equal parts. Support children by providing templates. Practise transferring sets of data in a tally chart into a pie chart by using a key and colouring a sector for each person. Ensure children understand that sectors of the same colour go next to each other.

### GOING DEEPER

Provide children with sets of data to transfer to a pie chart where each sector represents more than one person. For example:

| Fruit | Tally |
|---|---|
| pear | /// |
| banana | ⊬ℍ / |
| orange | ⊬ℍ //// |
| strawberry | ⊬ℍ / |

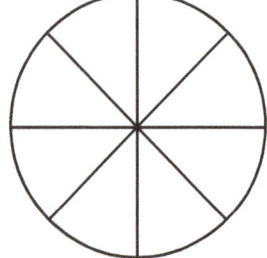

### KEY LANGUAGE

**In lesson:** pie chart, represent, same, different, tally chart, equal, sector, section, more, same

**Other language to be used by the teacher:** data, bar chart, percentage, fraction, part, whole, category, results, total

### STRUCTURES AND REPRESENTATIONS

Tally chart, bar chart, pie chart

### RESOURCES

**Optional:** pie charts, templates (circles split into 6, 8, 10, 12, 24), counters, cubes

 In the eTextbook of this lesson, you will find interactive links to a selection of teaching tools.

**Quick recap**

Ask children to sketch an example of a simple pie chart. Share examples and ask: *What information does your pie chart show?*

Unit 12: Statistics, Lesson 5

# Discover

**WAYS OF WORKING** Pair work

**ASK**
- Question 1 a): *How many different categories are there?*
- Question 1 a): *How many children are at the party in total?*
- Question 1 a): *How many sectors will be on the pie chart?*

**IN FOCUS** For question 1 a), children are required to use the picture of the fancy dress party to create a pie chart. They will need to decide how many categories there are and how many sectors there will be on the pie chart. Prompt discussion about how children will fill in the pie chart and whether they will use a key to represent each category.

**PRACTICAL TIPS** Provide children with blank pie chart templates, in this case circles divided into 12 sectors.

**ANSWERS**

Question 1 a):

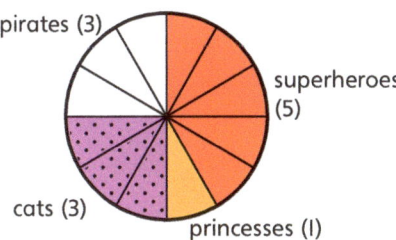

Question 1 b):

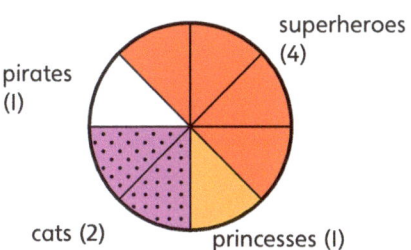

# Share

**WAYS OF WORKING** Whole class teacher led

**ASK**
- Question 1 a): *What does each sector of the pie chart represent?*
- Question 1 a): *How many categories or sections is the pie chart split into? What does each section represent?*

**IN FOCUS** It is important that children understand that each sector on the pie chart represents one person at the party and that each colour represents a different fancy dress category (a section of the pie chart). The pie chart in question 1 a) is divided into 12 sectors because there are 12 people. The pie chart in question 1 b) is divided into 8 sectors because there are 8 people.

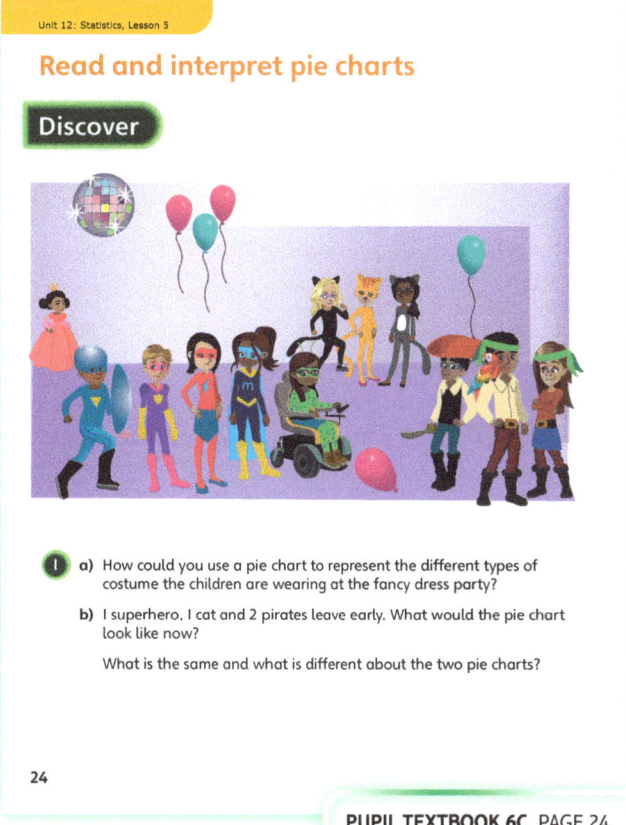

PUPIL TEXTBOOK 6C PAGE 24

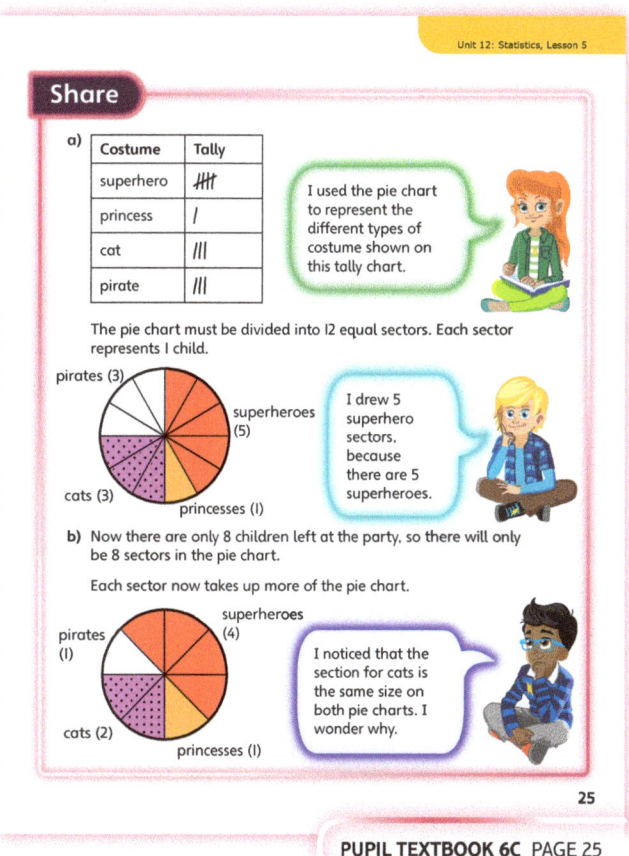

PUPIL TEXTBOOK 6C PAGE 25

# Think together

**WAYS OF WORKING** Whole class teacher led (I do, We do, You do)

**ASK**
- Question ①: *How many children are there altogether?*
- Question ②: *What does each coloured section represent?*

**IN FOCUS** In question ②, children are asked to compare two pie charts. Ask: *Can you count the sectors and identify that there were 3 children who chose rap music and now there are 5?*

In question ③, children need to identify that there are 8 sectors on the pie chart and 24 people, therefore each sector represents 3 people.

**STRENGTHEN** For question ③ a), if children are finding the concept of each sector representing more than one person challenging, give them some division examples:
- *If there are 9 sectors and 18 people, how many people does each sector represent?*
- *If there are 4 sectors and 20 people, how many people does each sector represent?*

**DEEPEN** For question ③ b), encourage children to consider different pie charts to represent the same data. For example, different numbers of sectors. The pie chart could have 32, 16 or 8 sectors. Ask: *Can you compare the pie charts?*

Children could also draw pie charts from previous questions with different numbers of sectors. Children should recognise that the number of sectors must be a factor of the total.

**ASSESSMENT CHECKPOINT** Use question ① to check that children can compare the information in two pie charts when there are a different number of sectors. Consider whether children can recognise that they will not be able to work out whether more children in Class 1 or Class 2 like singing just by comparing the size of the coloured sections.

**ANSWERS**

Question ①: Singing: true. More than a quarter of the children in Class 1 chose singing, whereas less than a quarter of the children in Class 2 chose singing. 4 out of 12 is more than 4 out of 20. Musical statues: false. Although the section representing musical statues is a quarter of each pie chart, it shows 3 (out of 12) for Class 1 and 5 (out of 20) for Class 2. So more children chose musical statues in Class 2 than in Class 1.

Question ②: 2 voted for rock and 2 voted for rap.

Question ③ a): 6 more people danced; 18 people did not sing.

Question ③ b):

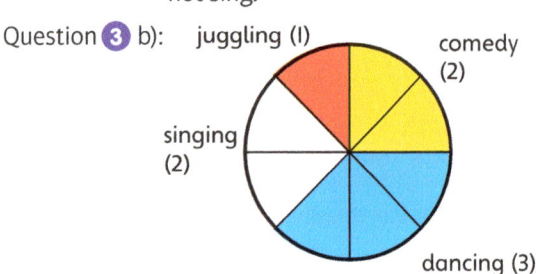

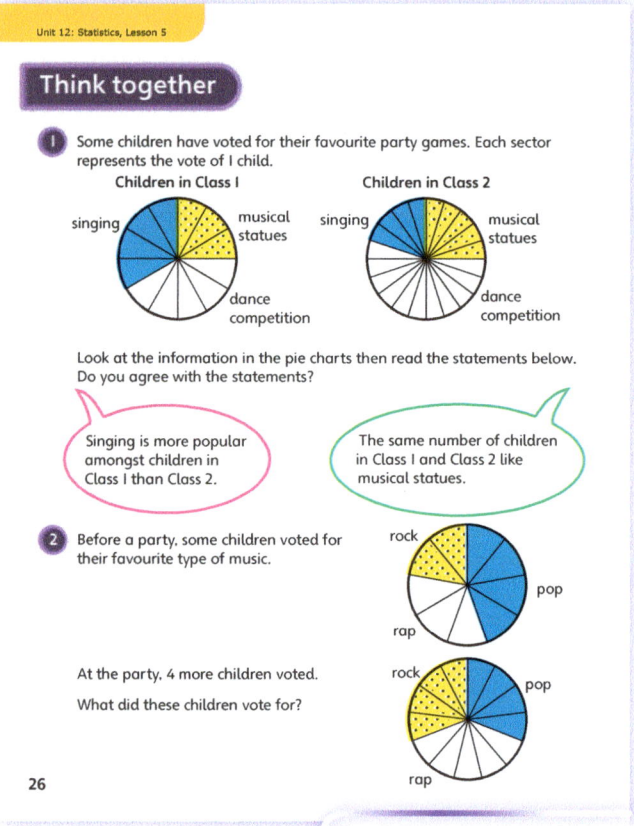

PUPIL TEXTBOOK 6C PAGE 26

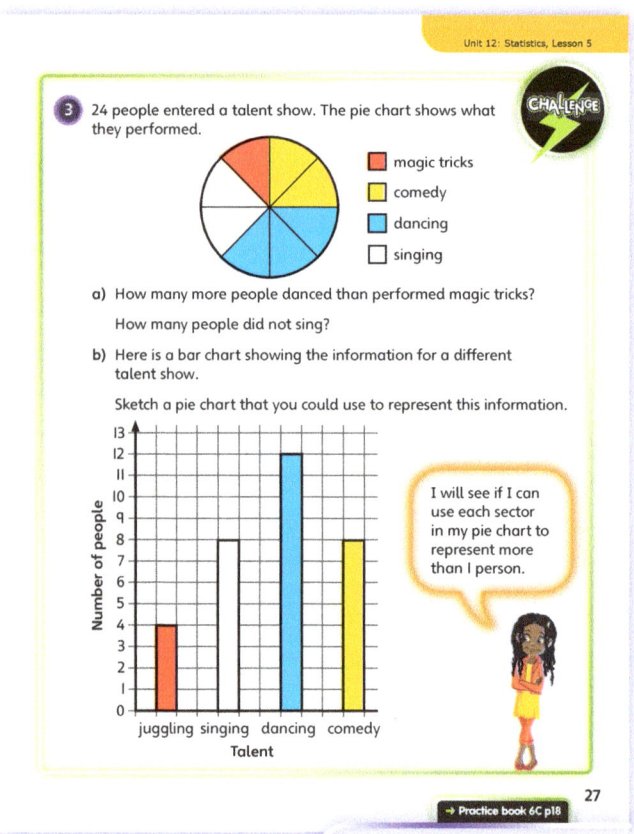

PUPIL TEXTBOOK 6C PAGE 27

Unit 12: Statistics, Lesson 5

# Practice

**WAYS OF WORKING** Independent thinking

**IN FOCUS** In question ①, children complete pie charts by transferring data from a tally chart and bar chart. Children are required to calculate how many people each sector on the pie chart represents.

In question ②, children must recognise that each section does not represent one football match; it represents a group of football matches, that were either won, lost or drawn. To solve the problem, children must calculate how many points each of the three sections of the pie chart represents before they can work out the total points of each team.

**STRENGTHEN** For question ①, discuss and model how to calculate what each sector represents.

**DEEPEN** For question ④, challenge children to draw different representations of the same pie charts, for example, with different numbers of sectors. Provide children with templates of pie charts, ready for them to work with.

**ASSESSMENT CHECKPOINT** Question ① gives you an opportunity to assess whether children are confident drawing pie charts to reflect information presented in different ways.

All questions allow you to assess children's understanding that a sector can represent different things, for example, people or points.

**ANSWERS** Answers for the **Practice** part of the lesson can be found in the *Power Maths* online subscription.

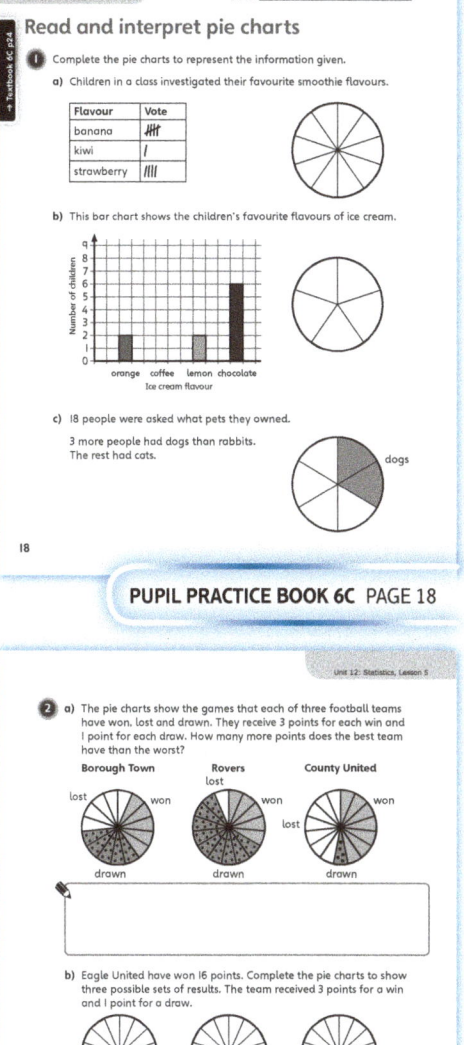

PUPIL PRACTICE BOOK 6C PAGE 18

PUPIL PRACTICE BOOK 6C PAGE 19

# Reflect

**WAYS OF WORKING** Independent thinking

**IN FOCUS** Children explain how to calculate what each sector of a pie chart represents. Encourage children to give examples.

**ASSESSMENT CHECKPOINT** Look for an explanation that shows that children understand that: the total number of people ÷ the number of sectors in the pie chart = how many people each sector represents.

**ANSWERS** Answers for the **Reflect** part of the lesson can be found in the *Power Maths* online subscription.

## After the lesson ⏸

- What percentage of children are confident reading and interpreting pie charts?
- How many children can sketch a basic pie chart?
- Did all children understand that a section of a pie chart can span more than one sector and that a sector can represent more than one person or item?

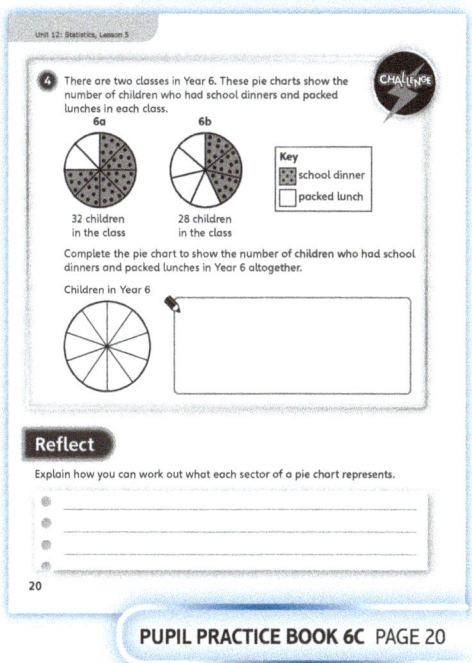

PUPIL PRACTICE BOOK 6C PAGE 20

63

Unit 12: Statistics, Lesson 6

# Pie charts and fractions

## Learning focus

In this lesson, children calculate the fractions represented in pie charts. They compare the categories by converting them into fractions of the pie chart.

## Before you teach

- Are children secure in shading and identifying fractions of circles?
- Are children able to use a key confidently?
- Do children understand the circle of the pie chart represents all of the results as a whole?

### NATIONAL CURRICULUM LINKS

**Year 6 Statistics**

Interpret and construct pie charts and line graphs and use these to solve problems.

### ASSESSING MASTERY

Children can calculate what fraction of a total each category is. They are able to say if a category is greater or less than a given fraction. They compare different pie charts taking into account the whole as well as what each section looks like. Children calculate the fractions represented by each sector. They are able to match statements to the correct pie chart.

### COMMON MISCONCEPTIONS

Children can mistake the number of sections as the fraction, for example, they may say that as there are 3 sections, then each is $\frac{1}{3}$. Ask:
- *How many parts is the whole split into here? Does each part look the same?*

Children may forget that the fractions of the pie chart must add up to 1. 1 is the whole. Ask:
- *What is the whole? When do you have the total?*

### STRENGTHENING UNDERSTANDING

Recap fractions of circles with the children. Provide circles and ask the children to shade $\frac{1}{2}, \frac{1}{4}, \frac{1}{3}, \frac{3}{4}$, etc. This will help children to visualise the fractions.

### GOING DEEPER

Go deeper by asking children to discuss and compare different pie charts split into different numbers of sectors, and where the sectors and sections represent different values.

### KEY LANGUAGE

**In lesson:** fraction, pie chart, sector, represent, divide, estimate

**Other language to be used by the teacher:** data, tally chart, bar chart, percentage, part, whole, category, results, total, section

### STRUCTURES AND REPRESENTATIONS

Tally chart, bar chart, pie chart

### RESOURCES

**Optional:** circles split into sectors for children to shade given fractions, counters, cubes

 In the eTextbook of this lesson, you will find interactive links to a selection of teaching tools.

## Quick recap

Ask children to draw a circle and split it into thirds. Then ask children to draw a circle and split it into fifths.

64

# Discover

**WAYS OF WORKING** Pair work

**ASK**

- Question 1 a): *How many sectors are in the circle?* (24: there are 24 hours in a day)
- Question 1 a): *What does each section represent?* (playing: 6 hours; eating: 4 hours; sleeping: 14 hours)

**IN FOCUS** In question 1, children are required to calculate what fraction a section of a pie chart represents. Encourage children to discuss the pie chart. Ask: *How many sectors does it have? What does each sector represent? What does the largest coloured section represent? Which is the smallest section?* Ask questions such as: *How many hours does Emily play for? How many hours does Emily sleep? Does Emily sleep for more or less than $\frac{1}{2}$ the day?*

**PRACTICAL TIPS** Provide children with images of fractions, i.e. a circle split into half, a circle split into quarters, a circle split into thirds, for them to compare the pie chart to. Check that children know how many hours are in the day and recap if necessary with a 24-hour clock.

**ANSWERS**

Question 1 a): $\frac{14}{24} = \frac{7}{12}$. Emily sleeps for $\frac{7}{12}$ of each day.

Question 1 b): Ebo is not correct. Emily spends $\frac{4}{24}$ of the day eating.
$\frac{4}{24} = \frac{1}{6}$ of the day

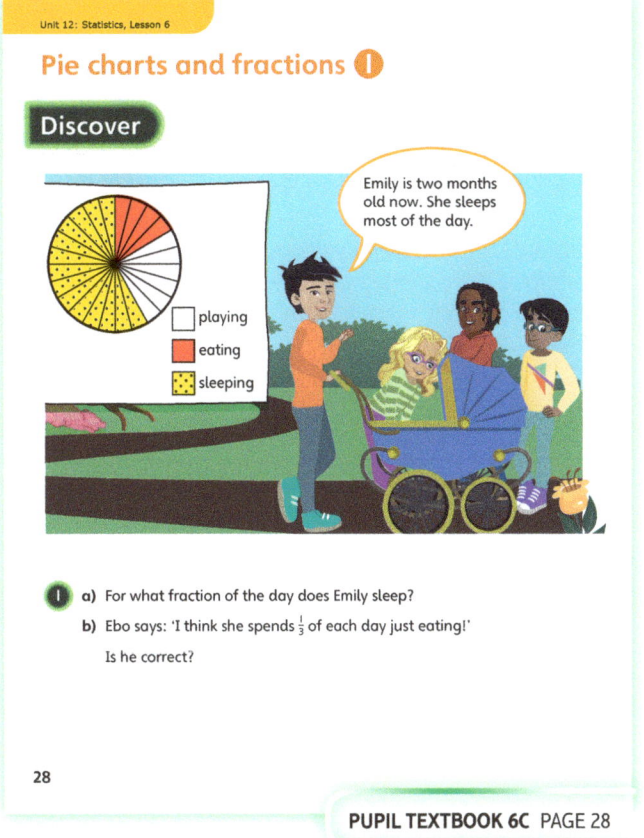

PUPIL TEXTBOOK 6C PAGE 28

# Share

**WAYS OF WORKING** Whole class teacher led

**ASK**

- Question 1 b): *What does each section on the pie chart represent?*
- Question 1 b): *How many hours does Emily spend eating? How can you show this as a fraction?*

**IN FOCUS** Question 1 b) provides a good opportunity for children to discuss fractions of circles. Ensure children understand that each sector on the pie chart represents one hour of the day and that each colour or pattern (section of sectors) represents a different activity in baby Emily's day. Ask: *Can you show each activity as a fraction? Can you simplify the fractions?*

In question 1 b), Ebo thinks Emily eats for $\frac{1}{3}$ of the day. Point out the model of the pie chart divided into thirds (total number of sectors divided by three). Ask: *How many sectors are there in a third?*

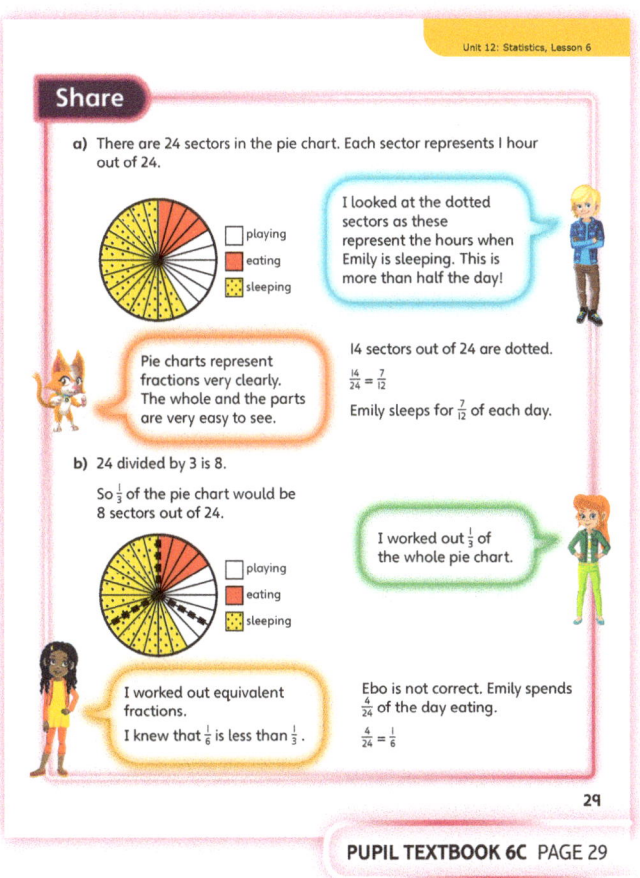

PUPIL TEXTBOOK 6C PAGE 29

# Think together

**WAYS OF WORKING** Whole class teacher led (I do, We do, You do)

**ASK**
- Question ❶: *What fraction of the whole does each colour represent? Can you simplify the fractions?*
- Question ❷: *How many sectors are there?*
- Question ❷: *How many hours does a sector represent?*

**IN FOCUS** Check children are working out how many hours each sector represents (question ❶: each sector is an hour; question ❷: each sector is 3 hours). Ensure children are able to simplify the fractions.

Remind children that the fractions of a pie chart must add up to 1. 1 is the whole. For example: $\frac{1}{2} + \frac{1}{8} + \frac{1}{8} + \frac{1}{4} = 1$

In question ❸, children need to consider the whole when comparing the two pie charts. In a) the chart represents 80 people; in b) it represents 30. The yellow dotted section represents approximately 15 people in the first pie chart. In the second pie chart 15 people would be half the pie chart, so a bigger section doesn't always mean more people chose that category, but is dependent on the whole.

**STRENGTHEN** Provide children with circles divided into fractions to support children in estimating the sections in question ❸. Highlight that the fractions of a pie chart must add up to 1. 1 is the whole, for example: $\frac{1}{2} + \frac{1}{8} + \frac{1}{8} + \frac{1}{4} = 1$

**DEEPEN** Expand on the challenge question by asking children to compare all the sections of the two pie charts. Do they fully understand that it is important to identify what the sections represent and that a larger section in a different pie chart can sometimes represent a smaller number?

**ASSESSMENT CHECKPOINT** Question ❶ will show whether children can calculate the fractions represented by sectors in a pie chart. Question ❷ checks that children recognise when a sector represents more than 1 hour. Can they explain why it is important to take the whole into consideration? Question ❸ assesses children's ability to estimate fractions in a pie chart without counting individual sectors.

**ANSWERS**

Question ❶: $\frac{1}{2}$ of Emily's time is spent sleeping.
$\frac{4}{24} = \frac{1}{6}$ of Emily's time is spent eating.
$\frac{8}{24} = \frac{1}{3}$ of Emily's time is spent playing.

Question ❷: $\frac{1}{8}$ of Emily's time is spent eating.
$\frac{3}{8}$ of her time is spent sleeping.
$\frac{1}{4}$ of her time is spent at school or playing.

Question ❸ a): A good estimate for the fractions:

| Ask for help | $\frac{1}{2}$ = 40 |
| Try to fix it | $\frac{3}{10}$ = 24 |
| Use a different device | $\frac{3}{20}$ = 12 |
| Do something else | $\frac{1}{20}$ = 4 |

Question ❸ b): A similar number of children would use a different device because, although the yellow section is bigger on the children's pie chart, not as many children were asked.

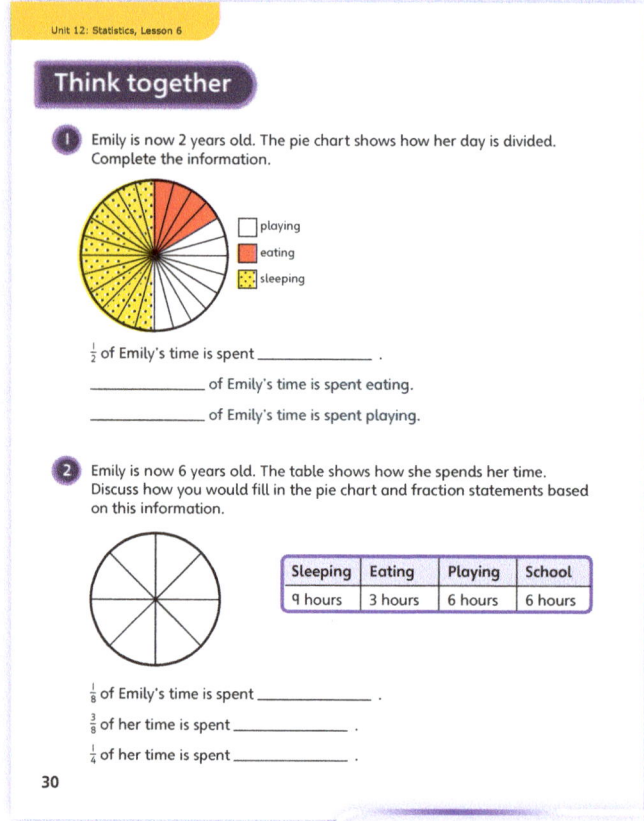

PUPIL TEXTBOOK 6C PAGE 30

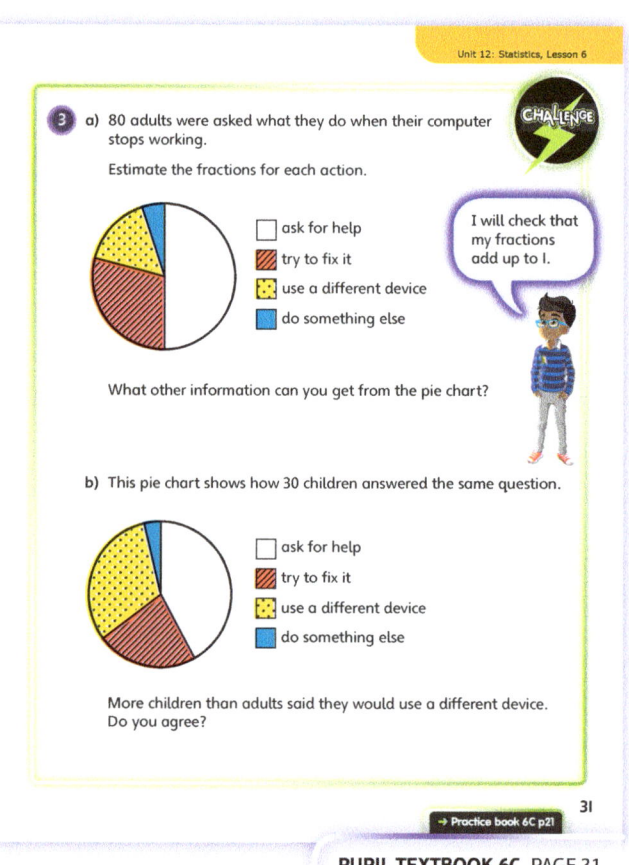

PUPIL TEXTBOOK 6C PAGE 31

Unit 12: Statistics, Lesson 6

## Practice

**WAYS OF WORKING** Independent thinking

**IN FOCUS** For question ❶, children find the fraction represented by a shaded sector in three pie charts. They will need to remember how many hours there are in a day because this is the whole for each pie chart.

For question ❹, children match statements to the correct pie chart. This requires understanding the need to consider the whole of each pie chart. Then they can calculate the numbers represented by the sections.

**STRENGTHEN** Recap how to calculate the value of each sector and section. Ask children to sketch and shade fractions of circles on an individual white board (or chalkboard) to familiarise themselves with the visual images of $\frac{1}{4}$, $\frac{1}{2}$, $\frac{1}{8}$ and $\frac{1}{3}$ of a circle.

**DEEPEN** For question ❸, challenge children to draw different representations of the same pie charts, for example, with different numbers of sectors and sections.

**THINK DIFFERENTLY** Question ❸ requires children to compare two pie charts and work out from them which school team has lost the most games. The teams have not played the same number of games, so children should realise that the fractions shown on each one will not be the same number. Children must explain their answer in words instead of showing it in a calculation. This should show whether they truly understand the importance of the whole.

**ASSESSMENT CHECKPOINT** Question ❺ requires children to show that their fraction estimates add up to 1. This will reinforce their understanding of the whole. The question also provides an opportunity to check children can calculate fractions of a 3-digit number.

**ANSWERS** Answers for the **Practice** part of the lesson can be found in the *Power Maths* online subscription.

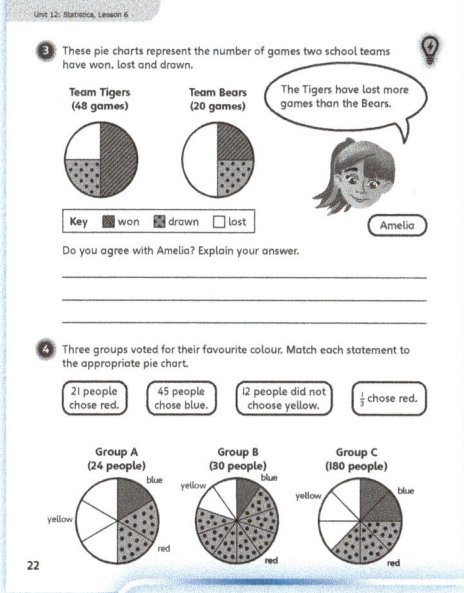

PUPIL PRACTICE BOOK 6C PAGE 21

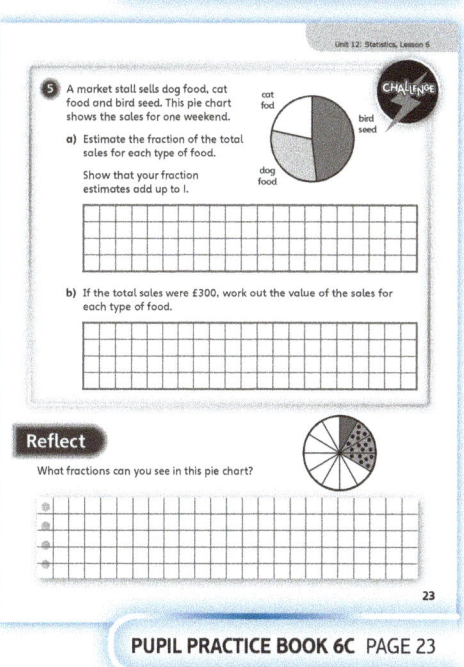

PUPIL PRACTICE BOOK 6C PAGE 22

## Reflect

**WAYS OF WORKING** Independent thinking

**IN FOCUS** Children are asked for the fraction represented by each section (group of sectors). Ensure children are simplifying fractions. Make sure children recognise that the fractions of a pie chart must add up to 1 and use this understanding to check their answers. $\frac{1}{12} + \frac{3}{12} + \frac{8}{12} = 1$.

**ASSESSMENT CHECKPOINT** This is a good question to assess which children have mastered fractions and pie charts, and which need more support.

**ANSWERS** Answers for the **Reflect** part of the lesson can be found in the *Power Maths* online subscription.

## After the lesson

- What percentage of the children are secure in calculating the fractions in a pie chart?
- How many children are able to estimate the fractions of a pie chart?
- Are there any misconceptions you need to pick up on before the next lesson?

PUPIL PRACTICE BOOK 6C PAGE 23

Unit 12: Statistics, Lesson 7

# Pie charts and fractions ❷

## Learning focus
In this lesson, children use given fractions of a pie chart, along with the total number of items the chart represents, to calculate the number of items in each category.

## Before you teach
- Are children secure in adding fractions?
- Are children secure in finding fractions of amounts? For example, $\frac{1}{6}$ of 30 = 5
- Do children understand the circle of the pie chart represents all of the results as a whole?

### NATIONAL CURRICULUM LINKS

**Year 6 Statistics**

Interpret and construct pie charts and line graphs and use these to solve problems.

### ASSESSING MASTERY

Children can use known facts about a pie chart to identify or calculate further information. They can use fractions of a pie chart to calculate the number of items represented in a category. Children can use the difference between two categories to calculate the value represented by a category. Children can confidently estimate fractions of a pie chart.

### COMMON MISCONCEPTIONS

Children may mistake the number of sections as the fraction, for example, they may say that as there are 3 sections, each is $\frac{1}{3}$. Ask:
- *How many sections are there? How many equal-sized sectors in each section? How can you express that as a fraction?*

Children may forget that the fractions of the pie chart must add up to 1. 1 is the whole. Ask:
- *What do the sections add up to?*

### STRENGTHENING UNDERSTANDING

Recap fractions of circles with the children. Provide circles and ask children to shade $\frac{1}{2}, \frac{1}{4}, \frac{1}{3}, \frac{3}{4}$, etc. This will help children to visualise the fractions.

### GOING DEEPER

Discuss and compare different pie charts. Ask children to create a pie chart and write their own questions about it.

### KEY LANGUAGE

**In lesson:** fraction, pie chart, section, right angle, exact, tally chart, sector

**Other language to be used by the teacher:** data, bar chart, percentage, part, whole, category, results, total

### STRUCTURES AND REPRESENTATIONS

Pie charts, bar models, arrays

### RESOURCES

**Mandatory:** counters

**Optional:** pie charts, circles split into sectors for children to shade given fractions, calendar

 In the eTextbook of this lesson, you will find interactive links to a selection of teaching tools.

## Quick recap

Ask children to draw a circle and split it into sixths. Then ask children to draw a circle and split it into tenths.

# Unit 12: Statistics, Lesson 7

## Discover

**WAYS OF WORKING** Pair work

**ASK**
- Question 1 a): *How many days are there in April?*
- Question 1 a): *How many days are there in $\frac{1}{3}$ of the month?*
- Question 1 b): *How many sectors are there in the pie chart for Cyprus?*
- Question 1 b): *What information can you gather from the pie chart?*

**IN FOCUS** Question 1 requires children to compare the fractions of two pie charts to identify how many days in April were sunny, cloudy or rainy. The pie charts have a different number of sectors to make children consider that the category sections don't represent numbers but fractions of the whole. They will practise using fractions in a pie chart to calculate numbers in a category.

**PRACTICAL TIPS** Show children a calendar to remind them how many days there are in April (30). Provide children with counters of three different colours to represent the sunny, rainy and cloudy days in April.

**ANSWERS**

Question 1 a): 5 days were sunny in London.

Question 1 b): 26 days were sunny in Cyprus.

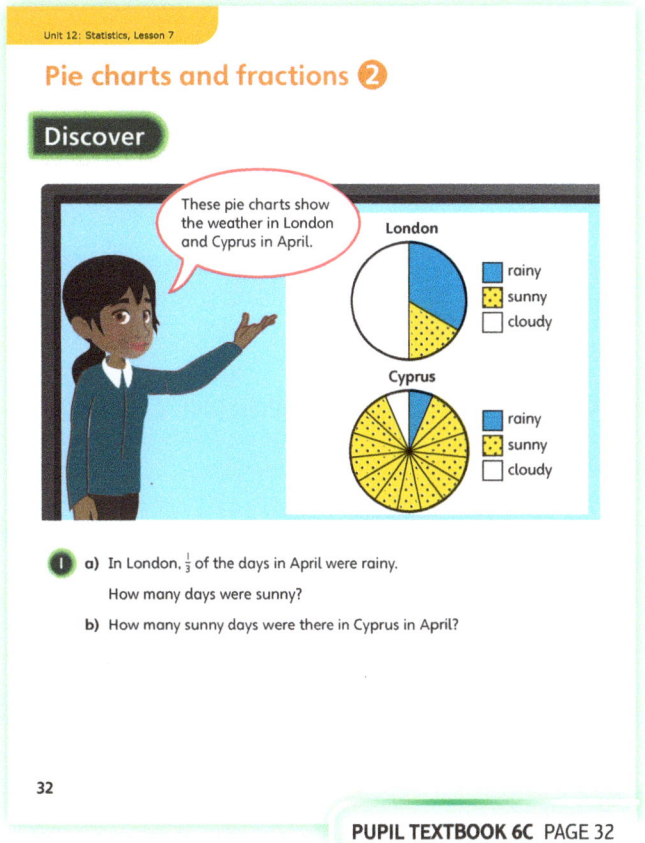

PUPIL TEXTBOOK 6C PAGE 32

## Share

**WAYS OF WORKING** Whole class teacher led

**ASK**
- Question 1 a): *Which method do you prefer and why?*
- Question 1 a) and b): *What does each section on the pie charts represent?*
- Question 1 a) and b): *What similarities are there between the pie charts?*

**IN FOCUS** Question 1 a) shows two methods to work out the answer. Compare the two methods and discuss which method children prefer and why. Provide children with counters to model the first method. Encourage children to draw a bar model representing the problem. This is an opportunity for children to compare different methods of working out a problem and realise that they may find some methods are better than others for different problems.

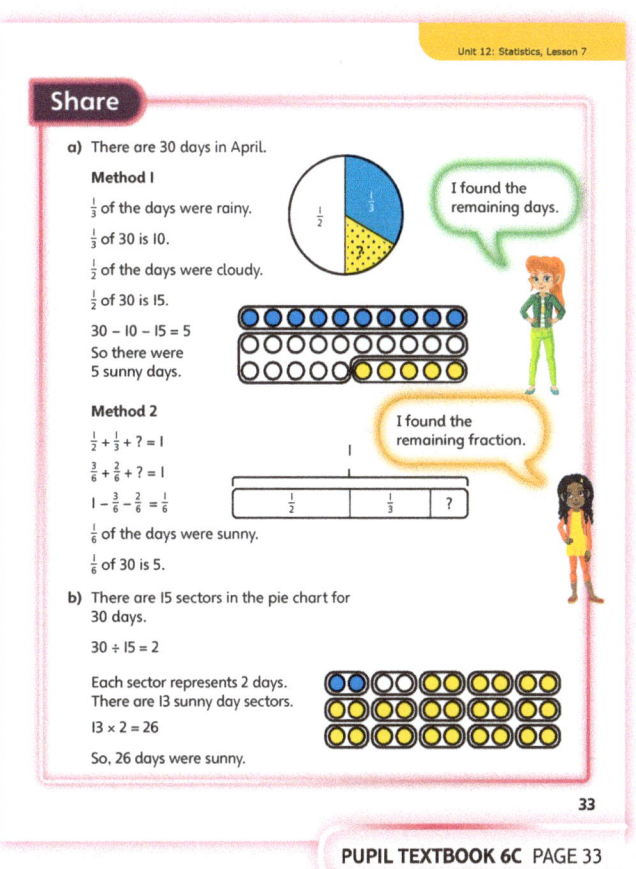

PUPIL TEXTBOOK 6C PAGE 33

69

# Think together

**WAYS OF WORKING** Whole class teacher led (I do, We do, You do)

**ASK**

- Question 2: *What information do you have? How can you use this information to solve the problem?*
- Question 3: *What do you notice in the pie charts (right angle)? How does that help you?*

**IN FOCUS** Question 1 a) gives children the opportunity to recap how to find what fraction represents a category. In question 1 b), they should realise that because they now know how many children are represented by one sector, they can work out the the total number of children. Children are learning to use information they have about the pie chart to calculate further information.

**STRENGTHEN** For question 1, remind children again that the fractions of a pie chart must add up to 1, for example, $\frac{1}{2} + \frac{1}{6} + \frac{2}{6} = 1$.

**DEEPEN** Provide children with a pie chart and challenge them to write their own questions about it. (They can use the question in question 2 as a guide.)

**ASSESSMENT CHECKPOINT** Question 1 will highlight whether children are confident about using information about a pie chart to calculate further information.

Question 3 assesses whether children are confident at estimating fractions of a pie chart. Ask: *Do you recognise that a right angle means the fraction is $\frac{1}{4}$?*

**ANSWERS**

Question 1 a): $\frac{1}{2}$ of the class like fish fingers.
$\frac{1}{6}$ of the class like popcorn.
$\frac{1}{3}$ of the class like strawberries.

Question 1 b): 24 people were asked.
$\frac{1}{3} = \frac{1}{6} + \frac{1}{6}$ so $\frac{1}{6} = 4$ items
$4 \times 6 = 24$

Question 2: 36 children said the winter holidays.
$45 \div 5$ sections = 9 people per section
$9 \times 4$ sections = 36 people

Question 3 a): Class 5 collected $\frac{1}{4}$ of 20 kg = 5 kg of paper.
Class 6 collected 10 kg of metal which is just under half of their total.
Class 6's total must be more than 20 kg.
Class 6 collected more than a $\frac{1}{4}$ of 20 kg.
Children may use an approximate fraction representing the metal in Class 6 and work out the total for Class 6 from that.

Question 3 b): The section is a bit less than treble 3·5, 10·5 kg.
An answer between 9 kg and 10 kg is a good approximation.

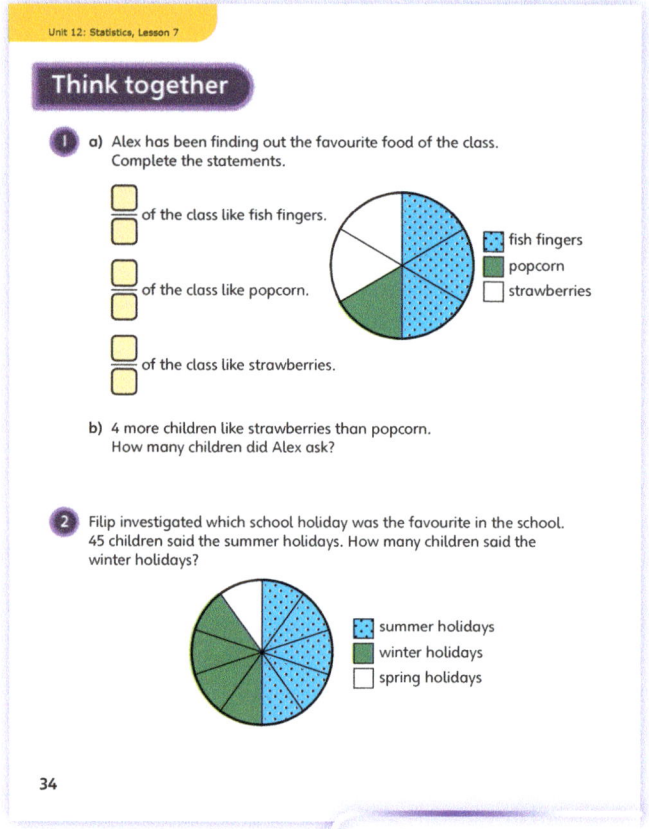

PUPIL TEXTBOOK 6C PAGE 34

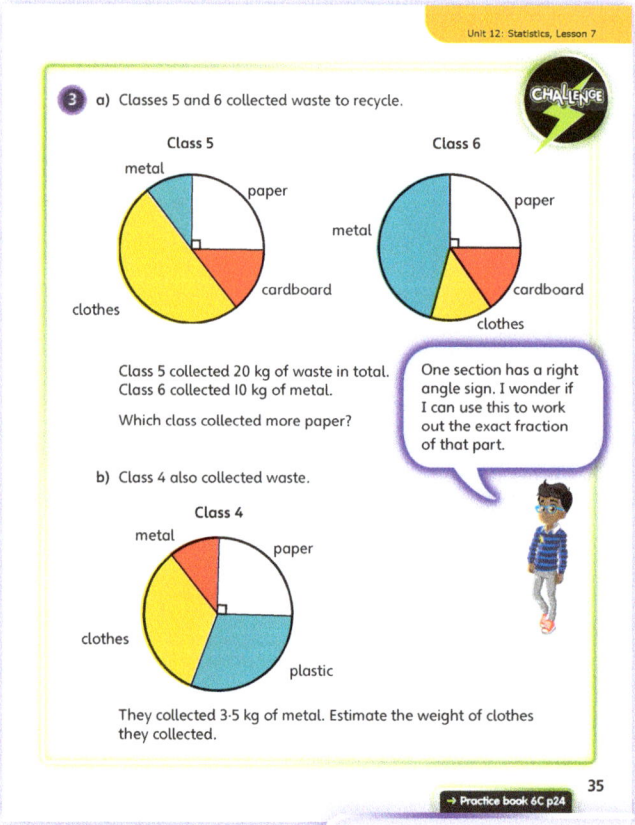

PUPIL TEXTBOOK 6C PAGE 35

Unit 12: Statistics, Lesson 7

# Practice

**WAYS OF WORKING** Independent thinking

**IN FOCUS** For question ①, children are given a piece of information to calculate further information from a pie chart. Encourage children to identify what they know about the pie chart and consider how to use this information. Ask: *What else does it tell you?*

Question ③ gives children practice at reading information from a pie chart to solve a problem. This requires them to calculate the numbers represented by fractions as well as vice versa. Do they see a step-by-step process for doing this? Ask: *What are the categories? Can you estimate the fractions? What information do you know? What do you need to find out?*

**DEEPEN** Challenge children to work in pairs and write a problem which gives the difference between two categories and requires their partner to calculate the total. They should sketch a pie chart to support the problem.

**ASSESSMENT CHECKPOINT** All questions test children's ability to interpret a pie chart.

Question ③ is a good question to use to check that children can use fractions of a pie chart to calculate totals in a category.

**ANSWERS** Answers for the **Practice** part of the lesson can be found in the *Power Maths* online subscription.

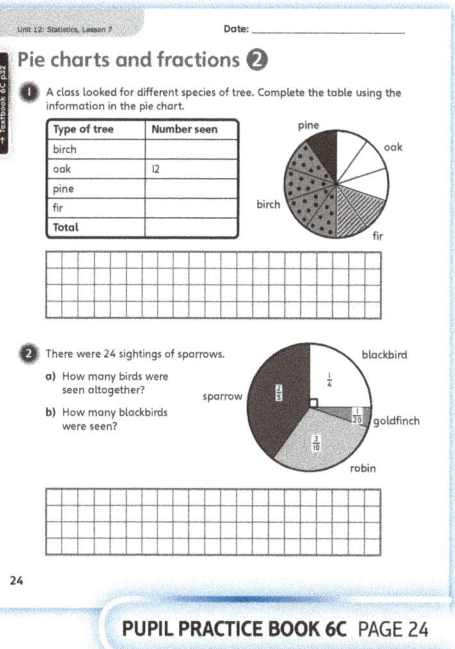

PUPIL PRACTICE BOOK 6C PAGE 24

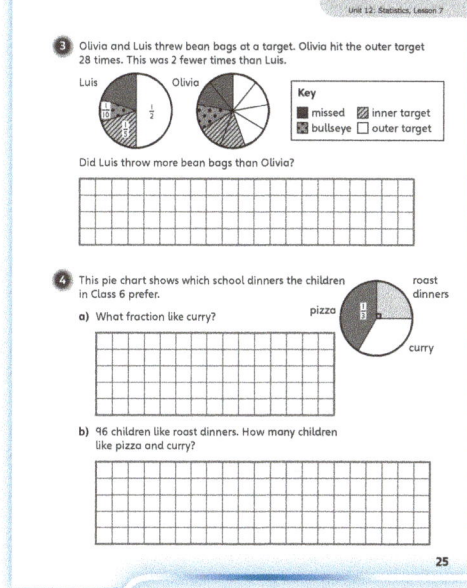

PUPIL PRACTICE BOOK 6C PAGE 25

# Reflect

**WAYS OF WORKING** Pair work

**IN FOCUS** Children are challenged to write their own problem and sketch a pie chart to match.

**ASSESSMENT CHECKPOINT** This question will allow children to demonstrate that they understand how to use a fraction of a pie chart to calculate the total/whole.

**ANSWERS** Answers for the **Reflect** part of the lesson can be found in the *Power Maths* online subscription.

## After the lesson

- Are all children secure in using information about the pie chart to calculate further information?
- Are children confident with calculating and estimating fractions of a pie chart?

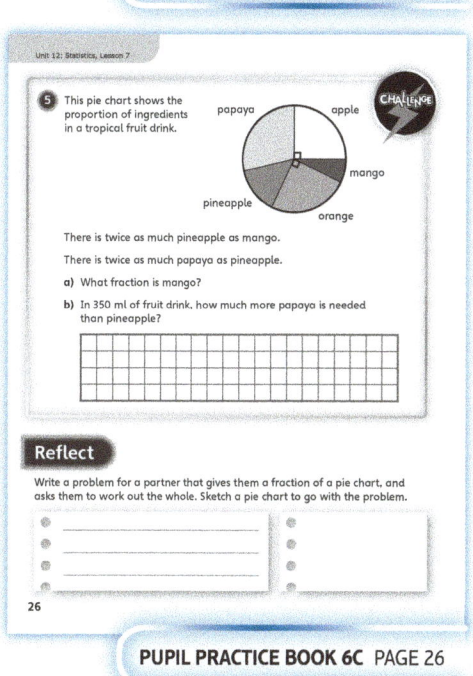

PUPIL PRACTICE BOOK 6C PAGE 26

Unit 12: Statistics, Lesson 8

# Pie charts and percentages

## Learning focus

In this lesson, children learn that the whole pie chart is represented by 100%. They compare and convert percentages of the pie chart to fractions. Children use percentages to calculate the value of each category.

## Before you teach

- Are children secure in calculating percentages?
- Can children convert percentages into fractions?
- Can children calculate angles in a circle?

### NATIONAL CURRICULUM LINKS

**Year 6 Statistics**

Interpret and construct pie charts and line graphs and use these to solve problems.

**Non-statutory guidance**

Pupils connect their work on angles, fractions and percentages to the interpretation of pie charts.

### ASSESSING MASTERY

Children know that 100% represents the whole pie chart. They can compare percentages of the pie chart to fractions. Children use percentages to calculate amounts. They can use knowledge of fractions and angles and convert percentages into fractions and angles.

### COMMON MISCONCEPTIONS

Some children may think degrees are the same as percentages. Ask:
- *What is the total number of degrees in a circle?* (360°) *What is the whole in percentages?* (100%)

### STRENGTHENING UNDERSTANDING

Children may need support converting percentages to fractions. Use bar models to support them. Recap percentages. Ask: *Can you find percentages of a given amount, for example: 70% of 150? 10% of 320?*

Practise converting percentages into fractions, for example: 50% = $\frac{1}{2}$, 25% = $\frac{1}{4}$, 20% = $\frac{1}{5}$.

Check that children know the angles of a circle equal 360°.

### GOING DEEPER

Explore the use of angles in pie charts. Ask: *Can you calculate the percentages of sections from given angles?*

### KEY LANGUAGE

**In lesson:** percentage, pie chart, fraction, accurate, estimate, sector, half, degree

**Other language to be used by the teacher:** angle, data, tally chart, bar chart, part, whole, category, results, total, section

### STRUCTURES AND REPRESENTATIONS

Pie chart, bar model, tally chart

### RESOURCES

**Optional:** counters, cubes, pie charts with degrees marked, circles split into sectors for children to shade given percentages, individual whiteboards

 In the eTextbook of this lesson, you will find interactive links to a selection of teaching tools.

## Quick recap

Challenge children to tell you the percentage equivalent of:

$\frac{1}{2}$   $\frac{1}{4}$   $\frac{3}{4}$   $\frac{9}{10}$

Unit 12: Statistics, Lesson 8

# Discover

**WAYS OF WORKING** Pair work

**ASK**
- Question 1 a): *What percentage of Mars's atmosphere is oxygen? How can you work it out?*
- Question 1 b): *What would $\frac{1}{5}$ of 100% be?*
- Question 1 b): *What information can you find in the pie chart?*

**IN FOCUS** Question 1 a) requires children to convert percentages to fractions to find what fractions of the atmosphere of Mars are nitrogen, argon and carbon dioxide. Ask: *What percentage of the atmosphere is carbon dioxide? How can you work this out?* Recap that a pie chart represents a whole and therefore the percentages in a pie chart add up to a total of 100%.

**PRACTICAL TIPS** Provide children with individual whiteboards or blackboards and encourage them to draw diagrams or bar models to help them work out the different percentages and fractions.

**ANSWERS**

Question 1 a): Nitrogen and Argon both = 2% = $\frac{2}{100}$ = $\frac{1}{50}$

Carbon dioxide = 100% - 4% = 96% = $\frac{96}{100}$ = $\frac{24}{25}$

Question 1 b): Oxygen = 100% – 78% – 1% = 21%

$\frac{1}{5}$ = $\frac{20}{100}$ = 20%

Aki's estimate is just 1% too small.

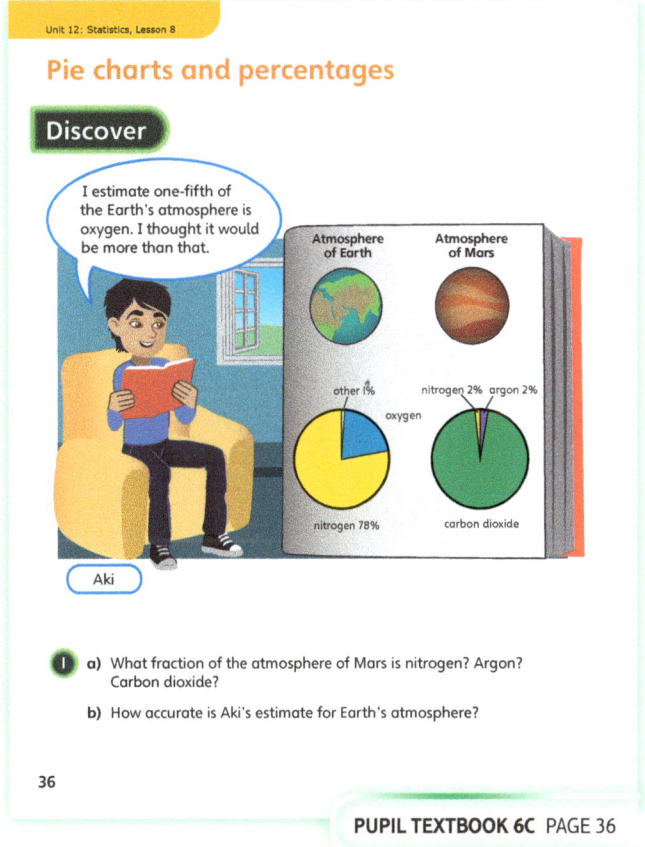

# Share

**WAYS OF WORKING** Whole class teacher led

**ASK**
- Question 1 a): *What do the percentages of a pie chart total?* (100%)
- Question 1 a): *Why did Flo check using the percentages?*
- Question 1 b): *Do you find the bar model helpful?*

**IN FOCUS** Question 1 b) shows how to use a bar model to calculate the missing percentage. Children should know that the pie chart total is 100% and can use this to calculate missing data. Ask children to draw bar models to show the percentages of each planet's atmosphere to give a visual model.

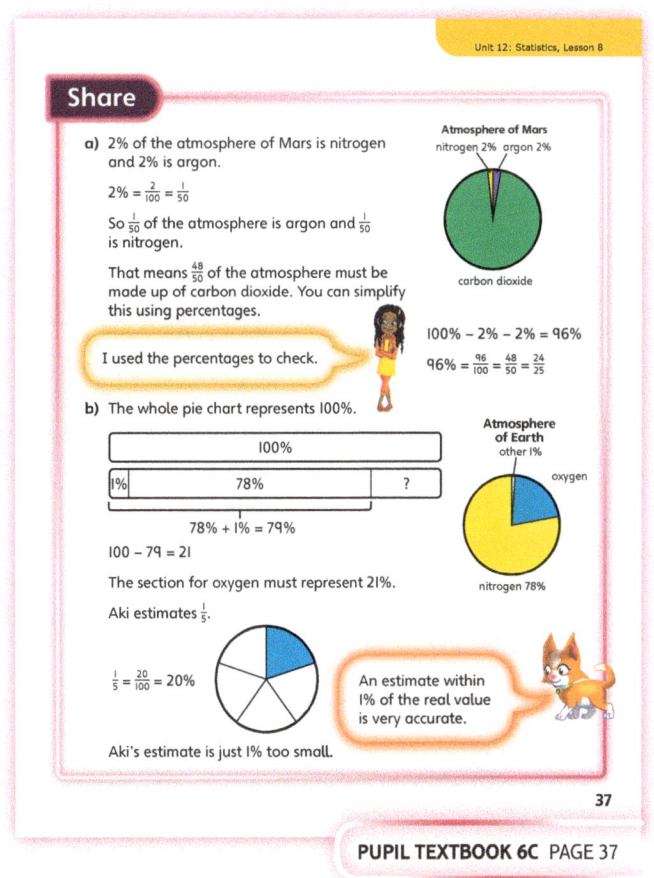

Unit 12: Statistics, Lesson 8

# Think together

**WAYS OF WORKING** Whole class teacher led (I do, We do, You do)

**ASK**

- Question ❶: *How many sectors is the pie chart divided into? What fraction of the whole are they?*
- Question ❷: *What percentage is the whole? What are the percentages converted to fractions?*
- Question ❸: *How many degrees are there in a circle? What information do you have about the categories?*

**IN FOCUS** Question ❶ requires children to understand that the pie chart is divided into 10 sectors (shown by the equally spaced marks around the outside). Each sector equals $\frac{1}{10}$ or 10% (100 ÷ 10 = 10).

In question ❷, children need to convert the percentages to fractions. When calculating the fraction of fruit and vegetables in the pie chart, children should note that these two sections need to be added together: 10% + 15% = 25% = $\frac{1}{4}$.

In question ❸ a), children should add up the given degrees and calculate the missing information.

36° + 72° + 90° + ?° = 360°
198 + 162 = 360
162° = jogging

They then convert this to a percentage

162 ÷ 360 = 0·45 = 45%

**STRENGTHEN** Use bar models to show children how percentages equate to fractions.

Ask children to draw bar models to find $\frac{1}{5}, \frac{1}{2}, \frac{1}{3}, \frac{3}{4}$.

**DEEPEN** Explore the use of angles in pie charts. Give children more pie charts with degrees marked. Ask them to calculate the percentages of sections from the angles.

**ASSESSMENT CHECKPOINT** Question ❷ involves calculating percentages, fractions and numbers in a category. It provides a good opportunity to assess whether children have truly mastered pie charts.

**ANSWERS**

Question ❶: Salt water = 70%
Land that can be farmed = 15%
Desert = 5%
Mountain = 5%
Snow/ice = 5%

Question ❷: More than one third of his food is bread = true
35% > 33% = $\frac{1}{3}$
Out of every 250 g, 50 g was cheese = true
$\frac{50}{250} = \frac{1}{5} = 20\%$
$\frac{1}{3}$ of his food was fruit and vegetables = false
15% + 10% = 25% = $\frac{1}{4}$ not $\frac{1}{3}$
He ate three times as much pasta as eggs = true
Eggs = 100% − (35 + 20 + 15 + 15 + 10)% = 5%
3 × 5% = 15%

Question ❸ a): 45% of people preferred jogging.

Question ❸ b): 192 people liked team sports.

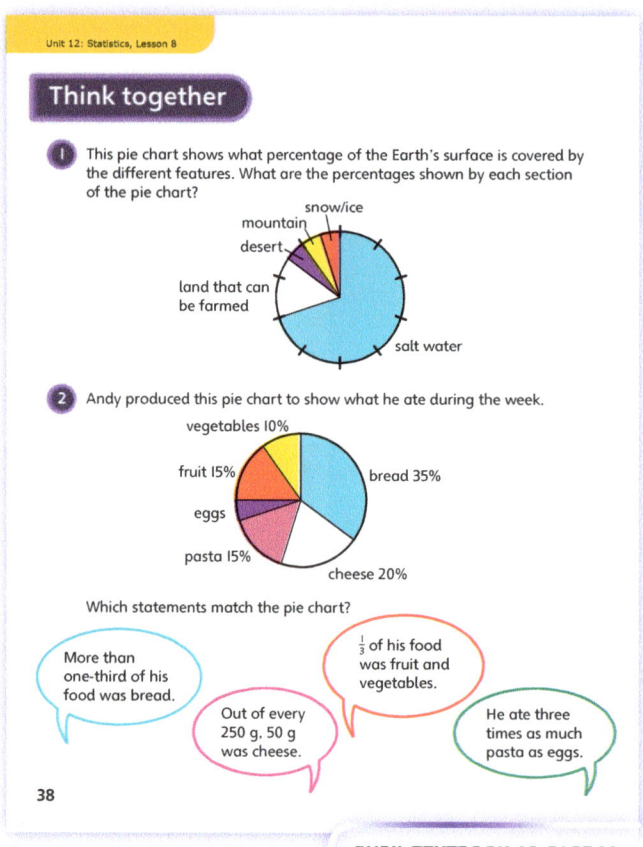

PUPIL TEXTBOOK 6C PAGE 38

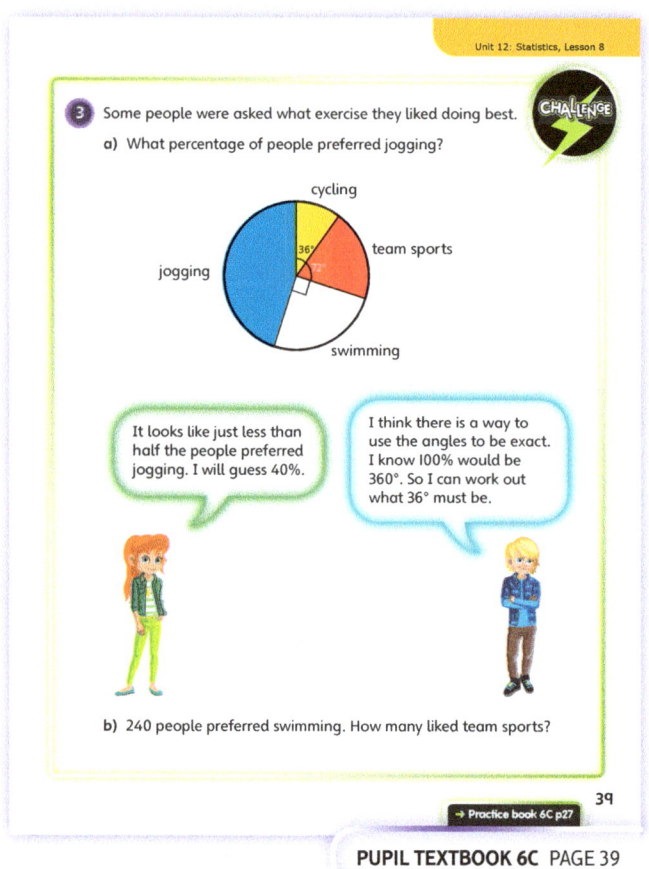

PUPIL TEXTBOOK 6C PAGE 39

74

# Unit 12: Statistics, Lesson 8

## Practice

**WAYS OF WORKING** Independent thinking

**IN FOCUS** In question ②, children must use percentages to work out how many people are in a category. This question includes a right angle. Children need to recognise that this means $\frac{1}{4}$ of the circle or 25% of the total.

In question ④, the information for one of the teams is supplied without a pie chart. Children may find it useful to draw a pie chart to represent this information to make it easier to compare the two teams.

**STRENGTHEN** If children are finding it a challenge to understand categories represented by degrees, remind them that there are 360° in a circle. So 180° = 50% = $\frac{1}{2}$; 90° = 25% = $\frac{1}{4}$. Suggest they draw bar models to show the equivalences.

**DEEPEN** Provide children with some information that is given in percentages and ask them to draw this as a pie chart. Challenge them to represent some of the percentages with degrees.

**ASSESSMENT CHECKPOINT** Question ③ tests children's understanding of how to work out what numbers some given percentages represent. Knowing that the three sections make up the whole, or 100%, and given the number for one category, children should be able to work out the numbers in the other categories.

**ANSWERS** Answers for the **Practice** part of the lesson can be found in the *Power Maths* online subscription.

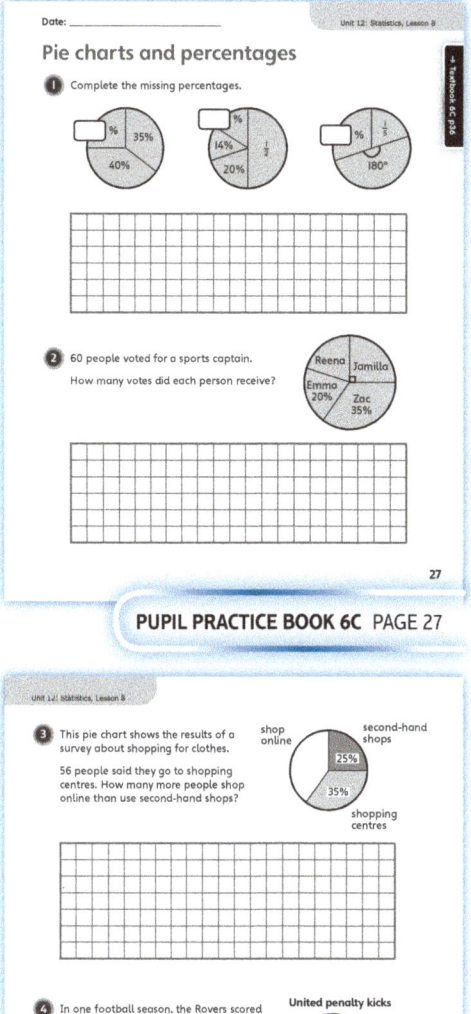

PUPIL PRACTICE BOOK 6C PAGE 27

PUPIL PRACTICE BOOK 6C PAGE 28

## Reflect

**WAYS OF WORKING** Independent thinking

**IN FOCUS** Children are challenged to draw a pie chart to show given percentages and a fraction. One percentage is missing so children calculate the missing percentage first: 25 ($\frac{1}{4}$) + 10 + 15 + ☐ = 100

**ASSESSMENT CHECKPOINT** The question contains a fraction and percentages. Children are asked to show how they know how to draw the pie chart and this will indicate whether they understand the concept of pie charts and the equivalence of fractions and percentages.

**ANSWERS** Answers for the **Reflect** part of the lesson can be found in the *Power Maths* online subscription.

### After the lesson ⏸
- Can children apply their knowledge of fractions and angles?
- Do you need to give any children further help with degrees in pie charts?

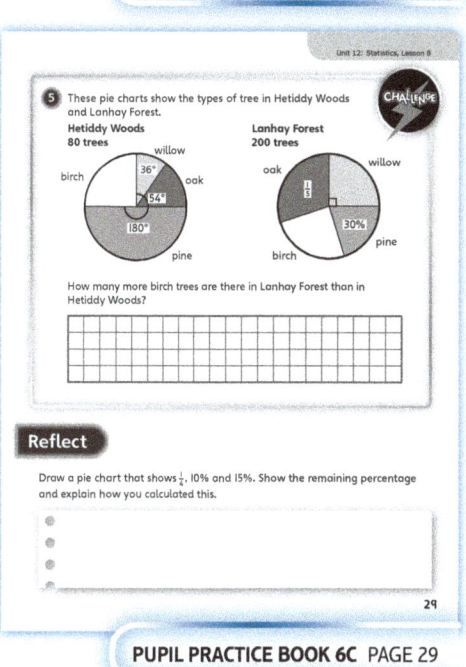

PUPIL PRACTICE BOOK 6C PAGE 29

Unit 12: Statistics, Lesson 9

# Introduction to the mean

### Learning focus
In this lesson, children learn to use the mathematical term 'mean' when referring to the average. They also consider two methods for calculating the mean of a set of numbers.

### Before you teach
- Are children secure in dividing 2-digit numbers?
- Are there any children who would benefit from pre-teaching the new vocabulary (mean) as a mathematical term?

### NATIONAL CURRICULUM LINKS

**Year 6 Statistics**

Calculate and interpret the mean as an average.

### ASSESSING MASTERY

Children can calculate the mean of a set of objects or numbers by sharing the total amount equally. Children can share sets of objects practically and then progress to finding the mean of a set of numbers using division. Children can confidently use, explain and understand the mathematical term 'mean' as calculating the average of a set of numbers by sharing the total equally between the number of people/objects.

### COMMON MISCONCEPTIONS

Some children may find the word 'mean' confusing as it is a homonym. Discuss the different meanings of the word 'mean': mathematical average (for example: 'What is the mean number of marshmallows on a stick?'), to be unkind (for example: 'It was mean to pull your sister's hair.'), and to represent something (for example: 'What does that mean?').

Another common misconception is that the greater the number of 'values' in a set then the greater the mean. Ask:
- Which is the set with the greatest mean? A: 4, 1, 1, 2; B: 2, 0, 0, 2; or C: 2, 0, 1, 0, 1, 0, 0, 0.

### STRENGTHENING UNDERSTANDING

Provide children with counters, cubes, marshmallows and other manipulatives to share sets of objects and find the mean average practically.

### GOING DEEPER

Focus on finding the mean of sets of numbers by dividing. Explore a variety of sets of numbers from real-life situations such as how tall sunflowers have grown, how many mini-beasts children have found, how much sponsor money children have collected, how many cars drive past school each day.

### KEY LANGUAGE

**In lesson:** average, mean, more, equal, even, size, set, total, share, greatest

**Other language to be used by the teacher:** calculate, divide, value

### STRUCTURES AND REPRESENTATIONS

Bar model, number lines

### RESOURCES

**Mandatory:** counters, cubes

**Optional:** marshmallows

 In the eTextbook of this lesson, you will find interactive links to a selection of teaching tools.

### Quick recap

Ask children to divide each of these numbers by 3:

21   36   180

Unit 12: Statistics, Lesson 9

# Discover

**WAYS OF WORKING** Pair work

**ASK**

- Question 1 a): *What does the term 'average' mean mathematically?*
- Question 1 a): *Do the children have an equal number of marshmallows? Is this fair?*
- Question 1 a): *How many marshmallows are there in total? How many children are there?*
- Question 1 b): *What if you shared 9 more marshmallows equally?*

**IN FOCUS** The questions introduce children to the term 'average'. Children should discuss the term and what it might mean mathematically. They can explore how to share the marshmallows so that everyone has the same number.

**PRACTICAL TIPS** Provide children with counters or cubes to represent the marshmallows and sort practically.

**ANSWERS**

Question 1 a): The mean (average) number of marshmallows on a stick is 9.

Question 1 b): The mean (average) number of marshmallows on a stick would be 11.

PUPIL TEXTBOOK 6C PAGE 40

# Share

**WAYS OF WORKING** Whole class teacher led

**ASK**

- Question 1 a): *What new language have you learnt? What does the term 'mean' mean mathematically?*
- Question 1 a): *How can you share the marshmallows equally? (27 divided by 3 = 9)*
- Question 1 b): *What two different ways can you use to find the 'mean'?*

**IN FOCUS** Question 1 a) shows children how to rearrange the groups of marshmallows so that everyone has an equal number. This requires an understanding of sharing objects equally. Ask: *Can you explain to a partner how to make the groups equal?* Question 1 b) asks children to consider what would happen if there were 6 more marshmallows and how this would affect the mean. Two methods are presented. Ask: *Which method do you prefer?*

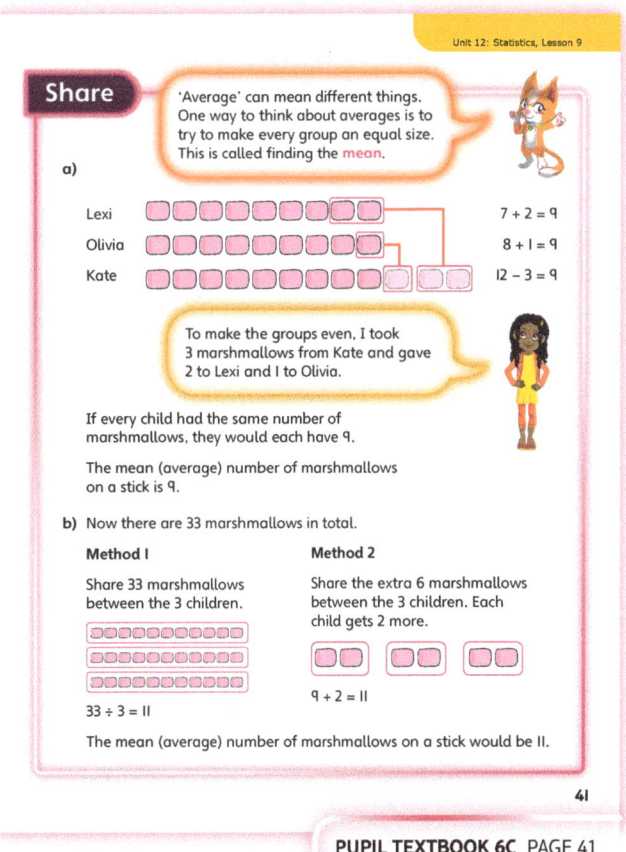

PUPIL TEXTBOOK 6C PAGE 41

# Think together

**WAYS OF WORKING** Whole class teacher led (I do, We do, You do)

**ASK**
- Question ❶: *What does 'mean' mean mathematically?*
- Question ❷: *How many cubes are there altogether?*
- Question ❸: *How many towers/children are there?*

**IN FOCUS** Question ❶ introduces a more varied number of marshmallows per person. Kate has many more than Bella, who has only 1. Children need to understand that, to find the mean, they need to make all the groups equal and will discover that they don't always have to take away from each group. Kate has the most, so most of the marshmallows will be taken from her and given to Bella. Question ❸ introduces the idea that some methods of finding the mean are better for different problems. Children are asked to discuss two methods to see what is different about them, then choose one to work out question ❸ b).

**STRENGTHEN** For question ❶, provide children with counters and ask them to rearrange the counters so each person has an equal number.

For question ❷, provide children with cubes to build towers.

**DEEPEN** For question ❷, ask children to build another set of towers that is different but has the same mean. Ask: *Can you explain why the mean is the same?*

**ASSESSMENT CHECKPOINT** Question ❶ will assess whether children understand that the mean is the average number, i.e. when all the groups in the set have the same number of marshmallows. Question ❷ will show whether children understand that two sets of different numbers can have the same mean if the total and number of groups are both the same. Although the towers are different sizes, there is the same number of towers in each set and the same number of cubes altogether.

**ANSWERS**

Question ❶: The mean (average) number of marshmallows is 7.

Question ❷ a): The mean number of cubes in each group of towers is 6.

Question ❷ b): The mean number of cubes in each group of towers is 6.
Both sets have 30 cubes in total shared between 5 towers.

Question ❸ a): Lee made towers of 8, 4 and 9 cubes, moving the cubes around to make towers of equal height.
Isla had added up the three numbers then divided by 3, the number of numbers.

Question ❸ b): Children should know to use Isla's method because making towers of those heights would not be practical.
The mean height of the four children is 130 cm.

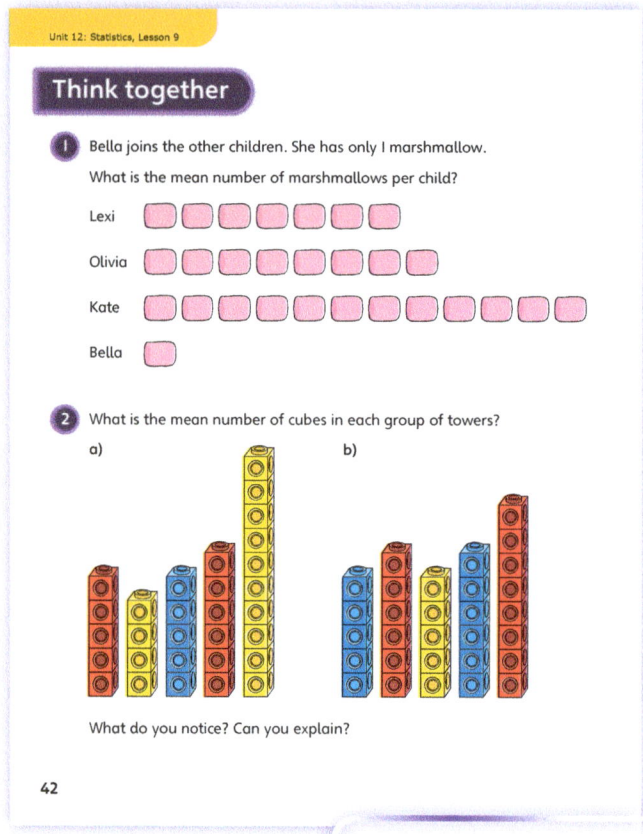

Unit 12: Statistics, Lesson 9

# Practice

**WAYS OF WORKING** Independent thinking

**IN FOCUS** Question 2 allows children to choose their method: drawing a diagram or calculating to find the mean number of marbles in a bag. In question 3, children are challenged to identify which sets have the same mean. Children will need to identify which sets have the same total and same number of dice (all the sets have the same number of dice in this example). Question 4 highlights the misconception that if there are more numbers in the set then the mean will be greater. Question 5 challenges children to find the mean of numbers on a number line. This provides a different visual representation. They should recognise that they can use the same method to find the mean each time.

**STRENGTHEN** Provide children with counters and cubes to rearrange. This will help them to see equal groups, which they can then draw.

**DEEPEN** Provide children with a set of data and challenge them to find as many different sets with the same mean as they can.

**ASSESSMENT CHECKPOINT** Question 2 will allow you to assess whether children can select an efficient method to find the mean.

Question 3 will show which children understand how different sets can have the same mean.

Question 4 will allow you to assess whether children understand that a greater number in a set does not result in a greater mean.

**ANSWERS** Answers to the **Practice** part of the lesson can be found in the *Power Maths* online subscription.

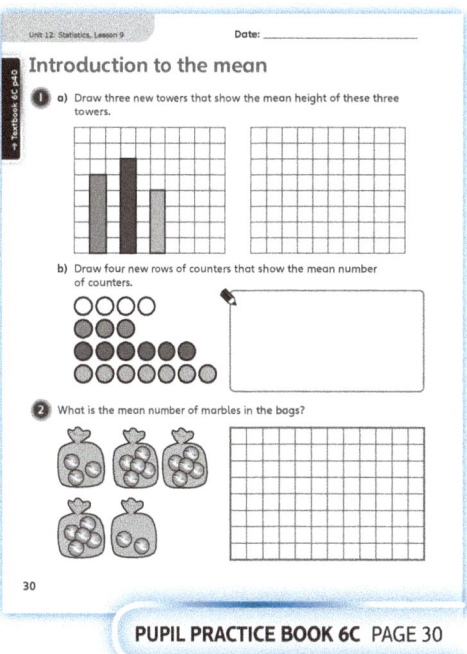

PUPIL PRACTICE BOOK 6C PAGE 30

PUPIL PRACTICE BOOK 6C PAGE 31

# Reflect

**WAYS OF WORKING** Independent thinking

**IN FOCUS** Children are required to explain two different methods to find the mean. They could draw a diagram or use counters/cubes to rearrange the groups so they are equal, or they could calculate by dividing (total ÷ number of groups = mean).

**ASSESSMENT CHECKPOINT** Can children use and explain two different methods to find the mean of a set of numbers?

**ANSWERS** Answers for the **Reflect** part of the lesson can be found in the *Power Maths* online subscription.

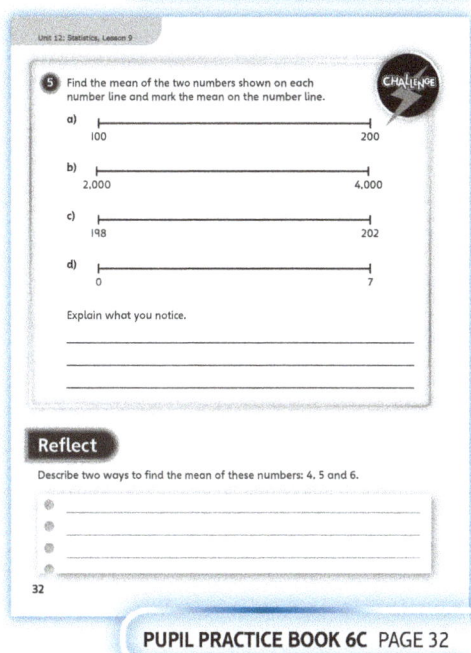

PUPIL PRACTICE BOOK 6C PAGE 32

## After the lesson

- What percentage of children understand the mathematical term 'mean'?
- What did the children find challenging and how could you address this next time?

Unit 12: Statistics, Lesson 10

# Calculate the mean

## Learning focus
In this lesson, children practise calculating the mean. Children explore using bar models as a visual representation. They consider situations when the mean is useful to compare groups of data.

## Before you teach
- Are children able to explain the mathematical term 'mean'?
- Are there any misconceptions from the previous lesson that need addressing?
- Are children secure in adding decimals with up to 2 decimal places?

### NATIONAL CURRICULUM LINKS

**Year 6 Statistics**

Calculate and interpret the mean as an average.

### ASSESSING MASTERY

Children can calculate the mean of a group of objects or numbers using bar models. They can calculate the mean by finding the total and dividing by the number of values in the group.

Children can identify and suggest situations where finding the mean is particularly useful to compare groups of data, for example, when the groups do not have an equal numbers of values.

### COMMON MISCONCEPTIONS

Some children may find the word 'mean' confusing as it is a homonym, a word that is spelt and pronounced the same but has several meanings. Discuss the different meanings of the word 'mean': mathematical average (for example: 'What is the mean number of marshmallows on a stick?'), to be unkind (for example: 'It was mean to pull your sister's hair.'), and to represent something (for example: 'What does that mean?').

### STRENGTHENING UNDERSTANDING

Provide children with cubes or counters and encourage them to use these to represent the different scores. This will give children a visual representation of the groups of numbers they are comparing. They can rearrange the cubes and explore whether the mean changes or stays the same.

### GOING DEEPER

Give children some problems to solve, in which they can use their understanding of the mean and division.

### KEY LANGUAGE

**In lesson:** highest, mean, compare, size, total, whole, lowest, set, greater,

**Other language to be used by the teacher:** average, share, even, equal, group, divide, calculate, data, value

### STRUCTURES AND REPRESENTATIONS

Bar model, towers of cubes

### RESOURCES

**Mandatory:** counters, cubes

**Optional:** dice

In the eTextbook of this lesson, you will find interactive links to a selection of teaching tools.

## Quick recap
Ask children to divide each of these numbers by 4:

10   30   25

# Unit 12: Statistics, Lesson 10

## Discover

**WAYS OF WORKING** Pair work

**ASK**

- Question 1 a): *Do the skaters have the same number of scores? Does this make it difficult to compare them?*
- Question 1 a): *Who had the highest/lowest score?*
- Question 1 a): *Who do you think won the competition? Why?*
- Question 1 b): *Can you think of different ways to compare the results?*

**IN FOCUS** In question 1 a), children are asked to find the mean of two skaters' scores. Remind children of the previous lesson on finding the mean. Recap the two methods used: making the scores equal using counters or cubes to share out the scores, or calculating the total and dividing by the number of scores in the group.

Question 1 b) will remind children that the mean provides a way to compare results when there is a different number of scores in the groups. Encourage lots of discussion about the skaters' scores.

**PRACTICAL TIPS** Provide children with cubes or counters to represent the skaters' scores.

**ANSWERS**

Question 1 a): Ambika's mean score is 6.
Jamie's mean score is 6·5.
Jamie had the higher mean score.

Question 1 b): Ambika received the highest score, but also the lowest score.
Her most common score was 5.
Jamie was more consistent. The judges all gave similar scores.
Her most common score was 6.

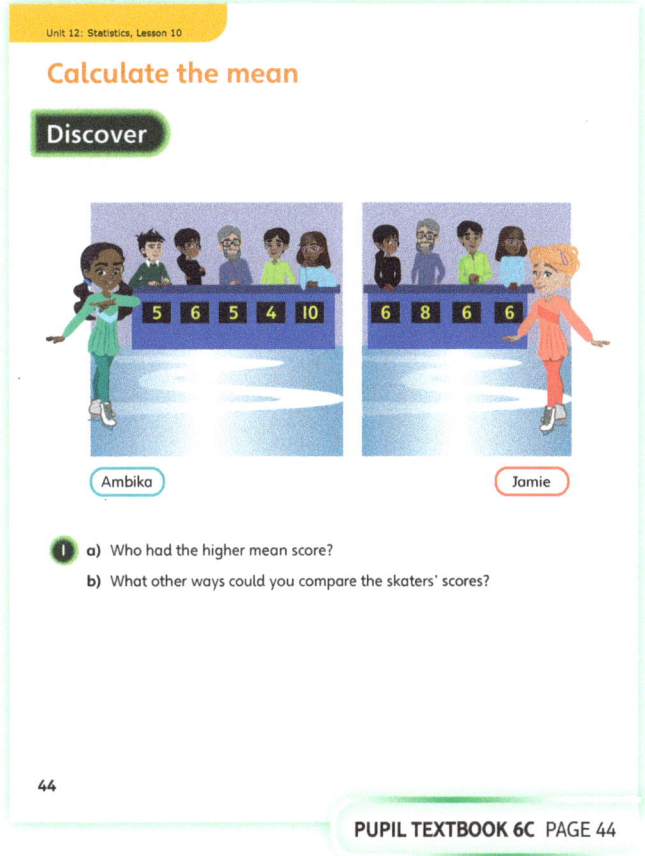

PUPIL TEXTBOOK 6C PAGE 44

## Share

**WAYS OF WORKING** Whole class teacher led

**ASK**

- Question 1 a): *Do you agree with the statements in the speech bubbles?*
- Question 1 a): *What method did you use to find the mean?*
- Question 1 a): *What do the bar models representing the results show you?*

**IN FOCUS** For question 1 a), children need to add the scores to find the total of each group and divide by the number of scores in the groups. Discuss the bar model used, explaining what it shows. Establish that it is difficult to compare the results as there is not the same number of scores in each group but that finding the mean provides a way to compare the results.

For question 1 b), discuss the statements comparing the skating results in detail.

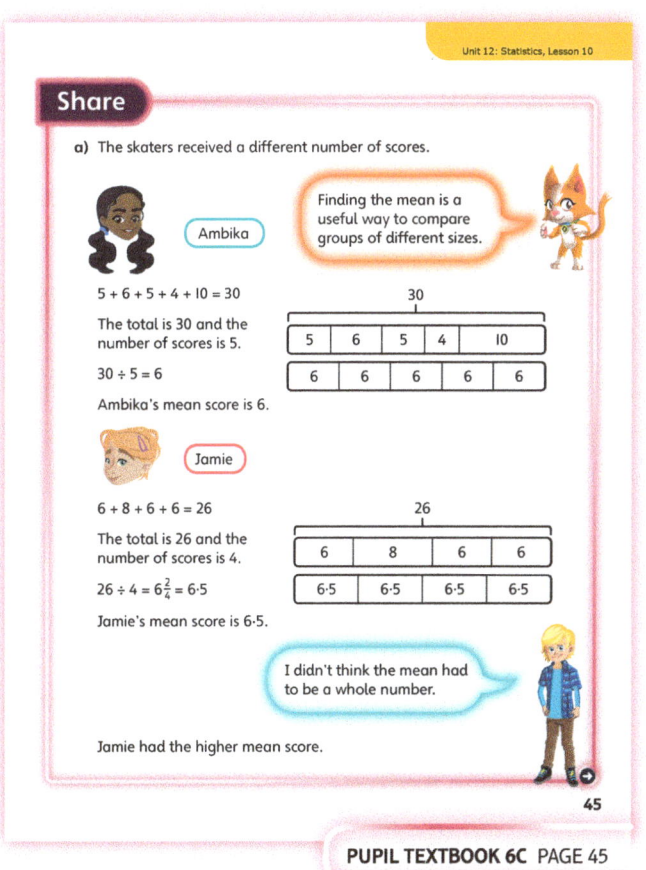

PUPIL TEXTBOOK 6C PAGE 45

# Think together

**WAYS OF WORKING** Whole class teacher led (I do, We do, You do)

**ASK**
- Question ❶: *What does 'mean' mean mathematically?*
- Question ❸: *Can different groups of data have the same mean?*
- *Can you give an example where the mean is particularly useful to compare groups of data?*

**IN FOCUS** Question ❶ asks children to compare scores by finding the mean. Question ❷ will show whether children are able to calculate the mean of a group of data. Question ❸ provides an opportunity to discuss that different groups of data can have the same mean. Explain that the mean is particularly useful in comparing groups of data that are not the same size or that do not have the same number of values in a group.

**STRENGTHEN** Provide children with counters and ask them to rearrange the counters so each person has an equal number. Support children to draw a bar model for each question/group of data to provide a visual model.

**DEEPEN** Give children groups of data and ask them to create a second group with the same mean.

| Group of data 1 | Mean | Group of data 2 (with the same mean) |
|---|---|---|
| 3, 4, 3, 4, 1 | 15 ÷ 5 = 3 | Example: 5, 5, 5 |
| 10, 11, 9, 10 | | |
| 1·5, 1·5, 1·2, 1·3 | | |
| 6, 6, 7, 8, 2, 2 | | |

**ASSESSMENT CHECKPOINT** Question ❷ will allow you to check that children understand mean is the average value of all the data in a set, regardless of how many numbers are in the set. Assess whether children are secure in calculating the mean.

Question ❸ will show whether children recognise that different groups of data can have the same mean.

**ANSWERS**

Question ❶: Mo's mean score is 7. Danny's mean score is 5·2.
Mo had the higher mean score. Danny had more scores to count.

Question ❷: Amelia's mean jump height is 1·3 m.
Richard's mean jump height is 125 cm.
Luis' mean jump height is 1·2 m. Children may give the answer 0·8 m if they include the no jump.

Question ❸: All of the mean scores are 2.

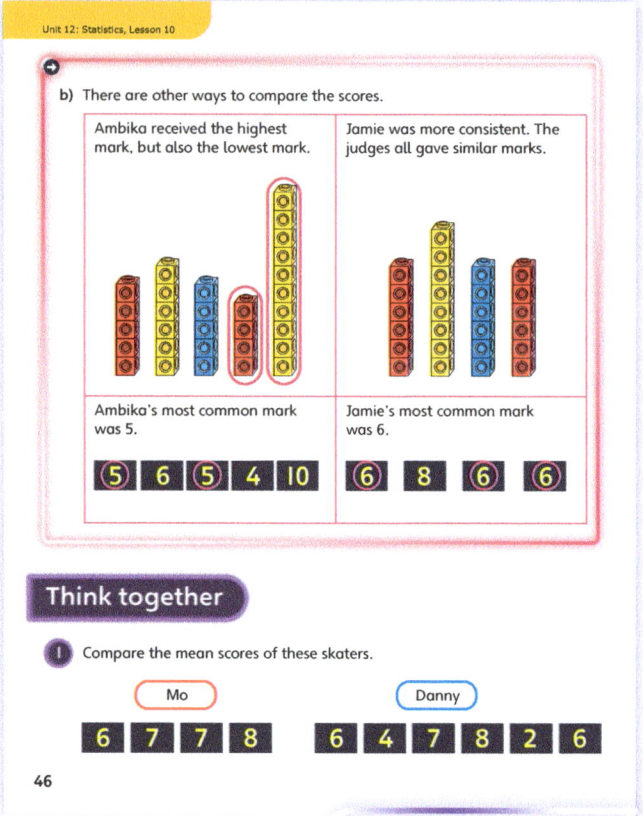

PUPIL TEXTBOOK 6C PAGE 46

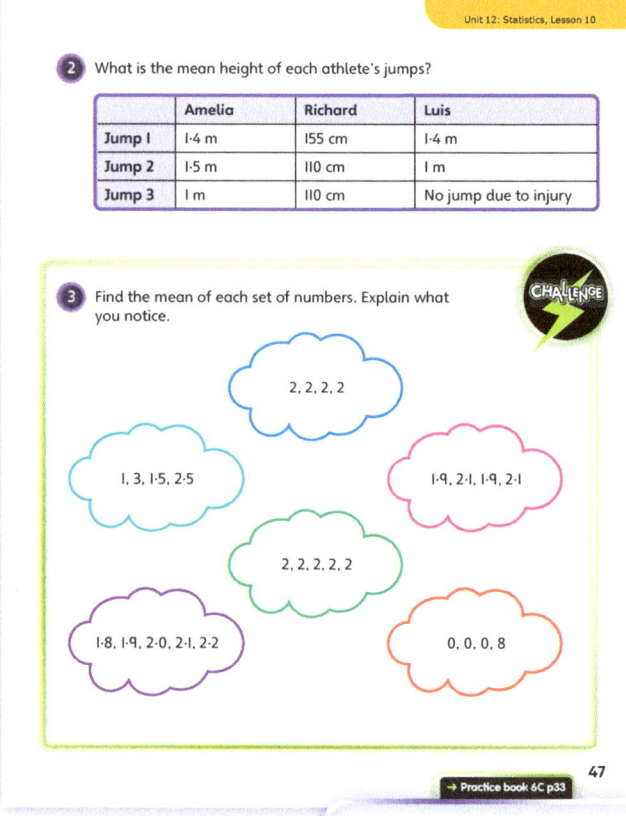

PUPIL TEXTBOOK 6C PAGE 47

Unit 12: Statistics, Lesson 10

# Practice

**WAYS OF WORKING** Independent thinking

**IN FOCUS** Question ❶ develops children's ability to calculate the mean of groups of data. Encourage children to use the bar models. Ask: *Can you describe the bar models and explain what they represent?*

The other questions will help children to realise that finding the mean is particularly useful when you need to compare groups of data of different sizes.

**STRENGTHEN** Support children to draw bar models. Provide templates for bar models if necessary.

**DEEPEN** Ask children to work in pairs or small groups. They roll a dice 5 times each, recording the results to create groups of data. Then they can swap with a partner to calculate the mean.

**ASSESSMENT CHECKPOINT** These questions will give you the opportunity to assess whether children recognise when it is useful to use the mean to compare groups of data. Ask: *Can you calculate the mean by dividing? Do you understand different groups can have the same mean?*

**ANSWERS** Answers for the **Practice** part of the lesson can be found in the *Power Maths* online subscription.

# Reflect

**WAYS OF WORKING** Independent thinking

**IN FOCUS** Children explain a method to find the mean. Children should confidently be able to write a clear step-by-step explanation of a method to find the mean of a group of numbers.

**ASSESSMENT CHECKPOINT** Look for explanations that include drawing a bar model to represent the data and calculating the mean by dividing.

**ANSWERS** Answers for the **Reflect** part of the lesson can be found in the *Power Maths* online subscription.

## After the lesson

- What percentage of children understand the mathematical term 'mean'?
- What did children find challenging and how could you address this next time?
- Are there any misconceptions you need to pick up on before next lesson?

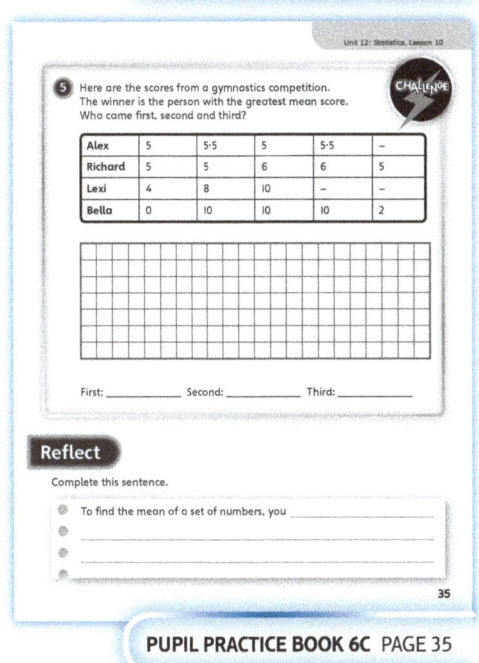

PUPIL PRACTICE BOOK 6C PAGE 33

PUPIL PRACTICE BOOK 6C PAGE 34

PUPIL PRACTICE BOOK 6C PAGE 35

83

Unit 12: Statistics, Lesson 11

# Problem solving – mean

## Learning focus
In this lesson, children solve problems involving the mean of a group of data. They learn to use the mean to calculate missing parts of data. Children secure their knowledge and understanding of finding the mean of a group of data.

## Before you teach
- Are there any misconceptions from the previous lesson that need addressing?
- Are children secure in multiplication facts?
- Can children use their understanding of the inverse to find missing numbers?

### NATIONAL CURRICULUM LINKS

**Year 6 Statistics**

Calculate and interpret the mean as an average.

### ASSESSING MASTERY

Children can calculate the mean of a group of data. Children use a given mean to find a missing part of the data group. They use diagrams and bar models to visually represent problems involving the mean. Children can solve problems involving the mean of a group of data.

### COMMON MISCONCEPTIONS

Some children may confuse finding the mean and the total: for example, finding the different ways 3 numbers can total 11 rather than have a mean of 11. Ask:
- *What are you being asked to find?*

### STRENGTHENING UNDERSTANDING

Explore simple missing number problems to begin with and look at how the same method is used when dealing with the mean.

2 + 5 + 4 + 6 + ☐ = 24; 2 + 5 + 4 + 6 + ☐ = mean of 4; 2 + 5 + 4 + 6 + ☐ = 6 × 4

Provide children with string or ribbon and encourage them to represent the different lengths of the snakes using the string or ribbon. This will give children a practical representation of the groups they are comparing.

### GOING DEEPER

Focus on finding groups of numbers that involve more difficult division skills. Explore a variety of groups of numbers from real-life situations.

### KEY LANGUAGE

**In lesson:** mean, represent, balance, even, odd, difference, greatest, least, whole, set

**Other language to be used by the teacher:** average, divide, share, equal, data, inverse, operation

### STRUCTURES AND REPRESENTATIONS

Bar model

### RESOURCES

**Mandatory:** counters, cubes

**Optional:** string or ribbon

 In the eTextbook of this lesson, you will find interactive links to a selection of teaching tools.

## Quick recap
Challenge children to find the mean of this set of numbers:

3, 10, 12, 15

Unit 12: Statistics, Lesson 11

# Discover

**WAYS OF WORKING** Pair work

**ASK**

- Question 1 a): *How many snakes are there?*
- Question 1 a): *How long are the snakes?*
- Question 1 a): *Can you draw a bar model or diagram to represent the problem?*
- Question 1 a): *Can you explain to a partner what the mean is?*
- Question 1 a): *What methods did you use in the last lesson to find the mean?*

**IN FOCUS** Question 1 a) asks children to find a missing piece of data in a group that they know the mean of. Children begin to explore problems involving the mean. Discuss the steps they need to take to work out the length of the fifth snake.

**PRACTICAL TIPS** Provide children with string, ribbon or cubes to represent the length of the snakes.

**ANSWERS**

Question 1 a): The fifth snake must be 15 cm long.

Question 1 b): The new snake is 26 cm long.

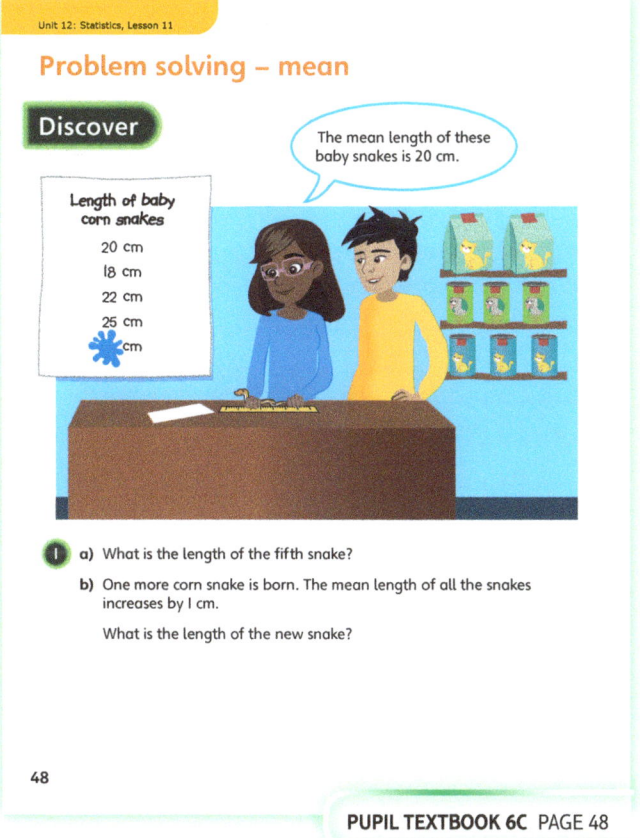

PUPIL TEXTBOOK 6C PAGE 48

# Share

**WAYS OF WORKING** Whole class teacher led

**ASK**

- Question 1 a): *What does the diagram show you?*
- Question 1 a): *Did anyone use a diagram to solve the problem presented in the Discover section?*
- Question 1 a): *Would this method work for other questions?*
- Question 1 b): *How can you check your answer?*
- Question 1 b): *Can you check your answer by adding the lengths of the snakes together?*

**IN FOCUS** In question 1 a), the visual representation shows children how to calculate the missing piece of data using the mean. Discuss what the diagram shows. Children could draw their own diagrams on individual whiteboards to show the problem and explain to a partner.

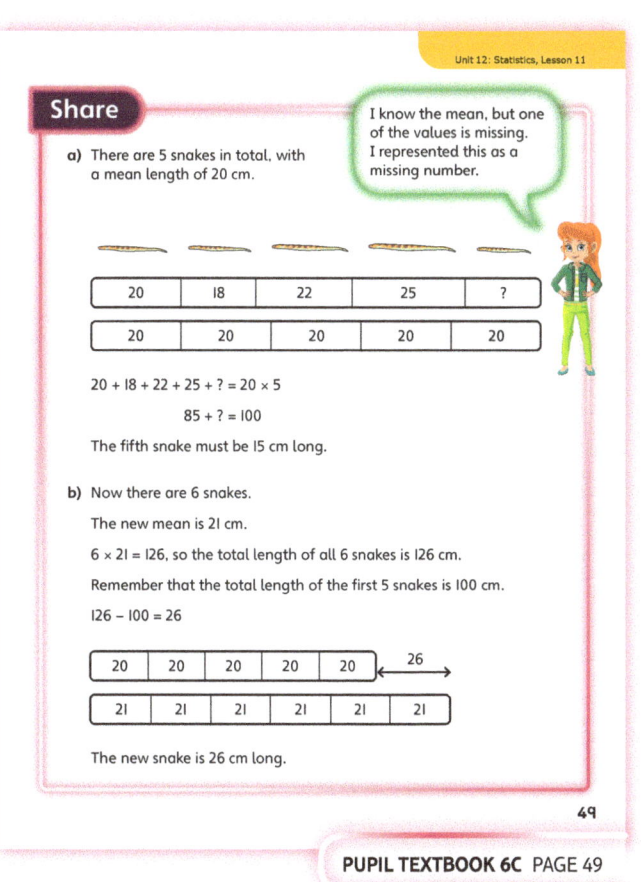

PUPIL TEXTBOOK 6C PAGE 49

85

# Think together

**WAYS OF WORKING** Whole class teacher led (I do, We do, You do)

**ASK**
- Question ❶: *How do the bar models help you?*
- Question ❷: *How many snakes are in the group?*
- Question ❷: *What do you need to find out first?*

**IN FOCUS** Question ❶ introduces data in the form of a bar chart. Children have the opportunity to recap on reading bar charts. Support children to use the bar model.

$2 + 5 + 4 + 6 + 1 + \square = 6 \times 4$    $18 + \square = 24$

Question ❷ practises finding a missing number when you know the mean. The bar model has less scaffolding, but children should be able to use this to work out the missing number.

$1 \cdot 1 + 1 \cdot 7 + 2 \cdot 1 + \square = 1 \cdot 5 \times 4$    $4 \cdot 9 + \square = 6$

Question ❸ has many different solutions. Children should compare their solutions with a partner to help them understand the fact that different groups of numbers can have the same mean.

**STRENGTHEN** To strengthen understanding, practise simple missing number problems to ensure children are familiar with the method and can select the inverse operation.

$34 + \square = 67$    $\square + 28 = 54$    $83 + \square = 112$

**DEEPEN** Give children groups of data (with one part missing) and the mean – challenge them to calculate the missing piece.

| Group of data | Mean |
|---|---|
| 3, 4, 5, 1, 1, ? | 3 |
| 10, 3, 2, 8, ? | 6 |
| 15, 12, 17, 3, ? | 10 |

**ASSESSMENT CHECKPOINT** Questions ❶ and ❷ will give you another opportunity to check that children are able to solve problems involving the mean.

Question ❸ can be used to check that children realise that different groups of numbers can have the same mean. Prompt discussion by pointing out Ash's comment.

**ANSWERS**

Question ❶: The height of the sixth tower is 6.

Question ❷: The mass of the last snake is 1·1 kg.

Question ❸: Three numbers with a mean of 11: any three numbers with a total of 33.
For example, 9, 11, 13 or 8, 12, 13.
Five numbers with a mean of 10: any 5 numbers with a total of 50.
For example, 2, 8, 10, 13, 17 (including 10) or 3, 8, 9, 13, 17 (not including 10).
Four numbers with a mean of 10 (total = 40) and a difference of four between highest and lowest numbers: only one answer of 8, 9, 11, 12.

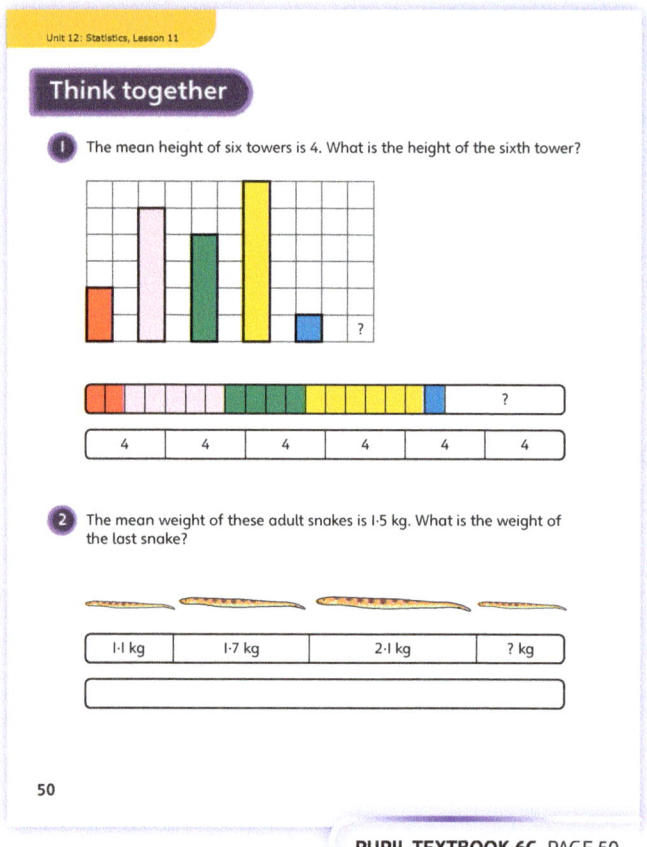

PUPIL TEXTBOOK 6C PAGE 50

PUPIL TEXTBOOK 6C PAGE 51

Unit 12: Statistics, Lesson 11

# Practice

**WAYS OF WORKING** Independent thinking

**IN FOCUS** Children practise using the mean to find missing numbers. Questions 3 and 5 introduce problems involving money and measures. Ask: *Can you apply the same methods to find the mean using numbers in these situations?*

**STRENGTHEN** Support children by providing cubes to investigate possible solutions. With question 5, discuss different ways to represent the mean – for example, $\frac{1}{4}$ litre is the same as 250 ml.

Provide coins and jugs for children to explore the problems practically.

**DEEPEN** Ask children to find the missing number in groups of data using the mean. Ask: *Can you find two missing numbers? Can you find the missing number when the mean is not a whole number?*

**THINK DIFFERENTLY** Question 5 asks children to calculate the possible volume of water contained in two jugs so the mean volume of five jugs is $\frac{1}{4}$ litre. This will test their ability to read different scales, as well as their understanding of calculations involving a mean. Check that they find numbers appropriate to the size of the jugs.

**ASSESSMENT CHECKPOINT** Question 1 assesses whether children recognise that there is often more than one solution to a problem.

Question 4 assesses whether children can find two missing numbers in a group of data using the mean.

**ANSWERS** Answers for the **Practice** part of the lesson can be found in the *Power Maths* online subscription.

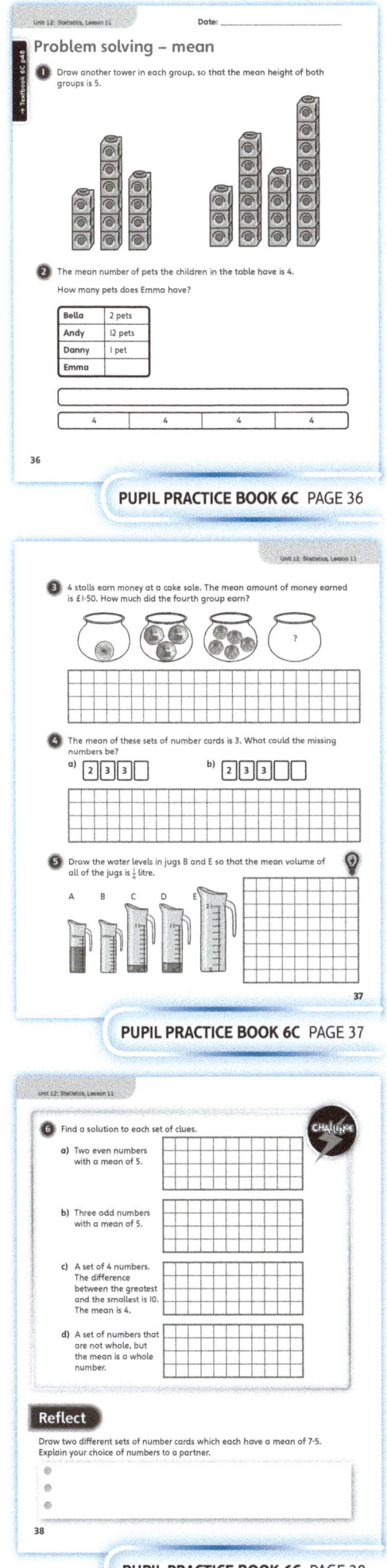

PUPIL PRACTICE BOOK 6C PAGE 36

PUPIL PRACTICE BOOK 6C PAGE 37

PUPIL PRACTICE BOOK 6C PAGE 38

# Reflect

**WAYS OF WORKING** Pair work, independent thinking

**IN FOCUS** Children are asked to choose two sets of numbers that have the same mean. In this problem, the mean is not a whole number and therefore requires children to use decimals and consider groups of data containing decimals. The statement does not specify how many numbers are in the group so there are many different solutions. Encourage children to explore solutions with different numbers of values in the group.

**ASSESSMENT CHECKPOINT** Do children recognise there is often more than one solution to a problem? Do they recognise that different groups of data can have the same mean? Can they find missing numbers when the mean is not a whole number?

**ANSWERS** Answers for the **Reflect** part of the lesson can be found in the *Power Maths* online subscription.

## After the lesson

- What percentage of children are confident using the mean to solve problems?
- Are there any misconceptions you need to pick up on before next lesson?

87

# End of unit check

> Don't forget the unit assessment grid in your *Power Maths* online subscription.

**WAYS OF WORKING** Group work adult led

**IN FOCUS**
- Question ❶ and question ❷ focus on the mean. Children demonstrate they can calculate the mean of a set of data by adding the data to find the total and then dividing by the number of values in the set.
- Questions ❸ and ❹ focus on pie charts. Children need to read and interpret the pie chart, considering fractions and percentages. In question ❹, children need to be careful because the two pie charts represent different numbers of children.
- Question ❺ focuses on line graphs. Children need to read two points on the graph and calculate the difference. One of the points is half-way between two intervals on the grid.

**ANSWERS AND COMMENTARY** Children calculate the mean from a set of data, demonstrate they can find missing data using the mean, read and interpret pie charts in terms of fractions and percentages and can interpret line graphs.

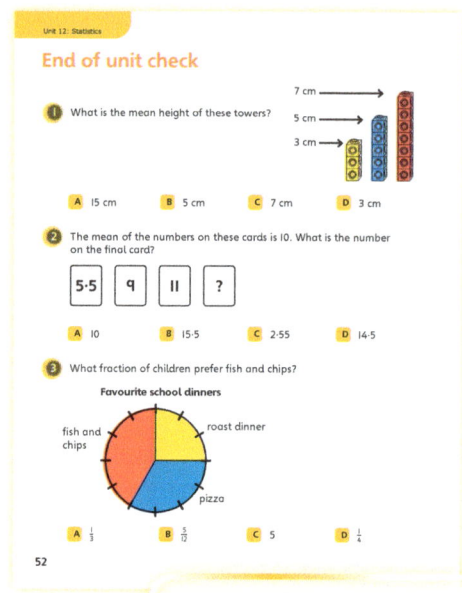

PUPIL TEXTBOOK 6C PAGE 52

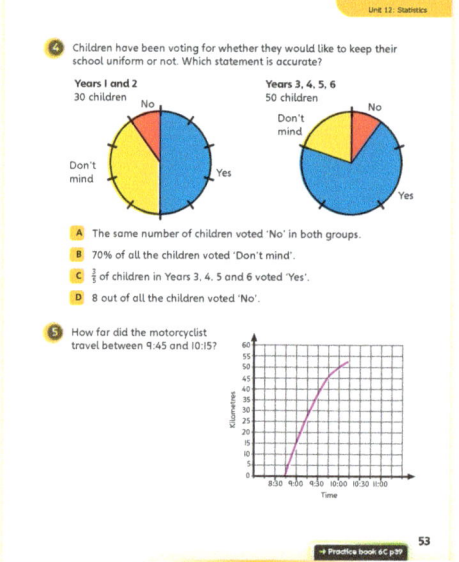

PUPIL TEXTBOOK 6C PAGE 53

| Q | A | WRONG ANSWERS AND MISCONCEPTIONS | STRENGTHENING UNDERSTANDING |
|---|---|---|---|
| 1 | B | A suggests children have added the data but not divided. | Mean = total ÷ number of values in a set. Give children sets of data and ask them to calculate the mean. Set 1: 3, 4, 5, 3 Set 2: 3·5, 5, 7·5 Set 3: 40, 30, 35, 25, 30 |
| 2 | D | A suggests children have given the mean as the answer but have not understood the question properly. C suggests children have added the data and divided by the mean. | |
| 3 | B | C suggests children have calculated how many of the 12 intervals represent fish and chips but not given the answer as a fraction. | Recap fractions and percentages of circles with children. Provide circles and ask children to shade $\frac{1}{2}, \frac{1}{4}, \frac{1}{3}, \frac{3}{4}$, etc. This will help children to visualise the fractions. |
| 4 | D | B shows children have miscalculated the percentage who don't mind. C shows children have miscalculated the fraction who voted 'Yes'. | |
| 5 | | The answer is 7·5 km. | Practise reading plotted points and in between plotted points from a line graph. |

# Unit 12: Statistics

## My journal

**WAYS OF WORKING** Independent thinking

**ANSWERS AND COMMENTARY**

Question ❶ asks children to create a conversion line graph. Children need to decide on an appropriate scale for the *x*-axis and *y*-axis and plot the points accurately before joining the dots with a line. Then children need to demonstrate they are able to use the graph to find the value of $19 in £. Ensure children use the graph to read the value of $19 rather than calculating from the data.

Question ❷ gives children the opportunity to really think about what they have learnt in this unit and formalise what they know about the advantages and disadvantages of different types of chart. Encourage them to look back at the lessons to help them remember what sort of things they might need to use a chart for.

## Power check

**WAYS OF WORKING** Independent thinking

**ASK**

- Can you calculate the mean of a set of numbers?
- Are you confident in reading pie charts and bar charts?
- How confidently can you create a line graph?
- Could you explain how to use the graph to find information?

## Power play

**WAYS OF WORKING** Pair work

**IN FOCUS** The **Power play** uses dice to generate data and then children have to plot the points onto a line graph. Use the **Power play** to develop children's confidence in plotting data onto a line graph.

**ANSWERS AND COMMENTARY** Encourage children to check their partner is plotting the data correctly onto the line graph. They need to be sure that at the end of the game, the line is in the correct place because this determines the winner of the game!

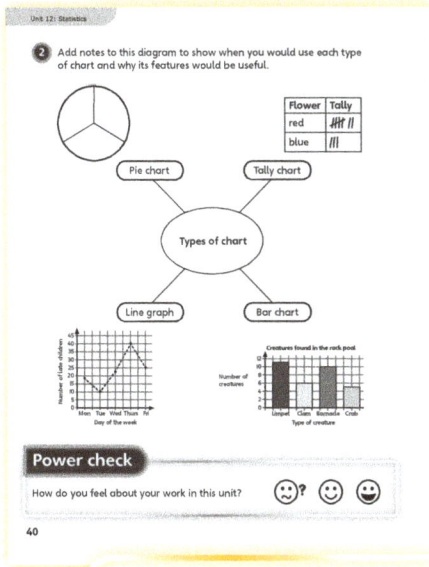

PUPIL PRACTICE BOOK 6C PAGE 39

PUPIL PRACTICE BOOK 6C PAGE 40

PUPIL PRACTICE BOOK 6C PAGE 41

## After the unit ⏸

- Are children able to suggest what type of graph and chart is most appropriate for different types of data/situations?
- Do children know when using the mean is most useful?

**Strengthen** and **Deepen** activities for this unit can be found in the *Power Maths* online subscription.

# Unit 13
## Geometry – properties of shapes

**Mastery Expert tip!** 'To develop confidence in properties of shapes, create opportunities for children to explore geometry in practical settings. For example, in art, children could use shapes to make pictures or make nets of shapes to form 3D shapes, or children could investigate shapes found in nature (such as hexagons in honeycomb).'

**Don't forget to watch the Unit 13 video!**

### WHY THIS UNIT IS IMPORTANT

This unit is important since it further develops children's understanding of the properties of shapes, drawing on a range of skills including using a protractor, angles in shapes, and applying knowledge of shape properties to accurately draw them. It encourages reasoning with shapes while also exploring different methods.

### WHERE THIS UNIT FITS

→ Unit 12: Statistics
→ **Unit 13: Geometry – properties of shapes**
→ Unit 14: Geometry – position and direction

In this unit, children extend their understanding of measuring angles to draw shapes accurately and explore the interior angles of shapes, building on prior knowledge of angles on a straight line. Children will continue to develop their reasoning skills by interpreting properties of circles and will focus on exploring 3D shapes when given 2D representations.

Before they start this unit, it is expected that children:
- can identify types of angle and use angle facts, such as angles around a point add up to 360° and angles on a straight line add up to 180°
- can measure lines using a ruler and know the properties of 2D and 3D shapes
- can multiply, divide, add and subtract numbers, and use a part-whole model and a bar model.

### ASSESSING MASTERY

Children who have mastered this unit are able to measure angles, draw accurately, calculate missing angles confidently using angle facts, solve multi-step problems and explore the properties of shapes.

| COMMON MISCONCEPTIONS | STRENGTHENING UNDERSTANDING | GOING DEEPER |
|---|---|---|
| When using a protractor children may incorrectly line it up or look at the wrong scale. | Encourage children to rotate their paper, so the baseline is horizontal and to ensure the crosshairs are at the vertex. Identifying the angle type can help them decide if the answer seems reasonable. | Ask children to explore and explain different ways of measuring angles using both scales on the protractor. Give children angles to measure which involve using angle facts, such as measuring a reflex angle. |
| When calculating a missing angle, children may not know which operation to use. | Showing the numbers on a bar model will help children understand which operations are needed. | Encourage children to further explore missing angle problems which include other angle facts, such as angles on a straight line or angles around a point. |
| Children may struggle to recognise 3D shapes from 2D representations. | Encourage children to use paper versions of the shapes, so they can manipulate them in a concrete way. | Encourage children to explore all possible ways of representing a 3D shape using a 2D form. |

# Unit 13: Geometry – properties of shapes

### UNIT STARTER PAGES

Introduce this unit using teacher-led discussion. Allow children time to discuss questions in small groups or pairs and then share ideas as a whole class. Children should be encouraged to use concrete resources where possible to make and explore multiple representations of shapes.

### STRUCTURES AND REPRESENTATIONS

**Bar model:** Allows children to translate problems into calculations and interpret the correct operation.

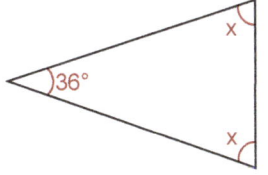
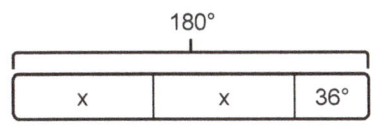

**Polygons:** Divide polygons into triangles so children can see how the sum of the interior angles of a polygon is always a multiple of 180°. This can help them to calculate the value of one interior angle.

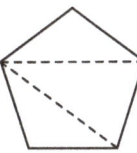

**Circles:** Children will be introduced to parts of a circle: circumference, radius and diameter.

**Nets:** Children will explore 2D representations of 3D shapes to further consolidate their understanding of the properties of shapes.

### KEY LANGUAGE

There is some key language that children will need to know as part of the learning in this unit.

➜ degrees, measurement, length
➜ angle, obtuse, acute, reflex, right angle, interior, vertically opposite angles
➜ protractor, baseline, crosshairs, scale
➜ vertex, edge, face
➜ parallel
➜ properties
➜ triangle, isosceles, equilateral, scalene
➜ regular, polygon, quadrilateral, parallelogram, kite, rhombus, trapezium
➜ diameter, radius, circumference, concentric, centre
➜ perimeter
➜ pyramid, tetrahedron, cylinder, prism, cuboid, cube
➜ nets
➜ isometric paper

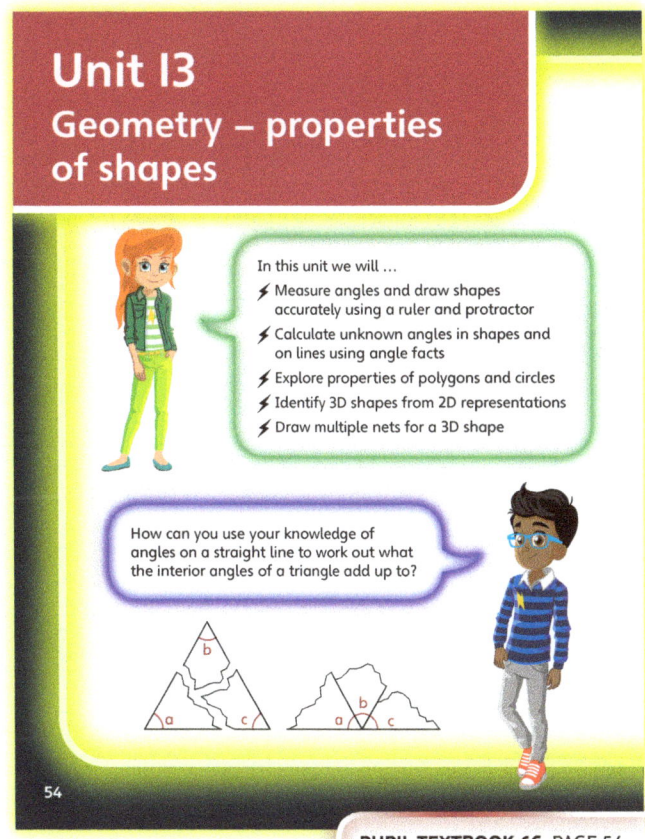

PUPIL TEXTBOOK 6C PAGE 54

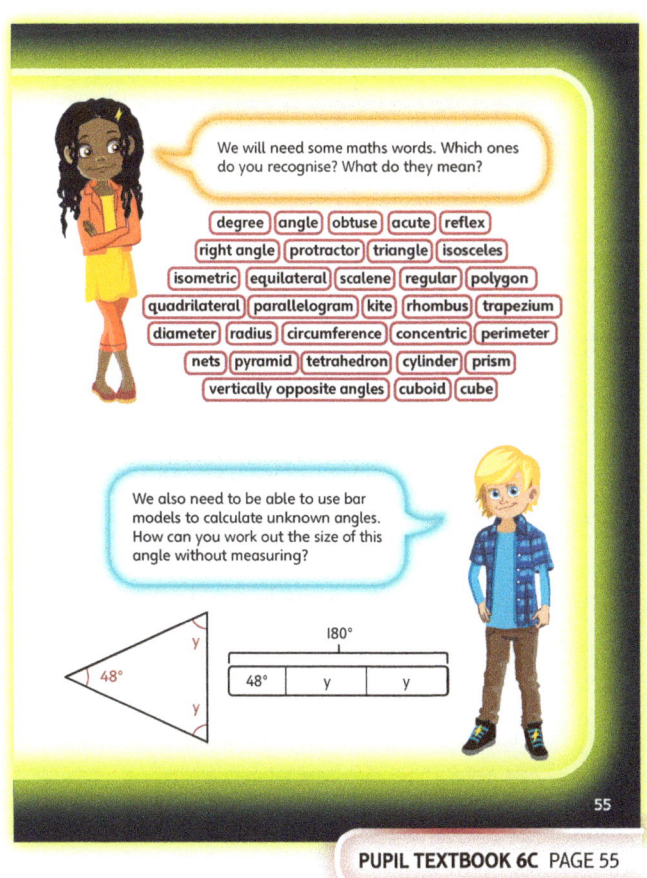

PUPIL TEXTBOOK 6C PAGE 55

Unit 13: Geometry – properties of shapes, Lesson 1

# Measure and classify angles

## Learning focus
In this lesson, children reinforce prior knowledge of angle types and understand how to measure angles using a protractor.

## Before you teach
- Can children identify types of angle?
- Do children know that angles around a point add to 360°?
- Can children identify interior angles?

### NATIONAL CURRICULUM LINKS

**Year 6 Geometry – properties of shapes**

Recognise angles where they meet at a point, are on a straight line, or are vertically opposite, and find missing angles.

### ASSESSING MASTERY

Children can confidently measure angles using a protractor, demonstrating an understanding of angle types. They can read the correct scale and give an accurate measurement while showing fluency in using known angle facts.

### COMMON MISCONCEPTIONS

Children may incorrectly line up the protractor to measure the angle, especially when the angle is oriented so that the baseline is not horizontal. Ask:
- *Have you positioned the baseline on top of the line that contains the angle and ensured the crosshairs are aligned at the vertex?*

Children may look at the wrong scale on the protractor and so read the incorrect measurement. Encourage them to draw an arrow between the baseline and the other line to help them see which scale to look at. Ask:
- *What type of angle do you think it is? Is your answer logical?*

### STRENGTHENING UNDERSTANDING

Show children incorrect and correct ways of lining up a protractor to measure an angle. Begin with angles that have a horizontal baseline and allow children to practise positioning the protractor on several different angles before they attempt to measure them. Next, move on to angles that are easy to measure, such as 60°; this is neither too small nor too big and is a multiple of 10. Once children are confident with this move on to angles that are multiples of 5.

### GOING DEEPER

Ask children to explore and explain different ways of measuring angles using both scales on the protractor. For example, they could use one line as the baseline and use one scale to measure the angle or they could use the other line as the baseline and use the other scale on the protractor.

Ask children to measure angles that are in different orientations (i.e. the baseline is not horizontal). Give children irregular shapes and ask them to measure the interior and exterior angles.

### KEY LANGUAGE

**In lesson:** measurement, angle, obtuse, **protractor**, baseline, crosshairs, scale, interior, regular, vertex

**Other language to be used by the teacher:** align, rotate, line up, accurate, degrees, acute, reflex

### STRUCTURES AND REPRESENTATIONS

Angles represented in lines and shapes

### RESOURCES

**Mandatory:** protractor

**Optional:** large whiteboard, protractor

 In the eTextbook of this lesson, you will find interactive links to a selection of teaching tools.

## Quick recap
Ask children to name as many different types of angles as they can. Challenge them to give you a definition of each angle.

# Unit 13: Geometry – properties of shapes, Lesson 1

## Discover

**WAYS OF WORKING** Pair work

**ASK**

- Question ❶ a): *How can you work out which angle is which?*
- Question ❶ b): *Why do you think Max got these answers? What mistake has he made?*

**IN FOCUS** Question ❶ a) introduces the concept of measuring angles using a protractor. Children also use their knowledge of types of angle to identify the obtuse angle.

Question ❶ b) addresses the common misconception of reading from the wrong scale when measuring angles with a protractor.

**PRACTICAL TIPS** You could introduce this topic using a whiteboard activity (similar to Jamilla's activity) and a large protractor, or ask children to measure angles around the classroom, possibly as part of a 'Scavenger Hunt' activity. It will be important for children to understand that a right angle is 90° and to get a 'feel' for angles that are less than or more than 90°, labelling them as acute and obtuse, respectively.

**ANSWERS**

Question ❶ a): A = 45°, B = 110° (the only obtuse angle) and C = 50°

Question ❶ b): Max has read the wrong scale. He started from the wrong side. He needs to measure the angle between the two lines.

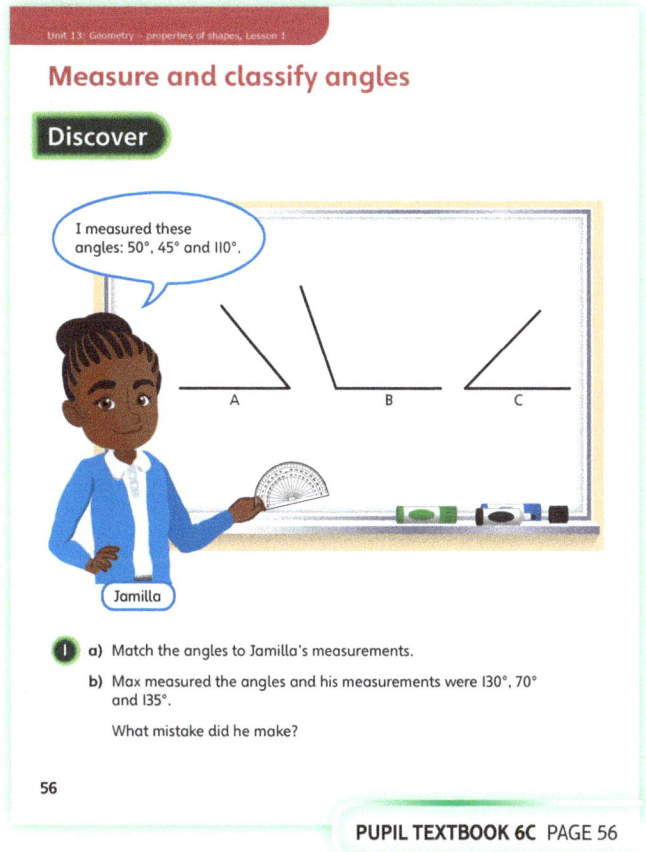

PUPIL TEXTBOOK 6C PAGE 56

## Share

**WAYS OF WORKING** Whole class teacher led

**ASK**

- Question ❶ a): *What types of angles are these? Can you match any without measuring the angle? How can you measure the other angles? What equipment can you use? How do you line up the protractor? Where are the crosshairs? What is the baseline? How do you know which scale to look at?*
- Question ❶ b): *What do you notice about the protractor? How do you know which scale to look at?*

**IN FOCUS** Question ❶ a) requires children to match the measurements to the diagrams. Encourage children to categorise the angles as obtuse and acute. Children should recognise that 110° is the only obtuse angle, so they can match this without measuring it. Watch out for children who try to guess the other angles. Discuss how to line up the protractor correctly, introducing key words such as baseline and crosshairs. Explain how to read from the correct scale as this is a common misconception. Ensure children are confident with the unit of degrees and the notation for this.

In question ❶ b), discuss the diagrams and ensure children understand which scale measures which angle.

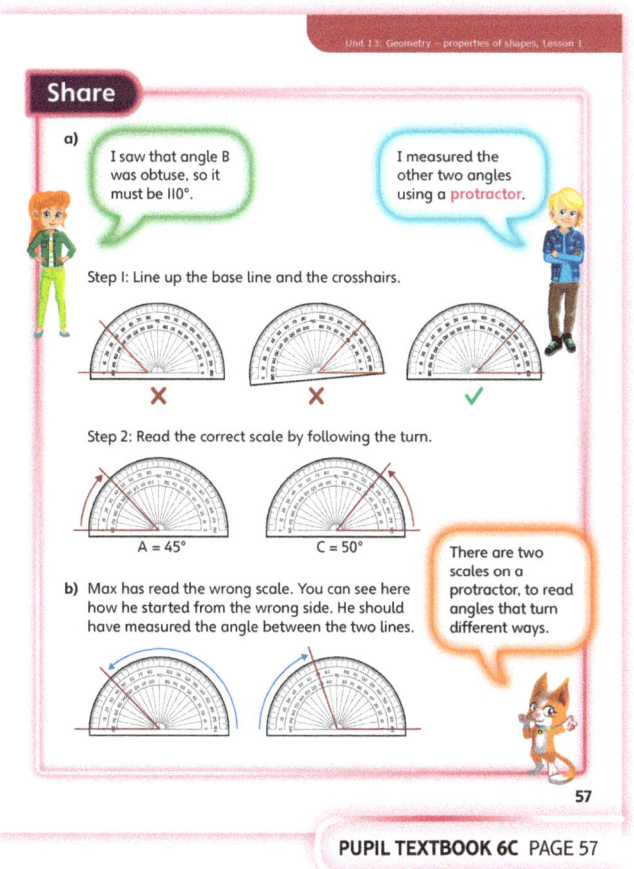

PUPIL TEXTBOOK 6C PAGE 57

93

# Unit 13: Geometry – properties of shapes, Lesson 1

## Think together

**WAYS OF WORKING** Whole class teacher led (I do, We do, You do)

**ASK**

- Question ❶: *How can you measure the angles? Which scale do you need to read? What number does the scale show? Is your answer accurate?*
- Question ❷: *Can you sort the angles into angle types? What is different about how the angles are drawn? How can you measure them?*
- Question ❸: *What does interior angle mean? How can you check if the pentagon is regular? What is special about a regular pentagon? How can you measure the interior angles?*

**IN FOCUS** Question ❶ requires children to measure the given angles. They will need to use a protractor, or their knowledge of angles on a straight line, for the third angle. Encourage children to read the scales accurately and watch out for children who round their answers.

Question ❷ asks children to sort angles into size order. It may be useful to encourage children to rotate the paper, so the baseline of each angle is horizontal.

Question ❸ presents children with angles in a different representation. It may be necessary to discuss the definition of interior angle and regular. Encourage children to identify the line they are going to use as a baseline first, then line up the protractor with the scale on top of the angle. In Shape B, the interior angle at vertex C is 90°; remind children that this is known as a right angle. Watch out for children who measure the exterior angle at vertex E on Shape B and remind them that the interior angle is a reflex angle. Children will need to use knowledge of angles around a point.

**STRENGTHEN** Encourage children to draw the angle onto the shape if it is not shown. Children can draw an arrow to help them identify which scale to read.

**DEEPEN** To deepen learning in question ❸, children could work out the exterior angles of each shape. Extend by asking children to draw their own angles, measure them and categorise them as acute, obtuse, reflex and right angles.

**ASSESSMENT CHECKPOINT** In questions ❶ and ❷, look for children who are confident in lining up the baseline and the crosshairs and those who give an accurate reading, demonstrating understanding of which scale to read.

In question ❸, look for children who are confident in using the correct lines to measure the angles while fluently using associated angle facts to measure reflex angles.

**ANSWERS**

Question ❶ a): 34°

Question ❶ b): 103°

Question ❶ c): 180°

Question ❷: From smallest to largest: C (55°), A (75°), D (120°), B (135°)

Question ❸: Shape A: A–E = 108° each
Shape B: A = 56°, B = 102°, C = 90°, D = 61°, E = 231°

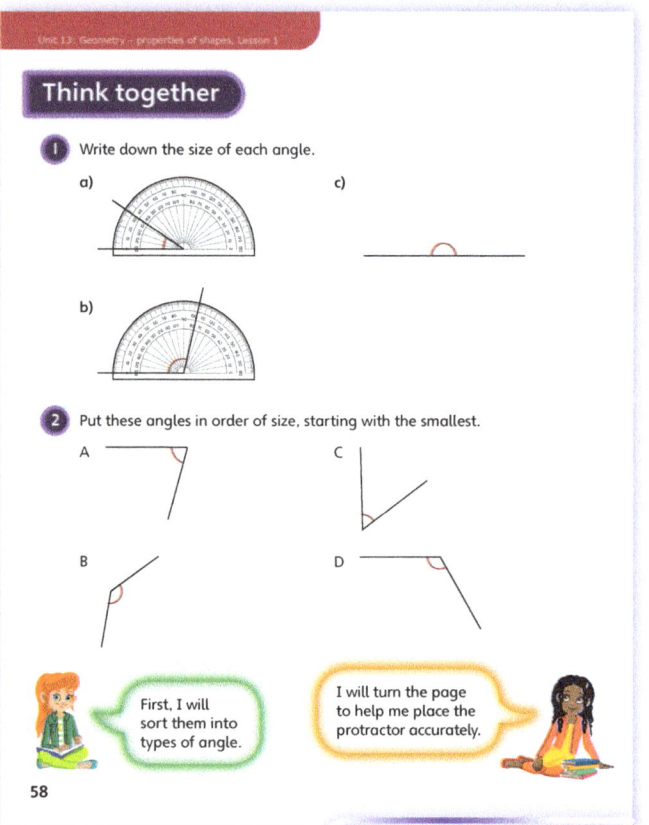

**PUPIL TEXTBOOK 6C** PAGE 58

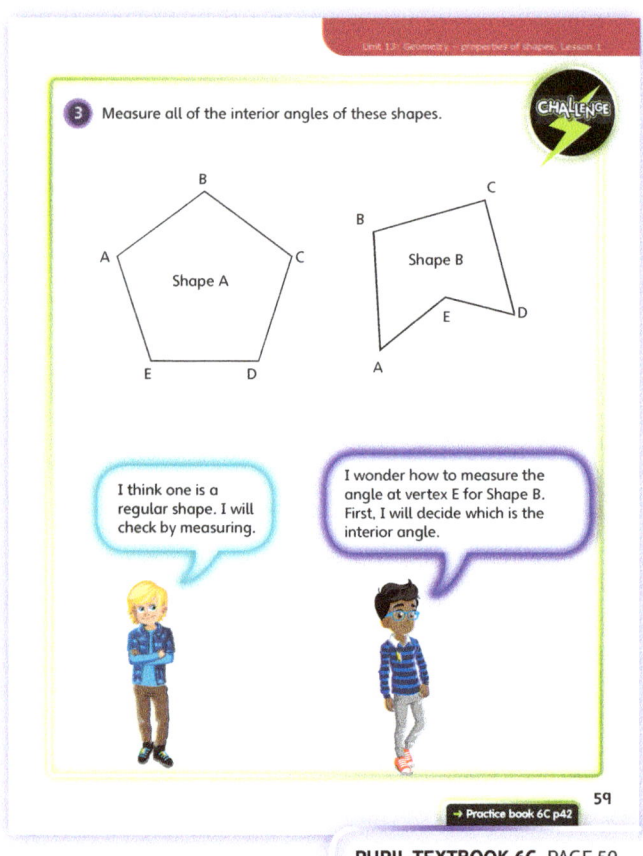

**PUPIL TEXTBOOK 6C** PAGE 59

# Unit 13: Geometry – properties of shapes, Lesson 1

## Practice

**WAYS OF WORKING** Independent thinking

**IN FOCUS** Questions ❶ and ❷ consolidate children's understanding of measuring angles using a protractor. Encourage children to rotate the page if necessary when the baseline is not horizontal.

In question ❸, children measure interior angles. Watch out for children who measure the exterior angle rather than the interior angle when it is a reflex angle. In question ❸ b), children may assume shape A is regular because the lengths are the same. Encourage children to measure all the interior angles and use their knowledge of angles in a regular shape.

In question ❺, children use their knowledge of symmetry and then measure the interior angles, noticing that some of the angles are the same.

**STRENGTHEN** To strengthen understanding, encourage children to identify and draw each angle on to the diagram before measuring, and to rotate the page so the baseline is horizontal.

**DEEPEN** Question ❺ can be extended by giving children squared paper and asking them to create their own symmetric shapes and to measure the interior angles. Deepen further by asking children to include an acute, obtuse and reflex angle in their shapes.

**THINK DIFFERENTLY** In question ❹, children may believe the angles are different because the lines are different lengths. Encourage children to measure each angle and explain their reasoning.

**ASSESSMENT CHECKPOINT** In questions ❶ and ❷, look for children confidently lining up the protractor, using the correct scale and taking accurate measurements.

In questions ❸ and ❺, look for children who can use the correct units in their measurements, show understanding of regular shapes and symmetry and deal with reflex angles.

In question ❹, look for children who can confidently explain why the angles are equivalent.

**ANSWERS** Answers for the **Practice** part of the lesson can be found in the *Power Maths* online subscription.

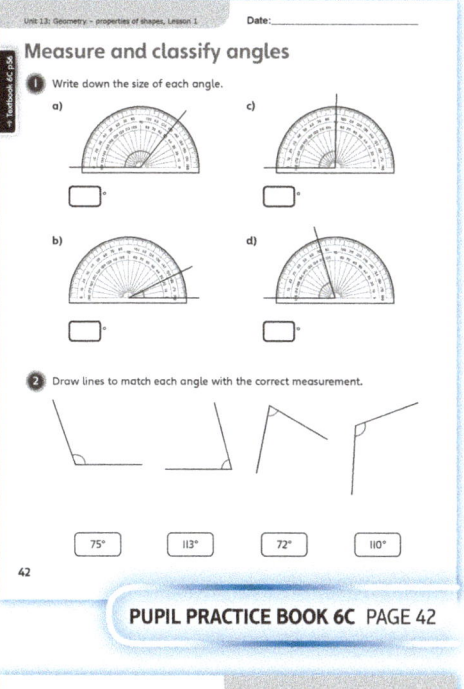

PUPIL PRACTICE BOOK 6C PAGE 42

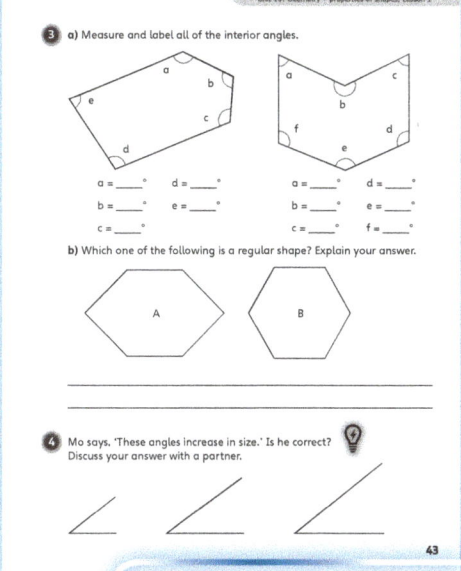

PUPIL PRACTICE BOOK 6C PAGE 43

## Reflect

**WAYS OF WORKING** Pair work

**IN FOCUS** Encourage children to discuss the misconceptions arising from the mistakes that have occurred in the lesson.

**ASSESSMENT CHECKPOINT** Look for children who are able to confidently explain mistakes, even if they did not make the mistake themselves, such as not lining up the protractor correctly or not reading the correct scale on the protractor.

**ANSWERS** Answers for the **Reflect** part of the lesson can be found in the *Power Maths* online subscription.

PUPIL PRACTICE BOOK 6C PAGE 44

## After the lesson

- Can children identify angle types and measure angles accurately?
- Can children accurately measure angles between two lines, interior angles of a shape and reflex angles?

Unit 13: Geometry – properties of shapes, Lesson 2

# Vertically opposite angles

## Learning focus
In this lesson, children will extend their understanding of angles to discover that vertically opposite angles are equal.

## Before you teach
- Do children know angles on a straight line add to 180°?
- Can children measure and draw angles with a protractor?
- Can children find missing angles in regular polygons, including triangles?

### NATIONAL CURRICULUM LINKS

**Year 6 Geometry – properties of shapes**

Recognise angles where they meet at a point, are on a straight line, or are vertically opposite, and find missing angles.

### ASSESSING MASTERY

Children understand that vertically opposite angles are equal using angles on a straight line which total to 180°. Children apply this understanding to solve missing angle problems, demonstrating fluency in associated angle facts.

### COMMON MISCONCEPTIONS

Children may think that any opposite angles are equal (for example, they may think angle w is equal to angle y or that angle x is equal to angle z). Ensure children understand that vertically opposite angles are only formed by a pair of crossing straight lines. Ask:
- How many lines are crossing?

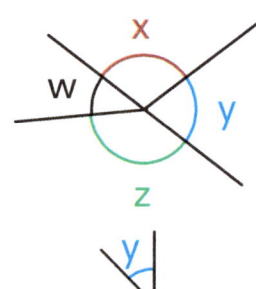

Another misconception occurs when the lines are different lengths or the angles are labelled with different curves (for example, children may think that angle x is not equal to angle y because of the way the angles have been marked or the fact that the lines are different lengths). Exposing children to examples like this and encouraging them to measure the angles using a protractor will help to strengthen understanding. Ask:
- If the marking for these angles were removed and you concentrated on just the angles, would they look a similar size?

### STRENGTHENING UNDERSTANDING

Encourage children to identify straight lines where they can use the fact that angles on a straight line total 180°. Build confidence by encouraging children to measure one angle using a protractor and predict the other angles before measuring to confirm.

### GOING DEEPER

Deepen learning by asking children to explore the different ways in which they can calculate a missing angle using a range of angle facts. Encourage children to discuss which methods are most efficient.

### KEY LANGUAGE

**In lesson: vertically opposite angle**, measurement, equal, calculate, pattern, cross, predict

**Other language to be used by the teacher:** properties, less, twice, degrees, triangle, regular, polygon, fifth

### STRUCTURES AND REPRESENTATIONS

Angles in crossing lines, angles on straight lines, bar models

### RESOURCES

**Mandatory:** paper, rulers, protractors, scissors, coloured paper, highlighter pens

**Optional:** tracing paper

 In the eTextbook of this lesson, you will find interactive links to a selection of teaching tools.

## Quick recap

Have a class discussion about angles and turns. Ask:
*How many degrees are in a half turn? How many degrees are in a whole turn?*

# Unit 13: Geometry – properties of shapes, Lesson 2

## Discover

**WAYS OF WORKING** Pair work

**ASK**

- Question ❶ a): *What is the size of angle a? How can you work out the size of angle b?*
- Question ❶ b): *What patterns can you see in the results? Why might this be?*

**IN FOCUS** In question ❶, children are introduced to the concept of vertically opposite angles being equal, building on the known angle fact of angles on a straight line.

**PRACTICAL TIPS** A practical way to introduce vertically opposite angles is with a paper activity. Ask children to draw intersecting lines, label the angles and cut them out (or use tracing paper) to see that the angles are the same.

**ANSWERS**

Question ❶ a): Experiment 3: b = 40°, c = 140°, d = 40°

Question ❶ b): Children could take one of the diagrams and write down the pairs of angles that lie on a straight line and add up to 180°. This shows that two opposite angles must be equal. For example, if b + c = 180° and b + a = 180°, then a = c (vertically opposite angles).

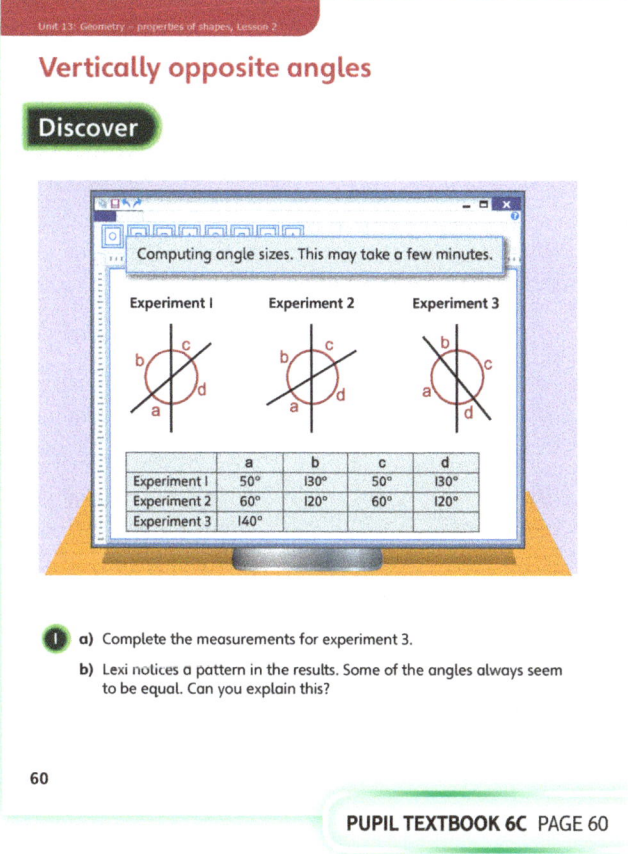

PUPIL TEXTBOOK 6C PAGE 60

## Share

**WAYS OF WORKING** Whole class teacher led

**ASK**

- Question ❶ a): *How can you work out the missing angles? Do you need to use a protractor? What angle fact could you use? What does the diagram show you?*
- Question ❶ b): *Which angles are equal? Why might this be? What do the bar models show you? What can you say about vertically opposite angles?*

**IN FOCUS** Question ❶ a) introduces children to vertically opposite angles by using the known fact of angles on a straight line. Encourage children to reason that angle b must equal 40° since angle a is 140° and angles a and b form a straight line. Show children the diagram to strengthen their understanding and repeat this process for the other angles.

Question ❶ b) requires children to find and explain patterns that occur within these results. It will be beneficial to refer children to the bar model that demonstrates how angle a must be equal to angle c, and angle b equal to angle d. Explore with children the straight lines that can be formed to show how these findings occur.

**STRENGTHEN** Watch out for children who think it is necessary to measure the angles with a protractor. Strengthen understanding by encouraging them to use the angle fact for angles on a straight line.

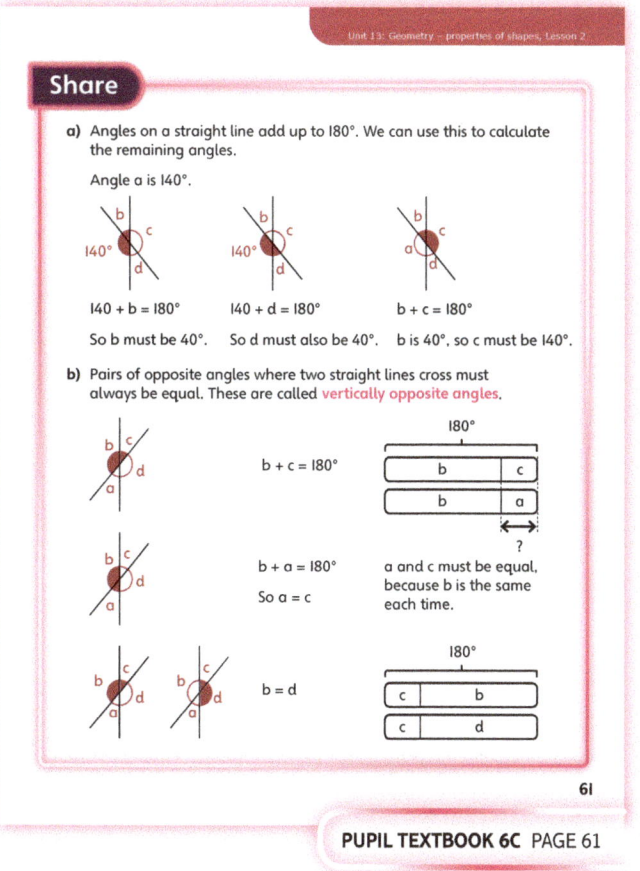

PUPIL TEXTBOOK 6C PAGE 61

# Unit 13: Geometry – properties of shapes, Lesson 2

## Think together

**WAYS OF WORKING** Whole class teacher led (I do, We do, You do)

**ASK**

- Question ❶: *Which angles make a straight line? Which angles are vertically opposite? Which angles can you calculate? Are you able to calculate them all?*
- Question ❷: *How can you draw pairs of straight lines that cross at different angles? What equipment will you need?*
- Question ❸: *Which angle rules do you need to use? Can you find the answers straight away? What other angles could you find first to help?*

**IN FOCUS** Question ❶ highlights a common misconception that all opposite angles are equal – watch out for children who assume that angle i in the last diagram is 62°.

Question ❷ reinforces vertically opposite angles being equal. Ensure children use a ruler to draw the lines. Encourage children to measure one of the angles with a protractor then predict the other angles using angle facts before checking they are correct using the protractor.

Question ❸ gives children an opportunity to explore angles and straight lines, while drawing on associated angle facts from previous lessons. Encourage children to discuss the order in which they found the angles.

**STRENGTHEN** Encourage children to identify which angles are vertically opposite. Ask: *Is this a pair of straight lines crossing? Can you check with a ruler? Which angles are vertically opposite?*

**DEEPEN** Question ❸ can be explored further by asking children to find other angles in the diagrams. Encourage children to explore the order in which the angles can be found, depending on which rule is used.

**ASSESSMENT CHECKPOINT** Questions ❶ and ❷ give an opportunity to assess children's understanding of the different methods for calculating angles in crossing lines. Children who need to measure the angles with a protractor each time are likely to need more support with this concept.

Question ❸ assesses children's ability to solve missing angle problems. Look for children who can draw on a range of angle facts, showing fluency in selecting the required operations to solve the problems. Children should also be able to describe the steps needed and the order in which they found the angles.

**ANSWERS**

Question ❶ a): a = 80°, b = 100°, c = 80°

Question ❶ b): d = 137°, e = 43°, f = 137°

Question ❶ c): g = unknown, h = 118°, i = unknown

Question ❷: Check that children have drawn a pair of crossing straight lines.

Question ❸ a): a = 25°, b = 80°, c = 75°, d = 80°

Question ❸ b): a = 38°, b = 142°, c = 52°

Question ❸ c): p = 38°, q = 72°, r = 70°

Question ❸ d): x = 108°

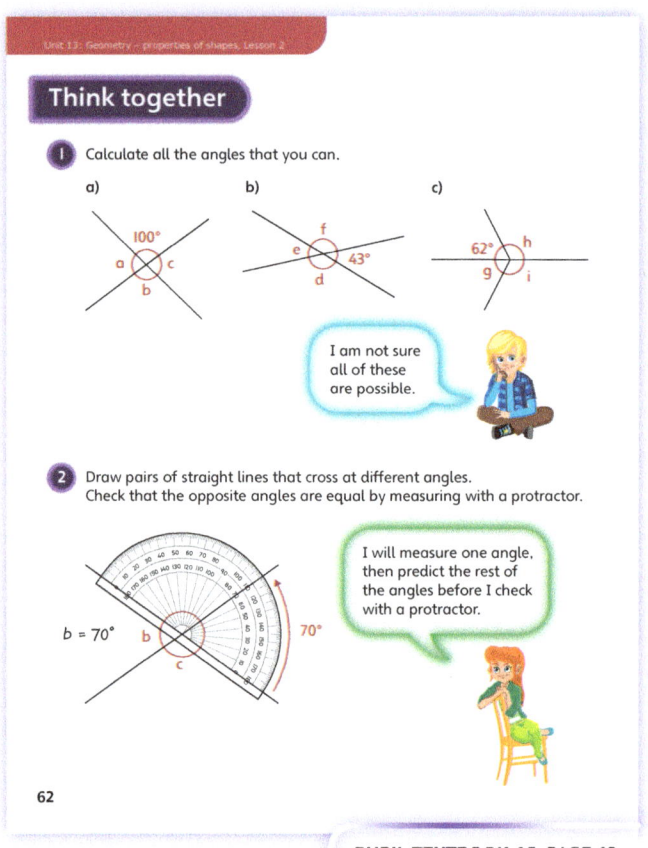

PUPIL TEXTBOOK 6C PAGE 62

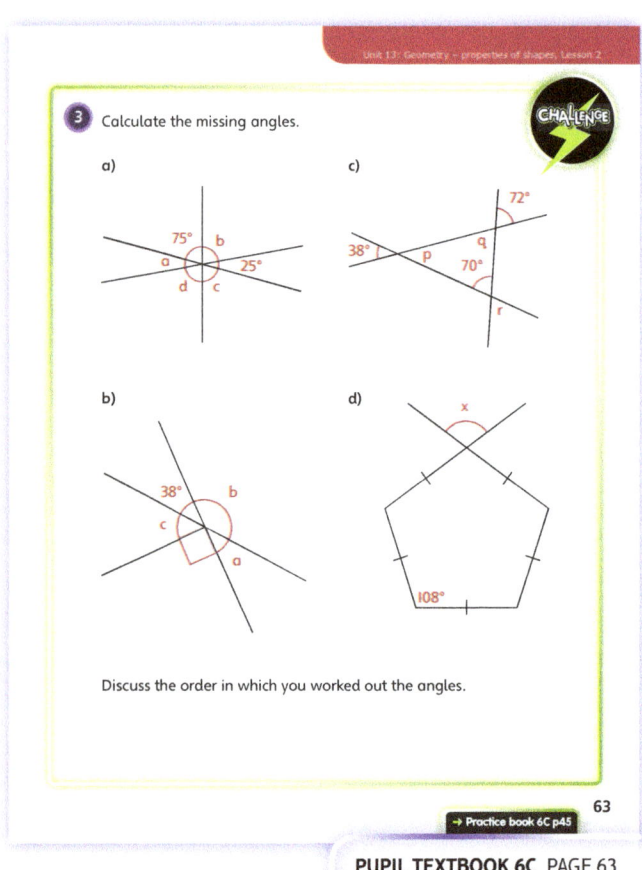

PUPIL TEXTBOOK 6C PAGE 63

# Unit 13: Geometry – properties of shapes, Lesson 2

## Practice

**WAYS OF WORKING** Independent thinking

**IN FOCUS** Questions ❶ and ❸ aim to consolidate children's understanding of vertically opposite angles and angles on a straight line.

Question ❷ addresses a common misconception where children think that any opposite angles are equal. Ensure they understand that vertically opposite angles are only formed by a pair of crossing straight lines.

Question ❻ asks children to calculate missing angles. Encourage them to discuss the order in which they found the angles and the angle facts used.

**STRENGTHEN** Strengthen learning by encouraging children to use bar models. It may also be useful to colour vertically opposite angles with a highlighter pen, especially in question ❺.

**DEEPEN** Extend question ❻ by asking children to draw similar problems with vertically opposite angles for a partner to find the unknown angles.

**ASSESSMENT CHECKPOINT** Questions ❶ to ❹ assess children's ability to calculate vertically opposite angles. Look for children confidently using this new angle rule, along with angles on a straight line.

In question ❺, look for children who can use angle facts to find the total of the given angles, showing fluency in identifying the required operations.

Question ❻ assesses children's ability to solve more complex missing angle problems. Children should be able to use associated angle facts, showing fluency in addition, subtraction and division.

**ANSWERS** Answers for the **Practice** part of the lesson can be found in the *Power Maths* online subscription.

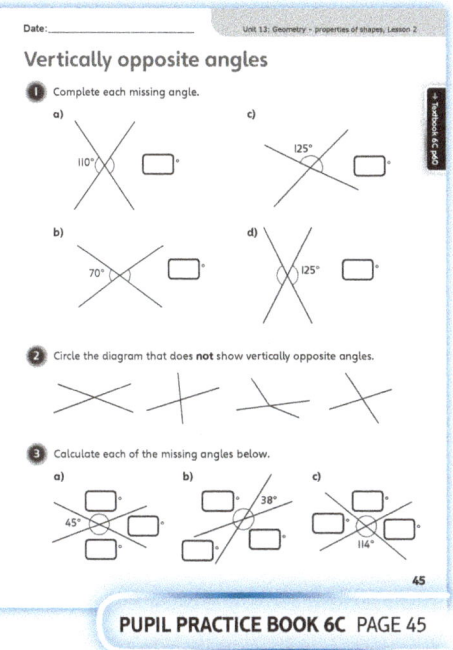
PUPIL PRACTICE BOOK 6C PAGE 45

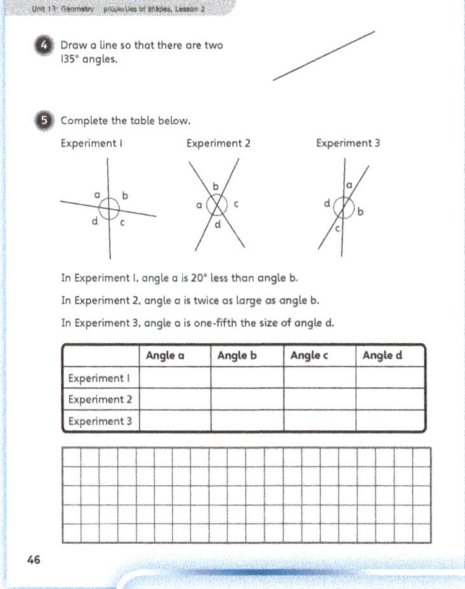
PUPIL PRACTICE BOOK 6C PAGE 46

## Reflect

**WAYS OF WORKING** Pair work

**IN FOCUS** This reflection question involves children explaining the steps that show vertically opposite angles are equal. Encourage children to use angle facts to justify their reasoning.

**ASSESSMENT CHECKPOINT** This reflection assesses children's understanding of vertically opposite angles. Look for children confidently explaining in their own words why they must be equal.

**ANSWERS** Answers for the **Reflect** part of the lesson can be found in the *Power Maths* online subscription.

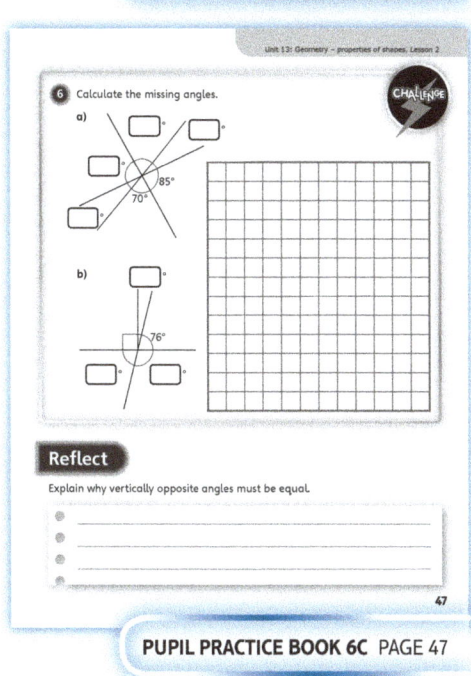
PUPIL PRACTICE BOOK 6C PAGE 47

### After the lesson ⏸

- Can children calculate missing angles on straight lines?
- Can children explain what makes vertically opposite angles and why they are equal?
- Can children calculate missing angles in shapes, drawing on a range of angle facts?

Unit 13: Geometry – properties of shapes, Lesson 3

# Angles in a triangle

### Learning focus
In this lesson, children will apply their knowledge of accurately drawing shapes and measuring angles to understand that angles in a triangle total 180°.

### Before you teach
- Can children accurately draw and measure shapes using a ruler and protractor?
- Do children know simple properties and the different types of triangle?
- Do children know angles on a straight line add to 180°?

#### NATIONAL CURRICULUM LINKS

**Year 6 Geometry – properties of shapes**

Compare and classify geometric shapes based on their properties and sizes and find unknown angles in any triangles, quadrilaterals and regular polygons.

Draw 2D shapes using given dimensions and angles.

#### ASSESSING MASTERY

Children can understand that the interior angles of a triangle total 180°, showing fluency in measuring angles, accurately drawing shapes and demonstrating an understanding of the sum of the angles on a straight line.

#### COMMON MISCONCEPTIONS

Children may incorrectly measure the interior angles of a triangle because they do not know how to use a protractor correctly. Develop competency by asking:
- *Which line are you going to use as the baseline? Where do you need to put the crosshairs? Which scale will you use?*

Another common misconception occurs when rearranging the interior angles of a triangle to form a straight line. This is important since it aids children's understanding of the sum of the angles in a triangle. Ensure children split the triangle into three sections (i.e. none are left behind) and then put the angles together, so all the straight lines meet together and the cut or torn edges are at the top and sides. Ask:
- *How can you position the angles to form a straight line?*

#### STRENGTHENING UNDERSTANDING

Start by asking children to add the interior angles of a range of triangles, to help them discover the total of 180°. Then move on to children measuring the angles and finally constructing the triangles themselves.

#### GOING DEEPER

Encourage children to draw their own triangles that are not to scale and label the interior angles, emphasising that they must total 180°. Give children triangles that are not accurately drawn and that have one unknown angle and ask them to use their new learning about the interior angles in a triangle to work out the missing angle.

#### KEY LANGUAGE

**In lesson:** angle, obtuse, acute, right angle

**Other language to be used by the teacher:** extend, accurate, sum, scale, rotate, degrees, protractor, baseline, crosshairs

#### STRUCTURES AND REPRESENTATIONS

Angles represented in triangles, angles on a straight line

#### RESOURCES

**Mandatory:** protractor, ruler

**Optional:** coloured paper to make into triangles to tear up

 In the eTextbook of this lesson, you will find interactive links to a selection of teaching tools.

### Quick recap
Ask children to sketch an example of a triangle. Then challenge them to estimate the size of each angle in their triangle.

# Unit 13: Geometry – properties of shapes, Lesson 3

## Discover

**WAYS OF WORKING** Pair work

**ASK**

- Question 1 a): *How can you accurately draw a triangle like this? What equipment do you need?*
- Question 1 b): *How can you check Ambika's solution?*

**IN FOCUS** Question 1 a) encourages children to use their knowledge of obtuse angles and the properties of triangles to discover that the challenge is impossible.
Question 1 b) develops this, requiring children to assess Ambika's solution using their knowledge of types of angle. This is a good opportunity to assess children's confidence with identifying angle types within a triangle. They should be able to see, without measuring, that the two smaller angles in the triangle are acute, so Ambika's measurements cannot be correct.

**PRACTICAL TIPS** The concept of angles in a triangle is introduced via an 'impossible' triangle. Explain to children that they will be attempting the challenge and encourage them to use their knowledge of angle types.

**ANSWERS**

Question 1 a): A triangle cannot have two obtuse angles because two sides of the triangle will never meet.

Question 1 b): Ambika's solution is incorrect. The right angle is correct, but the other angles are acute, so cannot be 130° and 140°. Ambika has **not** solved the challenge.

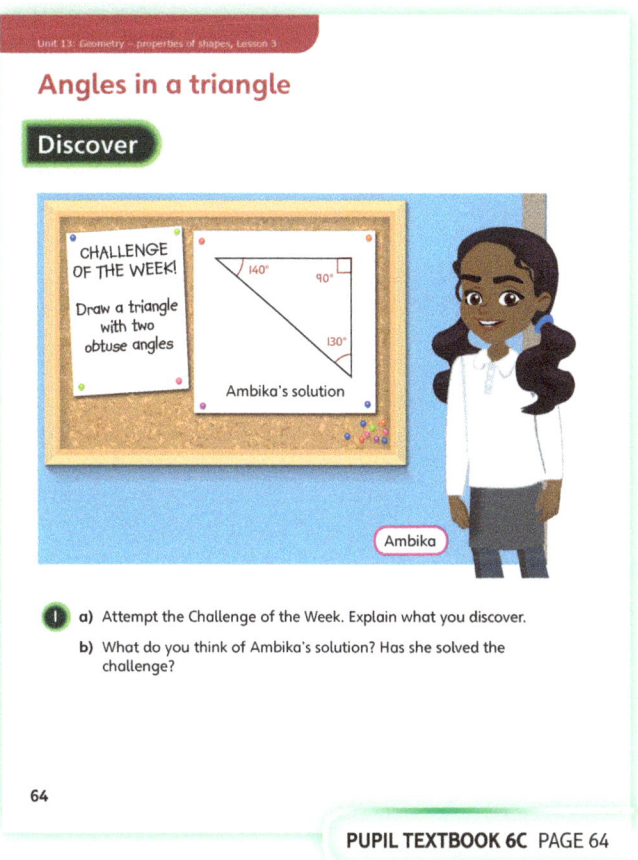

PUPIL TEXTBOOK 6C PAGE 64

## Share

**WAYS OF WORKING** Whole class teacher led

**ASK**

- Question 1 a): *How many sides does a triangle have? How many angles? Where can you start when drawing the triangle? What does it need to look like? What is an obtuse angle? Can you draw an obtuse angle? Can you draw another obtuse angle? Can you make a triangle? Could you complete this in a different way?*
- Question 1 b): *How can you check Ambika's solution? What could you use?*

**IN FOCUS** Question 1 a) requires children to attempt the challenge. Discuss the properties of a triangle, ensuring children know how a triangle might look. Encourage children to start by drawing a horizontal baseline, ensuring they leave enough room above. Check they understand the definition of an obtuse angle. Encourage children to draw an obtuse angle at each end of the line, then ask them to explain why it is impossible to create a triangle from these lines, reinforcing the properties of a triangle. Children could attempt the challenge again using different obtuse angles to confirm that it is impossible.

Question 1 b) requires children to assess Ambika's solution. This is important as it creates an opportunity to further explore types of angle in a triangle. Encourage children to use a protractor to check the 90° angle.

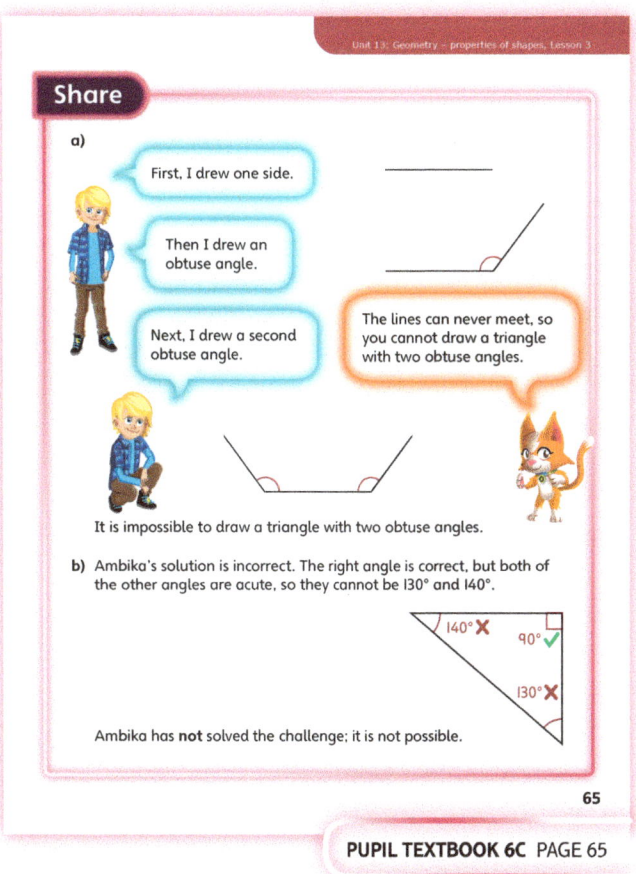

PUPIL TEXTBOOK 6C PAGE 65

101

Unit 13: Geometry – properties of shapes, Lesson 3

# Think together

**WAYS OF WORKING** Whole class teacher led (I do, We do, You do)

**ASK**
- Question ①: *How can you check the angle measurements? Which line will you use as the baseline?*
- Question ②: *Where will you begin? Which sides can you draw? Which angles can you draw? Can you extend the lines until they meet? What is the size of the missing angle? How can you check your drawing is accurate?*
- Question ③: *What different triangles can you draw? How can you put the angles together? Do they always form a straight line? What do you know about angles on a straight line? What can you say about angles in a triangle?*

**IN FOCUS** Question ① requires children to measure the interior angles in a triangle. Watch out for children who find the orientation of the triangles and angles challenging.

Question ② asks children to independently draw an accurate triangle in order to measure the unknown angle. Only one length is given so children will need to measure the angles and then extend the lines until they cross.

Question ③ gives children an opportunity to discover the sum of the interior angles of a triangle. Children are encouraged to use a range of triangles to investigate this, using their knowledge of angles on a straight line.

**STRENGTHEN** Encourage children to choose a line as a baseline and rotate the paper so this line is horizontal, ensuring they line up the crosshairs.

**DEEPEN** Question ① can be deepened by asking children to identify the types of triangle based on the correct angles.

Extend question ③ by encouraging children to look back at the previous questions and check if they follow their theories about angles in a triangle. Give children a triangle with one unknown angle and ask them to work out what it is by calculation, before measuring to check their answers.

**ASSESSMENT CHECKPOINT** Questions ① and ② will assess children's ability to measure angles within a triangle. Look for children confidently using a protractor to measure angles accurately using the correct scale.

In question ③, look for children who can draw different types of triangle and deduce that angles in a triangle add to 180°.

**ANSWERS**

Question ① a): The angles have all been measured correctly.

Question ① b): The angle labelled as 60° actually measures 40°.

Question ① c): The angle labelled as 60° actually measures 40°.

Question ②: Children should accurately draw the triangle and measure the angle as 90°.

Question ③ a): The three angles always form a straight line, no matter the order in which they are arranged.

Question ③ b): Children should conclude that the angles in a triangle always add up to 180°.

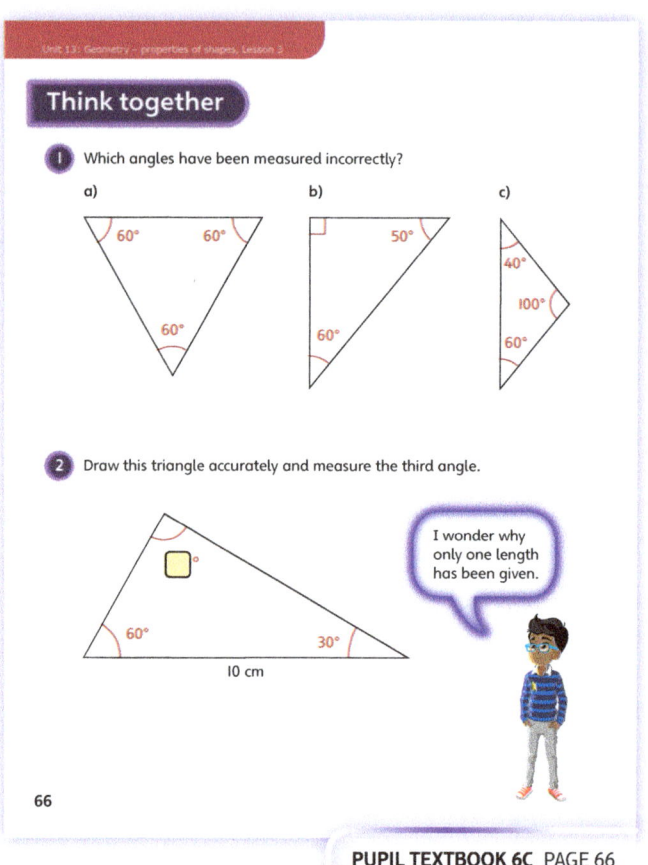

PUPIL TEXTBOOK 6C PAGE 66

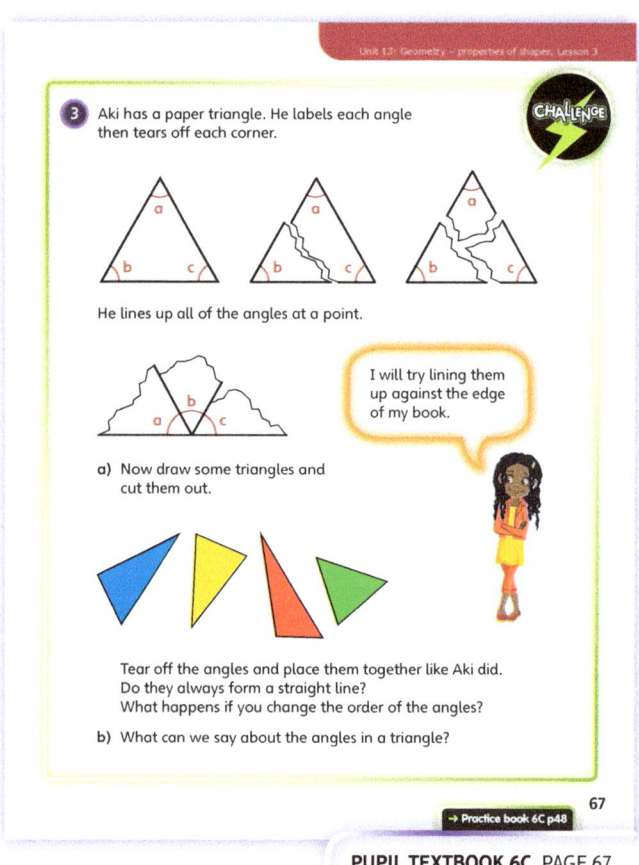

PUPIL TEXTBOOK 6C PAGE 67

# Unit 13: Geometry – properties of shapes, Lesson 3

## Practice

**WAYS OF WORKING** Independent thinking

**IN FOCUS** Question ❶ a) aims to consolidate children's understanding of measuring angles in a triangle. Encourage children to also consider the total of the interior angles. Question ❶ b) develops this, requiring children to accurately draw a triangle before measuring an unknown angle.

Question ❷ reinforces children's understanding of angles in a triangle forming a straight line and therefore summing to 180°.

Question ❸ requires children to analyse generalised statements about angles in triangles. Encourage them to experiment by drawing triangles to support the options they choose.

Question ❹ develops abstract thinking. Encourage children to use a ruler to join the dots, so that the lines are straight. Children then need to measure and label the angles in their triangles and add them using a suitable method.

**STRENGTHEN** Encourage children to rotate the page so the baseline is horizontal when measuring the interior angles of the triangles.

**DEEPEN** Extend question ❸ by encouraging children to make other statements that are sometimes true, always true or never true, and ask them to prove them using examples.

**ASSESSMENT CHECKPOINT** In questions ❶ and ❷, look for children confidently drawing lines using a ruler, measuring angles using a protractor, using the correct scale and taking accurate measurements.

In question ❸, look for children who are confident in explaining the statements using examples to support their reasoning.

**ANSWERS** Answers for the **Practice** part of the lesson can be found in the *Power Maths* online subscription.

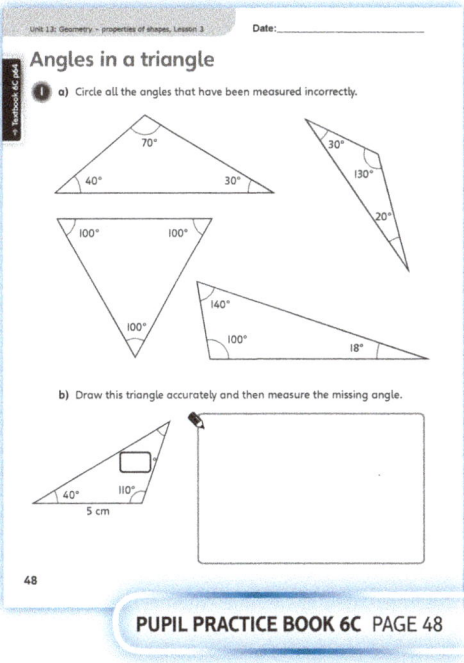

PUPIL PRACTICE BOOK 6C PAGE 48

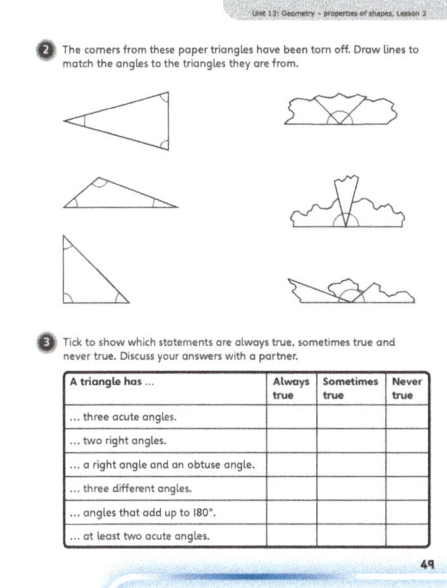

PUPIL PRACTICE BOOK 6C PAGE 49

## Reflect

**WAYS OF WORKING** Pair work

**IN FOCUS** This question checks children's understanding of angles in a triangle summing to 180°. Encourage children to explain how they know the total of the interior angles in a triangle.

**ASSESSMENT CHECKPOINT** Children should be able to explain that the angles sum to 180°, using their understanding of angles on a straight line.

**ANSWERS** Answers for the **Reflect** part of the lesson can be found in the *Power Maths* online subscription.

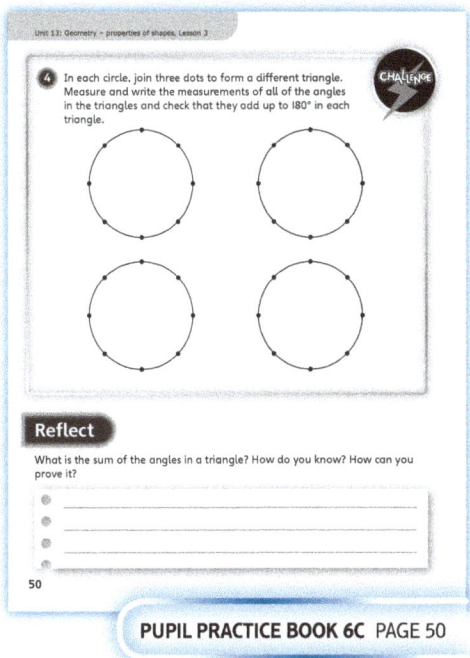

PUPIL PRACTICE BOOK 6C PAGE 50

## After the lesson

- Can children measure the interior angles of triangles?
- Can children accurately draw shapes and measure missing angles?
- Can children take the three interior angles of a triangle and form a straight line, linking this to their understanding that the angles in a triangle sum to 180°?

Unit 13: Geometry – properties of shapes, Lesson 4

# Angles in a triangle – missing angles

### Learning focus
In this lesson, children will extend their understanding of angles in a triangle and will apply their knowledge to calculate missing angles without using a protractor.

### Before you teach
- Can children measure angles using a protractor?
- Can children use a bar model?
- Do children know the angle rules for angles on a straight line and angles around a point?

#### NATIONAL CURRICULUM LINKS

**Year 6 Geometry – properties of shapes**

Compare and classify geometric shapes based on their properties and sizes and find unknown angles in any triangles, quadrilaterals and regular polygons.

#### ASSESSING MASTERY

Children can confidently calculate missing angles in a triangle without using a protractor, showing fluency in addition and subtraction and demonstrating an understanding of angle facts (such as angles around a point and angles on a straight line).

#### COMMON MISCONCEPTIONS

Children may try to use a protractor to measure all the angles, rather than calculating the angles using angle rules. Ensure children understand that not all diagrams are drawn to scale and that it would be time consuming to redraw all diagrams accurately, so it is more efficient to use the rule for angles in a triangle. Ask:
- *Can you check the angles given to see if the diagram is to scale? What do the three angles in a triangle always add up to?*

Children may not know which operation to use to calculate the missing angle. Showing the angles on a bar model will help children to understand which operations are needed. Ask:
- *What does this bar model show? How can you work out what is missing?*

#### STRENGTHENING UNDERSTANDING

To strengthen understanding, encourage children to use bar models for pictorial support. Children who need help with addition and subtraction could be encouraged to use a written method, such as the column method.

#### GOING DEEPER

Deepen learning by asking children to write down three angles that could be the three interior angles of a triangle, then ask them to draw the triangle. Encourage children to use other angle facts, such as angles on a straight line, by giving them missing angle problems that incorporate these facts.

#### KEY LANGUAGE

**In lesson:** angle, scale

**Other language to be used by the teacher:** degrees, protractor, right angle, efficient method, crosshairs, baseline

#### STRUCTURES AND REPRESENTATIONS

Triangles, bar model, angles on a straight line, angles around a point

#### RESOURCES

**Mandatory:** protractor, ruler

**Optional:** adhesive tape, dry-wipe pens, mini whiteboards

 In the eTextbook of this lesson, you will find interactive links to a selection of teaching tools.

### Quick recap

Ask children to sketch a triangle and then challenge them to estimate the size of each angle. Then ask them to find the total of their estimates. Discuss their findings as a class.

Unit 13: Geometry – properties of shapes, Lesson 4

# Discover

**WAYS OF WORKING** Pair work

**ASK**

- Question 1 a): *How can you work out the size of the angles? Do you need to measure both of them?*
- Question 1 b): *How is this triangle different to the triangle in question 1 a? Once you have measured the sizes of angles x and y, how can you find angle z without measuring?*

**IN FOCUS** Both parts of this question focus on the interior angles of a triangle. Children will use a protractor, but will also develop their understanding of using the sum of the interior angles of a triangle.

**PRACTICAL TIPS** Recap learning from the previous lesson with a practical activity creating triangles using adhesive tape and dry-wipe pens on mini whiteboards or desks. Encourage children to use known angle facts to work out the missing angles in the triangles.

**ANSWERS**

Question 1 a): b = 70° and c = 60°.

Question 1 b): x = 15° and y = 85°. Angles in a triangle add up to 180°, so z = 180° – 15° – 85° = 80°.

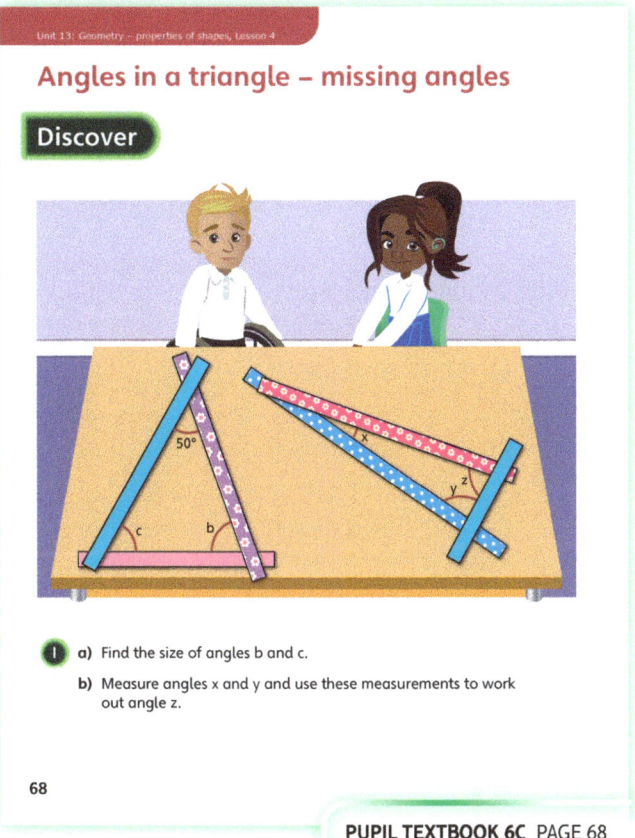

PUPIL TEXTBOOK 6C PAGE 68

# Share

**WAYS OF WORKING** Whole class teacher led

**ASK**

- Question 1 a): *How can you find the size of angle c? What do the angles in a triangle add up to? If you know two of the angles how can you work out the third angle? What do the diagrams show you? Do both methods give the same answer? How can you check your answers?*
- Question 1 b): *How many angles do you need to measure? What is the size of angle x? What is the size of angle y? How can you now work out the size of angle z?*

**IN FOCUS** Question 1 a) encourages children to use a protractor to measure one unknown angle, then use the angles in a triangle rule to calculate the third. Ensure children realise that they only need to measure one of the angles. Discuss the two possible methods for finding the other angle, using the bar model for pictorial support. Encourage children to check the answers by adding together 50°, 60° and 70°; they should recognise that the total should be 180°.

In question 1 b), none of the interior angles are labelled. Emphasise that it is only necessary to measure two angles, as the third can be calculated. Encourage discussion of the different methods for calculating the size of the third angle (i.e. adding then subtracting or just subtracting).

**STRENGTHEN** Encourage children to use a bar model for pictorial support.

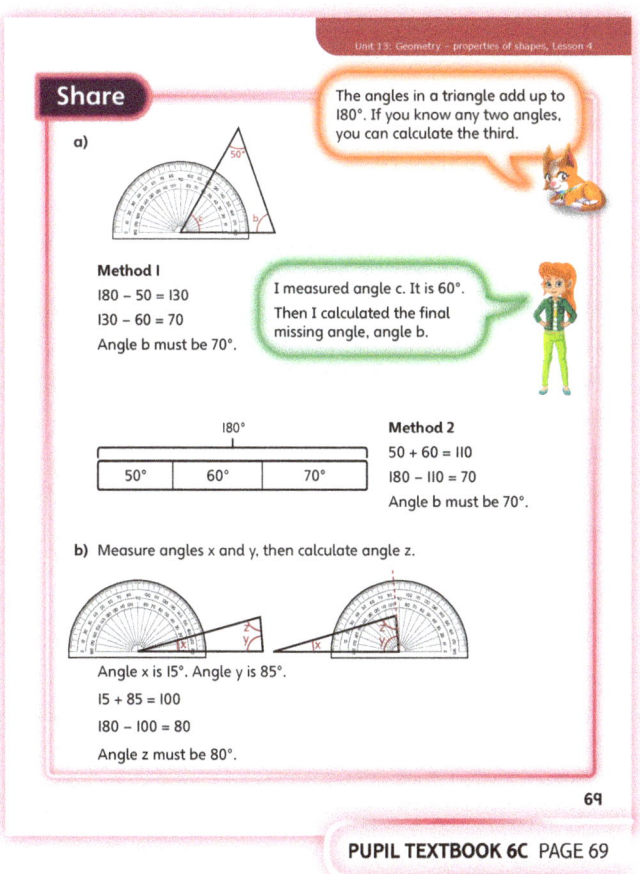

PUPIL TEXTBOOK 6C PAGE 69

# Unit 13: Geometry – properties of shapes, Lesson 4

## Think together

**WAYS OF WORKING** Whole class teacher led (I do, We do, You do)

**ASK**

- Question ❶: *How can you work out the missing angles? Do you need to use a protractor? Could you use a more efficient method? How can you check your answers?*
- Question ❷: *What do you know about the sum of angles a, b and c? Can you draw a bar model to help?*
- Question ❸: *How can you calculate the missing angles? What other angle rules do you know that could help?*

**IN FOCUS** Question ❶ reinforces calculating a missing angle in a triangle when given two of the angles. Encourage children to use their knowledge of the sum of the interior angles of a triangle. Watch out for children who try to measure the angles with a protractor – encourage them to use a more efficient method. With the third triangle, ensure children recognise the right angle as 90°. Encourage them to check their answers using inverse operations (i.e. by adding the three angles together).

Question ❷ is more complex and children are encouraged to use trial and error or a bar model to set up the problem.

Question ❸ gives children an opportunity to explore angles in a triangle using other known angle facts. It requires multiple steps for a solution. It will be beneficial to discuss the order in which the missing angles can be found. It may be necessary to reinforce the angle rules that are needed to calculate the missing angles.

**STRENGTHEN** Strengthen learning by encouraging children to draw a bar model to show the angles given, the missing angles and the total. This should help them to identify the operations needed to calculate the missing angles.

**DEEPEN** Question ❷ can be explored further by giving children similar problems where all the angles are missing.

Question ❸ can be deepened by asking children to explore the different methods for calculating angle c.

**ASSESSMENT CHECKPOINT** In question ❶, look for children who understand how to use the rule for angles in a triangle to find an unknown angle. Children who try to measure the angles using a protractor are likely to need more support with this concept.

In question ❸, look for children who can confidently work through the problems in a logical order using known angle facts, demonstrating fluency in addition and subtraction.

**ANSWERS**

Question ❶ a): a + 30° + 70° = 180°, so a = 80°.

Question ❶ b): b + 55° + 110° = 180°, so b = 15°.

Question ❶ c): c + 38° + 90° = 180°, so c = 52°.

Question ❷: a = 60°, b = 30°, c = 90°

Question ❸ a): a = 110°, b = 305°, c = 50°

Question ❸ b): Children should create an angle puzzle that requires finding a missing angle in a diagram using known angle facts.

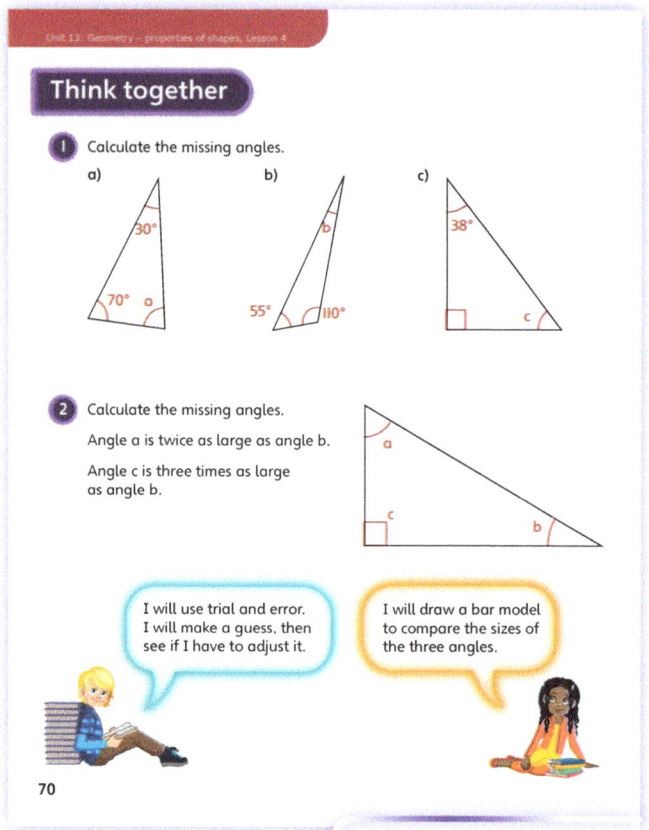

PUPIL TEXTBOOK 6C PAGE 70

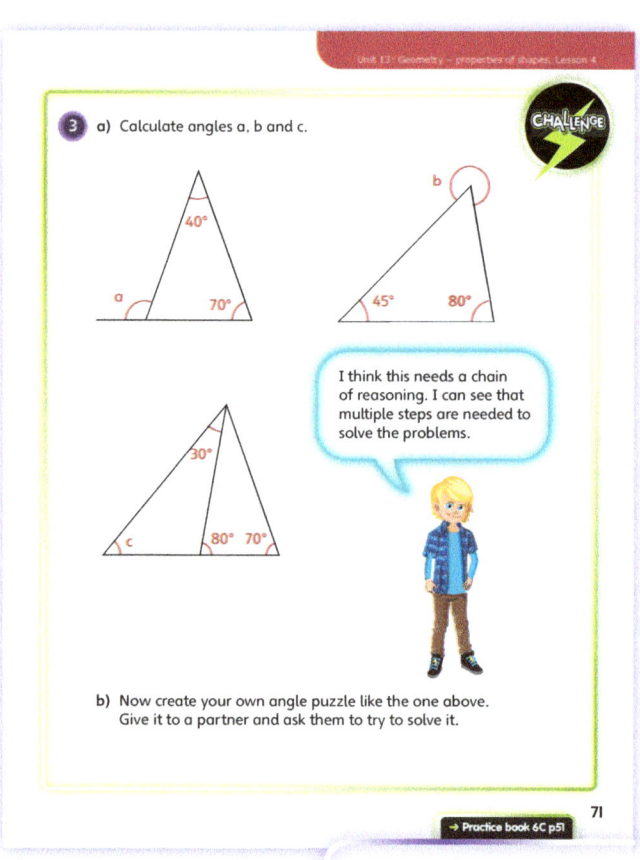

PUPIL TEXTBOOK 6C PAGE 71

Unit 13: Geometry – properties of shapes, Lesson 4

# Practice

**WAYS OF WORKING** Independent thinking

**IN FOCUS** Questions ❶ and ❷ aim to consolidate children's understanding of calculating a missing angle in a triangle. Watch out for children who find it challenging to measure the angles in question ❷ due to the orientation of the triangle – encourage them to rotate the paper, if necessary. Ensure children calculate the third angle rather than measuring it by encouraging them to show their working.

Question ❸ requires children to match three angles that could form the interior angles of a triangle. Encourage them to explore different possibilities.

In question ❹, children need to use other angle facts to calculate the missing angles. Reinforce angle rules and the interior angles of a triangle and encourage children to work through the questions in a logical order, showing their reasoning for each angle they calculate.

**STRENGTHEN** Strengthen learning by encouraging children to work out the missing angles in multiple steps (i.e. add the two known angles together, then subtract from 180°). Encourage children to draw bar models as this will help them to identify the required calculations.

**DEEPEN** Extend question ❺ by asking children to create their own missing angle problems using other known angle facts.

**ASSESSMENT CHECKPOINT** In questions ❶ and ❷, look for children confidently using the angles in a triangle rule to find the unknown angle.

In question ❺, look for children who can explain their working using known angle facts, showing fluency in addition and subtraction.

**ANSWERS** Answers for the **Practice** part of the lesson can be found in the *Power Maths* online subscription.

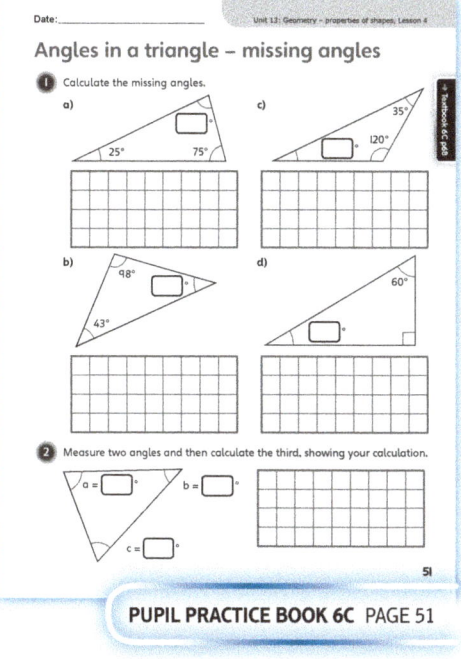

PUPIL PRACTICE BOOK 6C PAGE 51

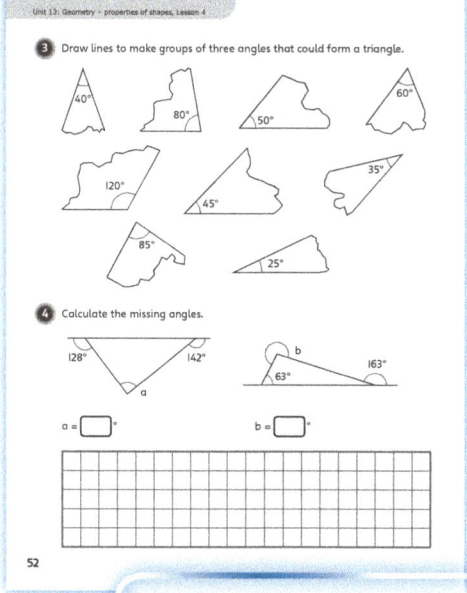

PUPIL PRACTICE BOOK 6C PAGE 52

# Reflect

**WAYS OF WORKING** Pair work

**IN FOCUS** This reflection question involves children drawing two different triangles that contain an interior angle of 50°, while explaining how they chose them. Encourage children to label all angles, and explain that clearly labelled diagrams do not need to be to scale.

**ASSESSMENT CHECKPOINT** Look for children confidently explaining that the other two angles need to total 130°, reliably using subtraction and confidently drawing triangles to represent their solutions.

**ANSWERS** Answers for the **Reflect** part of the lesson can be found in the *Power Maths* online subscription.

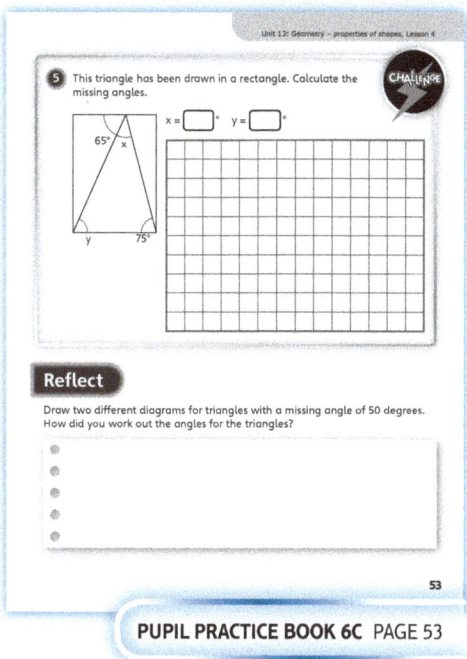

PUPIL PRACTICE BOOK 6C PAGE 53

# After the lesson

- Can children calculate the missing angle of a triangle when given two angles, without measuring?
- Do children understand that angles in a triangle add to 180°?
- Can children use known angle facts to solve missing angle problems?

Unit 13: Geometry – properties of shapes, Lesson 5

# Angles in a triangle – special cases

## Learning focus

In this lesson, children will understand how to calculate missing angles in an isosceles triangle given one of the other angles. Children will also solve problems that incorporate this.

## Before you teach

- Do children know the properties of isosceles triangles?
- Can children divide by a single digit, including finding half of a number?
- Do children know the angle rules for angles on a straight line and angles around a point?

### NATIONAL CURRICULUM LINKS

**Year 6 Geometry – properties of shapes**

Compare and classify geometric shapes based on their properties and sizes and find unknown angles in any triangles, quadrilaterals and regular polygons.

### ASSESSING MASTERY

Children can fluently find missing angles in isosceles and equilateral triangles using the sum of the interior angles of a triangle by adding, subtracting and dividing, showing understanding of other associated angle facts.

### COMMON MISCONCEPTIONS

Children may assume that the one given angle in an isosceles triangle is always the independent angle, particularly if it is at the top of the triangle. Before carrying out any calculations, ask:
- *Can you identify the lines that are the same length and the angles that are equal?*

Children may add or subtract the numbers without dividing, or vice versa. Use a bar model to address this misconception, to secure understanding and to encourage children to break down the method into steps. Ask:
- *What is shown in the bar model? What steps need to be taken?*

### STRENGTHENING UNDERSTANDING

Children who find it a challenge to calculate missing angles in isosceles triangles and equilateral triangles should be encouraged to revisit finding angles in scalene triangles by adding and subtracting. When solving missing angles problems, encourage children to use a bar model so they can visualise why they add or subtract and divide to find the unknown angles.

### GOING DEEPER

Encourage children to reason with angles in an isosceles triangle, for example by asking: *Is it possible to draw two different isosceles triangles that contain an angle of 40°? Can you draw two different isosceles triangles that contain an angle of 100°?*

### KEY LANGUAGE

**In lesson:** **isosceles**, equal, length, angle, degrees

**Other language to be used by the teacher:** equilateral

### STRUCTURES AND REPRESENTATIONS

Triangles, bar model

### RESOURCES

**Mandatory:** ruler, protractor, plain paper

**Optional:** straws or lollipop sticks (to make isosceles triangles)

 In the eTextbook of this lesson, you will find interactive links to a selection of teaching tools.

## Quick recap

Tell children that one angle of a triangle is 160°. Ask: *What could the other two angles be? How many different solutions can you find?*

# Unit 13: Geometry – properties of shapes, Lesson 5

## Discover

**WAYS OF WORKING** Pair work

**ASK**

- Question 1 a): *What types of triangle have been formed? How can you work out the missing angles?*
- Question 1 b): *Can you draw a diagram to help? Which angle could be 80°?*

**IN FOCUS** Question 1 a) introduces the concept of finding angles in isosceles triangles when given one of the angles.

Question 1 b) develops the concept of finding missing angles in an isosceles triangle and looks at the different angles that can be found.

**PRACTICAL TIPS** The context of making triangular frames could be introduced in a practical way, perhaps in an art lesson using straws or lollipop sticks of equal length, encouraging children to think about the angles formed in the triangles.

**ANSWERS**

Question 1 a): The two lengths are equal, so they form isosceles triangles. Angles a and b both equal 75°. Angles c and d both equal 40°.

Question 1 b): There are two possible solutions:
The 80° angle could be the angle between the equal sides. The other two angles would be 50°.
The 80° angle could be one of the equal angles. The other angle would be 20°.

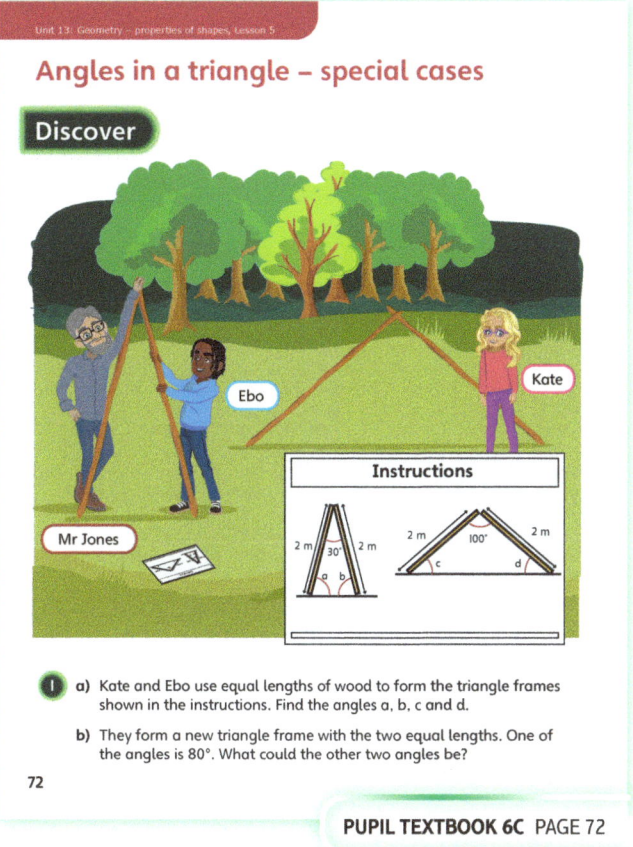

PUPIL TEXTBOOK 6C PAGE 72

## Share

**WAYS OF WORKING** Whole class teacher led

**ASK**

- Question 1 a): *Why are the triangles isosceles? What do you know about angles in an isosceles triangle? How can you calculate the missing angles using the bar models?*
- Question 1 b): *Why are there two solutions?*

**IN FOCUS** Question 1 a) requires children to use knowledge of isosceles triangles to calculate the missing angles. Discuss the marks used to indicate a triangle is isosceles and explain that two of the angles will be equal. Encourage children to use the bar models to reason that to find the missing angles they need to subtract the known angle from 180 and divide by 2. Ensure children understand that dividing by 2, and finding half of a number give the same answer.

In question 1 b), explore the possibilities that 80° could be the angle between the two equal sides, or could be one of the two equal angles. Some children may need help with this, so use bar models to represent both possibilities.

**STRENGTHEN** Strengthen learning by encouraging children to revisit finding angles in scalene triangles by adding and subtracting, given that angles in any triangle add to 180°. Return to isosceles triangles and use bar models to visualise why we add, or subtract and divide, to find unknown angles.

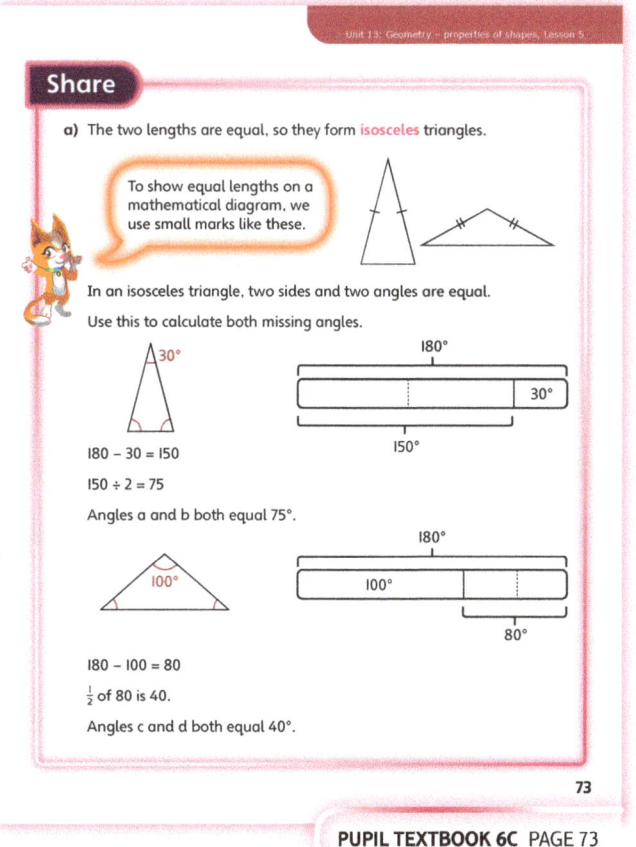

PUPIL TEXTBOOK 6C PAGE 73

109

Unit 13: Geometry – properties of shapes, Lesson 5

# Think together

**WAYS OF WORKING** Whole class teacher led (I do, We do, You do)

**ASK**

- Question ①: *Which angles are the same? How do you know? How can you calculate the missing angles? Could you draw a bar model to help?*
- Question ②: *How can you draw an isosceles triangle? How can you measure one of the angles? Does it matter which one? How can you calculate the other angles?*
- Question ③: *What other angle facts could help solve this?*

**IN FOCUS** Question ① requires children to calculate the missing angles when given one angle in an isosceles triangle. Watch out for children who assume 70° is the independent angle in part c) since it is at the top of the triangle; this can be a common misconception.

In question ②, children are required to independently draw a triangle and calculate angles. Look out for children who think they have to measure the angle between the two equal lengths. Encourage children to compare their answers with others.

Question ③ incorporates other angle facts. In the second problem, watch out for children who assume that the angles are the same because the lengths are the same. In the third problem, use a bar model to help children understand why they need to divide 180° by 3. Encourage children to complete each question in steps and show their reasoning.

**STRENGTHEN** To support understanding, encourage children to represent the calculations on a bar model. When solving question ③, encourage children to decipher the diagrams and consider other angle facts.

**DEEPEN** Question ③ can be explored further by giving children other problems that incorporate other angle facts.

**ASSESSMENT CHECKPOINT** Questions ① and ② assess children's ability to calculate missing angles in isosceles triangles. Look for children clearly explaining the steps needed and confidently using addition, subtraction and division to find the answers.

Question ③ assesses children's ability to find missing angles in a problem-solving context with no support or structure. If children can fluently use associated angle facts and then complete the calculations, while clearly explaining the steps, they are likely to have mastered this topic.

**ANSWERS**

Question ① a): The other two angles are 76°.

Question ① b): The other two angles are 34°.

Question ① c): The other two angles are 40°.

Question ②: There are many possible answers; the triangle must have two sides of length 75 mm and the three angles must add up to 180°.

Question ③: a = 75°   c = 72°   e = 130°
            b = 75°   d = 54°   f = 30°

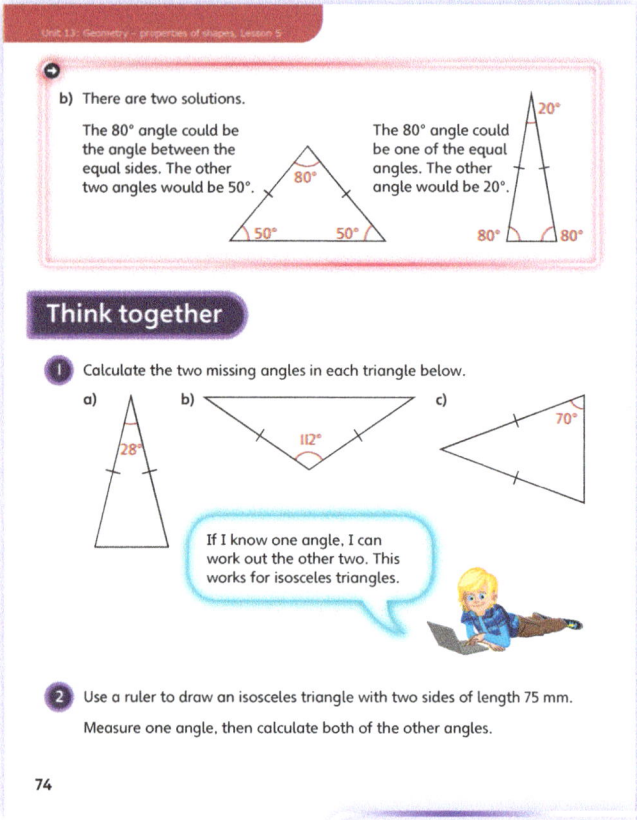

PUPIL TEXTBOOK 6C PAGE 74

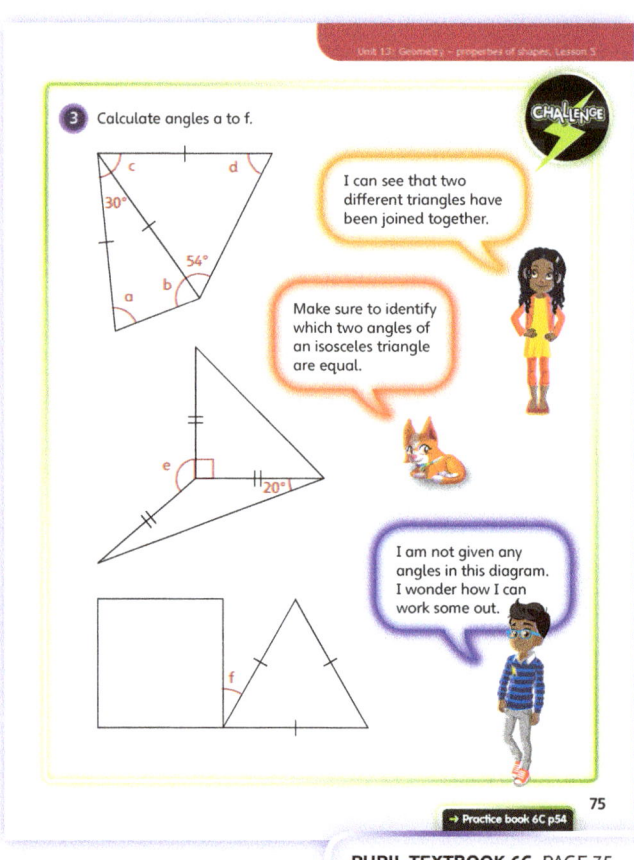

PUPIL TEXTBOOK 6C PAGE 75

110

# Unit 13: Geometry – properties of shapes, Lesson 5

## Practice

**WAYS OF WORKING** Independent thinking

**IN FOCUS** Question ❶ aims to consolidate children's understanding of the notation for equal lengths in isosceles triangles.

In question ❷, children practise calculating two unknown angles. Encourage them to write down their calculations and explain their steps.

Question ❸ develops children's understanding of identifying an isosceles triangle. Encourage them to use a ruler to measure the lengths, if necessary.

Question ❺ requires children to problem solve and use a range of angle facts to calculate the unknown angles.

**STRENGTHEN** To strengthen understanding, encourage children to represent the numbers on a bar model to help them identify the correct calculations.

**DEEPEN** Question ❹ can be explored further by asking: *What other triangles can you find where one angle is given and can only be drawn in one way? What is the smallest or biggest angle this could be?*

**THINK DIFFERENTLY** Question ❹ develops children's reasoning skills and encourages them to explore the different angles within an isosceles triangle. For Amelia's triangle, they should be able to reason that if 56° is one of the two equal angles, then the other two angles are 56° and 180° – 56° – 56° = 68°. If, instead, 56° is the single angle, then the other two angles are (180° – 56°) ÷ 2 = 62°. For Bella's triangle, 156° cannot be one of the equal angles because 156° + 156° = 312°, which is more than 180°. Encourage children to draw accurate diagrams to support their reasoning.

**ASSESSMENT CHECKPOINT** Questions ❶ and ❸ assess children's ability to identify isosceles triangles and mark equivalent lengths and angles, using the correct notation.

Question ❷ assesses children's ability to calculate missing angles in isosceles triangles. Look for children clearly explaining the steps needed and confidently using addition, subtraction and division and showing fluency when working abstractly.

In question ❺, children should be able to complete the calculations, recognising when to add, subtract or divide and demonstrating understanding of known angle facts.

**ANSWERS** Answers for the **Practice** part of the lesson can be found in the *Power Maths* online subscription.

## Reflect

**WAYS OF WORKING** Pair work

**IN FOCUS** This reflection gives children an opportunity to create a missing angle problem. Encourage them to draw on known angle facts.

**ASSESSMENT CHECKPOINT** Children should be able to confidently explain how to solve their problem, showing the steps required to reach the answer.

**ANSWERS** Answers for the **Reflect** part of the lesson can be found in the *Power Maths* online subscription.

### After the lesson ⏸

- Can children label isosceles triangles using the correct notation and calculate missing angles without measuring?
- Can children draw isosceles triangles and measure the interior angles?
- Can children use known angle facts to solve missing angle problems?

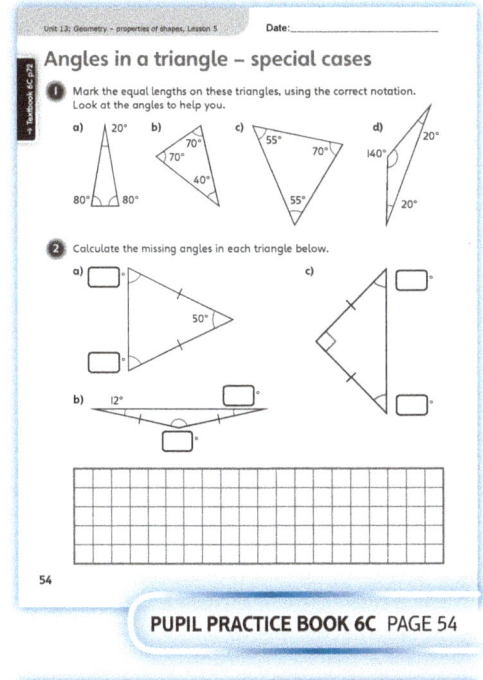

PUPIL PRACTICE BOOK 6C PAGE 54

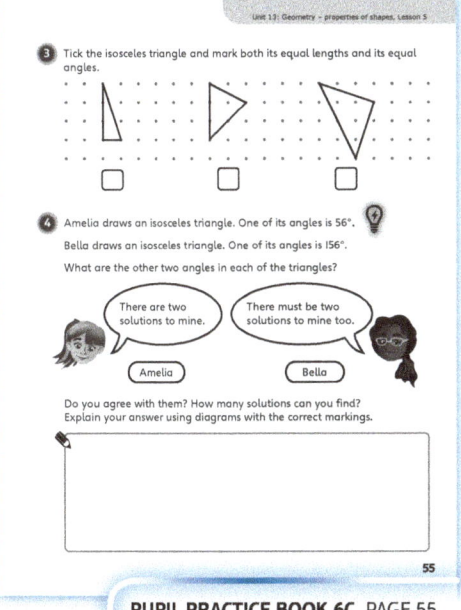

PUPIL PRACTICE BOOK 6C PAGE 55

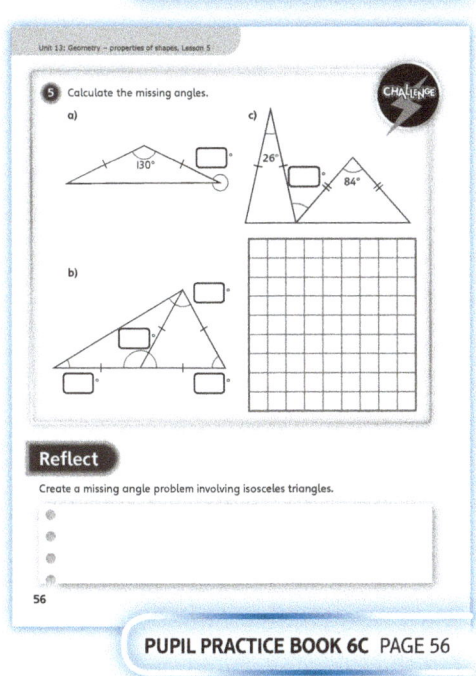

PUPIL PRACTICE BOOK 6C PAGE 56

111

Unit 13: Geometry – properties of shapes, Lesson 6

# Angles in quadrilaterals

### Learning focus
In this lesson, children will reinforce prior knowledge of the properties of shapes and extend their learning to understand the interior angles of a quadrilateral sum to 360°.

### Before you teach
- Do children know the properties of trapeziums and parallelograms?
- Can children add, subtract and divide numbers?
- Do children know the angle rules for angles on a straight line, angles around a point and the sum of the interior angles of a triangle?

#### NATIONAL CURRICULUM LINKS

**Year 6 Geometry – properties of shapes**

Compare and classify geometric shapes based on their properties and sizes and find unknown angles in any triangles, quadrilaterals and regular polygons.

#### ASSESSING MASTERY

Children can confidently describe properties of shapes and use these to discover that the interior angles of quadrilaterals add to 360°, demonstrating an understanding of other angle facts and showing fluency in addition, subtraction and division.

#### COMMON MISCONCEPTIONS

Children may not know the properties of shapes and so cannot apply this knowledge when exploring the interior angles of quadrilaterals. Children may not know the notation for properties of shapes (for example, they think that a small dash on two lines means that the lines are parallel and therefore identify the wrong shape). Ensure children are confident with properties of shapes by discussing these before completing the lesson. Ask:
- *What are the properties of this shape? What does this dash mean?*

#### STRENGTHENING UNDERSTANDING

Begin by revisiting properties of shapes and encourage children to describe the properties, focusing particularly on the interior angles. A matching activity could be useful. When exploring angles, encourage children to use paper versions of the shapes, so they can manipulate them to help strengthen understanding.

#### GOING DEEPER

Ask children to explore and explain different ways in which they can calculate a missing angle, discussing and deciding which is more efficient. Encourage children to reason and problem solve with angles in quadrilaterals asking: *Is it possible to have three obtuse angles in a quadrilateral?*

#### KEY LANGUAGE

**In lesson:** quadrilateral, isosceles, angle, degrees, shape, right angle, trapezium, scalene, equal, length, parallel, relationship

**Other language to be used by the teacher:** properties, interior, sum, parallelogram, calculate

#### STRUCTURES AND REPRESENTATIONS

Triangles, quadrilaterals

#### RESOURCES

**Mandatory:** coloured paper, scissors, protractors

 In the eTextbook of this lesson, you will find interactive links to a selection of teaching tools.

### Quick recap
Ask children to name as many different quadrilaterals as they can. Challenge them to give you a definition of each quadrilateral.

112

Unit 13: Geometry – properties of shapes, Lesson 6

# Discover

**WAYS OF WORKING** Pair work

**ASK**

- Question 1 a): *How can you describe the shapes left over? What properties could you describe?*
- Question 1 b): *What do you notice about the two triangles? What is the size of each angle in the triangle?*

**IN FOCUS** This question asks children to describe the properties of shapes while introducing the concept of the sum of the interior angles in a quadrilateral.

**PRACTICAL TIPS** The concept of angles in a quadrilateral could be introduced in a practical way using paper. Encourage children to explore the different shapes that can be formed, describing their properties.

**ANSWERS**

Question 1 a): The shape in step 1 is a rectangle. After step 2, a right-angled trapezium is left. (It has one pair of parallel sides, two right angles and sides of different lengths. The angles total: 60° + 120° + 90° + 90° = 360°.) After step 3, an isosceles trapezium is left. (It has two pairs of equal angles and one pair of parallel sides. The angles total: 60° + 120° + 60° + 120° = 360°.)

Question 1 b): A rectangle, two different parallelograms, and two different isosceles triangles can all be made by joining the two left-over triangles.

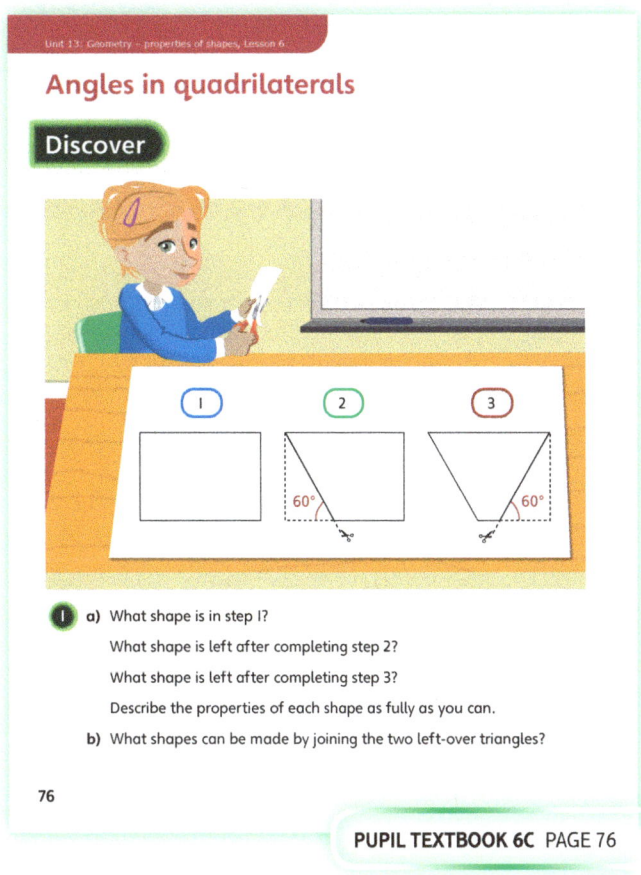

PUPIL TEXTBOOK 6C PAGE 76

# Share

**WAYS OF WORKING** Whole class teacher led

**ASK**

- Question 1 a): *What are the properties of the shapes? How do you show sides are parallel? The same length? What makes a shape a trapezium? What is the same about the shapes? What do you notice about the total of the interior angles?*
- Question 1 b): *What do you notice about the total of the interior angles?*

**IN FOCUS** Question 1 a) helps children to discover the sum of the interior angles of a quadrilateral. Encourage children to describe the properties of the shapes, using the diagrams to support this. Ensure children are confident with the different markings used for parallel sides and sides that are equal length. Encourage children to discuss what is the same about the shapes (i.e. they are quadrilaterals and the sum of the interior angles is 360°).

Question 1 b) requires children to form shapes from the two identical triangles. Reinforce previous learning by discussing the interior angles of the triangles that are formed and develop the new concept of angles in a quadrilateral.

**STRENGTHEN** It may be useful to begin by revisiting the properties of shapes, focusing particularly on the interior angles.

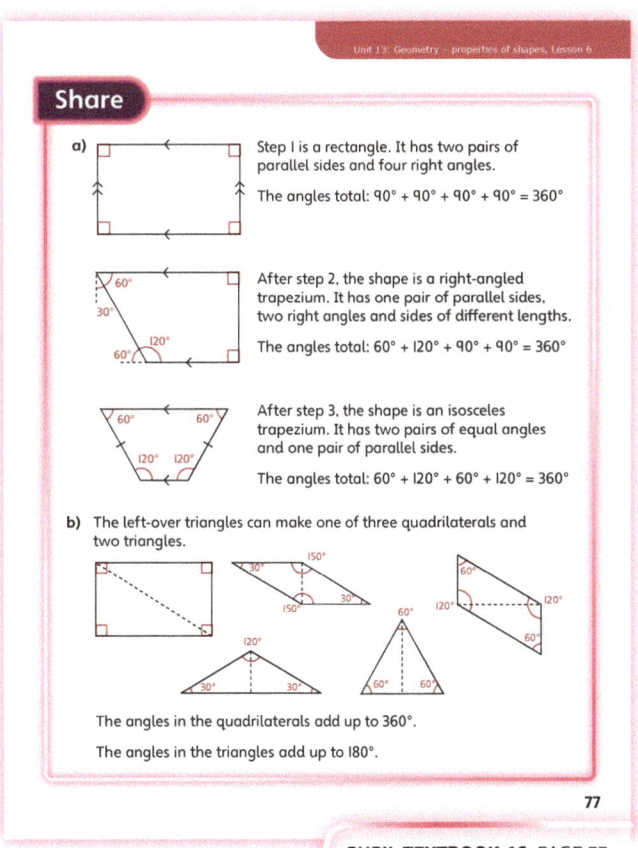

PUPIL TEXTBOOK 6C PAGE 77

# Think together

**WAYS OF WORKING** Whole class teacher led (I do, We do, You do)

**ASK**

- Question ❶: *How has the shape been formed? What shape is left over? What are the properties of the shape? What do you notice about the sum of the interior angles?*
- Question ❷: *What are the properties of the shapes? What do the markings on the shapes tell you?*
- Question ❸: *What shapes are shown? What are the properties of each shape? How can you work out the answers?*

**IN FOCUS** Question ❶ requires children to identify the shape left over, and to describe the properties, given the pictorial representations. Encourage them to explore and discuss if the angles always total to the same number.

In question ❷, encourage children to use the properties of the shapes to calculate the angles, rather than trying to measure them with a protractor.

Question ❸ presents children with some quadrilaterals where the angles are not numerical. Encourage children to make their own versions and manipulate the angles to explore the relationships between them. For example, they will be able to see that some of the angles are equal by placing one on top of the other.

**STRENGTHEN** To support understanding, encourage children to make paper versions of each shape to help them describe the properties and explore the interior angles.

**DEEPEN** For question ❸, children could be encouraged to draw their own quadrilaterals and explore other relationships between the angles.

**ASSESSMENT CHECKPOINT** In question ❶, look for children who are able to describe the properties of the parallelogram and find the total of the interior angles.

In questions ❷ and ❸, look for children who are confident using properties of shapes and angle facts to find the missing angles. Watch out for children who try to measure the angles with a protractor as they are likely to need more support with this concept.

**ANSWERS**

Question ❶: A parallelogram is left. There are always 360° in a parallelogram. The angles total 60° + 120° + 60° + 120° = 360°.

Question ❷ a): 75° + 105° + 75° + 105° = 360°

Question ❷ b): 115° + 115° + 65° + 65° = 360°

Question ❷ c): 73° + 90° + 90° + 107° = 360°

Question ❷ d): 101° + 79° + 101° + 79° = 360°

Question ❸: Children should notice that opposite angles in each shape are equal, and that the pairs of angles next to each other in each shape add up to 180°.

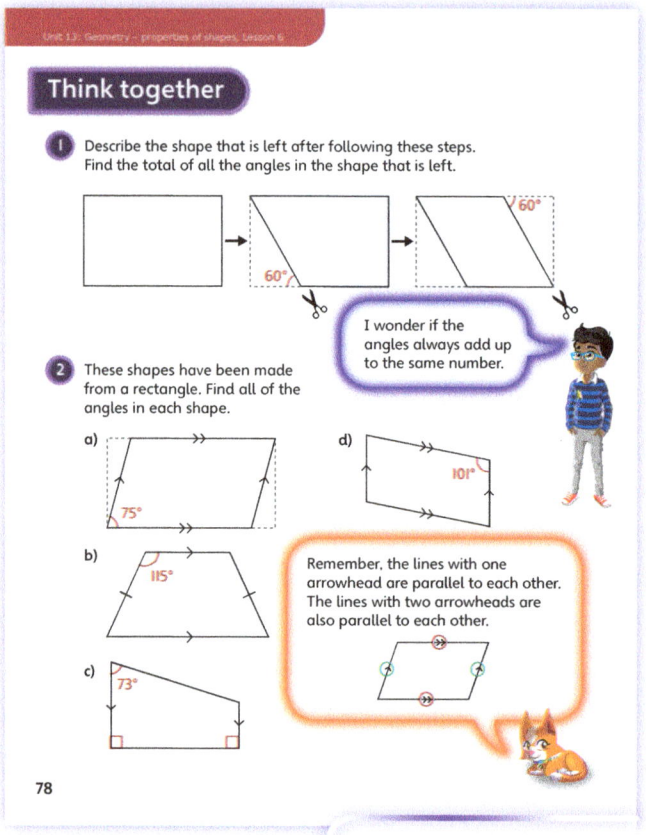

PUPIL TEXTBOOK 6C PAGE 78

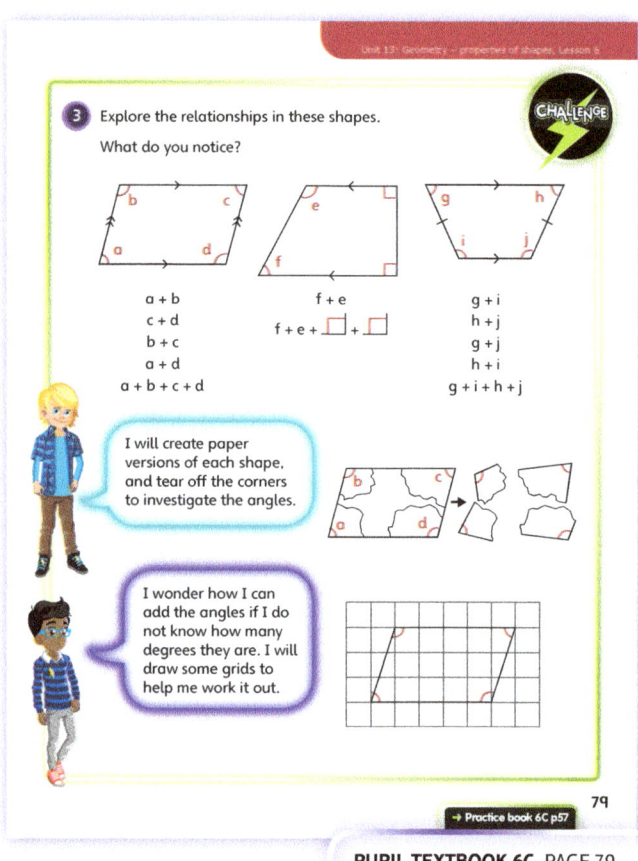

PUPIL TEXTBOOK 6C PAGE 79

# Unit 13: Geometry – properties of shapes, Lesson 6

## Practice

**WAYS OF WORKING** Independent thinking

**IN FOCUS** Question 2 asks children to find missing angles using the sum of the interior angles of a quadrilateral. Encourage them to work through the calculations in steps and show their working.

Question 6 focuses on two quadrilaterals in particular and asks children to explore the different ways they can be created. Encourage children to think about the different types of trapezium they could draw and to focus on the total of the interior angles.

**STRENGTHEN** To strengthen understanding, encourage children to use bar models to represent the numbers and identify the calculations needed to find missing angles. Children may find it helpful to make shapes out of paper to help them explore the properties.

**DEEPEN** Extend question 5 by asking children to write other statements about shapes that are always true, sometimes true and never true.

**THINK DIFFERENTLY** Question 5 aims to develop children's reasoning with angles in quadrilaterals. There is no prompting or visual representation, so encourage children to explain their answers using diagrams.

**ASSESSMENT CHECKPOINT** Questions 1 and 3 give an opportunity to assess children's ability to name and label shapes. Look for children confidently using properties of shapes.

In questions 2 and 4, look for children who demonstrate understanding of the sum of the interior angles of quadrilaterals, while showing fluency in selecting the correct operations to find the unknown.

Question 5 assesses children's ability to reason with quadrilaterals by focusing on the interior angles. Look for children who can confidently reason, justifying their answers with diagrams.

Question 6 assesses children's ability to draw parallelograms and trapeziums. Look for children who can confidently draw a variety of these shapes demonstrating an understanding of their properties.

**ANSWERS** Answers for the **Practice** part of the lesson can be found in the *Power Maths* online subscription.

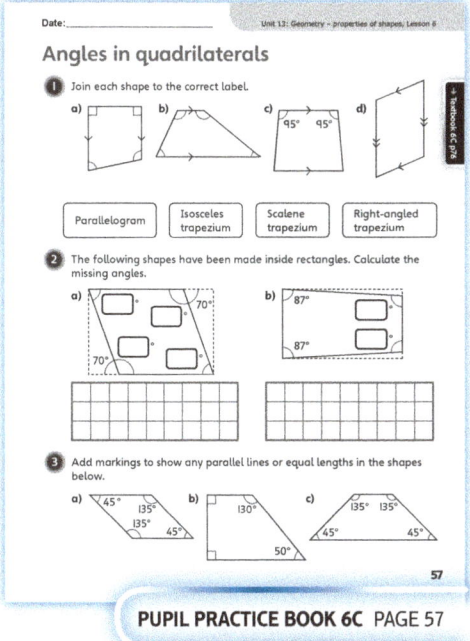

PUPIL PRACTICE BOOK 6C PAGE 57

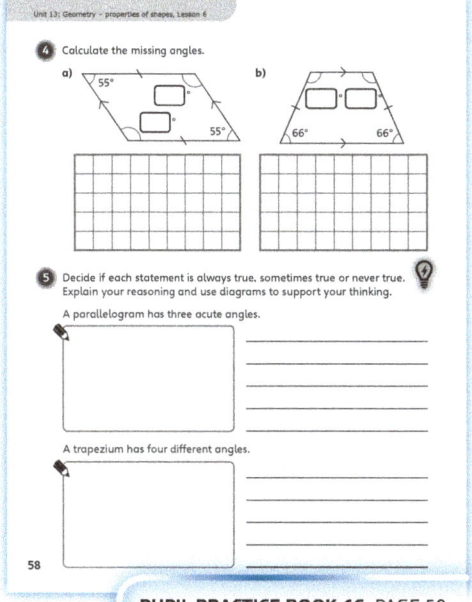

PUPIL PRACTICE BOOK 6C PAGE 58

## Reflect

**WAYS OF WORKING** Pair work

**IN FOCUS** This reflection gives children an opportunity to show their understanding of the total of the angles in quadrilaterals. Encourage children to explain the sum of the angles as well as drawing a diagram.

**ASSESSMENT CHECKPOINT** Children should be able to explain that the interior angles sum to 360°.

**ANSWERS** Answers for the **Reflect** part of the lesson can be found in the *Power Maths* online subscription.

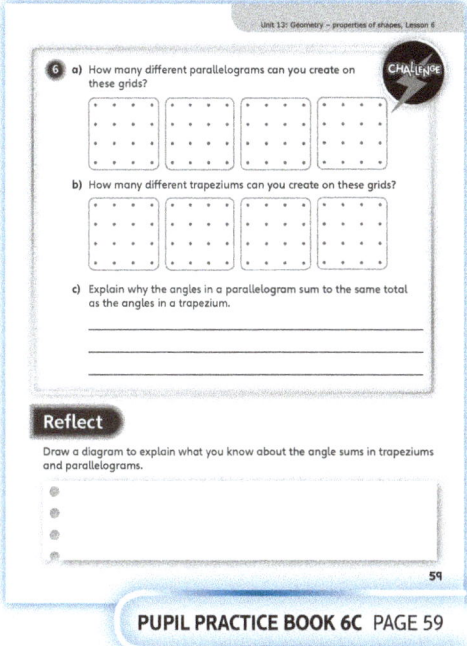

PUPIL PRACTICE BOOK 6C PAGE 59

## After the lesson

- Can children name and describe quadrilaterals and their properties?
- Can children correctly label the properties of quadrilaterals?
- Can children understand why angles in a quadrilateral sum to 360° and use this fact to calculate missing angles in quadrilaterals?

Unit 13: Geometry – properties of shapes, Lesson 7

# Angles in polygons

### Learning focus
In this lesson, children will develop their understanding of the sum of the angles in quadrilaterals and extend this to calculate the sum of the interior angles in other polygons, then use these to find missing angles.

### Before you teach
- Do children know the properties of polygons?
- Can children confidently add, subtract, multiply and divide numbers, and work with decimal answers?
- Do children know that the sum of the interior angles in a triangle is 180°?

## NATIONAL CURRICULUM LINKS

**Year 6 Geometry – properties of shapes**

Compare and classify geometric shapes based on their properties and sizes and find unknown angles in any triangles, quadrilaterals and regular polygons.

## ASSESSING MASTERY

Children understand that angles in a quadrilateral total 360° and can find the total of the angles in polygons. They can confidently use this learning to calculate missing angles in shapes showing fluency in addition, subtraction, multiplication and division, while demonstrating knowledge of associated angle facts.

## COMMON MISCONCEPTIONS

Children may focus on the numbers given in a shape and ignore right angles when they are labelled with a square. Encourage children to identify all angles before carrying out any calculations. Ask:
- *What does labelling an angle with a square mean?*

Another misconception may occur when the shape is not regular, for example, children may mistake arrowheads for triangles and use 180° as the total of the interior angles rather than 360°. Ask:
- *Is this a triangle or not?*

Children may think three angles are required to work out a missing angle in a quadrilateral. Encourage them to consider the properties of the shapes they are dealing with. Ask:
- *Can you work out the two missing angles?*

## STRENGTHENING UNDERSTANDING

If children find it challenging to calculate missing angles in polygons, recap finding missing angles in triangles and quadrilaterals. Children will also need a sound understanding of the properties of shapes. When calculating missing angles, encourage children to use a bar model to identify the calculations needed and to complete the calculations in steps, showing each stage of their working.

## GOING DEEPER

Children could be encouraged to calculate the sum of the angles in polygons with many sides and to solve missing angle problems involving these. Give children some missing angle problems in word format where they also have to use their knowledge of properties of shapes to solve the problem.

## KEY LANGUAGE

**In lesson:** quadrilateral, total, sum, angle, shape, measure, calculate, triangle, pentagon, hexagon, heptagon, kite, rhombus, regular, polygon

**Other language to be used by the teacher:** method, degrees, properties, interior, vertex

## STRUCTURES AND REPRESENTATIONS

Quadrilaterals and polygons

## RESOURCES

**Mandatory:** ruler, coloured paper, scissors, protractors

 In the eTextbook of this lesson, you will find interactive links to a selection of teaching tools.

### Quick recap
Ask children to name as many different polygons as they can. Challenge them to give you a definition of each polygon.

Unit 13: Geometry – properties of shapes, Lesson 7

# Discover

**WAYS OF WORKING** Pair work

**ASK**

- Question 1 a): *Which angles will stay the same? Which angles will be different?*
- Question 1 b): *What is the angle total of Lexi's quadrilateral? How can you be sure the total will always be the same?*

**IN FOCUS** Question 1 b) introduces children to the concept of the sum of the interior angles of any quadrilateral equalling 360°. It will be important to ensure that children are confident with the sum of the angles in a triangle.

**PRACTICAL TIPS** The context in this lesson is joining two triangles together to make a quadrilateral. This could be made into a practical activity where children make their own triangles from paper and form quadrilaterals while discussing the angles that are created and the sum of the angles.

**ANSWERS**

Question 1 a): The angles in Lexi's quadrilateral have a total of 40 + 80 + 165 + 75 = 360°.

Question 1 b): Children may notice that any quadrilateral can be split into two triangles, so the total of all the angles in a quadrilateral must be 180° × 2 = 360°.

# Share

**WAYS OF WORKING** Whole class teacher led

**ASK**

- Question 1 a): *What does the diagram show you? How can you calculate the new angles that are created? What operation do you need to use? What is the total of these angles?*
- Question 1 b): *What shapes can be made from quadrilaterals? Is this true for any quadrilateral? What can you say about the total of the angles in a quadrilateral?*

**IN FOCUS** Question 1 a) aims to help children understand how quadrilaterals can be created by putting two triangles together. Explore with children which angles will stay the same and which angles are newly formed in the quadrilateral. Use the diagram to help children understand that to calculate the angles in the quadrilateral it is necessary to add. Emphasise how these angles total 360° and reinforce links with the previous lesson.

Question 1 b) develops this concept by giving children an opportunity to explore a range of quadrilaterals that are split into two triangles. Ensure children are confident with the sum of the angles in triangles and use the diagram for pictorial support.

**STRENGTHEN** In question 1 b), it may be beneficial for children to draw their own quadrilaterals and see how they can be split into two triangles to strengthen their understanding of this concept.

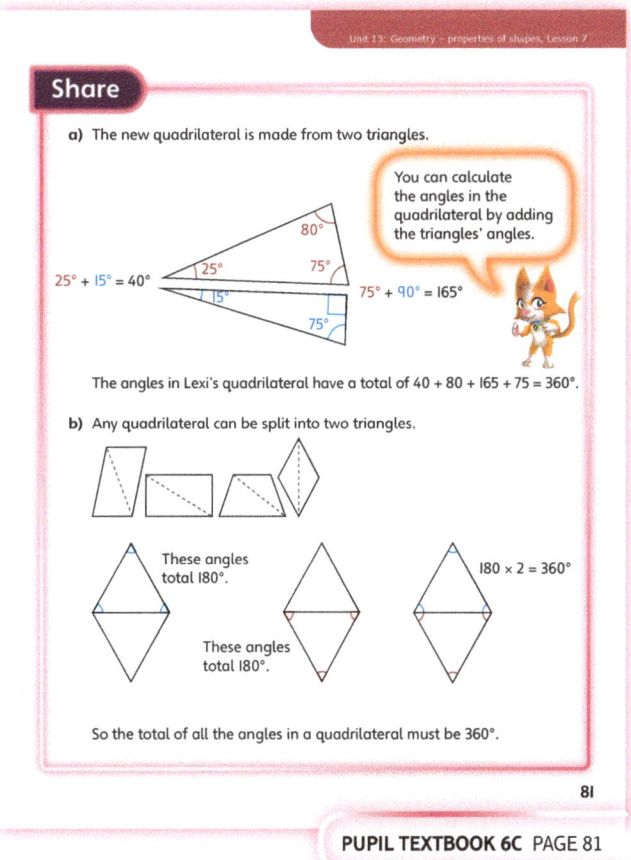

117

# Think together

**WAYS OF WORKING** Whole class teacher led (I do, We do, You do)

**ASK**

- Question 1: *What do the angles add up to? How can you work out the missing angles?*
- Question 2: *What are the properties of a kite and a rhombus? Which angles would you need to know?*
- Question 3: *How many triangles can you see in the polygons? What does this tell you about the interior angles of the polygons?*

**IN FOCUS** Question 1 requires children to calculate missing angles in a quadrilateral when given three of the angles. Watch out for children who mistake shape c) for a triangle. Encourage children to do their calculations in steps and show their working.

Question 2 develops children's thinking about the angles required to work out other missing angles. Encourage children to consider the properties of these shapes.

Question 3 introduces the sum of the interior angles in other shapes. It may be beneficial to revisit the definitions of polygon and regular.

**STRENGTHEN** To strengthen understanding, encourage children to represent the numbers on a bar model to help them decide which operations they need to use.

**DEEPEN** Extend question 3 by asking: *Can you find the total of the interior angles in other polygons?* Give children some irregular polygons with some angles labelled and ask them to calculate one unknown angle.

**ASSESSMENT CHECKPOINT** Question 2 assesses children's ability to recall the properties of shapes. If children think it is necessary to measure three angles, in order to calculate the rest, they are likely to need more support.

In question 3, children should be able to use the total of the interior angles to calculate one of the angles confidently using division.

**ANSWERS**

Question 1 a): 360° − 120° − 95° − 60° = 85°

Question 1 b): 360° − 98° − 87° − 72° = 103°

Question 1 c): 360° − 90° − 30° − 30° = 210°

Question 2 a): Two angles: one of the side angles (which are equal) and one of the other two.

Question 2 a): Any one of the angles.

Question 3: Hexagon: 6 sides, 4 triangles, 180 × 4, 720°
Heptagon: 7 sides, 5 triangles, 180 × 5, 900°
a is an angle in a regular pentagon, so
a = 540° ÷ 5 = 108°.
b is an angle in a regular hexagon, so
b = 720° ÷ 6 = 120°.
c is an angle in a regular heptagon, so
c = 900° ÷ 7 = 128·57° (to 2 decimal places).

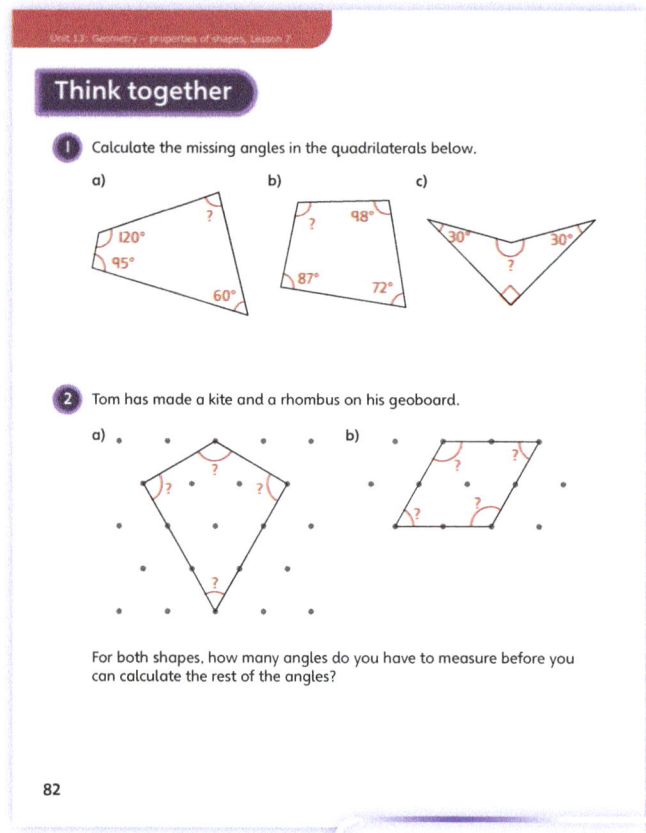

PUPIL TEXTBOOK 6C PAGE 82

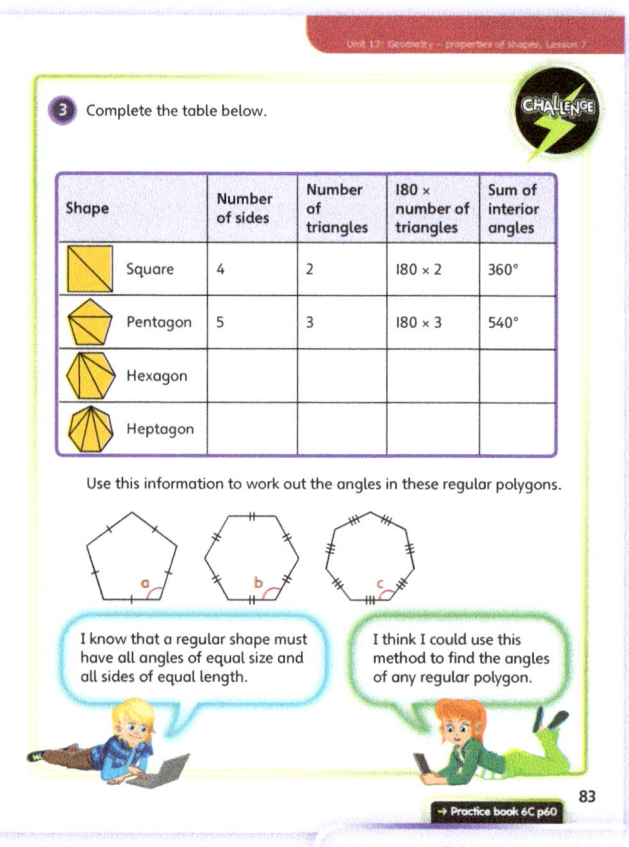

PUPIL TEXTBOOK 6C PAGE 83

Unit 13: Geometry – properties of shapes, Lesson 7

# Practice

**WAYS OF WORKING** Independent thinking

**IN FOCUS** Question ❶ develops children's understanding of using the sum of the interior angles of quadrilaterals to find unknown angles. Question ❷ allows children to find incorrect angles and consolidates using a protractor.

Question ❸ asks children to split polygons into triangles to work out the total of the interior angles. Watch out for children who overlap the triangles or do not have all the vertices of the triangles touching the edges of the polygons.

Question ❺ is more abstract – encourage children to split the decagon into triangles to help.

In question ❻, children need to use other angle facts and explore all the possible angles that can be found on the diagram.

**STRENGTHEN** If children are finding it a challenge to calculate missing angles in polygons, remind them of the total of the interior angles and encourage them to use a bar model to show what they know and what they need to find.

**DEEPEN** Extend question ❺ by encouraging children to find the interior angles of other polygons with more than 10 sides. In question ❻, challenge children to find all the angles in the second diagram.

**THINK DIFFERENTLY** Question ❹ addresses the misconception related to children drawing triangles incorrectly in shapes. Encourage children to explain why splitting the shape in this way does not work.

**ASSESSMENT CHECKPOINT** In questions ❸, ❹ and ❺, look for children fluently using multiplication and those who are able to draw triangles confidently where each vertex touches the edges of the polygons.

In question ❻, children should be able to fluently use the total of the interior angles in polygons to find one interior angle, while confidently using other angle facts and explaining their steps and reasoning.

**ANSWERS** Answers for the **Practice** part of the lesson can be found in the *Power Maths* online subscription.

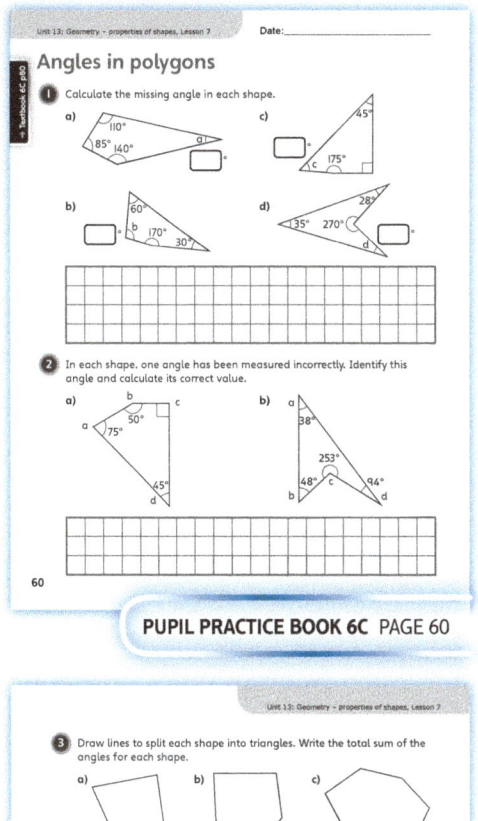

PUPIL PRACTICE BOOK 6C PAGE 60

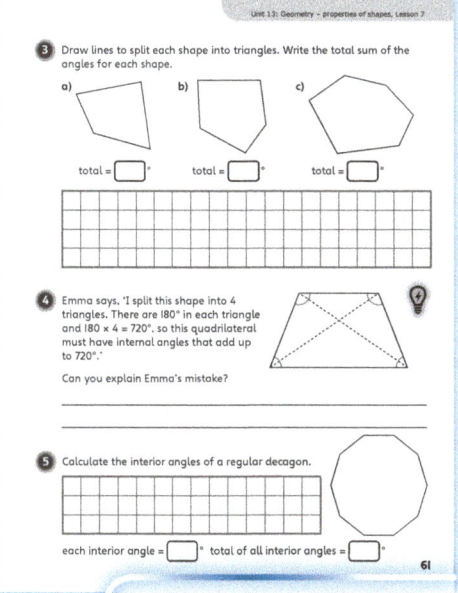

PUPIL PRACTICE BOOK 6C PAGE 61

# Reflect

**WAYS OF WORKING** Pair work

**IN FOCUS** This reflection gives children an opportunity to work backwards and create a problem with a specific answer. Encourage them to draw a diagram to represent the problem and to use more than one operation if possible. Encourage children to describe the steps needed to answer the problem, writing their explanation in their own words. Ask them to give their problem to a partner to check.

**ASSESSMENT CHECKPOINT** Look for children fluently working backwards to create a problem, using their understanding of inverse operations while confidently checking their work and their partner's.

**ANSWERS** Answers for the **Reflect** part of the lesson can be found in the *Power Maths* online subscription.

# After the lesson

- Can children accurately draw triangles inside polygons?
- Can children calculate missing angles and solve problems in polygons, using the properties of shapes?
- Can children write their own problems?

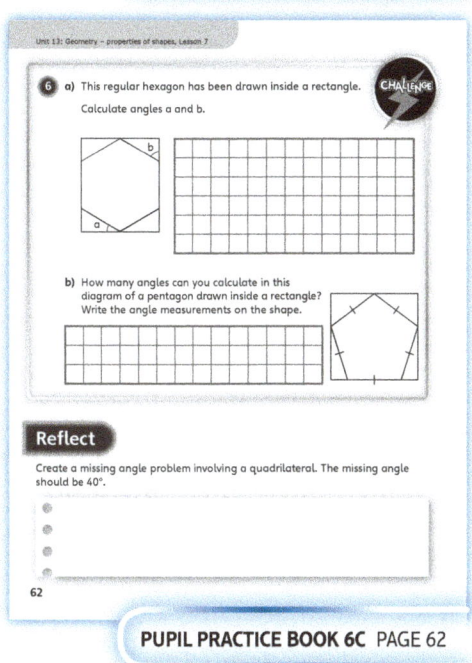

PUPIL PRACTICE BOOK 6C PAGE 62

119

Unit 13: Geometry – properties of shapes, Lesson 8

# Circles

### Learning focus

In this lesson, children will understand that as the number of vertices increases an equal distance from the centre, a circle is formed. They will learn the definition of radius and diameter and can solve problems involving radius and diameter.

### Before you teach

- Can children use a ruler to measure lines?
- Do children understand the word perimeter?
- Can children find the length of an equilateral triangle when given the perimeter?

#### NATIONAL CURRICULUM LINKS

**Year 6 Geometry – properties of shapes**

Illustrate and name parts of circles, including radius, diameter and circumference and know that the diameter is twice the radius.

#### ASSESSING MASTERY

Children can recognise that a circle is formed by creating many points that are equal distances from the centre. They can identify the radius and diameter and calculate with them. They can use multiplication and division fluently, drawing circles accurately and solving problems, explaining the steps in their own words.

#### COMMON MISCONCEPTIONS

Children may think the radius goes from the centre of a circle in a horizontal or vertical direction only. Expose children to diagrams of circles that show the radius can be in any orientation from the centre. Ask:
- *Can you draw the radius at any angle?*

When asked to draw a circle given a diameter, children may forget to divide by 2 to find the radius. Encourage them to identify the radius and diameter before completing any questions and to check their answers. Ask:
- *Which is longer, the radius or the diameter? If the diameter is x, how can you work out the radius?*

#### STRENGTHENING UNDERSTANDING

Children who have difficulty identifying the radius from the diameter should draw this on the circle to help them see that they need to divide the diameter by 2. Children who find it a challenge to draw circles using a pair of compasses could be encouraged to rotate the paper instead as children often find this easier.

#### GOING DEEPER

Children can be encouraged to solve more complex problems involving circles. For example ask: *In a diagram of 5 concentric circles the smallest circle has a radius of 6 cm. The diameter of each circle increases by 1 cm. What is the diameter of the largest circle?* Ask children to explore the different methods they can use to solve the problems.

#### KEY LANGUAGE

**In lesson:** distance, vertices, triangle, quadrilateral, radius, circle, centre, pair of compasses, concentric, diameter

**Other language to be used by the teacher:** approximate, twice, equal, vertex, perimeter

#### STRUCTURES AND REPRESENTATIONS

Polygons, circles

#### RESOURCES

**Mandatory:** pair of compasses, ruler, paper, string, pin (to hold string)

**Optional:** 2p and 5p coins, counters

 In the eTextbook of this lesson, you will find interactive links to a selection of teaching tools.

### Quick recap

Have a class discussion about shapes. Ask: *What kind of shapes do you see in nature? How do these compare with shapes that you see in maths lessons?*

Unit 13: Geometry – properties of shapes, Lesson 8

# Discover

**WAYS OF WORKING** Pair work

**ASK**

- Question 1 a): *What shape will three people form? What shapes will be formed as more people join?*
- Question 1 b): *What shape will the second class form?*

**IN FOCUS** This question introduces children to placing points an equal distance from a centre and exploring the shapes that are formed.

**PRACTICAL TIPS** It will be beneficial to use counters to represent the class in the **Discover** scenario, so children have an overhead view. This will help them to see the shapes formed.

**ANSWERS**

Question 1 a): Three children will form a triangle around Amelia. Four children will form a quadrilateral. As more children join, the shape will have more vertices and it will start to form a circle.

Question 1 b): The second class will form another circle. The radius will be 6 m, so it will be larger.

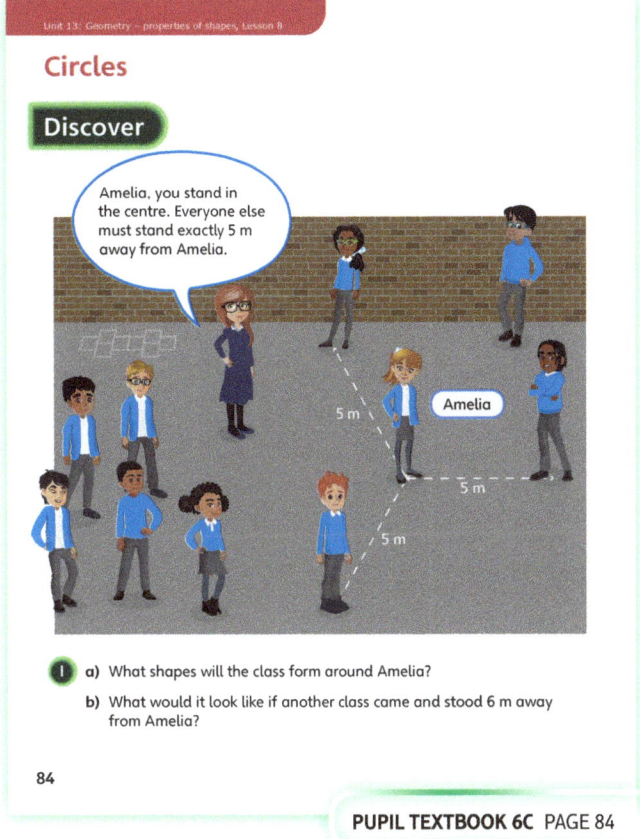

PUPIL TEXTBOOK 6C PAGE 84

# Share

**WAYS OF WORKING** Whole class teacher led

**ASK**

- Question 1 a): *What do the diagrams show? What shape is formed when three people stand around Amelia? How about four people? Or five people? What happens as more people stand around Amelia? What shape is created? What is the distance from the centre called in a circle? How can you draw a circle? What equipment do you need?*
- Question 1 b): *What shape will the second class form? Will the circle be smaller or bigger than the first one? How do you know? What is the special name for circles with the same centre?*

**IN FOCUS** Question 1 a) asks children to explore the different shapes created by points placed around a central location. It would be beneficial to act this out with children, maybe using a smaller distance than 5 m.

Children should recognise that, as more people join, a circle is eventually formed. Define the term radius and discuss how to draw a circle using the correct equipment (a pair of compasses).

Question 1 b) further develops the concept of equal distance from the centre and introduces the meaning of concentric circles. It will be useful to discuss how concentric circles can be drawn using a pair of compasses and a ruler.

**STRENGTHEN** In question 1 a), encourage children to look at the diagram to strengthen their understanding of the concept that as the number of vertices increases the shape will eventually become a circle.

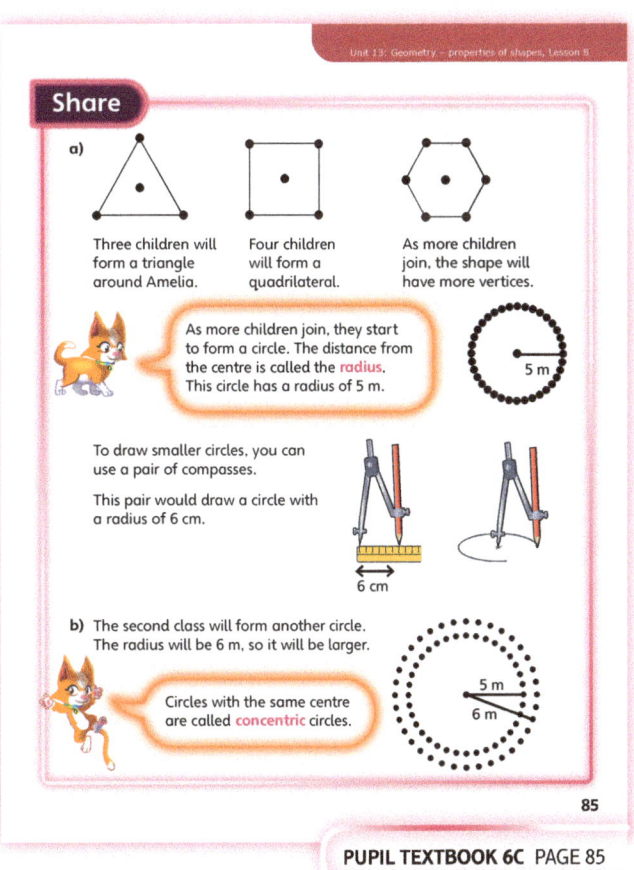

PUPIL TEXTBOOK 6C PAGE 85

Unit 13: Geometry – properties of shapes, Lesson 8

# Think together

**WAYS OF WORKING** Whole class teacher led (I do, We do, You do)

**ASK**
- Question 1: *How can you identify the radius? Which direction does it go in? What equipment do you need? How can you ensure your answer is accurate?*
- Question 2: *What do you need to draw first? Which circle should you start with? Does it matter?*
- Question 3: *What is the diameter? How could this help? How can you find the diameter of a circle?*

**IN FOCUS** Question 1 develops children's understanding of identifying and measuring the radius. Ensure children are confident using the centre of the circle to measure the radius. Explore with them how the radius can go in any direction and always be the same.

In question 2, children are encouraged to use a pair of compasses, string or a ruler. Encourage them to explain which piece of equipment will give them the most accurate copy.

In question 3, ensure children measure the widest part of the circles by estimating where the diameter is and then adjusting as necessary.

**STRENGTHEN** When drawing circles with a pair of compasses, it can be useful to encourage children to rotate the page rather than the compasses.

**DEEPEN** Extend question 2 by asking children to create other concentric circle patterns. Encourage them to calculate the distance between the circumference of the circles and ask if this will always be the same.

**ASSESSMENT CHECKPOINT** Question 1 assesses children's ability to identify and measure the radius of a circle. Look for children who are confident with the definition and can use a ruler accurately.

In question 2, look for children who can measure accurately using the correct equipment and those who create an accurate copy of the design.

Question 3 assesses children's ability to identify and measure the diameter and radius of a circle. Look for children who can confidently divide the diameters by 2 using an appropriate method. If children simply guess where the centre is, they may need more support.

**ANSWERS**

Question 1 a): 2 cm

Question 1 b): 3 cm

Question 2: Children should accurately copy the design with the measurements given.

Question 3 a): 3·1 cm

Question 3 b): 5 cm

Question 3 c): 2·9 cm

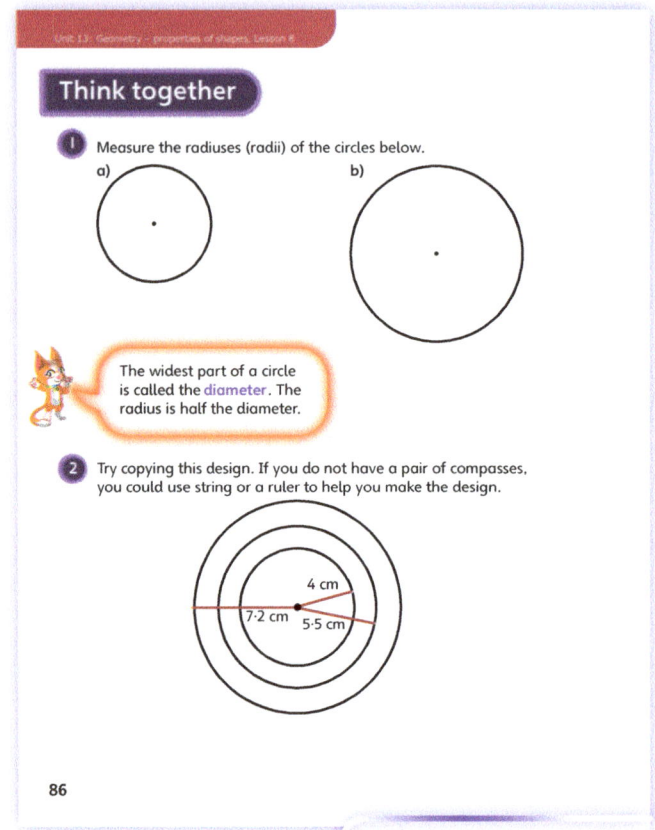

PUPIL TEXTBOOK 6C PAGE 86

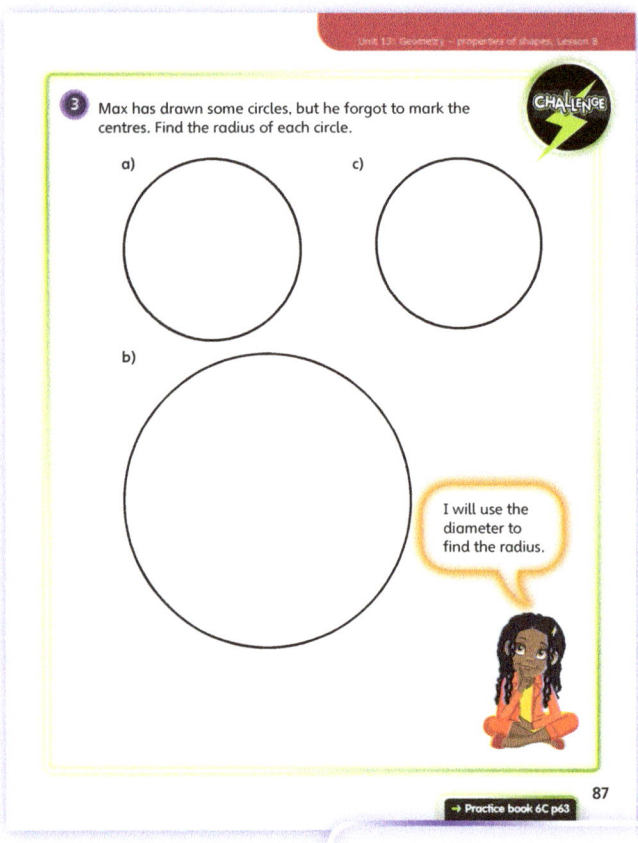

PUPIL TEXTBOOK 6C PAGE 87

# Unit 13: Geometry – properties of shapes, Lesson 8

## Practice

**WAYS OF WORKING** Independent thinking

**IN FOCUS** Question ❶ requires children to make dots an equal distance from the centre. Encourage children to spread the dots to create a circle.

Questions ❷, ❸ and ❹ develop children's understanding of the radius and diameter. Watch for children who try to use a ruler in question ❹.

In question ❻, explore with children the type of triangle shown and encourage them to reason about how they could calculate the length of one side. Children may need a reminder of the definition of perimeter. Encourage children to show their method clearly and use the correct units for their answers.

**STRENGTHEN** In question ❸, encourage children to represent the sentences on diagrams to support their thinking. Get them to replace the *x* with a number to help them decide if the statement is correct.

**DEEPEN** Extend questions ❺ and ❻ by asking children to explain and explore the different ways in which the answers can be calculated.

Deepen learning in question ❻ by asking children to draw other shapes on tessellated circles.

**THINK DIFFERENTLY** In question ❺, look out for children who divide by the wrong amount (for example, divide 13 cm by 5 since there are 5 coins). Encourage children to show their method clearly and to use the correct units.

**ASSESSMENT CHECKPOINT** Questions ❷, ❸ and ❹ assess children's ability to work with the radius and diameter of a circle.

In questions ❺ and ❻, look for children fluently using division or multiplication in their calculations, while explaining the different steps in their own words.

**ANSWERS** Answers for the **Practice** part of the lesson can be found in the *Power Maths* online subscription.

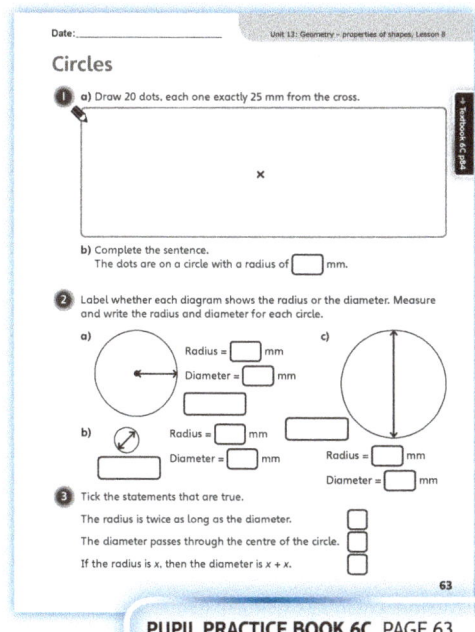

PUPIL PRACTICE BOOK 6C PAGE 63

PUPIL PRACTICE BOOK 6C PAGE 64

## Reflect

**WAYS OF WORKING** Pair work

**IN FOCUS** This reflection question checks children's understanding of drawing a circle when given a diameter. It addresses a common misconception where children may draw a circle with a radius of 4 cm rather than a diameter of 4 cm.

**ASSESSMENT CHECKPOINT** Children should be able to describe the steps needed to draw the circle. Look for children who recognise the need to divide by 2 to calculate the radius and who identify the correct equipment to draw an accurate circle.

**ANSWERS** Answers for the **Reflect** part of the lesson can be found in the *Power Maths* online subscription.

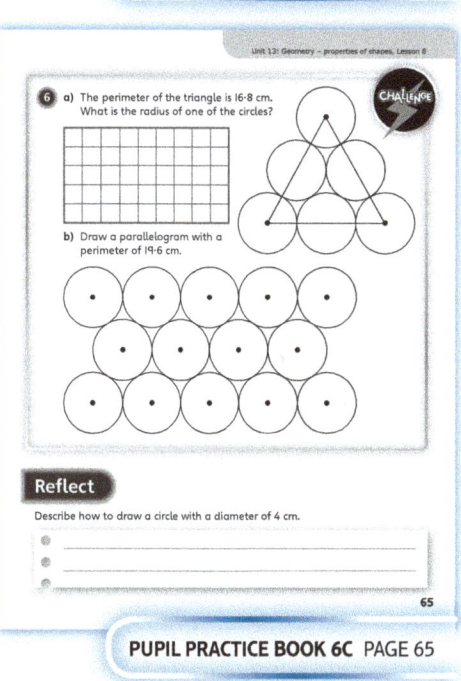

PUPIL PRACTICE BOOK 6C PAGE 65

## After the lesson ⏸

- Can children differentiate between the radius and diameter of a circle and solve problems involving these lengths?
- Can children accurately draw a circle and describe the steps required?
- Can children draw concentric circles?

Unit 13: Geometry – properties of shapes, Lesson 9

# Parts of a circle

### Learning focus
In this lesson, children will learn more about the parts of a circle and their properties.

### Before you teach
- Do children understand the terms radius, diameter and perimeter?
- Can children reliably measure using a ruler and a protractor?
- Can children calculate missing angles in triangles using angle facts?

#### NATIONAL CURRICULUM LINKS

**Year 6 Geometry – properties of shapes**

Illustrate and name parts of circles, including radius, diameter and circumference and know that the diameter is twice the radius.

#### ASSESSING MASTERY

Children can confidently identify the radius, diameter and circumference of a circle and can measure these accurately. They can draw shapes in circles and explore the properties of them, showing fluency in measuring angles and calculating unknown angles, demonstrating an understanding of associated angle facts.

#### COMMON MISCONCEPTIONS

Children may not understand that the radius of a circle can come from the centre at any angle and, thus, they may find it a challenge to identify isosceles triangles. To address this misconception, it is important to expose children to circles with the radius and diameter marked at different angles. Ask:
- *Can the radius be drawn at an angle that is not horizontal or vertical?*

#### STRENGTHENING UNDERSTANDING

To support children with drawing shapes within circles, provide circles with either the diameter or the radius pre-drawn. It may be beneficial for children to practise drawing a radius and diameter on a circle in different orientations before attempting to draw triangles.

#### GOING DEEPER

Children could be encouraged to investigate a range of shapes that can be drawn in circles, to develop their understanding of the parts of a circle. For example, you could challenge children to draw a hexagon in a circle by accurately drawing six equilateral triangles from the centre.

#### KEY LANGUAGE

**In lesson:** circumference, diameter, radius, perimeter, polygon, centre, triangle, angle, isosceles

**Other language to be used by the teacher:** measure, shapes, properties, accurate, twice, equilateral, kite, parallelogram, trapezium, rhombus

#### STRUCTURES AND REPRESENTATIONS

Circles, triangles, polygons

#### RESOURCES

**Mandatory:** string, ruler, pin (to hold string)

**Optional:** rope (for outdoor activities), squared paper, pair of compasses

 In the eTextbook of this lesson, you will find interactive links to a selection of teaching tools.

### Quick recap
Ask children to sketch a circle with a radius of 5 cm. Ask: *What would a circle look like if it had a diameter of 5 cm instead?*

# Discover

**WAYS OF WORKING** Pair work

**ASK**

- Question 1 a): *What equipment is needed to measure the edge of the bike wheel?*
- Question 1 b): *What is the radius? What is the diameter?*

**IN FOCUS** Question 1 a) introduces children to the circumference of a circle. Question 1 b) develops this, requiring children to explore the longest length, using their knowledge of radius and diameter. This is a good opportunity to assess children's confidence with these definitions.

**PRACTICAL TIPS** Children could be introduced to the circumference of circles in a practical setting, such as measuring the circumference of a circular object outside. Encourage them to use string/rope to understand the circumference is the distance around the outside of a circle.

**ANSWERS**

Question 1 a): Method 1: Wrap a piece of rope or string around the circumference, then unwrap it and measure it in a straight line.
Method 2: Choose a point on the wheel and roll it until the point returns to the starting position. The distance it has rolled is the circumference.

Question 1 b): The circumference is always longer than its radius or diameter.

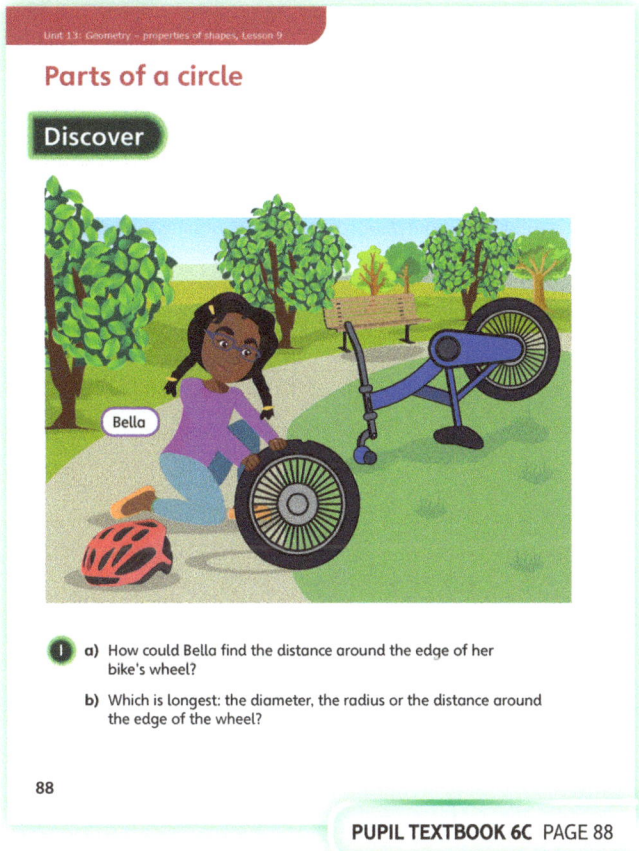

PUPIL TEXTBOOK 6C PAGE 88

# Share

**WAYS OF WORKING** Whole class teacher led

**ASK**

- Question 1 a): *What is the name for the distance around the edge of a circle? What is this similar to? In method 1, how could you measure the piece of string or rope? In method 2, how would you measure the distance travelled?*
- Question 1 b): *What does a radius look like? A diameter? Which is longer? Is the circumference bigger or smaller?*

**IN FOCUS** Question 1 a) introduces the term 'circumference'. Watch out for children who think a valid way of measuring the circumference would be to put a ruler around the outside of the circle. Explain that a more accurate way of measuring the circumference is needed. Explore methods 1 and 2 with children. When discussing method 2, emphasise the need to mark a dot on the circle so the measurement is accurate. It would be beneficial to complete this activity in a physical way, so children can see how the wheel (i.e. circle) moves rather than just looking at the diagram.

In question 1 b), encourage children to compare the radius and diameter first so they can eliminate one of these parts. Use the diagrams to support their understanding that the circumference is longest.

**STRENGTHEN** It may be useful to link the concept of circumference with children's prior knowledge of the perimeter of polygons, using diagrams.

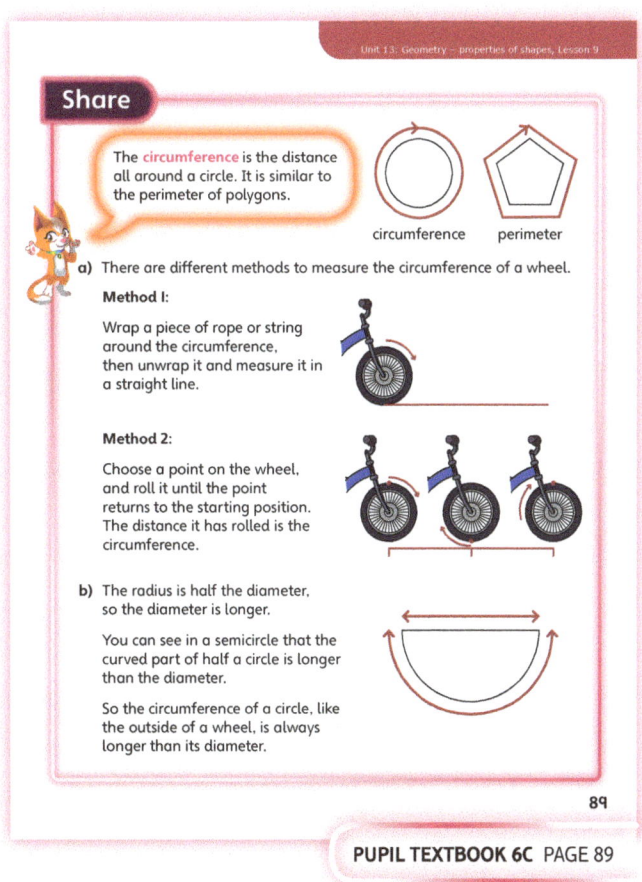

PUPIL TEXTBOOK 6C PAGE 89

Unit 13: Geometry – properties of shapes, Lesson 9

# Think together

**WAYS OF WORKING** Whole class teacher led (I do, We do, You do)

**ASK**
- Question ❶: *What can you use to measure accurately?*
- Question ❷: *What is the word for the length from the centre of a circle to the circumference? What type of triangles are formed? Why? Is it possible to create any different types of triangle if the centre is always used?*
- Question ❸ a): *What is the same and what is different about the triangles? What do you notice about the angles?*
- Question ❸ b): *How has Isla split up the triangle? What type of triangles are the smaller ones? How do you know? What is the total of angles a + a + b + b? What does this tell you about the total of one angle a and one angle b? Can you explain Isla's reasoning?*

**IN FOCUS** Question ❶ supports children in developing their understanding of the circumference of a circle and asks them to measure using a piece of string. Encourage children to work in pairs in order to measure more accurately.

Question ❷ gives children an opportunity to explore the types of triangle that can be formed within a circle. Encourage them to think about the two lines that come from the centre of the circle and consequently the types of triangles formed. Encourage children to use a protractor to check an equilateral triangle, if they try to create one.

Question ❸ requires children to explore triangles in circles with the diameter as an edge. Children should notice that the angle between the lines that touch the circumference is always a right angle. This is explained in question ❸ b).

**STRENGTHEN** To help children measure the circumference of the circle, encourage them to make paper versions of circles and try method 2 from the **Share** section.

**DEEPEN** Questions ❷ and ❸ extend children's understanding of the parts of circles by drawing triangles within them. Encourage children to explore other shapes they could draw using parts of a circle to deepen this further.

**ASSESSMENT CHECKPOINT** In question ❶, look for children who measure accurately and use the correct units.

Questions ❷ and ❸ give an opportunity to assess children's ability to use parts of circles to draw triangles while understanding more complex reasoning, showing fluency in types of triangle and measuring angles.

**ANSWERS**

Question ❶ a): 12 cm

Question ❶ b): 17·5 cm

Question ❷: Alex can form an isosceles triangle or an equilateral triangle.

Question ❸ a): Children may notice that the angle at the circumference of the circle is 90° in both cases. Children may also point out that the other two angles add up to 90°.

Question ❸ b): Children may notice that if a + a + b + b = 180°, then a + a = 90° and b + b = 90°. So, a + b = 90°, showing that the angle at the circumference is a right angle.

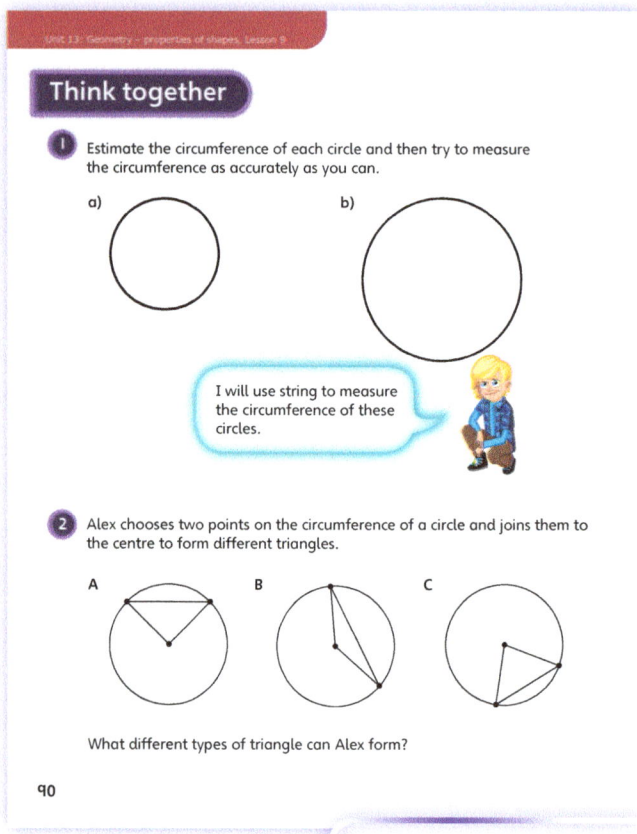

PUPIL TEXTBOOK 6C PAGE 90

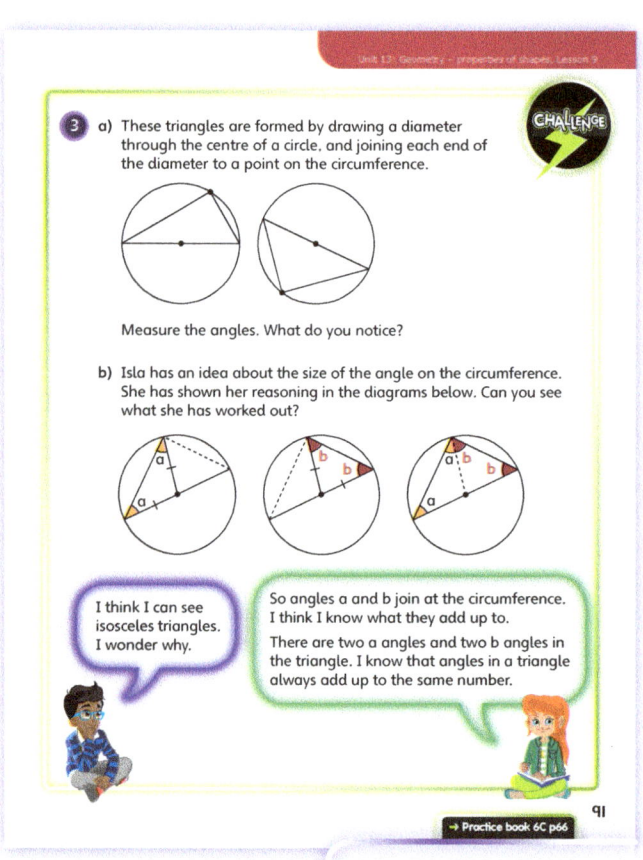

PUPIL TEXTBOOK 6C PAGE 91

# Unit 13: Geometry – properties of shapes, Lesson 9

## Practice

**WAYS OF WORKING** Independent thinking

**IN FOCUS** Question ❶ consolidates children's understanding of identifying parts of a circle from a diagram.

Question ❸ looks at creating other shapes in a circle. Ensure children are confident with the properties of each shape by discussing them beforehand.

Question ❹ develops children's understanding of the 90° angle at the circumference. Question ❺ requires children to demonstrate an understanding of area and develops the concept of counting squares to find the area.

**STRENGTHEN** If children are finding it challenging to draw shapes inside circles, draw the first line for them and ask them to complete the shape.

**DEEPEN** Question ❺ can be explored further by asking children to find areas of other circles drawn on squared paper.

**THINK DIFFERENTLY** In question ❷, children should be able to reason that any triangle formed by joining two points on the circumference with each other and with the centre of the circle will be an isosceles triangle. This is because two sides of the triangle will be radii of the circle and so equal in length. When calculating angles, watch out for children who try to measure all the angles. They should in fact be able to measure just one angle and use it to determine the sizes of the others. Can children explain this?

**ASSESSMENT CHECKPOINT** Questions ❷, ❸ and ❹ assess children's ability to create shapes inside circles. Children should be able to identify and use parts of the circle to accurately form these shapes, showing fluency in measuring angles and calculating missing angles.

Question ❺ gives an opportunity to assess children's ability to approximate the area of a circle. Children should be able to count the full squares and half squares to find an estimate for the area.

**ANSWERS** Answers for the **Practice** part of the lesson can be found in the *Power Maths* online subscription.

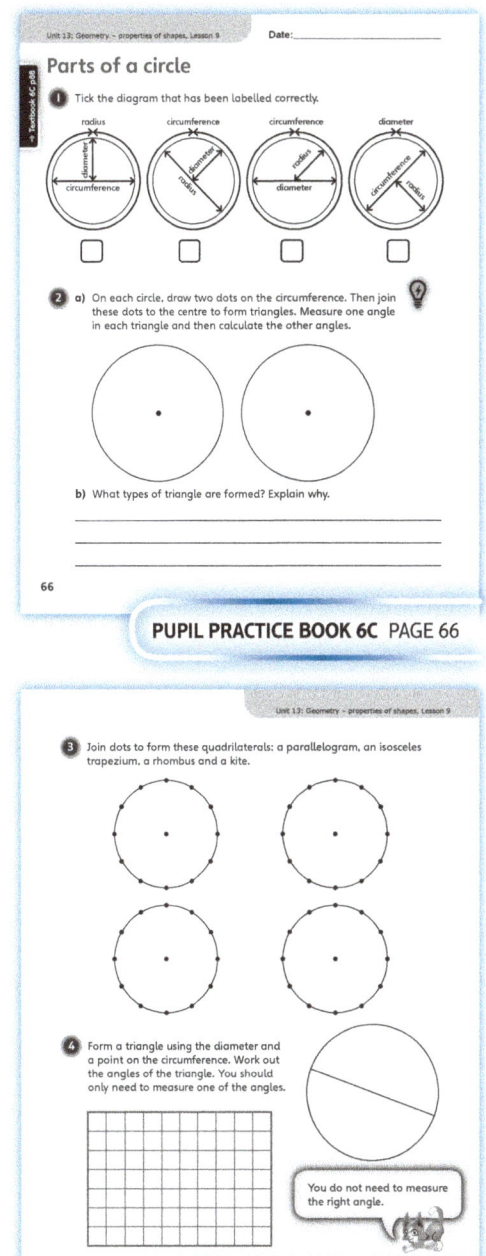

## Reflect

**WAYS OF WORKING** Independent thinking

**IN FOCUS** This reflection question will allow you to assess children's understanding of how to draw an isosceles triangle using a circle. Encourage children to describe the steps using key language.

**ASSESSMENT CHECKPOINT** Children should be able to describe the process confidently, clearly explaining the steps in their method and showing fluency with the parts of a circle and the properties of shapes.

**ANSWERS** Answers for the **Reflect** part of the lesson can be found in the *Power Maths* online subscription.

### After the lesson

- Can children confidently identify the radius, diameter and circumference of a circle, and measure the circumference of a circle using appropriate equipment?
- Can children draw shapes within circles and reason with shapes and angles inside circles?
- Can children find an approximate area of a circle by counting squares?

127

Unit 13: Geometry – properties of shapes, Lesson 10

# Draw shapes accurately

## Learning focus

In this lesson, children will understand how to draw shapes accurately using a ruler and a protractor. Children also explore drawing shapes on dotted paper.

## Before you teach

- Can children draw and measure lines and angles?
- Do children know the definition of midpoint and can they find a midpoint by dividing by 2?
- Do children know the properties of a square, rectangle, parallelogram, kite and rhombus?

### NATIONAL CURRICULUM LINKS

**Year 6 Geometry – properties of shapes**

Draw 2D shapes using given dimensions and angles.

### ASSESSING MASTERY

Children can accurately draw shapes to scale, measuring and drawing straight lines to the nearest millimetre and drawing angles to the nearest degree, demonstrating an understanding of right angles.

### COMMON MISCONCEPTIONS

Children may incorrectly draw the length of a line or the size of an angle because they do not know how to use a ruler or protractor correctly. Remind them how to use a ruler and protractor to measure lines and angles before they start looking at drawing shapes accurately. Ask:

- Can you copy this shape accurately?

Children may draw the lines or angles the wrong way around (for example, if a shape has a length of 8 cm on the left-hand side and 9 cm on the right-hand side, this needs to be the same on the scale drawing). Ask:

- What type of angle have you drawn? Does the shape look accurate?

### STRENGTHENING UNDERSTANDING

Start by asking children to construct accurate copies of angles between two lines where the baseline is horizontal, the lengths of the lines are rounded to the nearest centimetre and the angles are multiples of 10. It may be useful to provide the baseline so children only need to draw the angle and the other line.

### GOING DEEPER

Give children diagrams of shapes that are not accurately drawn and that have missing lengths and ask them to accurately draw the shapes and find the actual lengths of the unknown sides. Provide descriptions of shapes and ask children to draw them from the words rather than from a diagram.

Ask children to draw an irregular polygon on a blank piece of paper then measure the size of the angles and the length of the sides. Children can then swap with a partner and make an accurate copy of their shape.

### KEY LANGUAGE

**In lesson:** protractor, midpoint, right angle, parallelogram, extend, length

**Other language to be used by the teacher:** accurate, halving, isometric, degrees, baseline, crosshairs, scale, interior, kite, rhombus

### STRUCTURES AND REPRESENTATIONS

Angles represented in lines and shapes

### RESOURCES

**Mandatory:** protractor, ruler, blank paper

**Optional:** dotted paper

 In the eTextbook of this lesson, you will find interactive links to a selection of teaching tools.

## Quick recap

As a class, discuss different methods for drawing right angles. Ask: *How many different methods can you think of?*

# Unit 13: Geometry – properties of shapes, Lesson 10

## Discover

**WAYS OF WORKING** Pair work

**ASK**

- Question 1 a): *How can you accurately draw the square? What equipment will you need?*
- Question 1 b): *How can you find the midpoint of each side?*

**IN FOCUS** Question 1 introduces the concept of drawing a shape accurately using a ruler and a protractor. Children will need to use their knowledge of right angles, midpoints and halving numbers.

**PRACTICAL TIPS** Encourage children to experiment with finding midpoints and using this to draw shapes within shapes, perhaps using coloured paper to demonstrate the different shapes they can make.

**ANSWERS**

Question 1 a): Children should accurately draw a square with a side length of 12 cm, using a ruler and protractor.

Question 1 b): Refer to the completed diagram in the **Share** section of the Textbook.

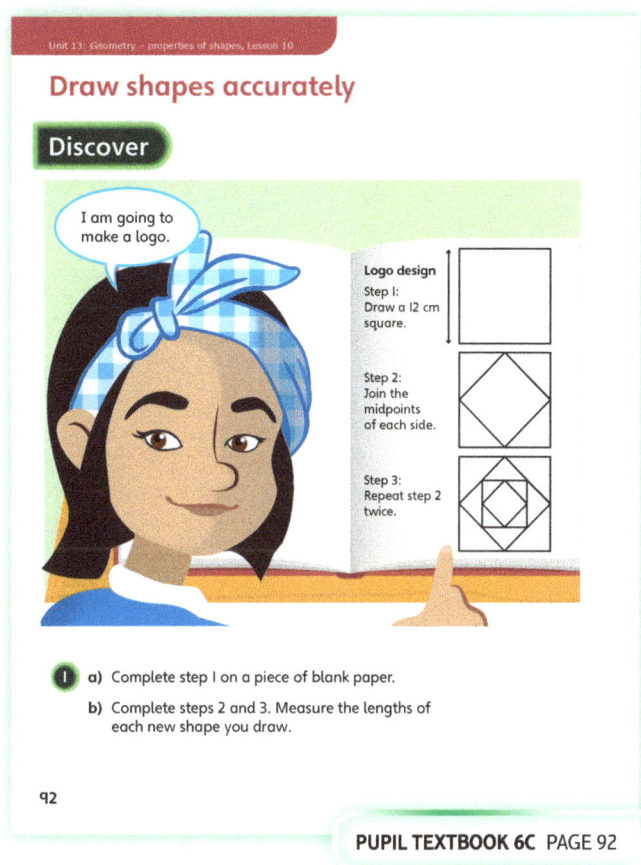

PUPIL TEXTBOOK 6C PAGE 92

## Share

**WAYS OF WORKING** Whole class teacher led

**ASK**

- Question 1 a): *Where could you start when drawing the square? What are the interior angles of a square? What can you use to make sure each angle is accurate? What do you know about the lengths of the sides? Can you check your square is correct by measuring?*
- Question 1 b): *What does midpoint mean? How can you find the midpoint? Can you draw another square?*

**IN FOCUS** Question 1 a) requires children to accurately draw a square, starting with a 12 cm horizontal line. Make sure they leave enough room above to draw the vertical lines. Children are required to use blank paper so they have to use a protractor to measure and draw the angles. Remind them that the interior angles of a square are right angles (90°). Encourage children to follow the steps described in **Share**, rotating the paper if necessary so the baseline is horizontal when measuring and drawing the angles. Encourage children to check their square is accurate by measuring the length of each line and the size of each angle.

For question 1 b), children are required to complete the logo. Discuss the definition of midpoint and ensure children are confident with dividing numbers by 2 using a suitable method. Encourage children to accurately measure the midpoint of each line using a ruler, then to join up these points. Children should realise that it is not necessary to use a protractor for this part. Encourage children to measure accurately, to the nearest millimetre, and to check that the sides of each square are the same.

**DEEPEN** Encourage children to draw other shapes within shapes using midpoints – for example, parallelograms inside rectangles.

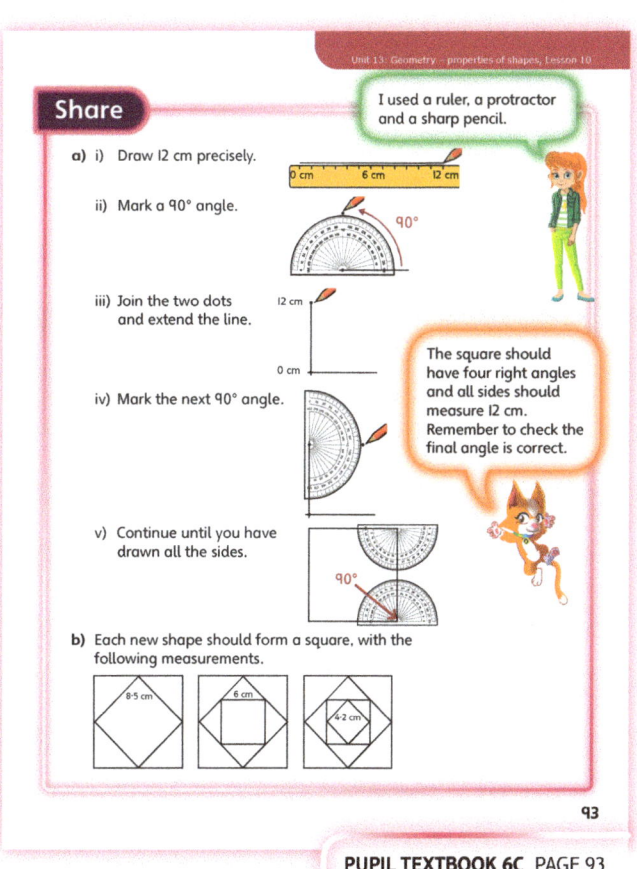

PUPIL TEXTBOOK 6C PAGE 93

# Unit 13: Geometry – properties of shapes, Lesson 10

## Think together

**WAYS OF WORKING** Whole class teacher led (I do, We do, You do)

**ASK**

- Question ❶: *How can you draw these angles? How can you use your ruler accurately? How can you line up your protractor? How can you check your drawing is accurate?*
- Question ❷: *Where will you begin? Which sides and angles can you draw? Can you extend the lines until they meet? What are the lengths of the missing sides? How can you check your drawings are accurate?*
- Question ❸: *What are the properties of parallelograms? How can you complete the shapes to make parallelograms? Can you use the dots and lines to help? How can you check your drawings are accurate?*

**IN FOCUS** Question ❶ requires children to draw angles and lines accurately using a ruler and protractor. Encourage children to try to draw the angles in a similar orientation, but explain that as long as the lengths and angle sizes are correct then they have completed an accurate copy. Encourage children to check their drawings by measuring all lines and angles when finished.

Question ❷ asks children to draw an accurate quadrilateral. They will need to draw lines and angles in a particular order to find the lengths of the unknown sides. The lines will need to be extended until they cross. Crossed lines do not need to be rubbed out.

Question ❸ requires children to complete the drawings of parallelograms. It may be necessary to discuss the definition and properties of a parallelogram.

**STRENGTHEN** To support understanding of drawing shapes, give children a starting line and guide them through the steps needed to complete the shapes accurately.

**DEEPEN** The final part of question ❸ allows children to explore multiple solutions, so encourage them to suggest several different parallelograms.

**ASSESSMENT CHECKPOINT** In question ❶, look for children confidently measuring to the nearest millimetre and using a protractor correctly and accurately.

In questions ❷ and ❸, look for children who can identify where to start and can work through the steps to draw the shapes in a logical order.

**ANSWERS**

Question ❶ a) to c): Children should accurately draw the lines and angles using a ruler and protractor.

Question ❷: Children should accurately draw the shape using a ruler and protractor.

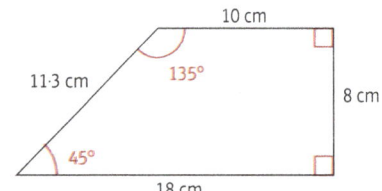

Question ❸: Check children have completed their diagrams accurately. Note that there are various possible answers to question ❸ c).

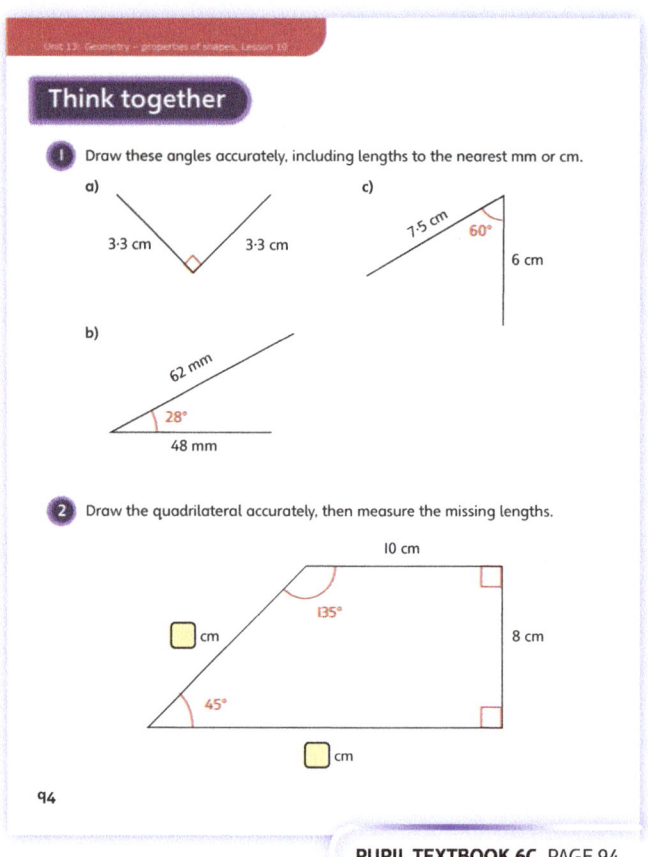

PUPIL TEXTBOOK 6C PAGE 94

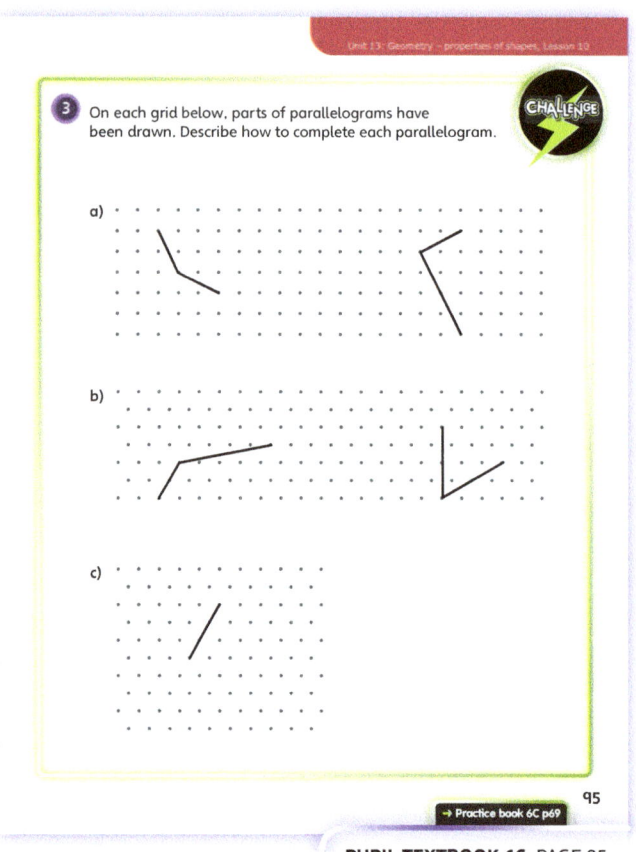

PUPIL TEXTBOOK 6C PAGE 95

130

# Unit 13: Geometry – properties of shapes, Lesson 10

## Practice

**WAYS OF WORKING** Independent thinking

**IN FOCUS** Question ❶ aims to consolidate children's understanding of drawing angles using a protractor.

Question ❷ builds on the **Think together** question. Watch out for children who try to measure the lengths and angles on the diagram given and those who copy the diagram in the wrong order and guess the length of the top line.

In question ❻, children are required to use their knowledge of the area and interior angles of rectangles to make accurate scale drawings. Encourage them to use a suitable written method, such as short division, to find the length of the missing sides. Ensure children use a protractor to accurately draw the interior right angles and encourage them to label all lengths and angles on their diagrams.

**STRENGTHEN** To strengthen learning, remind children to rotate the page so baselines are horizontal when drawing shapes.

**DEEPEN** Extend question ❺ by encouraging children to explore the different ways they can make the shapes using isometric paper.

Deepen learning with question ❻ by asking children to make accurate drawings of different shapes that have a certain area. This could include triangles as well as rectangles.

**ASSESSMENT CHECKPOINT** In questions ❶ and ❷, look for children confidently drawing lines using a ruler, lining up the protractor, using the correct scale and taking accurate measurements.

In questions ❸, ❹ and ❺, look for children who can confidently use known properties of shapes to complete the diagrams.

In question ❻, look for children who can confidently divide and work with with decimal answers and who can draw accurate rectangles, demonstrating understanding of the size of the interior angles.

**ANSWERS** Answers for the **Practice** part of the lesson can be found in the *Power Maths* online subscription.

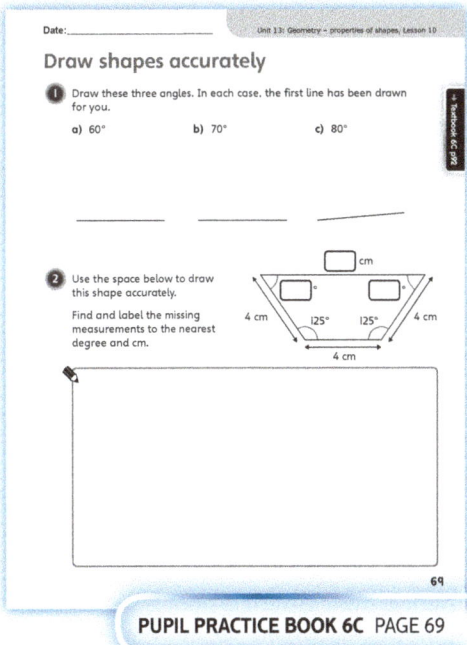

PUPIL PRACTICE BOOK 6C PAGE 69

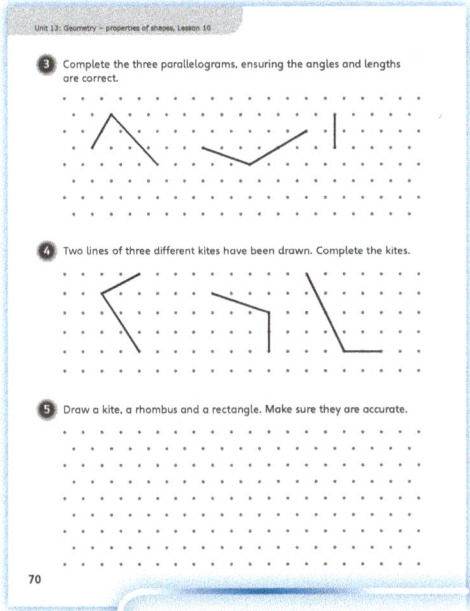

PUPIL PRACTICE BOOK 6C PAGE 70

## Reflect

**WAYS OF WORKING** Pair work

**IN FOCUS** This reflection gives an opportunity for children to describe how to draw an angle and what mistakes to avoid. Encourage them to reflect on the lesson and recall any mistakes or misconceptions.

**ASSESSMENT CHECKPOINT** Look for children who are able to confidently explain the steps needed to draw the angle accurately and who can highlight the mistakes to avoid.

**ANSWERS** Answers for the **Reflect** part of the lesson can be found in the *Power Maths* online subscription.

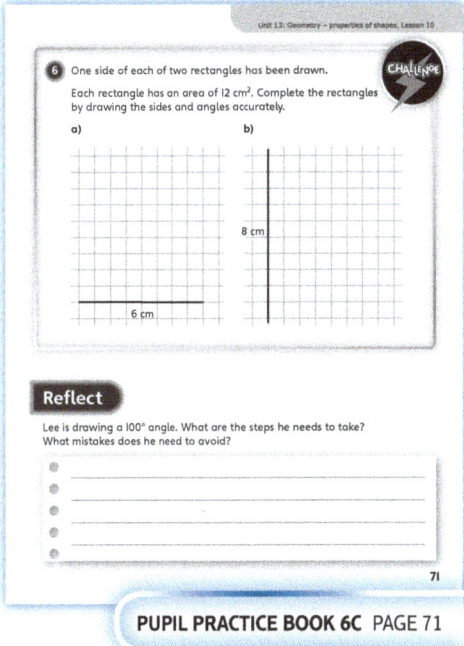

PUPIL PRACTICE BOOK 6C PAGE 71

> ## After the lesson
> - Can children accurately draw angles, lines and shapes, and measure missing lines and angles?
> - Can children complete drawings of shapes on dotted paper?

Unit 13: Geometry – properties of shapes, Lesson 11

# Nets of 3D shapes

### Learning focus
In this lesson, children will use their understanding of the properties of 3D shapes to develop their ability to identify shapes from nets and draw nets.

### Before you teach
- Can children recognise and name 3D shapes?
- Can children identify the properties of 3D shapes?

### NATIONAL CURRICULUM LINKS

**Year 6 Geometry – properties of shapes**

Recognise, describe and build simple 3D shapes, including making nets.

### ASSESSING MASTERY

Children can confidently identify 3D shapes from nets using the properties of shapes and can sketch nets, demonstrating understanding of the different ways in which nets can be represented.

### COMMON MISCONCEPTIONS

Children may focus on just some of the shapes of the faces in the net and become mixed up between 3D shapes. For example, children may see a triangular face and assume it must be a net for a pyramid. Also, children may forget to include one of the faces (usually the face that would be seen as the 'top' of a 3D shape). Ensure children are confident with identifying 3D shapes and their properties before completing this lesson. Ask:
- *Have you looked at all of the faces?*

Children may draw the correct faces for the net but join them in such a way that it would be impossible to fold up the net to make a 3D shape where all the edges touch. Ask:
- *Which edges will meet when the net is folded to make a 3D shape?*

### STRENGTHENING UNDERSTANDING

Encourage children to consolidate learning by focusing on paper versions of nets, so they can manipulate them to make 3D shapes.

### GOING DEEPER

Children could be challenged to explore all the possible nets for a particular 3D shape.

Give children a 3D shape with measurements on it and ask them to create a net that is to scale and can be folded to make an accurate copy of the 3D shape.

### KEY LANGUAGE

**In lesson:** nets, 3D, 2D, shape, face, sketch, overlap, pentagonal-based pyramid, **tetrahedron**, square-based pyramid, triangular prism, cuboid, **isometric** paper

**Other language to be used by the teacher:** accurate, form, edge, vertex, draw, cylinder, hexagonal-based pyramid, pentagonal prism, hexagonal prism

### STRUCTURES AND REPRESENTATIONS

Nets, 3D shapes

### RESOURCES

**Mandatory:** paper, scissors, ruler, protractor

**Optional:** paper nets

 In the eTextbook of this lesson, you will find interactive links to a selection of teaching tools.

### Quick recap

Ask children to name as many different 3D shapes as they can. Challenge them to give you a definition of each shape.

Unit 13: Geometry – properties of shapes, Lesson 11

# Discover

**WAYS OF WORKING** Pair work

**ASK**

- Question 1 a): *What is a net? What shapes do you recognise in the nets? Can you link these to 3D shapes?*
- Question 1 b): *What are the properties of a pentagonal-based pyramid? What is a pyramid?*

**IN FOCUS** Question 1 a) will introduce children to identifying 3D shapes from 2D nets. Question 1 b) gives children an opportunity to explore the concept of nets by sketching a net for a 3D shape.

**PRACTICAL TIPS** You could give children copies of the nets or ask them to draw their own versions. They can then physically fold the nets to discover the 3D shapes that will be created. It may be best to do this activity after children have tried the problem themselves, to reinforce the concepts discussed.

**ANSWERS**

Question 1 a): Triangular prism, square-based pyramid and tetrahedron (four triangular faces)

Question 1 b): Various nets can be drawn for a pentagonal-based pyramid. Two suggestions are shown in the **Share** section of the Textbook.

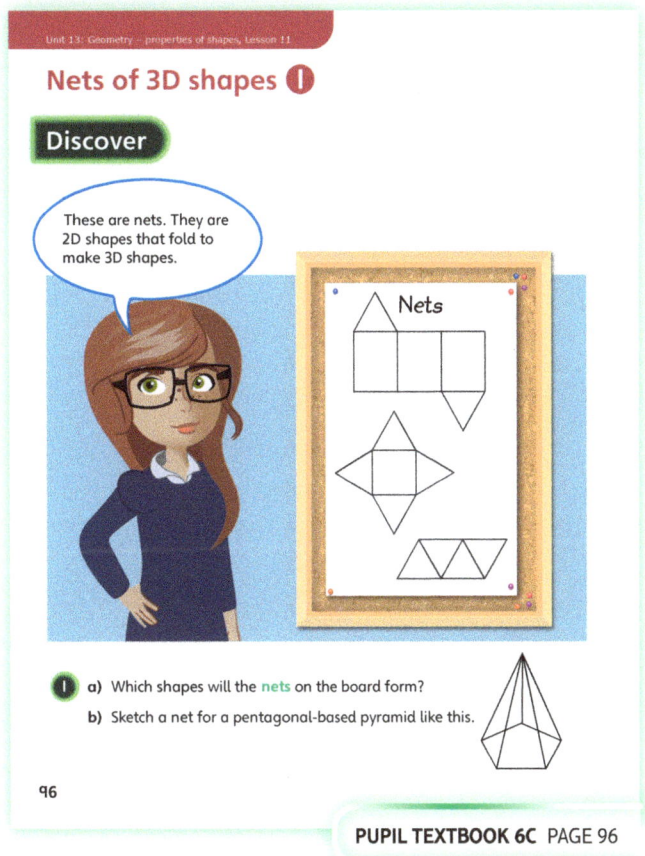

PUPIL TEXTBOOK 6C PAGE 96

# Share

**WAYS OF WORKING** Whole class teacher led

**ASK**

- Question 1 a): *What faces do the nets show? What 3D shapes have these faces? What are the properties of a prism? What are the properties of a pyramid?*
- Question 1 b): *What faces must the net contain? What does the diagram show? Are there any other ways to make a net? How can you check your answer?*

**IN FOCUS** In question 1 a), encourage children to use the descriptions of the 3D shapes and compare them with the nets, but ensure they do not rely on the diagrams of the 3D shapes to name them. Children should realise that they need to analyse the properties of the nets to identify the 3D shapes formed.

In question 1 b), discuss the key properties of a pentagonal-based pyramid and explore with children the different ways that the net can be sketched. Discuss the difference between a *sketch* and an accurate *drawing* – the net needs to be easily identifiable but does not need to be completely accurate or to scale. Emphasise the need to check that the net would fold to make a pentagonal-based pyramid.

**STRENGTHEN** Strengthen learning by using paper versions of the nets, so children can manipulate them in a concrete way.

**DEEPEN** Extend question 1 b) by challenging children to find all the possible nets for a pentagonal-based pyramid.

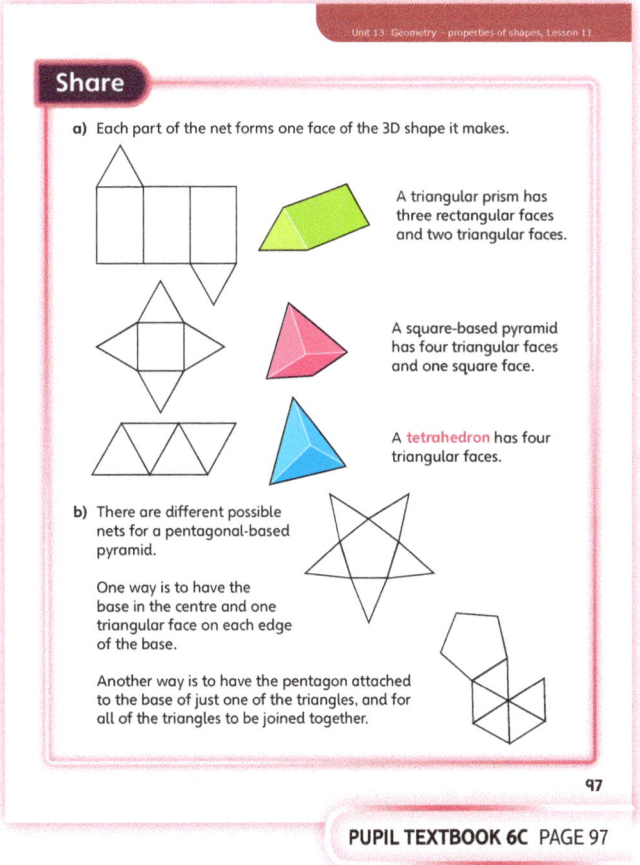

PUPIL TEXTBOOK 6C PAGE 97

# Think together

**WAYS OF WORKING** Whole class teacher led (I do, We do, You do)

**ASK**

- Question ❶: *What are the properties of a cuboid? Can you tell if any of the nets would **not** form a cuboid based on their properties? Which faces need to be next to each other? Would any of the faces overlap when folded to make a 3D shape?*
- Question ❷: *What are the properties of each shape? Where would the faces need to be on the nets? How can you check your answers?*
- Question ❸: *What shape is shown? What are its properties? How can you draw an accurate net?*

**IN FOCUS** In question ❶, children should be encouraged to consider the properties of a cuboid and then visualise the nets forming to make a 3D shape, thinking about any overlapping that would occur.

Question ❷ builds on the **Discover** section asking children to sketch a range of nets. Encourage children to discuss the properties of the shapes first, highlighting the number of faces and the faces that will need to be next to each other in the net. Remind children to check that their nets will form the 3D shapes after sketching them. Watch out for children who are unsure where to place the circles for the cylinder. Since the rectangular part wraps round the circles, the circles can be placed anywhere along the edge of the rectangle.

Question ❸ is more challenging: children are required to identify the shape and its properties and create an accurate drawing of its net. Children will need to ensure all the lengths in the net correspond to the lengths that are labelled on the 3D shape. Explore different techniques for drawing the net accurately and discuss Ash's suggestion.

**STRENGTHEN** To support understanding, children can explore the shapes using paper versions of the nets.

**DEEPEN** Question ❶ can be deepened by asking children to explore all the possible ways of correctly representing a net for a cuboid. Questions ❷ and ❸ can be extended by challenging children to sketch and draw the nets in different ways.

**ASSESSMENT CHECKPOINT** Question ❶ assesses children's ability to identify nets that form a cuboid. Questions ❷ and ❸ develop this, giving an opportunity to assess children's ability to sketch and draw accurately nets of 3D shapes.

**ANSWERS**

Question ❶: Only net D will form a cuboid.

Question ❷: Examples of the nets are:

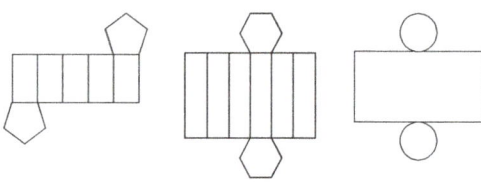

Question ❸: Children should draw a regular hexagon with sides of 4 cm and then construct an isosceles triangle attached to each side of the hexagon. The triangle should have sides of 4 cm, 8 cm and 8 cm.

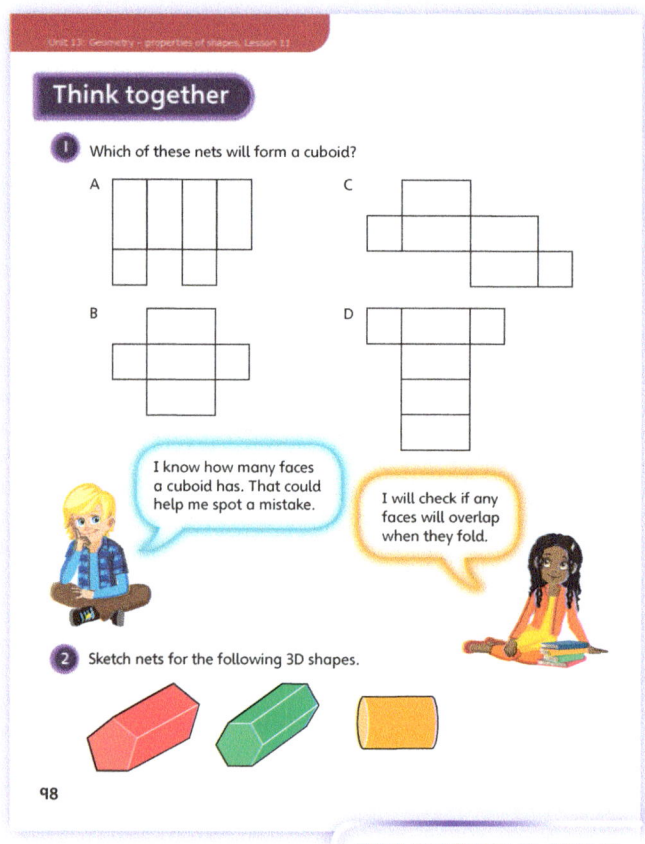

**PUPIL TEXTBOOK 6C** PAGE 98

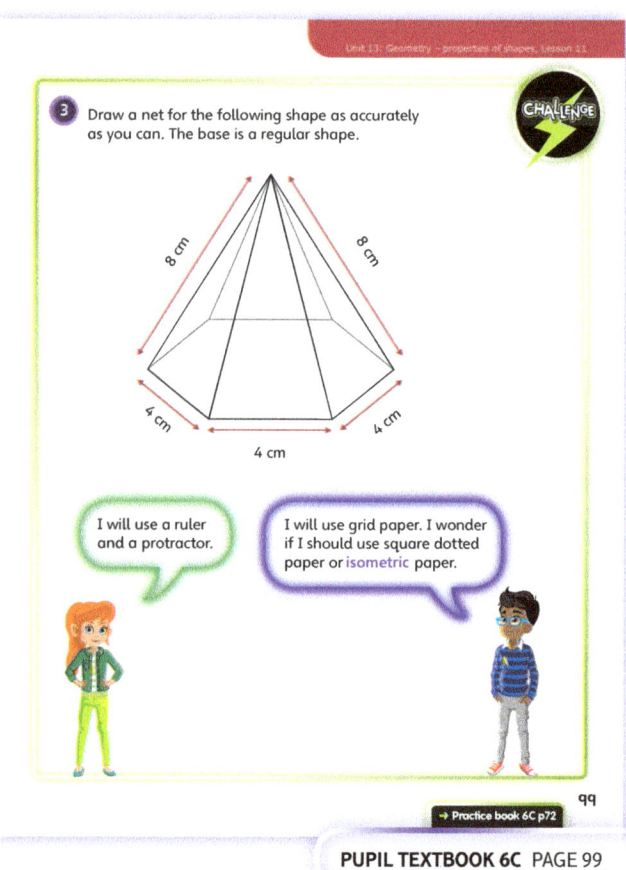

**PUPIL TEXTBOOK 6C** PAGE 99

# Unit 13: Geometry – properties of shapes, Lesson 11

## Practice

**WAYS OF WORKING** Independent thinking

**IN FOCUS** Question ❶ aims to consolidate children's understanding of nets by asking them to complete a matching activity. Encourage children to look at the properties of each 3D shape (for example, how many faces, edges or vertices each one has) and try to identify a net with the same properties.

Question ❷ develops children's understanding of nets being represented in different ways.

Questions ❸ and ❹ require children to apply their knowledge of nets. Encourage them to think about which edges will meet. Children will also need a ruler and pencil to complete question ❹, as they will need to divide the vertical faces into two parts.

In question ❺, children transition from recognising nets to actually drawing a net. There are different ways of drawing this net, but look for children having a sound understanding of which faces will meet when the net is folded up.

**STRENGTHEN** Strengthen learning by encouraging children to represent the nets on paper and to cut them out, so they can make the 3D shapes.

**DEEPEN** Extend question ❺ by challenging children to draw the net in a different way.

**ASSESSMENT CHECKPOINT** Questions ❸ and ❹ provide an opportunity to assess children's ability to reason with nets and visualise which faces will be where when the 3D shape is formed.

In question ❺, look for children who can demonstrate understanding of where the faces need to be so the net forms a cuboid.

**ANSWERS** Answers for the **Practice** part of the lesson can be found in the *Power Maths* online subscription.

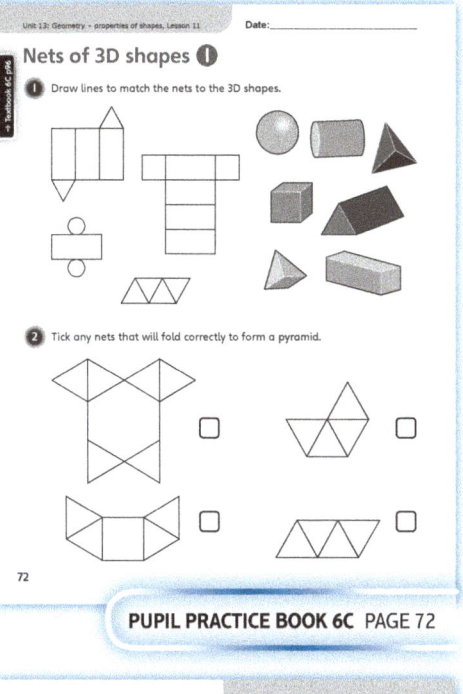

**PUPIL PRACTICE BOOK 6C** PAGE 72

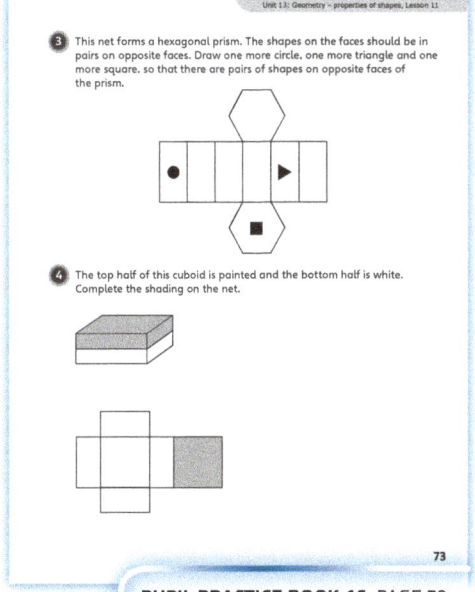

**PUPIL PRACTICE BOOK 6C** PAGE 73

## Reflect

**WAYS OF WORKING** Independent thinking

**IN FOCUS** This reflection asks children to draw a net of a pyramid. Discuss the different pyramids they could draw, encouraging them to reflect on the pyramids they have met in the lesson. Children should be able to describe the properties of pyramids compared with other 3D shapes, for example, prisms.

**ASSESSMENT CHECKPOINT** Look for children confidently choosing an appropriate pyramid and drawing an accurate net.

**ANSWERS** Answers for the **Reflect** part of the lesson can be found in the *Power Maths* online subscription.

## After the lesson ⏸

- Can children match a net to its 3D representation?
- Can children name a 3D shape when given its net?
- Can children identify which nets will fold correctly to form a 3D shape and draw a net accurately?

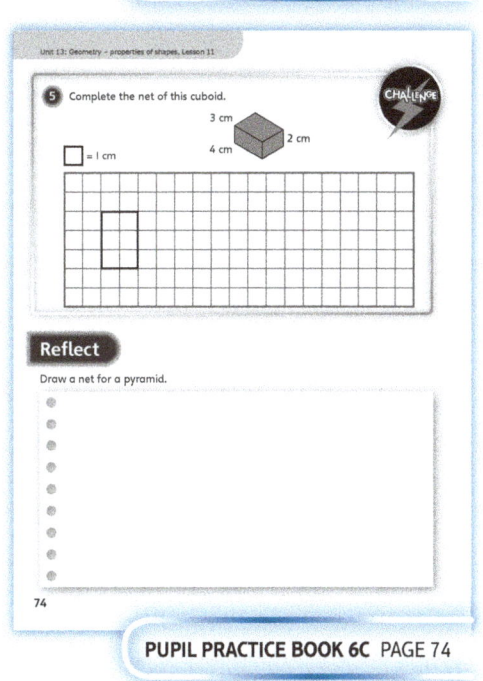

**PUPIL PRACTICE BOOK 6C** PAGE 74

Unit 13: Geometry – properties of shapes, Lesson 12

# Nets of 3D shapes 2

### Learning focus
In this lesson, children will build on their knowledge of nets of 3D shapes by exploring the multiple nets of a cube in the context of dice.

### Before you teach
- Can children identify the properties of a cube?
- Can children sketch nets?

#### NATIONAL CURRICULUM LINKS

**Year 6 Geometry – properties of shapes**

Recognise, describe and build simple 3D shapes, including making nets.

#### ASSESSING MASTERY

Children can confidently identify nets that will form cubes and can sketch nets, demonstrating understanding of faces that are opposite in cubes and the different ways in which the nets of a cube can be represented.

#### COMMON MISCONCEPTIONS

Children may not include all six faces of a cube in its net. Ensure they are confident with the properties of a cube. Ask:
- *How many faces make a cube?*

Children may draw the correct number of faces for the net of a cube, but have faces that overlap or edges that do not meet when the net is folded. When working with patterns on nets of cubes, children often get the patterns in the wrong place. Ask:
- *Which edges will meet when the net is folded? Which faces will be opposite each other when the net is folded?*

#### STRENGTHENING UNDERSTANDING

Children should be encouraged to strengthen learning by using construction materials to make cubes. They can also focus on paper versions of nets.

#### GOING DEEPER

Encourage children to deepen learning by exploring different patterns on the nets of a cube. Give them a picture of a cube that has a pattern on the faces and ask them to create the net. Ask: *Can you find more than one solution using different nets?*

#### KEY LANGUAGE

**In lesson:** nets, cube, form, face, opposite, dice, sketch, solution, view, construction, fold

**Other language to be used by the teacher:** total, edge, sides

#### STRUCTURES AND REPRESENTATIONS

Nets of cubes, cubes

#### RESOURCES

**Mandatory:** paper, scissors, ruler

**Optional:** dice, cubes, geometric construction set

 In the eTextbook of this lesson, you will find interactive links to a selection of teaching tools.

### Quick recap

As a class, discuss the properties of a cube. Ask: *How many different facts can you tell me about cubes?*

Unit 13: Geometry – properties of shapes, Lesson 12

# Discover

**WAYS OF WORKING** Pair work

**ASK**

- Question 1 a): *What 3D shape is a dice? Which faces are opposite one another? How can you work out which net is correct?*
- Question 1 b): *Which faces would be opposite each other?*

**IN FOCUS** Question 1 a) introduces children to the properties of a dice and asks them to identify the net that forms a correct dice. Question 1 b) gives children an opportunity to explore the various ways in which the dots on a net of a dice can be displayed.

**PRACTICAL TIPS** You could give children paper versions of the nets, to fold. However, children will need to be able to reason in an abstract way, so it may help to complete the practical activity after children have thought about the problem. This concept could also be introduced during an art session with children decorating the different sides of a cube and examining how the faces of the net fit together.

**ANSWERS**

Question 1 a): The net must fold to make a cube and opposite faces of the dice must total 7. Only net D is correct.

Question 1 b): There are multiple solutions. The opposite faces have been colour coded. Pairs totalling 7 must go on the same colour. Here is one solution:

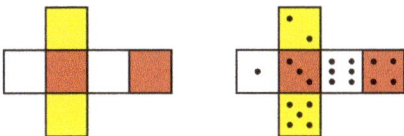

# Share

**WAYS OF WORKING** Whole class teacher led

**ASK**

- Question 1 a): *Which numbers must be opposite each other? How do you know? Which faces are opposite each other in the nets shown? How do you know? Do all the nets form cubes correctly? Which net is correct?*
- Question 1 b): *Which faces must be opposite each other? What total must the numbers make? What does the diagram show? Are there any other ways to make a net of a cube?*

**IN FOCUS** Question 1 a) introduces children to the properties of a net for a dice. First discuss with children what 3D shape a dice is and then discuss the properties before asking children which pairs of numbers total 7. Encourage children to analyse the given nets based on which faces are opposite one another. Children should realise that numbers which are next to each other in the net cannot be opposite each other in the 3D shape. With net B highlight that this would not form a cube correctly. This is an important concept that children need to be able to identify.

In question 1 b), encourage children to discuss which faces are opposite on the net of the cube and challenge them to explore all possible solutions.

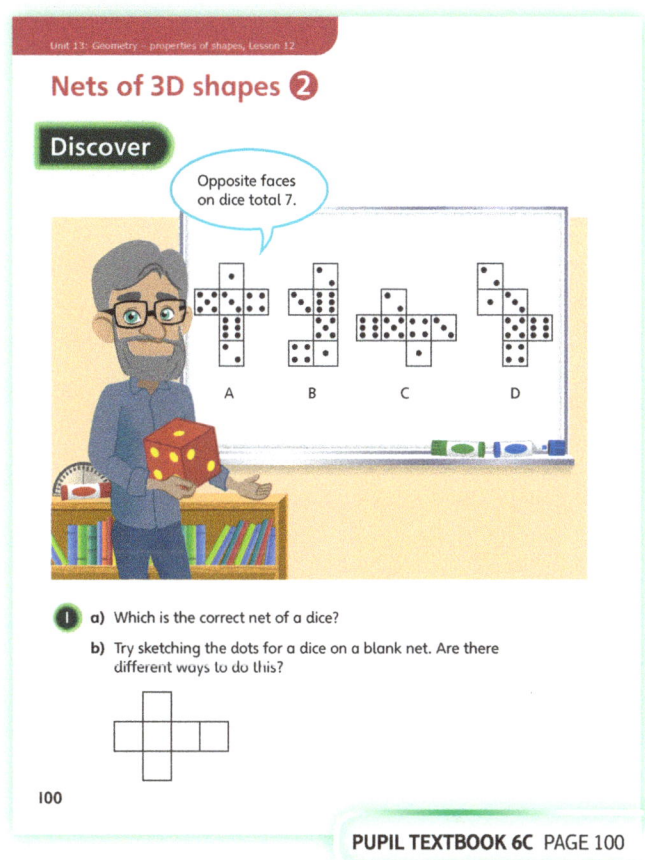

PUPIL TEXTBOOK 6C PAGE 100

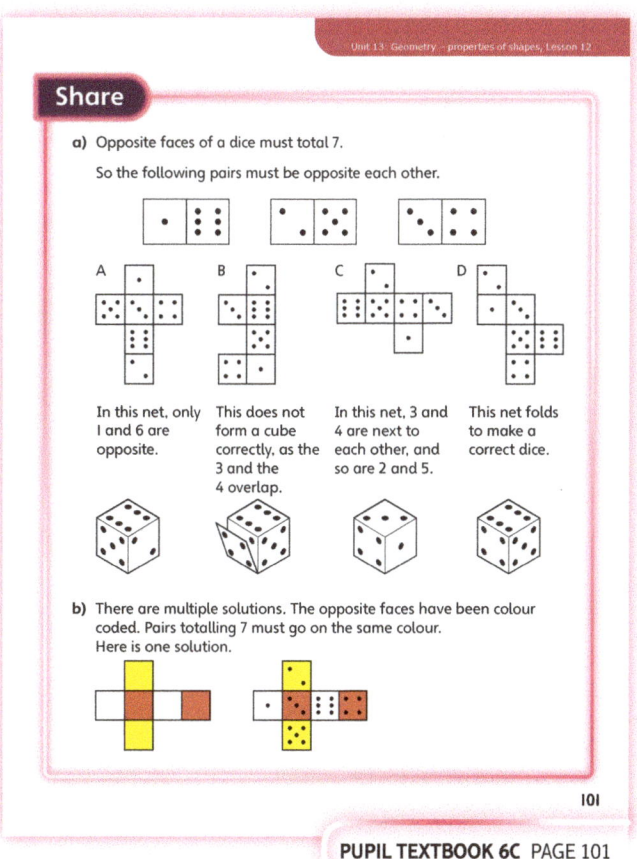

PUPIL TEXTBOOK 6C PAGE 101

137

Unit 13: Geometry – properties of shapes, Lesson 12

# Think together

**WAYS OF WORKING** Whole class teacher led (I do, We do, You do)

**ASK**

- Question ❶: *Can you tell if any of the nets would not form a cube? Would any of the faces overlap when folded to make a 3D shape?*
- Question ❷: *Are there any that you can rule out easily?*
- Question ❸: *How many faces need to be drawn?*

**IN FOCUS** Question ❶ aims to develop understanding of forming cubes from nets and addresses common misconceptions. Encourage children to consider the properties of a cube and to visualise each net folding to make a cube, thinking about any overlapping that would occur.

Question ❷ asks children to identify the cubes that could have been formed from a net. Watch out for children making common mistakes, such as choosing A because it shows three triangles even though it would be impossible for the faces to meet in this way. Encourage children to attempt the problem abstractly before making a paper version to fold and check.

Question ❸ allows children to explore the different possible nets of a cube. Discuss nets that are drawn in different orientations, as per Dexter's comment.

**STRENGTHEN** Encourage children to explore the shapes using paper versions of the nets or concrete materials.

**DEEPEN** Question ❷ can be deepened by asking children to explore all the possible views of the cube from this net. Challenge children by giving them another patterned cube and asking them to draw the net or vice versa.

**ASSESSMENT CHECKPOINT** Question ❶ assesses children's ability to identify nets that form a cube. Question ❷ develops this, giving an opportunity to assess children's ability to work out how the cube could look once it is formed. Look for children who can confidently identify which views are possible using a paper version or otherwise.

Question ❸ assesses children's ability to find nets of cubes. Look for children who can systematically work through the problem to find all possible solutions.

**ANSWERS**

Question ❶: Nets A and D correctly form a cube.

Question ❷: Diagrams C and D are views of the cube.

Question ❸: Reena is correct. There are eleven different nets that form a cube.

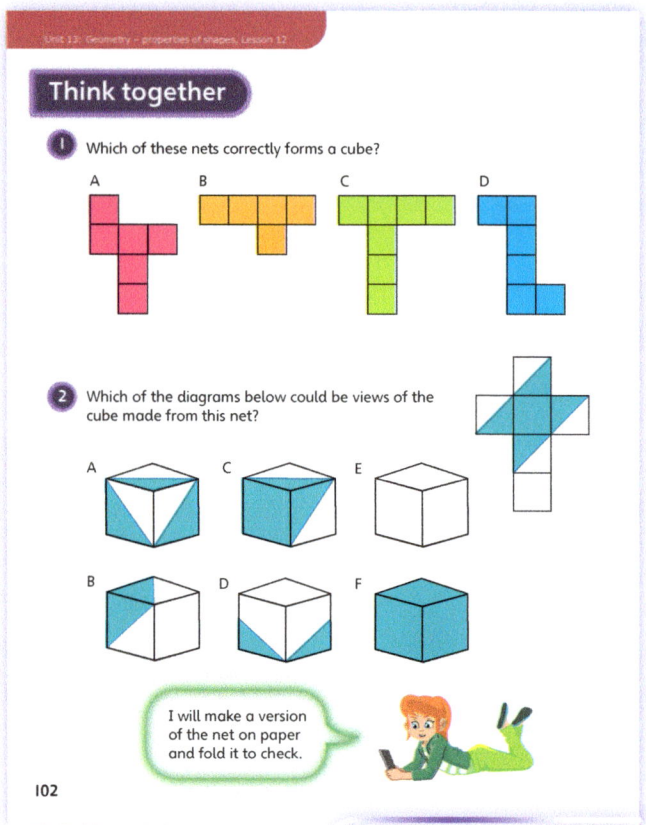

PUPIL TEXTBOOK 6C PAGE 102

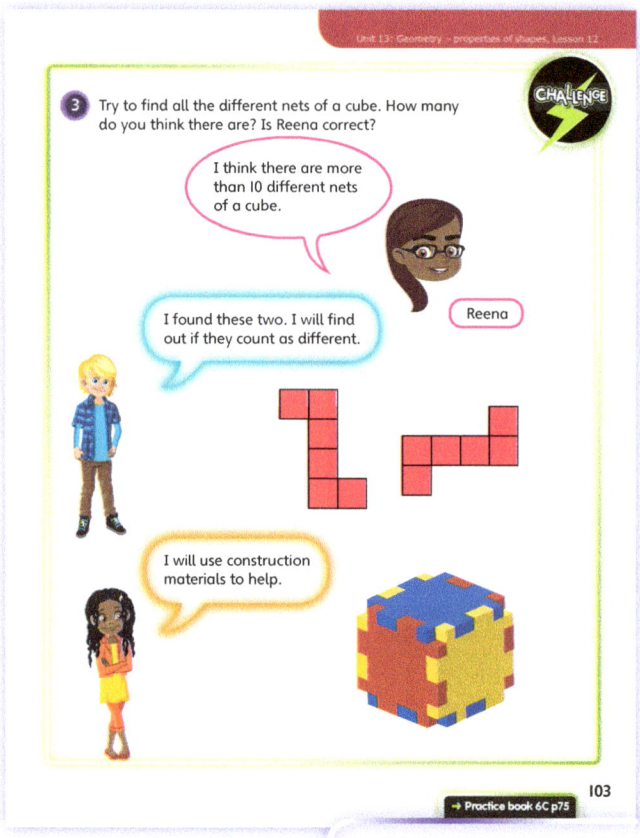

PUPIL TEXTBOOK 6C PAGE 103

# Unit 13: Geometry – properties of shapes, Lesson 12

## Practice

**WAYS OF WORKING** Independent thinking

**IN FOCUS** Questions ① to ③ aim to consolidate children's understanding of representing the net of a cube in different ways. The questions gradually reduce scaffolding by progressing from nets given, to completing a net, to drawing nets independently where children will need to identify opposite faces.

Question ④ allows children to apply their knowledge of nets in a different context and develops children's understanding of which vertices will meet when a cube is formed.

Question ⑤ asks children to use their knowledge of nets and volume to answer the question.

**STRENGTHEN** When identifying and sketching nets, encourage children to represent the nets on paper and cut them out, so they can make the 3D shapes. Ask: *How do the 3D shapes help you check the nets are correct? What faces are opposite each other? Do any of the sides overlap?*

**DEEPEN** Question ④ can be explored further by challenging children to draw the net in a different way.

**ASSESSMENT CHECKPOINT** Questions ① and ② assess children's ability to identify nets of a cube and complete nets when given four of the faces.

Question ③ gives an opportunity to assess children's ability to draw nets of cubes independently. Look for children who can confidently draw the net in three different ways, demonstrating understanding of opposite faces.

Question ④ assesses children's ability to complete a pattern on a net. Look for children who can complete this abstractly or those who make a paper version correctly, demonstrating an understanding of where the vertices and edges will meet so the pattern is formed correctly.

**ANSWERS** Answers for the **Practice** part of the lesson can be found in the *Power Maths* online subscription.

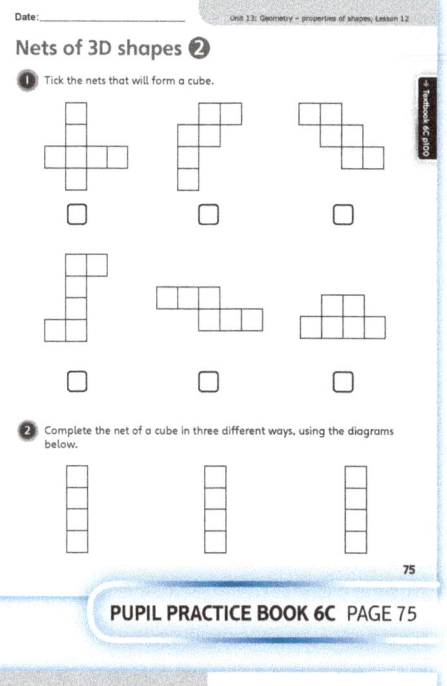

PUPIL PRACTICE BOOK 6C PAGE 75

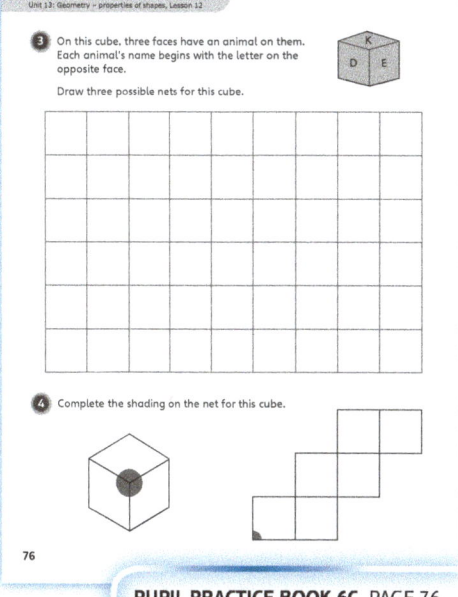

PUPIL PRACTICE BOOK 6C PAGE 76

## Reflect

**WAYS OF WORKING** Independent thinking or pair work

**IN FOCUS** This reflection gives an opportunity to check children's understanding of identifying nets that form a cube. Encourage children to explain in their own words and to draw on key language, such as faces and edges.

**ASSESSMENT CHECKPOINT** Look for children who can confidently identify if a net will form a cube, demonstrating understanding of the properties of a cube and the edges of faces that will meet.

**ANSWERS** Answers for the **Reflect** part of the lesson can be found in the *Power Maths* online subscription.

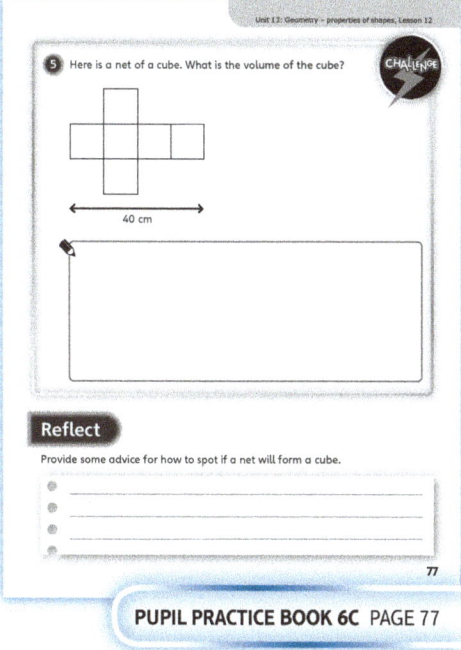

PUPIL PRACTICE BOOK 6C PAGE 77

### After the lesson ⏸

- Can children identify opposite faces on the net of a cube?
- Can children identify which nets will form a cube?
- Can children complete nets of cubes, including nets of cubes that contain patterns?

# Unit 13: Geometry – properties of shapes

# End of unit check

**Don't forget the unit assessment grid in your Power Maths online subscription.**

**WAYS OF WORKING** Group work teacher led

**IN FOCUS**
- Question ❶ assesses children's ability to use a protractor to measure an angle.
- Questions ❷, ❸ and ❺ assess children's ability to use angle facts to calculate missing angles in shapes and on lines. Question ❺ is more of a problem-solving question.
- Question ❹ assesses children's knowledge of the properties of shapes.
- Question ❻ is a SATs-style question which allows children to apply their skills to draw a 2D representation of a 3D shape. Encourage children to draw the net accurately.

**ANSWERS AND COMMENTARY** Children who have mastered the concepts in this unit are able to confidently measure angles, understand and recall facts about angles in shapes and lines, fluently use shape properties to reason and accurately draw and recognise nets of 3D shapes.

In questions ❸ and ❺, encourage children to label any angles they know or can work out. If necessary, remind them that a right angle is 90°. Strengthen understanding by encouraging children to use a written method, such as the column method, for their calculations.

In question ❻, encourage children to identify the properties of the cuboid and to discuss the length and width of the faces. Common misconceptions include not drawing the correct number of faces, not drawing equivalent faces opposite one another, or drawing faces so that they will overlap when the net is folded to make the 3D shape.

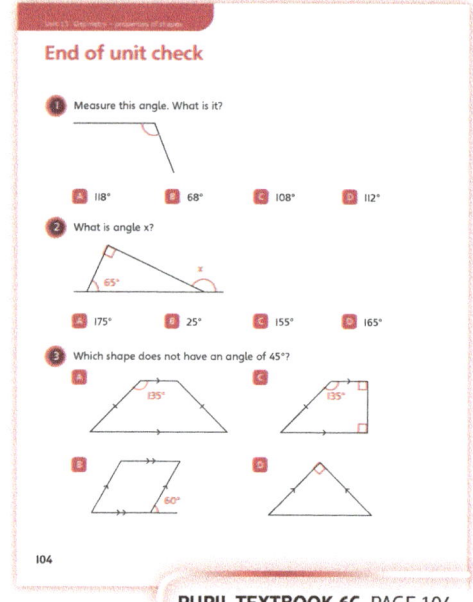

**PUPIL TEXTBOOK 6C** PAGE 104

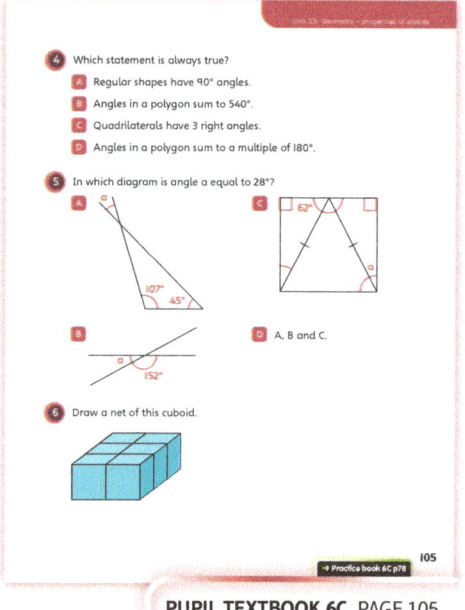

**PUPIL TEXTBOOK 6C** PAGE 105

| Q | A | WRONG ANSWERS AND MISCONCEPTIONS | STRENGTHENING UNDERSTANDING |
|---|---|---|---|
| 1 | D | A and C suggest that children have misread the numbers or not aligned the protractor correctly. B suggests children have looked at the wrong scale. | Encourage children to rotate the paper, so the baseline is at the bottom. |
| 2 | C | A and D suggest that children have miscalculated when adding the numbers. B suggests children have worked out the unknown in the triangle. | Encourage children to write on any angles they know or can work out. Recap the relevant angle rules. |
| 3 | B | Other answers suggest that children do not have a sound understanding of the properties of shapes or have miscalculated. | Encourage children to discuss the properties of each shape. |
| 4 | D | | |
| 5 | D | | |
| 6 | Correct net | Look out for and correct any common misconceptions. | Children could draw their net on paper and cut it out to check their answer. |

# Unit 13: Geometry – properties of shapes

## My journal

**WAYS OF WORKING** Independent thinking

**ANSWERS AND COMMENTARY**

Question **1** requires children to work out missing angles by using their knowledge of the properties of angles in a triangle rather than by measuring with a protractor. Using the information given, children should work out that they need to divide the bar model into 10 equal sections. p occupies one section, r occupies 3 sections and q occupies 6 sections.

p = 18°, q = 108°, r = 54°

Question **2** aims to consolidate angle facts and assesses understanding of the steps needed to find unknown angles. Look for children who can identify where to start, confidently explain the steps needed using angle facts, demonstrate understanding of the properties of a square and show fluency in addition and subtraction.

a = b = h = 63°, c = 99°, d = 72°, e = g = 81°, f = 117°

Question **3** requires children to work 'backwards' to identify the 3D shapes that nets will make. Look for children who can confidently describe how they can identify if a net will form a 3D shape, demonstrating understanding of the properties of shapes and edges of faces that will meet.

A: not a net; B: pyramid; C: pyramid; D: cube; E: prism; F: not a net; H: prism

## Power check

**WAYS OF WORKING** Independent thinking

**ASK**

- *How confident do you feel about the properties of shapes?*

## Power puzzle

**WAYS OF WORKING** Pair work or small groups

**IN FOCUS** Use this activity to assess children's understanding of shape properties. Look for children who make the same polygons, but in different orientations – encourage them to make unique polygons each time.

**ANSWERS AND COMMENTARY** There are various answers to this puzzle.

Encourage experimentation with each polygon made and ask children to name the shapes and discuss their properties using key words, such as regular or irregular. Watch out for children who join the triangles like this: this is not a polygon. To be a polygon, each side must intersect with other sides at two distinct vertices.

This question can be explored further by encouraging children to investigate the lines of symmetry and the interior angles of the polygons.

## After the unit

- Can children measure angles and draw shapes accurately?
- Can they calculate unknown angles in shapes and on lines using known angle facts and the properties of shapes?
- Can children draw and identify nets of 3D shapes?

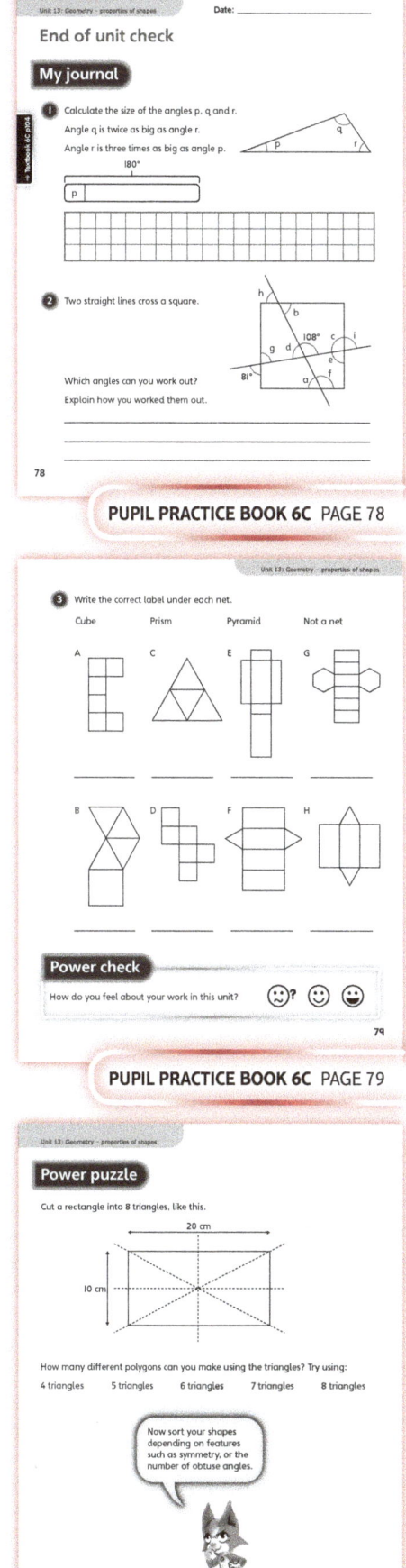

PUPIL PRACTICE BOOK 6C PAGE 78

PUPIL PRACTICE BOOK 6C PAGE 79

PUPIL PRACTICE BOOK 6C PAGE 80

**Strengthen** and **Deepen** activities for this unit can be found in the *Power Maths* online subscription.

# Unit 14
## Geometry – position and direction

**Mastery Expert tip!** 'My class really liked it when we played practical games, such as coordinate battleships and guess my shape, which involved them practising and using the skills from this unit in a fun, games-based way.'

**Don't forget to watch the Unit 14 video!**

### WHY THIS UNIT IS IMPORTANT

This unit exposes children to coordinates in all four quadrants for the first time. Children are encouraged to combine their knowledge of the properties of shapes with their coordinate knowledge and to reason and solve problems involving shapes on a coordinate grid. This provides a great opportunity to develop their problem solving and reasoning skills and allows them to make connections between areas of mathematics. Finally, this unit is important as it exposes children to translations and reflections on a coordinate grid for the first time.

### WHERE THIS UNIT FITS

→ Unit 13: Geometry – properties of shapes
→ **Unit 14: Geometry – position and direction**
→ Unit 15: Problem solving

This unit builds on work in Year 5, when children were introduced to coordinates being used to describe the positions of points on grids, and when they developed the skill of plotting coordinates in the first quadrant. It also builds upon work on the properties of shapes, and it encourages children to make connections between the properties of shape and coordinates to solve increasingly complex problems involving shapes in all four quadrants.

Before they start this unit, it is expected that children:
- know that a pair of coordinates describes the position of a point within a grid
- can plot coordinates in the first quadrant
- can read coordinates in the first quadrant
- understand key properties of a range of shapes, for example, the number of vertices, the relationship between side lengths, and the number of sides of a range of common regular and irregular polygons.

### ASSESSING MASTERY

Children who have mastered this unit can plot and read coordinates in all four quadrants. They can identify coordinates that form the vertices of a range of common shapes, and they can solve increasingly complex problems involving shapes in all four quadrants. They can reflect points and shapes on a coordinate grid in the x- and y-axes as well as in simple diagonal lines, and they can carry out multi-step translations and reflections. Finally, children are able to extend these skills to problems where they are given just the coordinates and no coordinate grid.

| COMMON MISCONCEPTIONS | STRENGTHENING UNDERSTANDING | GOING DEEPER |
|---|---|---|
| Children may start with the y-axis, leading to transposed coordinates, for example, (⁻3,4) becomes (4,⁻3). | Encourage children to use a mnemonic such as 'y's up that x is across' or 'go along the corridor then up the stairs'. | Increase the complexity of the problems one stage at a time. For example, children could consider what the different possibilities are when completing a shape based on two given pairs of coordinates. They should also be encouraged to begin to create their own problems involving shapes and reflections or translations for others to solve. |
| Children may incorrectly identify properties of shapes and therefore make incorrect connections and assumptions when seeing them on a coordinate grid. | Encourage children to draw or manipulate the shapes separately and identify their properties, then support children in applying these properties to the problem they are facing involving a coordinate grid. | |

# Unit 14: Geometry – position and direction

### UNIT STARTER PAGES

Talk through the key learning points and the key vocabulary as a class.

### STRUCTURES AND REPRESENTATIONS

**Coordinate grid with one quadrant:** Children are reintroduced to coordinate grids with just one quadrant. They will plot coordinates in the first quadrant.

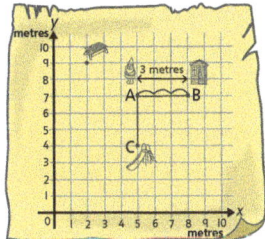

**Coordinate grid with four quadrants:** Children are then introduced to coordinate grids which show all four quadrants. They will use these to plot coordinates in all four quadrants, work out missing coordinates in shapes and reason about shapes using their coordinates.

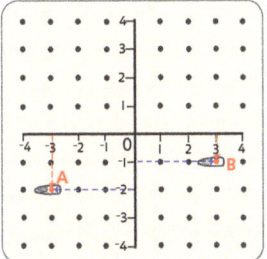

**Zero-centred number line:** Children may also benefit from using a 0-centred number line and thinking about how it relates to the $x$- and $y$-axes of a coordinate grid. This will help them to correctly identify where to plot coordinates with positive or negative values.

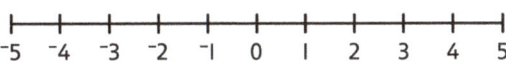

### KEY LANGUAGE

There is some key language that children will need to know as part of the learning in this unit:

→ plotting, coordinates, quadrant, four quadrants, point, axis, axes, $x$-axis, $y$-axis, grid, $x$-coordinate, $y$-coordinate, positive, negative

→ vertices, vertex, square, side, rectangle, triangle, equilateral, oblong, shape, irregular, hexagon, identical, similar, parallelogram

→ perimeter, metre (m), distance, length, long

→ horizontal, vertical

→ half-way, line, properties, value, reason

→ translate, translation, reflect, reflection, original, left, down, up, right, mirror, away, diagonal

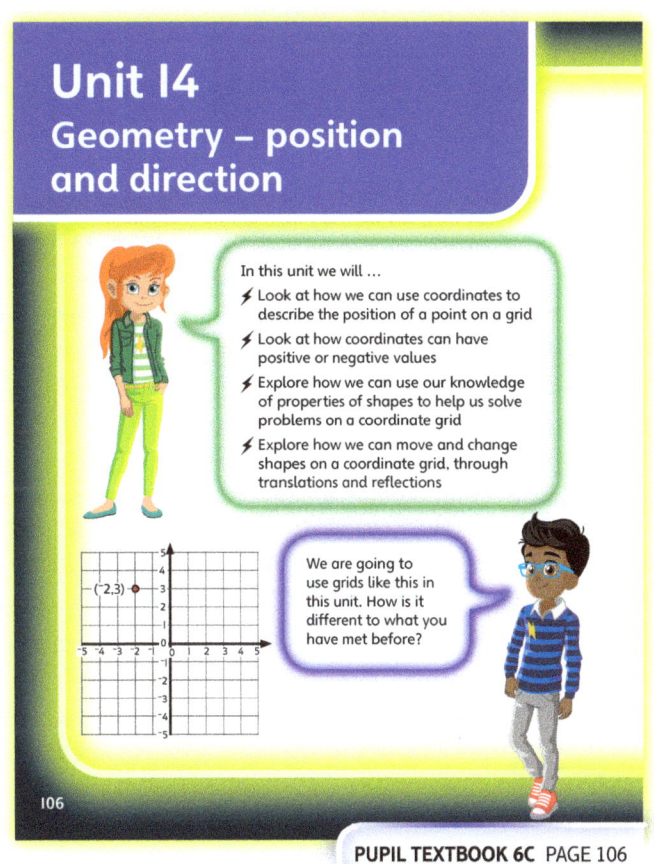

PUPIL TEXTBOOK 6C PAGE 106

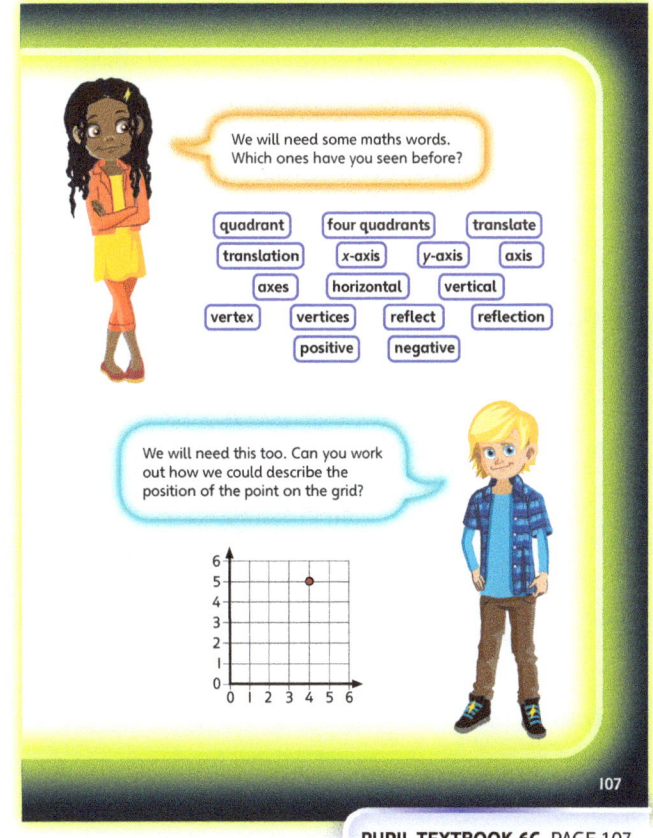

PUPIL TEXTBOOK 6C PAGE 107

Unit 14: Geometry – position and direction, Lesson 1

# The first quadrant

### Learning focus
In this lesson, children will revisit how to plot coordinates in the first quadrant. They will solve problems that involve reasoning using the properties of shape, and their coordinate knowledge.

### Before you teach
- Are children secure in their knowledge of the properties of shapes that they covered in Year 5?
- Are children able to plot and identify coordinates in the first quadrant?

### NATIONAL CURRICULUM LINKS

**Year 6 Geometry – position and direction**

Describe positions on the full coordinate grid (all four quadrants).

### ASSESSING MASTERY

Children can accurately plot coordinates in the first quadrant. Children can solve problems that involve completing the missing vertices of shapes, and applying their knowledge of shape properties.

### COMMON MISCONCEPTIONS

Children may misremember the names of each axis, calling the x-axis the y-axis and vice versa. Ask:
- *What do you call the horizontal axis? What do you call the vertical axis? How can you remember this?*

Children may think the coordinates are written with the y-axis value first, rather than the x-axis value. Ask:
- *Which axis value do you write first? Is there a saying you could use to help you remember this, such as 'You go along the corridor (x) before you go up the stairs (y)'?*

### STRENGTHENING UNDERSTANDING

Encourage children to physically plot coordinates in the first quadrant and to use matchsticks and other items to create shapes. They can then use these to reason about the properties of shapes and investigate the answers to the problems presented in this lesson. For example, they can use matchsticks to represent two side lengths of a square and investigate what this shows about the values of the other vertices.

### GOING DEEPER

Encourage children to create their own problems involving shapes on a coordinate grid for others to solve. Ask children if they can work out the minimum amount of information they must give for the problem to be solvable.

### KEY LANGUAGE

**In lesson:** plotting, coordinates, quadrant, point, vertices, vertex, horizontal, vertical, axis, **x-axis**, **y-axis**, grid, identical, symmetrical

**Other language to be used by the teacher:** properties, oblong

### STRUCTURES AND REPRESENTATIONS

Coordinate grids with the first quadrant

### RESOURCES

**Mandatory:** coordinate grids with the first quadrant

**Optional:** matchsticks, counters

 In the eTextbook of this lesson, you will find interactive links to a selection of teaching tools.

### Quick recap

Lead a class discussion about what the coordinate pair (2,5) means. Ask: *What does it not mean?* For example, it means 2 along and 5 up. It does not mean 5 along and 2 up.

Unit 14: Geometry – position and direction, Lesson 1

# Discover

**WAYS OF WORKING** Pair work

**ASK**

- Question 1 a): *What information can you use from the diagram to help you solve this problem?*
- Question 1 a): *What do you know about the properties of squares? How can you use this information to help you solve the problem?*
- Question 1 a): *How can you work out the coordinates for the missing vertex?*
- Question 1 b): *What does 'perimeter' mean? How can you use the information from the diagram to help you calculate it?*

**IN FOCUS** Question 1 a) encourages children to visually reason about properties of a square and asks them to complete the square, based on three given vertices. Children are expected to identify that the sides of a square are all the same length, and understand that they are then able to work out the coordinates of the missing vertex.

**PRACTICAL TIPS** Provide children with practical experiences of plotting coordinates and completing shapes, including using counters or other objects to mark coordinates, and using matchsticks to create polygons on the coordinate grid and explore their properties.

**ANSWERS**

Question 1 a): D is at the coordinate (8,4).

Question 1 b): The perimeter is 3 × 4 = 12 metres.

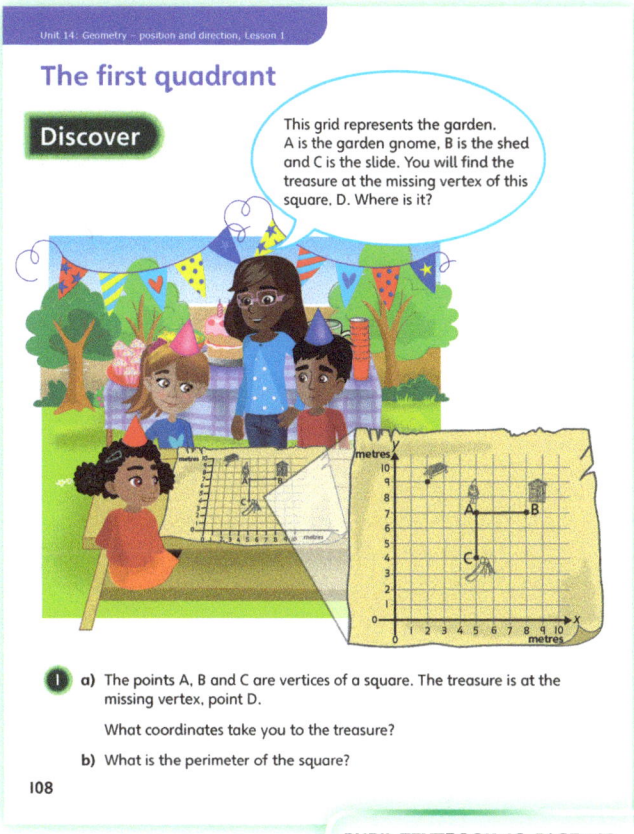

PUPIL TEXTBOOK 6C PAGE 108

# Share

**WAYS OF WORKING** Whole class teacher led

**ASK**

- Question 1 a): *How can you use your knowledge of the properties of squares to help you?*
- Question 1 a): *Could you work out the coordinates of the missing vertex in a different way?*
- Question 1 b): *What information could you use to help you work out the perimeter of the square?*

**IN FOCUS** In question 1 a), children are encouraged to work out the length of a given side of the square, and therefore reason that the missing points must be the same distance down from (8,7) or right from (5,4). It is important that children understand that they could use either (8,7) or (5,4) along with their knowledge of the side length in order to calculate the coordinates of the missing vertex.

In question 1 b), children are encouraged to draw on their knowledge that the perimeter of a square is 4 times the length of one side, and to use this and the given side length to calculate the perimeter of the square.

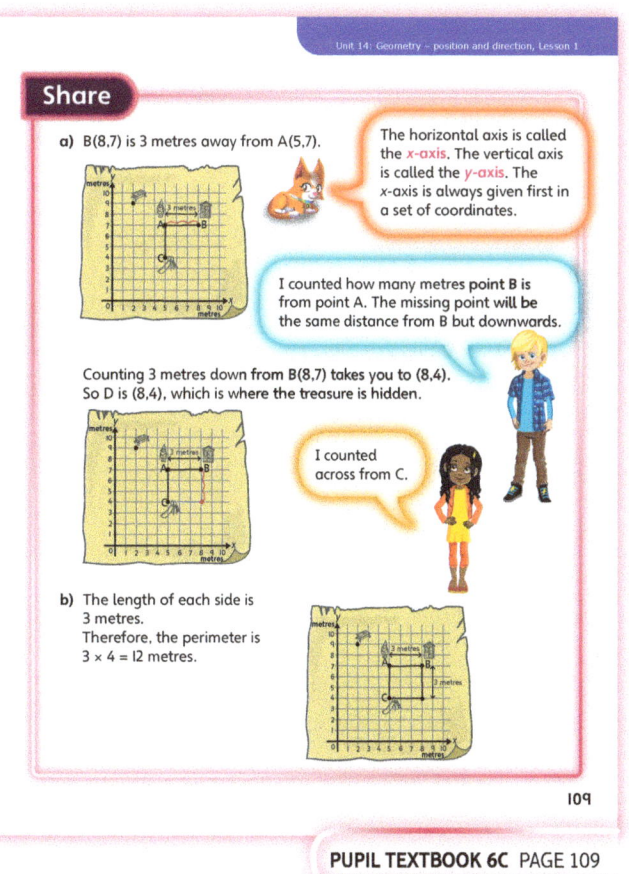

PUPIL TEXTBOOK 6C PAGE 109

# Unit 14: Geometry – position and direction, Lesson 1

## Think together

**WAYS OF WORKING** Whole class teacher led (I do, We do, You do)

**ASK**

- Questions 1 a) and b): *What do you know about the properties of rectangles and squares that could help you answer this question?*
- Question 1 a): *Can you point to where the missing vertex will be? What coordinates is this point at?*
- Question 1 b): *How long is each side of this square? Can you use this to help you work out the missing vertices? Is there more than one possible set of answers for this question? Why is this?*
- Question 2: *How can you work out the missing coordinates without a coordinate grid? Can you use the properties of a rectangle to help you?*

**IN FOCUS** Question 2 introduces children to working out the missing coordinates of shapes that are not presented on a grid. This requires them to apply the knowledge and strategies developed in **Discover**, **Share** and question 1 of this section. They should complete the missing coordinates by using the properties of shapes to calculate them. For example, they should understand that point C is vertically above point B, and will therefore share the same x-axis value as point B.

**STRENGTHEN** To support children in working out the missing vertices in question 2 where a grid is not provided, initially create a similar style question on a coordinate grid. Ask children what they notice about the x and y values of each vertex, and then encourage them to apply the same reasoning to question 2.

**DEEPEN** Children should be encouraged to reason about and use the properties of a wider range of shapes in order to solve coordinate problems in the first quadrant. Question 3 provides some initial exposure to this. Children could be encouraged to create their own problems for partners that use a wider range of shapes.

**ASSESSMENT CHECKPOINT** Use questions 1 a) and b) to assess whether children can apply their knowledge of the properties of shapes to solve problems presented on a coordinate grid. Do they understand why Astrid says she could count up or across?

**ANSWERS**

Question 1 a): (4,3)

Question 1 b): (1,2) and (1,6) or (9,2) and (9,6)

Question 2: B (8,4), C (8,7), D (3,7)

Question 3: A (13,7), B (4,13)

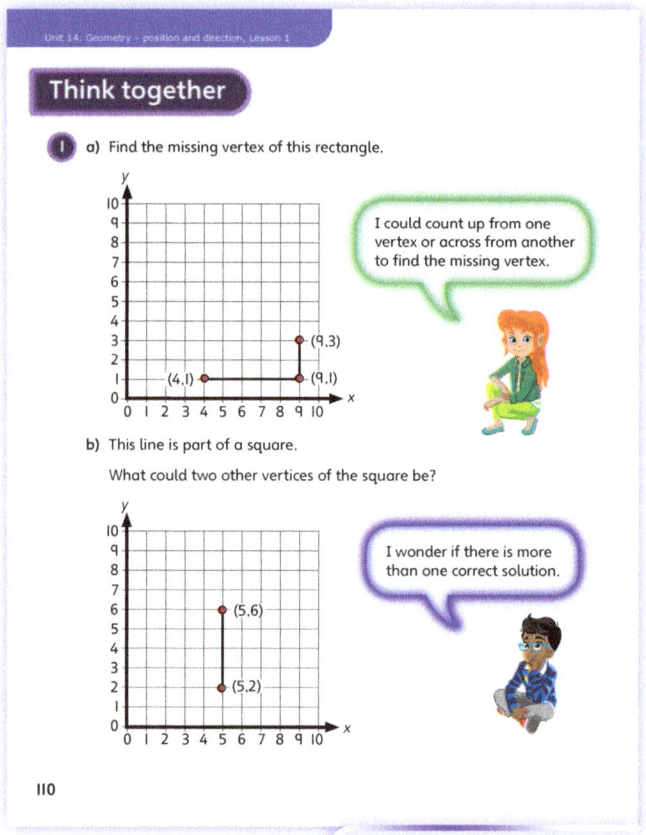

PUPIL TEXTBOOK 6C PAGE 110

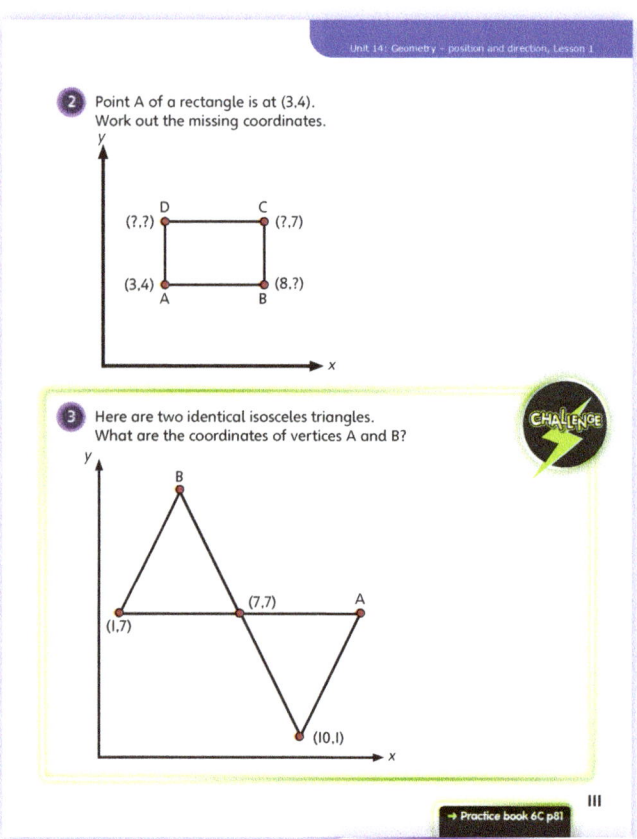

PUPIL TEXTBOOK 6C PAGE 111

Unit 14: Geometry – position and direction, Lesson 1

# Practice

**WAYS OF WORKING** Independent thinking

**IN FOCUS** Question ❹ and the first grid of question ❷ introduce children to shapes that are presented on a diagonal on a coordinate grid. Children should be encouraged to calculate the length of each side based on the *x* and *y* values of the two given vertices, and to check that their complete shape looks correct (it should look like a square).

**STRENGTHEN** Questions ❸ a) and b) present a problem that could have two different solutions. To help children find both sets of coordinates, encourage them to physically represent the problem on a coordinate grid, using matchsticks or other items to represent the given line. Encourage them to manipulate the item or items used to represent the side, exploring where the coordinates would be if the square (in part a) or rectangle (in part b) extended either side of the given line.

**DEEPEN** Children should be encouraged to extend their knowledge to multiple shapes on the same grid. Question ❺ provides some opportunity to explore this. Ask: *If shapes are identical, what does this mean? How can you use this to help you solve more complex problems involving coordinates and the properties of shapes?*

**ASSESSMENT CHECKPOINT** Use question ❹ to assess whether children can calculate missing vertices. Check that they remember which coordinate to write first.

**ANSWERS** Answers for the **Practice** part of the lesson can be found in the *Power Maths* online subscription.

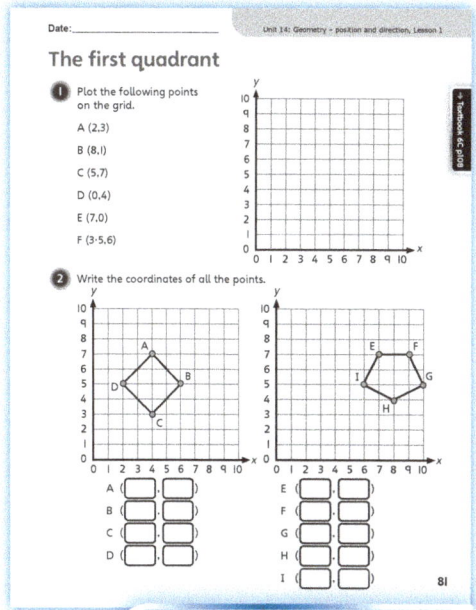

PUPIL PRACTICE BOOK 6C PAGE 81

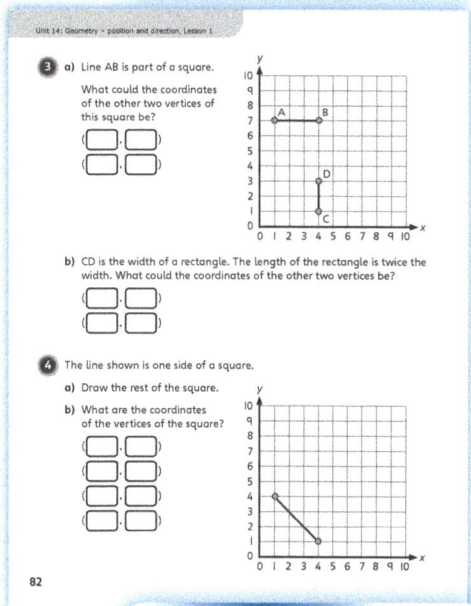

PUPIL PRACTICE BOOK 6C PAGE 82

# Reflect

**WAYS OF WORKING** Independent thinking

**IN FOCUS** This **Reflect** activity is designed to draw out children's understanding of points placed on the axes: that if a point is on the *x*-axis then the *y*-coordinate is equal to 0, and vice versa.

**ASSESSMENT CHECKPOINT** Use this question to assess whether children understand how the axes relate to each other, and that a point placed on an axis will have a 0 coordinate.

**ANSWERS** Answers for the **Reflect** part of the lesson can be found in the *Power Maths* online subscription.

## After the lesson

- Are all children secure at plotting and identifying points in the first quadrant? How will you address any misconceptions about this through same-day interventions before children are exposed to coordinates in four quadrants in Lesson 2?
- Can you make cross-curricular links between coordinates in one quadrant and other subjects, for example GPS coordinates in Geography or PE?

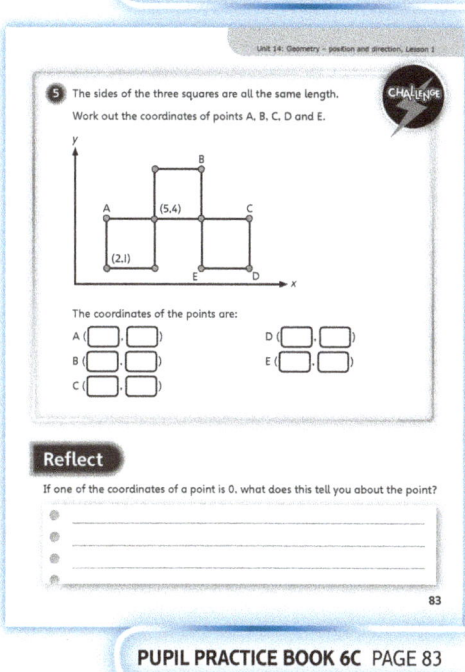

PUPIL PRACTICE BOOK 6C PAGE 83

147

Unit 14: Geometry – position and direction, Lesson 2

# Read and plot points in four quadrants

### Learning focus
In this lesson, children are introduced to plotting coordinates in all four quadrants.

### Before you teach
- Are children secure with plotting and reading coordinates in the first quadrant from Lesson 1 in this unit?
- Are there any common misconceptions around plotting coordinates from Lesson 1? If so, how will you adapt your teaching so that these can be addressed in this lesson?

### NATIONAL CURRICULUM LINKS

**Year 6 Geometry – position and direction**

Describe positions on the full coordinate grid (all four quadrants).

### ASSESSING MASTERY

Children can read the coordinates of points that are plotted in all four quadrants and can plot these. Children can begin to develop their problem solving and reasoning abilities, including simple reasoning about shapes. They should also be able to identify common errors.

### COMMON MISCONCEPTIONS

When plotting coordinates, children may plot the first coordinate against the *y*-axis rather than the *x*-axis. Ask:
- *Which axis do you plot against first? What do you call this axis? Is there a saying you could use to help you remember this, such as `You go along the corridor (x) before you go up the stairs (y)'?*

Children may plot negative values as positive values. For example, they may plot (⁻3,⁻4) at (3,4). Ask:
- *What is the value of the coordinate? Is it before or after 0? Where is this on the axis? What are the coordinates where both axes cross each other?*

### STRENGTHENING UNDERSTANDING

Encourage children to physically plot coordinates in all four quadrants. If you have a gridded area on your school playground, this would be an ideal opportunity to ask children to stand at given coordinates.

When plotting or reading values, it can be helpful to make the link between the axis and a 0-centred number line. Children can also record a '+' (positive) and '⁻' (negative) sign at the appropriate ends of each axis, to help them remember which coordinates are positive and which are negative. Drawing the axes with two different colours (one for the positive and one for the negative section of each axis) can also help children when plotting coordinates that have a negative value.

### GOING DEEPER

Encourage children to begin to solve problems involving the properties of shapes in all four quadrants. For example, children could try to find the missing vertex of a square or rectangle.

### KEY LANGUAGE

**In lesson:** plotting, coordinates, point, grid, negative, *x*-axis, *y*-axis, **four quadrants**, positive, value

**Other language to be used by the teacher:** vertices, vertex, horizontal, vertical

### STRUCTURES AND REPRESENTATIONS

Coordinate grids with all four quadrants, 0-centred number line

### RESOURCES

**Mandatory:** coordinate grids with all four quadrants

**Optional:** matchsticks

 In the eTextbook of this lesson, you will find interactive links to a selection of teaching tools.

### Quick recap
Count back together as a class from 10 to ⁻10.

# Discover

**WAYS OF WORKING** Pair work

**ASK**

• Question 1 a): *What do you notice about the coordinate grid in this problem?*
• Question 1 a): *How can you use the information on the diagram to help you?*
• Question 1 a): *How do you read coordinates? Does this work for plotting points on a four-quadrant grid?*
• Question 1 b): *Why do you think this coordinate has a negative value? Where would this point be represented along the x-axis?*

**IN FOCUS** This activity introduces children to a coordinate grid that has more than one quadrant, and to coordinates that have a negative value. Children should be encouraged to make connections between plotting coordinates in the first quadrant and plotting coordinates in all four quadrants.

**PRACTICAL TIPS** Provide children with practical experiences of plotting coordinates in all four quadrants. This should augment the experience of reading and pointing to coordinates that they will gain through the **Discover**, **Share** and **Think together** sections.

**ANSWERS**

Question 1 a): The coordinates of ship A are (⁻3,⁻2).
The coordinates of ship B are (3,⁻1).

Question 1 b):

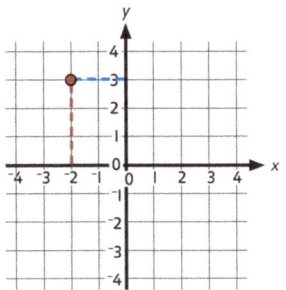

# Share

**WAYS OF WORKING** Whole class teacher led

**ASK**

• Question 1 a): *How can you work out the coordinates of ships A and B?*
• Question 1 a): *How can you use your knowledge of plotting coordinates from your last maths lesson to help you?*
• Question 1 a): *How can you work out the x and y values for each point? What happens when a value is below 0?*
• Question 1 b): *How can you make sure you are plotting this point against the correct places on the x- and y-axes?*

**IN FOCUS** Children are exposed to a range of coordinates in all four quadrants, including those that have two negative values, for example (⁻3,⁻2), as well as those that have a positive and a negative value, for example (3,⁻1). Some children may not understand why there are four quadrants and how these relate to negative and positive values.

PUPIL TEXTBOOK 6C PAGE 112

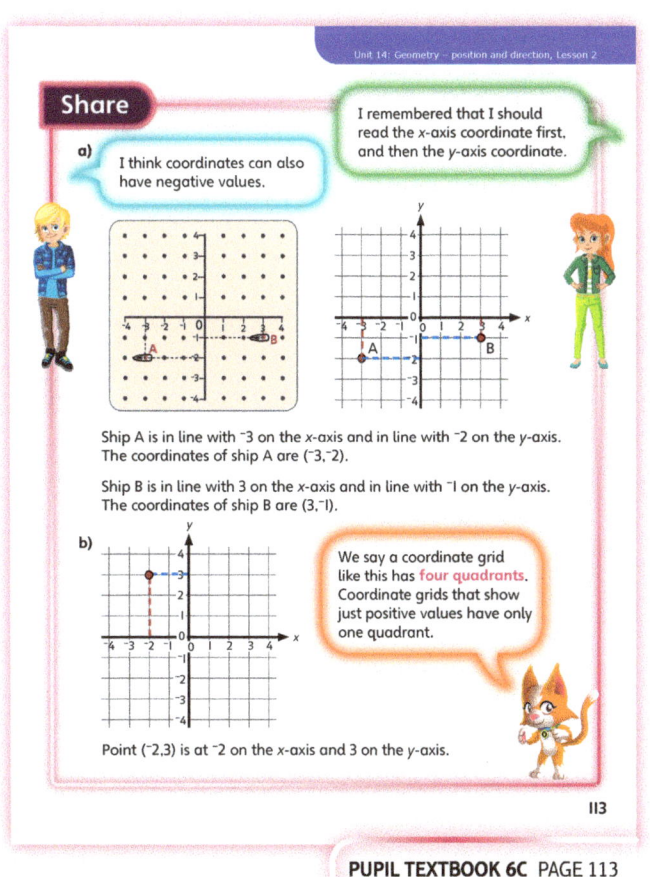

PUPIL TEXTBOOK 6C PAGE 113

Unit 14: Geometry – position and direction, Lesson 2

# Think together

**WAYS OF WORKING** Whole class teacher led (I do, We do, You do)

**ASK**
- Question 1 a): *Do you record the x- or y-axis value first?*
- Question 1 a): *How do the lines drawn on the grid for ship A help you?*
- Question 1 b): *If the value is negative, which part of the x- or y-axis is it on?*
- Question 2: *Has Mark plotted all the coordinates in the right order? Has he plotted all the negative values correctly?*

**IN FOCUS** Question 2 explores some common misconceptions and errors that occur when plotting in all four quadrants and shows how they can be avoided.

**STRENGTHEN** Children may be unsure where to plot positive and negative values. Encourage them to write a plus or minus sign at the appropriate ends of each axis in their books, as a reminder.

**DEEPEN** Give children missing vertex problems and challenge them to reason using the properties of shapes in grids with four quadrants.

**ASSESSMENT CHECKPOINT** Use all questions to assess whether children can read and plot coordinates in all four quadrants. Point out the dashed lines in question 1 a), which are there to help. Do children understand how positive and negative values relate to the quadrants?

**ANSWERS**

Question 1 a): A (5,⁻2); B (⁻4,⁻2); C (⁻3,3); D (3,2)

Question 1 b):

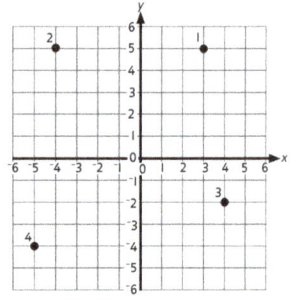

Question 2: A should be (⁻4,1). Mark has put the coordinates in the wrong order.
C should be (5,⁻3). Mark has not read the x-coordinate correctly.
D should be (0,⁻2). Mark has put the coordinates in the wrong order.

Question 3: (1,1), (2,1), (2,⁻1) (1,⁻1)

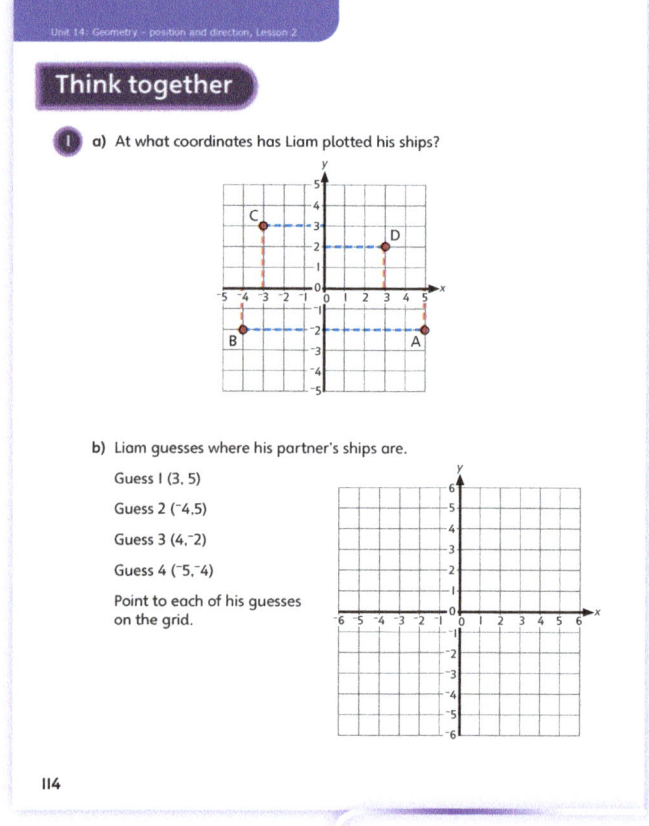

**PUPIL TEXTBOOK 6C** PAGE 114

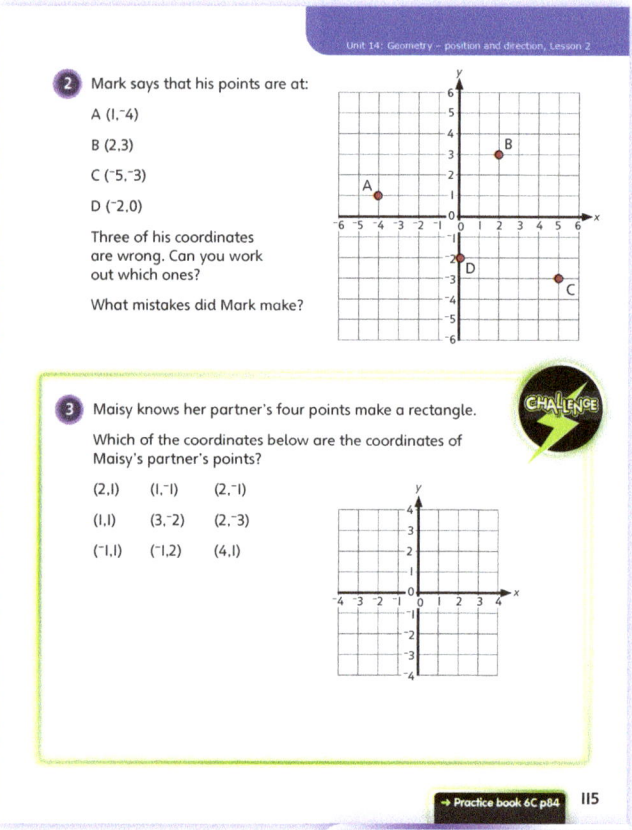

**PUPIL TEXTBOOK 6C** PAGE 115

# Unit 14: Geometry – position and direction, Lesson 2

## Practice

**WAYS OF WORKING** Independent thinking

**IN FOCUS** Question ➋ introduces children to basic reasoning about shapes based on coordinates. They are expected to plot the coordinates on a coordinate grid and then to identify which shape the coordinates could be the vertices of.

**STRENGTHEN** To help children identify the shapes formed by the coordinates in question ➋, encourage them to use matchsticks or other objects to join the vertices so that they are able to see the outlines of the shapes.

**DEEPEN** Children should be encouraged to begin to solve missing vertices and coordinates problems, reasoning about the properties of shapes to help them. For example, ask: *What coordinates would I need to plot to complete this square?*

**THINK DIFFERENTLY** Question ➌ asks children to explain a common misconception when plotting coordinates. They will need to understand that you get to a different point if you do not write or plot coordinates in the correct order.

**ASSESSMENT CHECKPOINT** Use question ➋ to assess if children can accurately plot coordinates in all four quadrants. They should be able to see if they have gone wrong and why by looking at the resulting shapes.

**ANSWERS** Answers for the **Practice** part of the lesson can be found in the *Power Maths* online subscription.

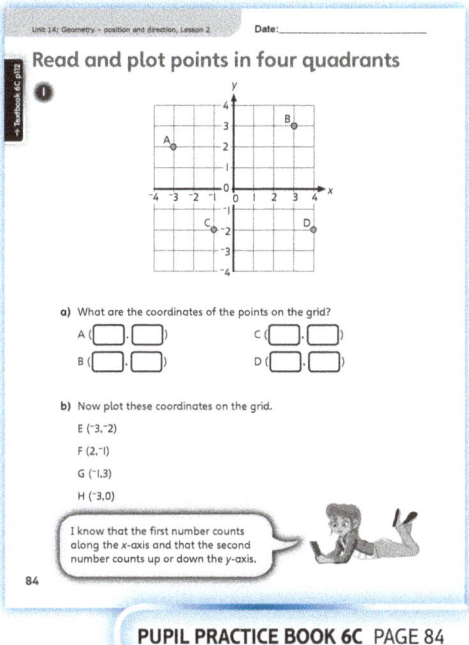

PUPIL PRACTICE BOOK 6C PAGE 84

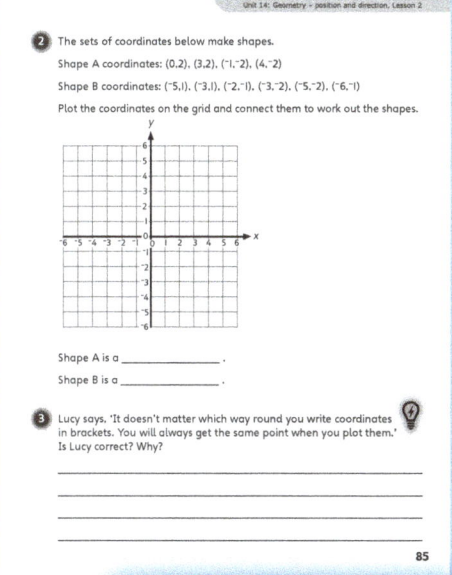

PUPIL PRACTICE BOOK 6C PAGE 85

## Reflect

**WAYS OF WORKING** Independent thinking

**IN FOCUS** This **Reflect** activity encourages children to reflect on the similarities and differences between plotting coordinates in one quadrant and plotting them in four quadrants.

**ASSESSMENT CHECKPOINT** Use this question to assess whether children can connect their knowledge of plotting coordinates in one quadrant with the knowledge they have gained in this lesson about plotting coordinates in all four quadrants.

**ANSWERS** Answers for the **Reflect** part of the lesson can be found in the *Power Maths* online subscription.

## After the lesson ⏸

- Are all children secure in plotting coordinates in all four quadrants?
- How could you address any insecurities through same-day interventions, before children begin to use these skills as part of Lesson 3 in this unit?

PUPIL PRACTICE BOOK 6C PAGE 86

Unit 14: Geometry – position and direction, Lesson 3

# Translations

### Learning focus
In this lesson, children are introduced to translating shapes on a coordinate grid.

### Before you teach
- Are children secure with plotting and reading coordinates in all four quadrants covered in Lesson 2 in this unit?
- How will you address any common misconceptions at the start of this lesson?

### NATIONAL CURRICULUM LINKS

**Year 6 Geometry – position and direction**

Draw and translate simple shapes on the coordinate plane, and reflect them in the axes.

### ASSESSING MASTERY

Children can translate shapes that are presented on a coordinate grid. They can explain translations in terms of a coordinate grid, for example 'the shape has been translated 2 to the right and 3 down'.

### COMMON MISCONCEPTIONS

Children may not realise that all the vertices of a translated shape must be moved in the same way. Draw children's attention to the fact that a shape after a translation is identical to the original shape. Ask:
- *What do you notice about shapes after a translation? Let's translate this shape by [for example] 4 right. What has happened to the coordinates of each point? Have they all moved by the same amount?*
- *Does this mean that the shape itself has changed?*

### STRENGTHENING UNDERSTANDING

Encourage children to draw and cut out copies of the shapes that are being translated. They can place these on the grid and slide them across and up or down to new positions. This will help them to explore what happens to the coordinates of each of the points as they move.

### GOING DEEPER

Encourage children to explore translation problems which involve both horizontal and vertical translation, in both positive and negative directions.

### KEY LANGUAGE

**In lesson:** plotting, translation, *x*-axis, *y*-axis, coordinates, vertices, irregular, grid, identical

**Other language to be used by the teacher:** quadrants

### STRUCTURES AND REPRESENTATIONS

Coordinate grids with all four quadrants

### RESOURCES

**Mandatory:** coordinate grids with all four quadrants

 In the eTextbook of this lesson, you will find interactive links to a selection of teaching tools.

### Quick recap
Ask children to draw any two points on a coordinate grid with four quadrants. Then ask them to describe how to move from one point to the other.

# Discover

**WAYS OF WORKING** Pair work

**ASK**

- Question 1 a): *What do you think the question means when it asks us to translate a shape?*
- Question 1 a): *What information can you use from the diagram to help you solve this problem?*
- Question 1 b): *What words will you use in your description?*

**IN FOCUS** This activity encourages children to begin to explore the translation of shapes in all four quadrants.

**PRACTICAL TIPS** Provide children with practical experiences of translating shapes, including on their own coordinate grids. Ensure children are comfortable with the language of translation, including up, down, left, right and units.

A very helpful way of identifying a translation is to pick a corner in the original shape, and then find that same corner in the translated shape and consider what translation is needed to move from one point to another.

**ANSWERS**

Question 1 a):

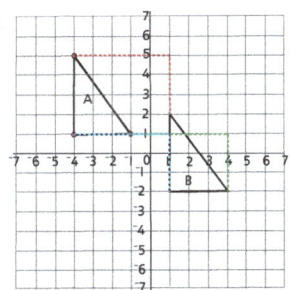

Question 1 b): Shape A has been translated 2 units left and 7 units down onto shape C.

# Share

**WAYS OF WORKING** Whole class teacher led

**ASK**

- Question 1 a): *If you translate a shape, what does it mean you are doing to it?*
- Question 1 a): *Can anyone work out the position of the translated shape in another way?*
- Question 1 b): *Does the translated shape look identical to the original shape?*

**IN FOCUS** Children should be encouraged to recognise that when they translate a shape, all the vertices of that shape move by the same amount and the resulting translated shape is identical to the original but in a new location.

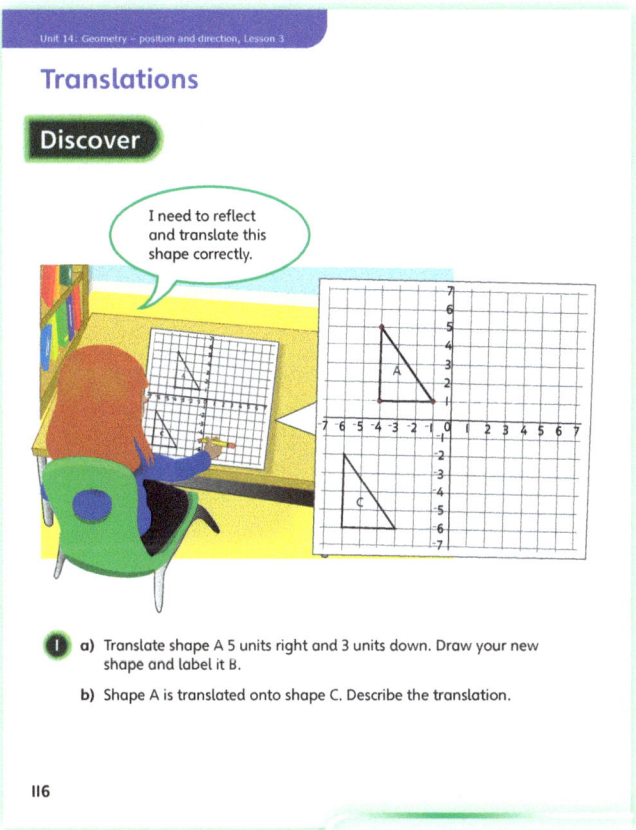

PUPIL TEXTBOOK 6A PAGE 116

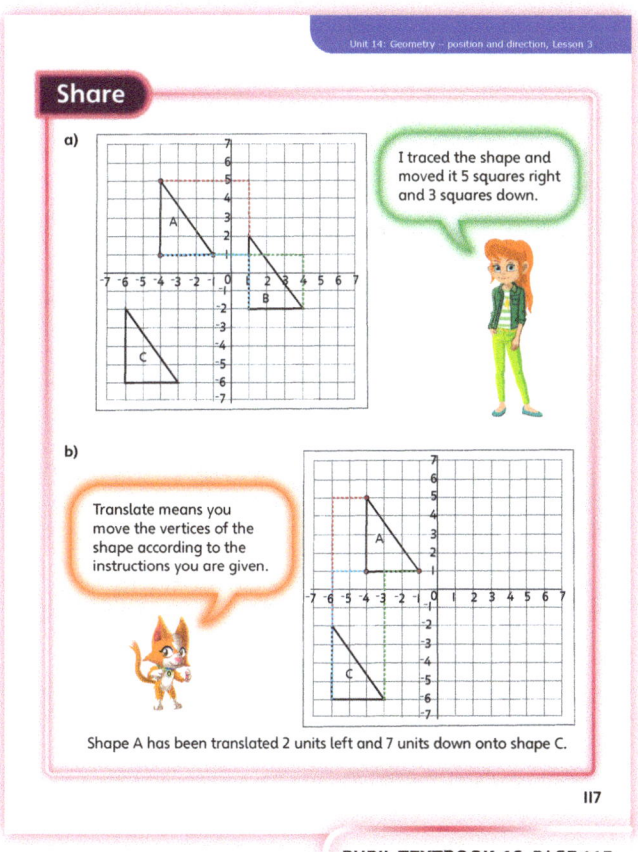

PUPIL TEXTBOOK 6C PAGE 117

# Think together

**WAYS OF WORKING** Whole class teacher led (I do, We do, You do)

**ASK**
- Question ❶: *Will shape E look the same as shape D? How do you know?*
- Question ❷: *How can you identify the translation?*
- Question ❸: *Which point are you going to move first?*

**IN FOCUS** Question ❷ invites children to identify a translation based on two identical shapes (rather than complete a translation themselves). They should be encouraged to explore how one of the vertices of the shape has been moved to make the corresponding vertex of the second shape, and then check that this translation and relationship is the same for the other vertices of the shapes.

**STRENGTHEN** To support children when translating shapes, it can be useful to physically represent the problem by making the shape out of paper or other material. This shape can then be physically moved along the course of the translation, which helps to reinforce the fact that the shapes are identical after the translation.

**DEEPEN** Question ❸ b) introduces children to the concept of identifying a translation based on knowing only one of the new coordinates, without a visual representation. They should be encouraged to move a paper copy of the shape around the grid. They should use this to explore and define all the possible translations, depending on which vertex of shape D moves to the new coordinates each time. Ask: *Have we found every possible answer? How do you know?*

**ASSESSMENT CHECKPOINT** Use question ❶ to assess whether children can accurately find the new location of a shape based on a given translation. Use question ❷ to assess whether children can define a translation based on seeing where a shape has moved from and to on the grid.

**ANSWERS**

Question ❶:

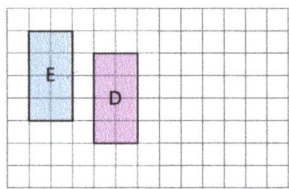

Question ❷: Shape F has been translated 2 units right and 5 units down to become shape G.

Question ❸ a):

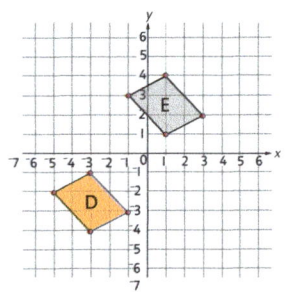

Question ❸ b): Possible answers: 5 right 1 down, 3 right 1 up, 5 right 2 up or 7 right.

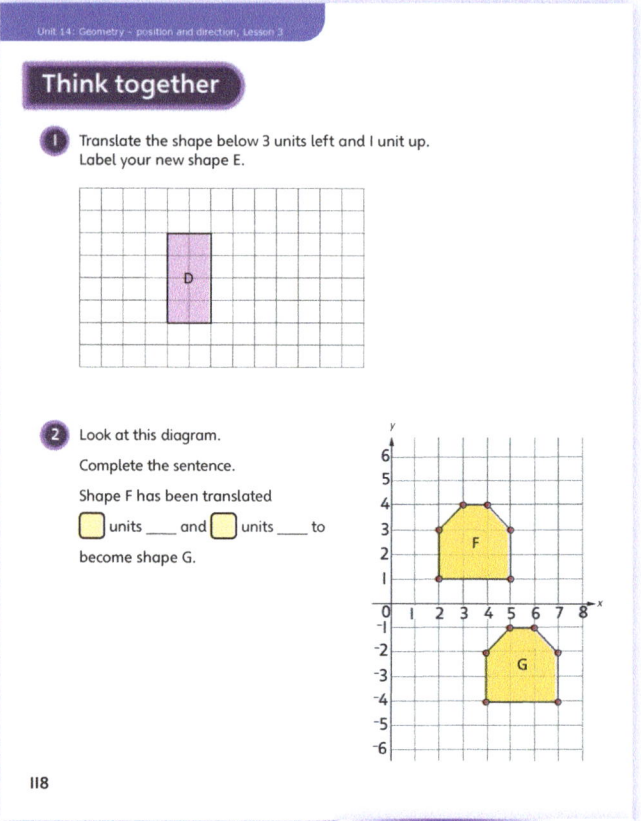

**PUPIL TEXTBOOK 6C** PAGE 118

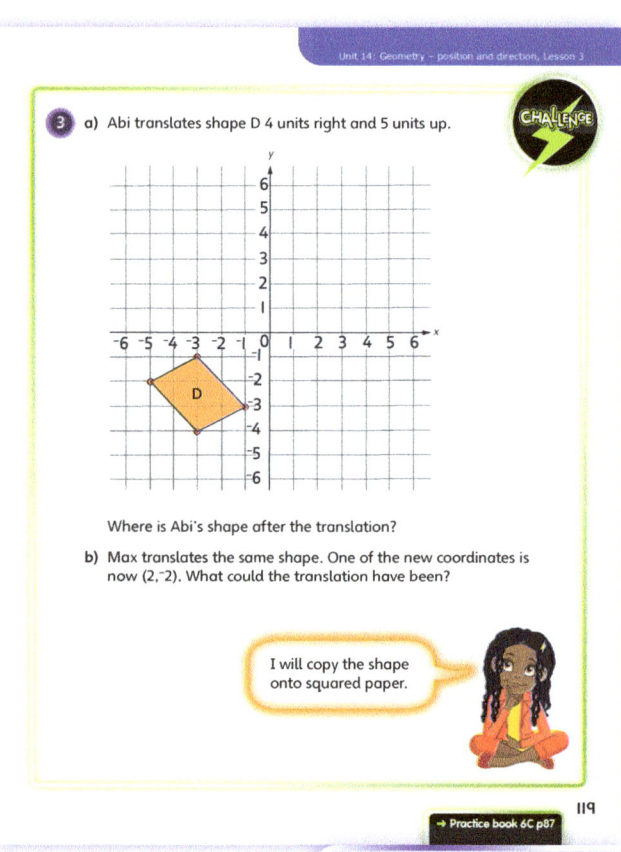

**PUPIL TEXTBOOK 6C** PAGE 119

Unit 14: Geometry – position and direction, Lesson 3

# Practice

**WAYS OF WORKING** Independent thinking

**IN FOCUS** Questions ① to ④ give children the opportunity to draw the new location of shapes based on given translations. In question ⑤, children define a series of translations to describe how a given shape moves around the grid.

**STRENGTHEN** In question ③, children can identify the effect of a series of translations by making their own copy of shape E, which they can slide right, down and then left on the grid. They can then draw round their shape to show the new locations of shape F and shape R. Discuss how the shape itself does not change, only its position.

**DEEPEN** In question ④, children translate shapes on the coordinate grid, including translations into different quadrants. They should list the coordinates of the vertices of each shape and explore what happens to these when the shape is translated. Can they predict what the coordinates of the new shape will be just by knowing the coordinates of the original shape and the translation? For example, the top left corner of the rectangle is (⁻5,3) and the translation is 3 units right and 4 units down, can they predict that the coordinate of the new top left corner will be (⁻5 + 3, 3 – 4)?

**ASSESSMENT CHECKPOINT** Use question ⑤ to assess whether children can identify translations.

**ANSWERS** Answers for the **Practice** part of the lesson can be found in the *Power Maths* online subscription.

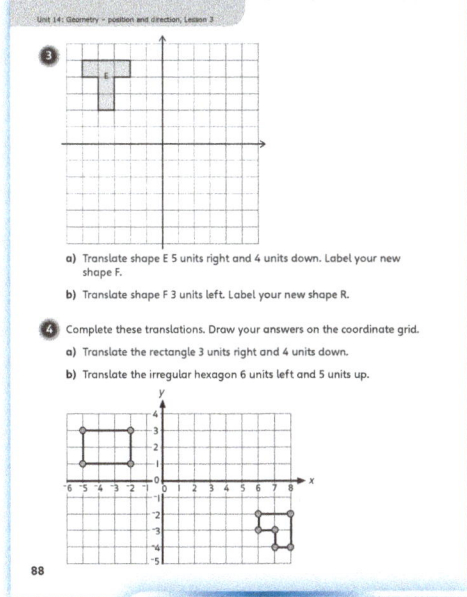

PUPIL PRACTICE BOOK 6C PAGE 87

PUPIL PRACTICE BOOK 6C PAGE 88

# Reflect

**WAYS OF WORKING** Independent thinking

**IN FOCUS** This **Reflect** activity encourages children to draw and describe a translation on a coordinate grid with four quadrants. A sentence scaffold is not provided, so children will need to recall the key vocabulary of translation from the lesson when constructing their description.

**ASSESSMENT CHECKPOINT** Use this question to assess whether children can explain what effect translating has on a shape.

**ANSWERS** Answers for the **Reflect** part of the lesson can be found in the *Power Maths* online subscription.

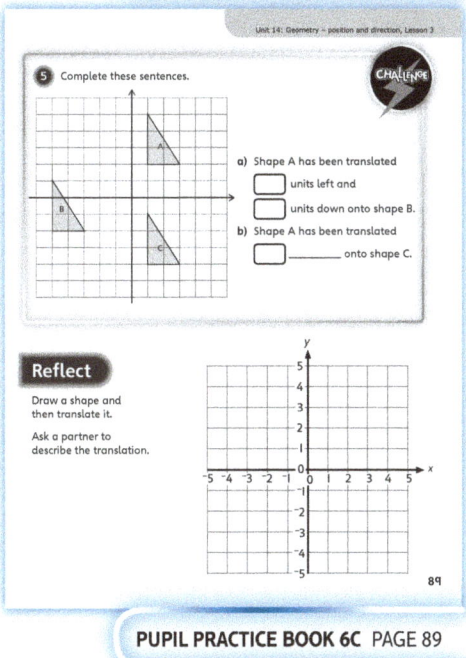

PUPIL PRACTICE BOOK 6C PAGE 89

# After the lesson

- Are all children secure in translating shapes? How will you address any individual misconceptions?
- Are children confident in using the vocabulary of translation?

Unit 14: Geometry – position and direction, Lesson 4

# Reflections

### Learning focus
In this lesson, children are introduced to reflecting shapes on a coordinate grid.

### Before you teach
- Are children secure in their knowledge of reflections from Year 5, when they experienced reflections that were not on a coordinate grid?
- Are children familiar with using a mirror to see a reflection?

#### NATIONAL CURRICULUM LINKS

**Year 6 Geometry – position and direction**

Draw and translate simple shapes on the coordinate plane, and reflect them in the axes.

#### ASSESSING MASTERY

Children can reflect shapes that are presented on a coordinate grid. They can explain reflections in terms of a coordinate grid, for example 'the shape has been reflected in the *y*-axis'.

#### COMMON MISCONCEPTIONS

Children may struggle to identify the axis or line that a shape has been reflected in. Encourage children to use a mirror to investigate the impact that reflecting the shape in each axis/line would have on the original shape, and which image matches the reflection they are trying to describe. Ask:
- *How could you check if this shape is reflected in [for example] the x-axis?*

#### STRENGTHENING UNDERSTANDING

Encourage children to use mirrors to help them identify and describe the effect of reflections. For example, when reflecting in the *x*-axis, invite children to place a mirror along the *x*-axis, and note the effect this reflection has on the shape, and the position that the reflected shape is in. Then invite them to draw this reflection on the coordinate grid, before drawing their attention to the effect the reflection has had on the coordinates of each vertex of the shape.

#### GOING DEEPER

Encourage children to explore problems that combine both a translation and a reflection.

#### KEY LANGUAGE

**In lesson:** plotting, translation, reflection, *x*-axis, *y*-axis, mirror, coordinates, vertices, irregular, grid, identical

**Other language to be used by the teacher:** quadrants

#### STRUCTURES AND REPRESENTATIONS

Coordinate grids with all four quadrants

#### RESOURCES

**Mandatory:** coordinate grids with all four quadrants

**Optional:** mirror

 In the eTextbook of this lesson, you will find interactive links to a selection of teaching tools.

### Quick recap
Ask children to draw any one point on a coordinate grid with four quadrants. Ask: *How far is your point from the x-axis? How far is your point from the y-axis?*

# Unit 14: Geometry – position and direction, Lesson 4

## Discover

**WAYS OF WORKING** Pair work

**ASK**

- Question 1 a): *What information can you use from the diagram to help you solve this problem?*
- Question 1 a): *What does it mean to reflect the shape? What do you think it means to reflect the shape in the x-axis?*
- Question 1 a): *Is there anything you could use to explore the effect of reflecting this shape?*

**IN FOCUS** This activity encourages children to begin to explore the reflection of shapes in all four quadrants. They are introduced to the vocabulary of reflecting shapes across an axis for the first time.

**PRACTICAL TIPS** Ensure children have had the experience of using a mirror to reflect shapes and of exploring the effect of this reflection on the position of the reflected image.

**ANSWERS**

Question 1 a):

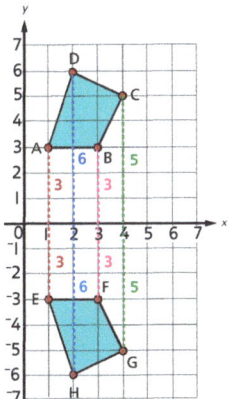

Question 1 b):

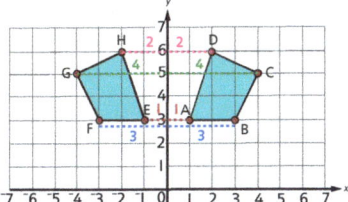

## Share

**WAYS OF WORKING** Whole class teacher led

**ASK**

- Question 1 a): *How can you work out the coordinates of the reflected shape? Can anyone see a different way?*
- Question 1 a): *Can you place a mirror on the x-axis? What do you notice about the position of the reflected shape in relation to the x-axis?*
- Questions 1 a) and b): *Can you point to the axis that you are reflecting the shape in?*
- Questions 1 a) and b): *Does the reflected shape look identical to the original shape?*

**IN FOCUS** Children are encouraged to explore the effect of reflecting shapes. They should be encouraged to notice that when they reflect shapes, the reflected shape is the same distance away from the axis of reflection as the original shape.

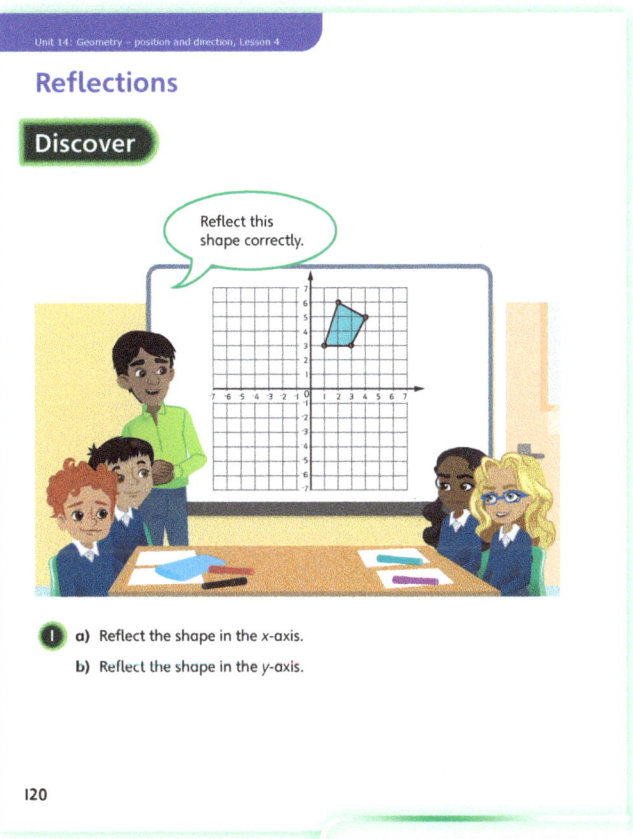

PUPIL TEXTBOOK 6C PAGE 120

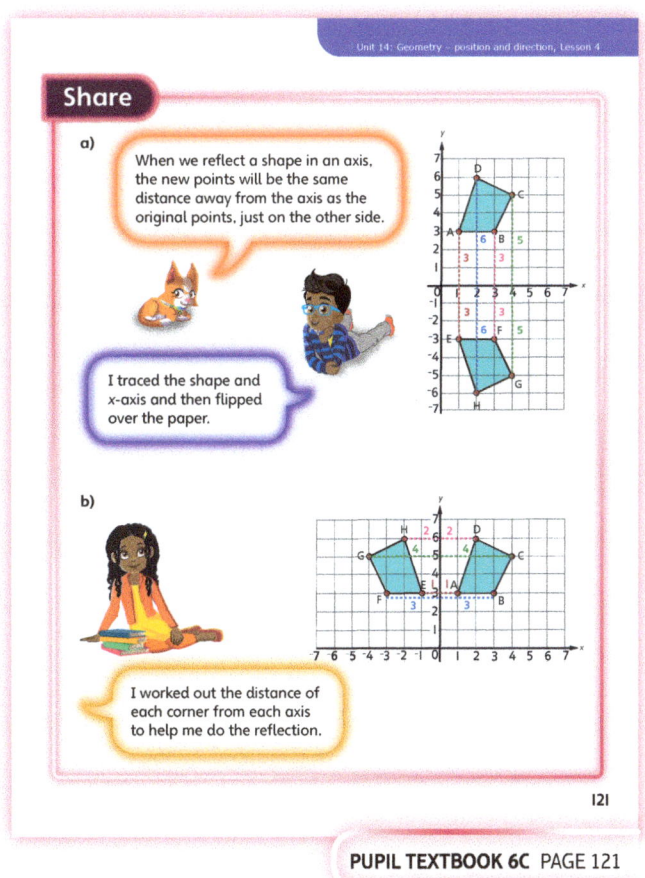

PUPIL TEXTBOOK 6C PAGE 121

# Think together

**WAYS OF WORKING** Whole class teacher led (I do, We do, You do)

**ASK**

- Question 2: *What axes are you reflecting the shapes in? Can you point to them?*
- Question 2 b): *Does reflecting the shape in the y-axis produce the same result as reflecting it in the x-axis? Why?*
- Question 3: *What equipment could help you to check this question?*

**IN FOCUS** For question 1, ensure children look closely at where the line of reflection is and use this to accurately place the reflected shape. They should notice that the original shape is the same distance from the line of reflection as the new shape is.

**STRENGTHEN** To support children when reflecting shapes, it can be useful to physically represent the problem by copying or tracing and then flipping the shape. Alternatively children can place a mirror on the line of reflection to help them envisage where the reflected shape will be.

**DEEPEN** Children should begin to reflect shapes in lines other than the axes, for example, reflecting shapes in a diagonal line. Encourage children to explore the impact that the angle and position of the line of reflection has on the reflected shape.

**ASSESSMENT CHECKPOINT** Use question 1 to assess whether children can accurately reflect shapes in a given mirror line. Use questions 2 a) and b) to assess whether children can accurately reflect shapes in both axes.

**ANSWERS**

Question 1 a):

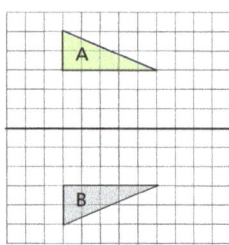

Question 1 b):

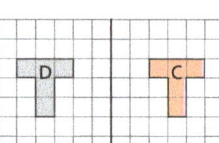

Questions 2 a) and b):

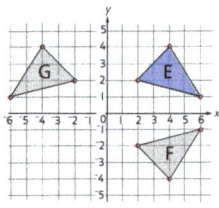

Question 3:

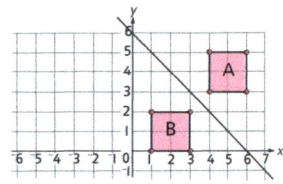

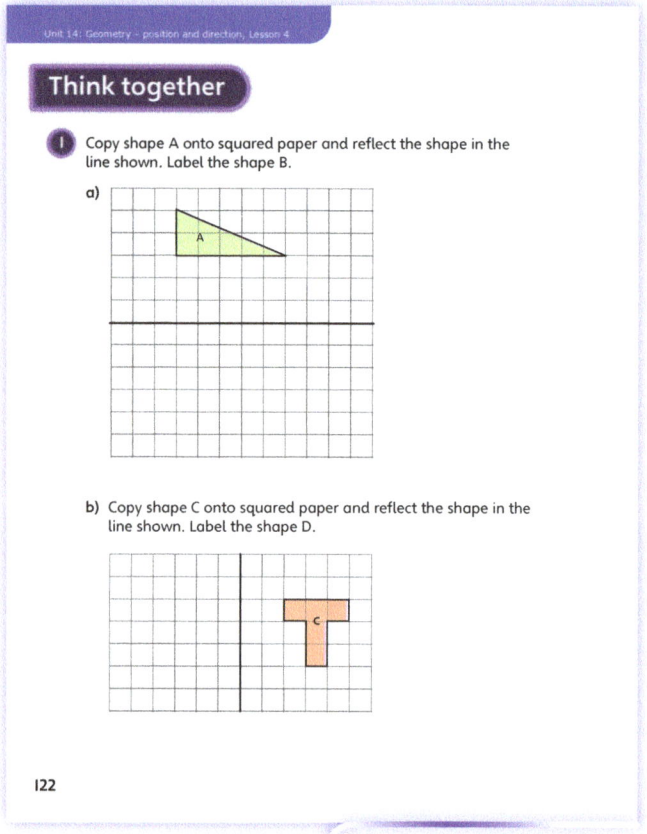

PUPIL TEXTBOOK 6C PAGE 122

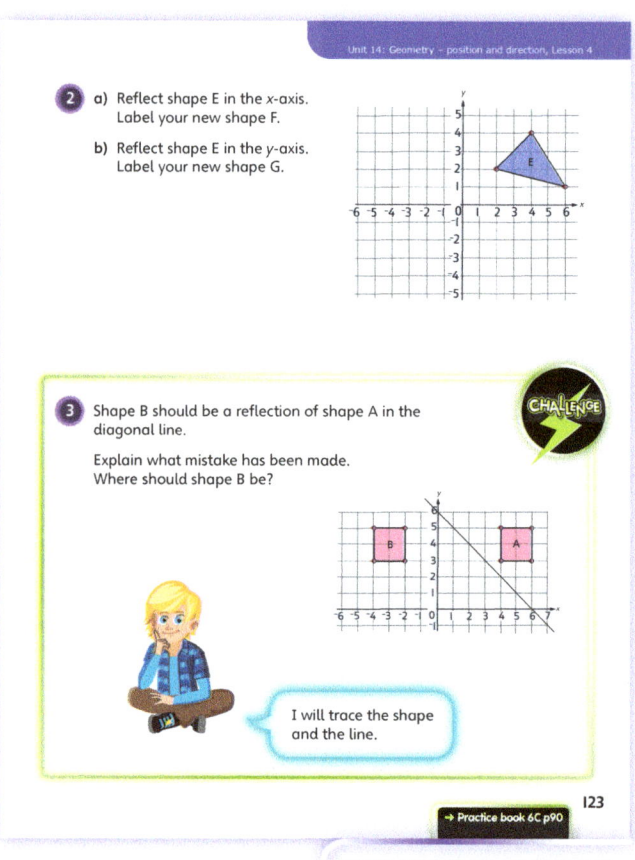

PUPIL TEXTBOOK 6C PAGE 123

Unit 14: Geometry – position and direction, Lesson 4

# Practice

**WAYS OF WORKING** Independent thinking

**IN FOCUS** Question 5 gives children practice at reflecting shapes in the y-axis of a coordinate grid and the use of this to find the new coordinates of the vertices of the reflected shape. Children will need to draw on their learning from earlier questions in order to develop their approach for working out the coordinates.

**STRENGTHEN** In question 4, to help children identify the effect of a reflection in a diagonal line, ensure that children explore this initially using a mirror, and that they are encouraged to draw the position of the reflected shape based on what they have seen in the mirror. Having two copies of the problem and working in pairs (so one can hold the mirror on one copy of the problem, and the other can draw the answer on the second copy, and then switch over) can be helpful.

**DEEPEN** Children should be encouraged to explore reflections that are followed by translations and vice versa. They should notice that carrying out a reflection followed by a translation does not give the same result as carrying out the same translation followed by the same reflection.

**THINK DIFFERENTLY** Question 4 gives children exposure to the reflection of a shape in a diagonal line. Children should be encouraged to use mirrors to check that they are plotting the reflection in the diagonal line correctly.

**ASSESSMENT CHECKPOINT** Use question 3 to assess whether children can carry out reflections in the x-axis and the y-axis of a coordinate grid with four quadrants.

**ANSWERS** Answers for the **Practice** part of the lesson can be found in the *Power Maths* online subscription.

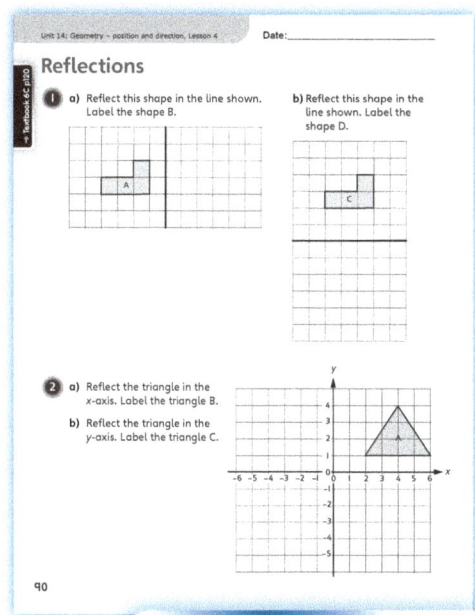

**PUPIL PRACTICE BOOK 6C** PAGE 90

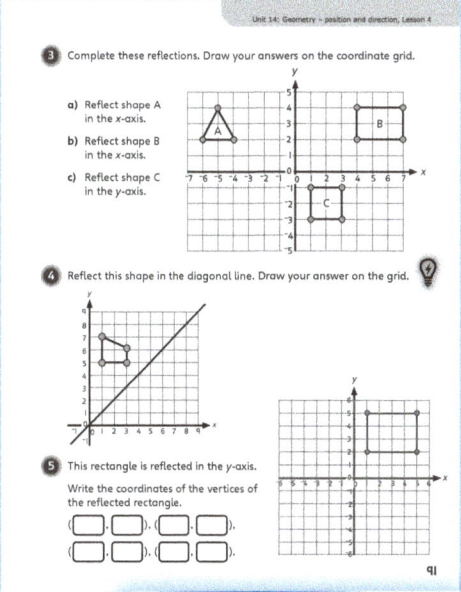

**PUPIL PRACTICE BOOK 6C** PAGE 91

# Reflect

**WAYS OF WORKING** Independent thinking

**IN FOCUS** This **Reflect** activity encourages children to discuss whether a reflected or translated image is exactly the same as the original shape. You might like to discuss how having the same side lengths and angles makes two shapes the same, even if they are facing opposite ways.

**ASSESSMENT CHECKPOINT** Use this question to assess whether children can explain what effect reflecting or translating has on the resulting shapes.

**ANSWERS** Answers for the **Reflect** part of the lesson can be found in the *Power Maths* online subscription.

## After the lesson

- Are all children secure in translating and reflecting shapes? How will you address any individual misconceptions through same-day interventions before children use these skills as part of Lesson 5?
- Are there any common misconceptions that you need to incorporate into your teaching of the next lesson in which children will use and apply their knowledge of translating and reflecting shapes to a wider range of problems?

**PUPIL PRACTICE BOOK 6C** PAGE 92

# Unit 14: Geometry – position and direction, Lesson 5

# Solve problems with coordinates

## Learning focus
In this lesson, children extend their ability to reason about shapes based on their properties and to solve problems that involve coordinates in all four quadrants.

## Before you teach
- Are children secure with plotting and reading coordinates in all four quadrants from Lesson 2 in this unit?
- Were there any common misconceptions about the properties of shapes and using these on a coordinate grid in the first quadrant from Lesson 1? How will you address these during this lesson?

### NATIONAL CURRICULUM LINKS

**Year 6 Geometry – position and direction**

Describe positions on the full coordinate grid (all four quadrants).

Draw and translate simple shapes on the coordinate plane, and reflect them in the axes.

### ASSESSING MASTERY

Children can solve problems that involve reasoning about shapes in all four quadrants. They can find the coordinates of the missing vertices of shapes, including when a grid is not provided. Children can also reason about identical and similar shapes and use their reasoning to solve problems and find missing coordinates.

### COMMON MISCONCEPTIONS

Children may misremember the names of each axis, calling the *x*-axis the *y*-axis and vice versa, which will mean errors when plotting and reading coordinates. Ask:
- *What do you call the vertical axis? Is there a saying you could use to help you remember that this is the vertical axis? Which axis do you record first in your coordinates? Do you remember the saying 'You go along the corridor (x) before you go up the stairs (y)'?*

Children may not realise that identical shapes share all the same properties. They may therefore not be able to transfer the properties between identical shapes in order to help them solve missing coordinate problems. Ask:
- *What does it mean when shapes are identical? What is the same about them? How can you use this to help you solve problems?*

### STRENGTHENING UNDERSTANDING

Encourage children to physically plot coordinates in all four quadrants, and to use matchsticks or other items to create shapes, so that they are able to physically manipulate the shapes and begin to reason about their properties. They can also use these resources to create identical shapes, and see the connections between these shapes, including seeing that they have all the same properties, such as side lengths.

### GOING DEEPER

Encourage children to create their own problems involving shapes in all four quadrants for others to solve. Ask: *What makes your problem hard or easy to solve? Why?*

### KEY LANGUAGE

**In lesson:** coordinates, properties, *x*-axis, *y*-axis, vertex, *x*-coordinate, *y*-coordinate, translation, grid, vertices

**Other language to be used by the teacher:** quadrant, horizontal, vertical

### STRUCTURES AND REPRESENTATIONS

Coordinate grids with all four quadrants, 0-centred number line

### RESOURCES

**Mandatory:** coordinate grids with all four quadrants

**Optional:** matchsticks, counters

In the eTextbook of this lesson, you will find interactive links to a selection of teaching tools.

## Quick recap
Tell children that one corner of a square is at (2,2). Ask: *What could the coordinates of the other three corners be?*

Unit 14: Geometry – position and direction, Lesson 5

# Discover

**WAYS OF WORKING** Pair work

**ASK**

- Question ❶ a): *What information can you use from the diagram to help you solve this problem?*
- Question ❶ a): *What do you know about the properties of squares?*
- Question ❶ a): *How could you work out the length of the side of the shape when you don't have a grid to help you?*
- Question ❶ b): *What do you think it means when the two squares are identical? Can you use what you know about the first square to help you find the coordinates for points F, G and H? Can you work out how the first square has been translated to form the second square?*

**IN FOCUS** This activity encourages children to visually reason about the properties of two identical squares, and asks them to find the coordinates of the different vertices of two squares. Children need to understand that identical shapes share all the same properties.

**PRACTICAL TIPS** Provide children with practical experiences of plotting coordinates and completing shapes in all four quadrants, including using counters or other objects to mark coordinates, and matchsticks or other objects to create polygons on the coordinate grid.

**ANSWERS**

Question ❶ a): The coordinates of vertex C are (4,5).
The coordinates of vertex D are (1,5).

Question ❶ b): The missing coordinates for shape Q are:
F (6,⁻5), G (6,⁻2) and H (3,⁻2).

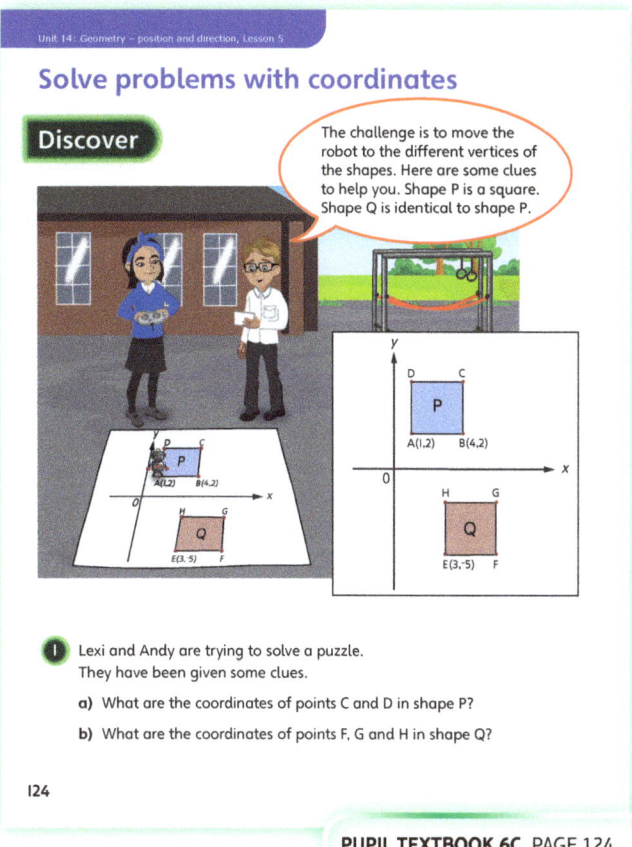

PUPIL TEXTBOOK 6C PAGE 124

# Share

**WAYS OF WORKING** Whole class teacher led

**ASK**

- Question ❶ a): *How can you work out the coordinates of the missing vertices?*
- Question ❶ a): *How can you use your knowledge of the properties of squares to help you?*
- Question ❶ a): *How can you work out the length of the sides? How can you use these to help you work out the coordinates of points C and D?*
- Question ❶ b): *What do you know about the second square?*
- Question ❶ b): *How can you work out the coordinates of points F, G and H? Can you use your knowledge of translating shapes to help you?*

**IN FOCUS** In question ❶ a), children are encouraged to first work out the length of a given side of the square that is in the first quadrant. A grid is not provided, meaning children need to reason about the length of the sides of the shape based on the *x* and *y* values of the coordinates of given vertices. In question ❶ b), they are then expected to use the knowledge that the two squares are identical, along with the properties of squares (all side lengths the same), to work out the translation that would move the first square to the second, and therefore work out the missing coordinates of the vertices of the second square.

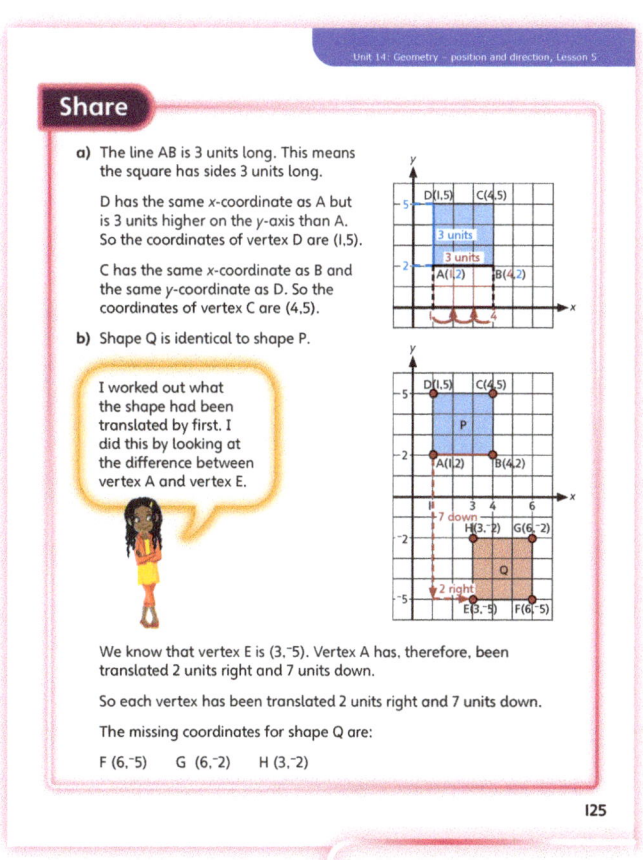

PUPIL TEXTBOOK 6C PAGE 125

161

Unit 14: Geometry – position and direction, Lesson 5

# Think together

**WAYS OF WORKING** Whole class teacher led (I do, We do, You do)

**ASK**
- Question ❶: *What do you know about the properties of a square that could help you answer this question?*
- Question ❶ a): *How can you work out the length of a side of this square? What do you know about the sides?*
- Question ❶ a): *Can you use the length of the sides of the square to help you work out points B and C?*
- Question ❶ b): *What does it mean when you say the squares are 'identical'?*
- Question ❶ b): *Can you work out how the first square has been translated to make the second square?*

**IN FOCUS** Question ❷ asks children to work out the value of missing coordinates of shapes that are not presented on a grid. This requires them to apply their knowledge and strategies developed in **Discover**, **Share** and question ❶ of this section, and to complete the missing coordinates by using the properties of an isoceles triangle (it is symmetrical).

**STRENGTHEN** Children may become confused when calculating a translation that goes into a different quadrant and may not realise that this may create a negative value for the coordinates. For example, a translation 2 units left from (1,3) goes to (⁻1,3). Encourage children to use a 0-centred number line to help them calculate the impact of the translations on the coordinates. For example, when translating a *y*-axis value of 4 down by 6 units, use a number line to support the calculation of 4 – 6 = ⁻2.

**DEEPEN** Children should be encouraged to reason about and use the properties of a wider range of shapes in order to solve coordinate problems in all four quadrants. This should include identical shapes and shapes with points lying on an axis where one coordinate is 0, for example, (1,0). Question ❸ provides some initial exposure to this. Children could be encouraged to create their own problems for partners that use a wider range of shapes.

**ASSESSMENT CHECKPOINT** Use questions ❶ a) and b) to assess whether children can apply their knowledge of the properties of shapes to solve problems in all four quadrants.

**ANSWERS**

Question ❶ a): Point B (4,1)
Point C (4,4)

Question ❶ b): Point E (⁻6,⁻5)
Point F (⁻3,⁻5)
Point G (⁻3,⁻2)

Question ❷ a): The coordinates of point C are (3,2).

Question ❷ b): B has moved to (⁻2,7).
C has moved to (⁻1,4).

Question ❸: C (1,0); D (3,0); E (1,5)

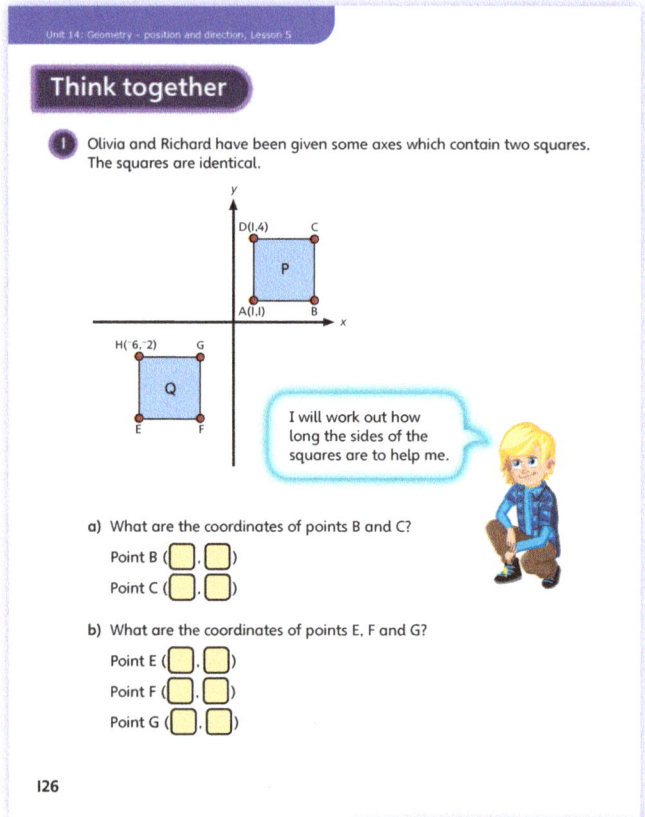

PUPIL TEXTBOOK 6C PAGE 126

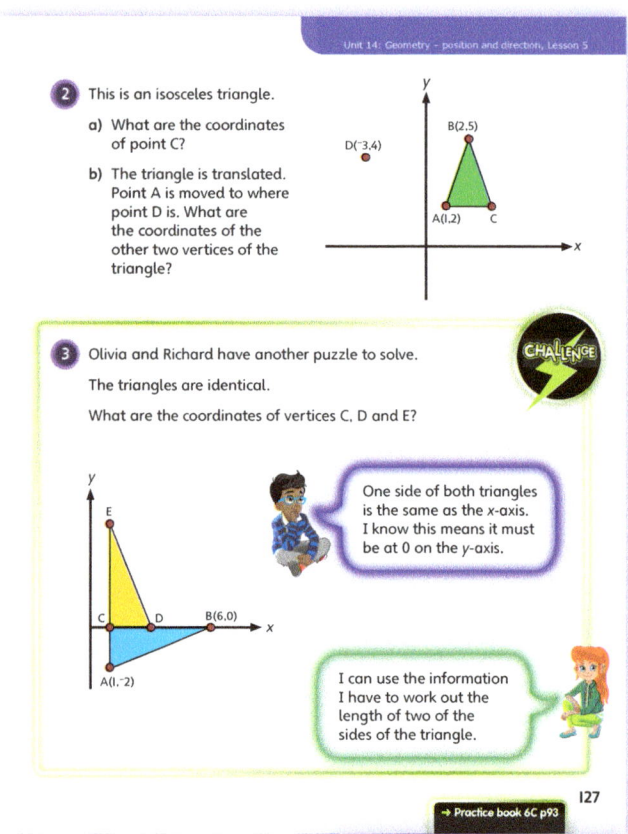

PUPIL TEXTBOOK 6C PAGE 127

Unit 14: Geometry – position and direction, Lesson 5

# Practice

**WAYS OF WORKING** Independent thinking

**IN FOCUS** Question ③ exposes children to coordinates of a point located on one of the axes. Children should be able to identify that this represents a '0' value for the 'opposite' coordinate to the axis on which it lies. For example, if a point lies on the y-axis, then this means its x-axis value is 0.

Question ④ introduces children to shapes that are related to each other by a scale factor (in this case, a scale factor of 2, or double). They need to understand the effect this has on the length of the sides: the length of the sides on the larger shape will be twice the length of the sides on the smaller shape.

**STRENGTHEN** To help children identify the effect that a given translation has on a coordinate (that the translation increases or decreases the value of a coordinate), encourage them to mark a '+' (positive) and '−' (negative) on the relevant ends of both axes. Ask: *Is the shape being moved towards the positive or negative end of the axis? Does this mean you need to add or subtract to work out the translated coordinates?*

**DEEPEN** Children should be encouraged to extend their knowledge to a wider range of shapes, and reason about more than two shapes on the same axes. Question ⑤ provides some opportunity to explore this. Ask: *If shapes are identical, what does this mean? What do you know about the properties of parallelograms?* Finally, invite children to begin to create their own similar problems for others to solve.

**ASSESSMENT CHECKPOINT** Use question ③ to assess whether children can extend their knowledge to a range of different shapes by answering this question about isosceles (symmetrical) triangles. They should understand what the half-way coordinate is on the x-axis.

**ANSWERS** Answers for the **Practice** part of the lesson can be found in the *Power Maths* online subscription.

# Reflect

**WAYS OF WORKING** Independent thinking

**IN FOCUS** This **Reflect** activity encourages children to reflect on what they found challenging in the lesson. It may be that they found it difficult to identify and draw reflections and translations without the help of a grid or numbers on the two axes. They should now be able to solve problems without a grid and explain how they will go about this.

**ASSESSMENT CHECKPOINT** Use this question to assess whether children have got to grips with the most challenging parts of the lesson. Encourage them to say whether they found a problem too challenging to solve.

**ANSWERS** Answers for the **Reflect** part of the lesson can be found in the *Power Maths* online subscription.

## After the lesson

- Are all children secure at solving problems involving properties of shapes in all four quadrants? How will you address any misconceptions through same-day interventions?
- This completes children's work on coordinates in Year 6. How will you incorporate work on coordinates into other curriculum areas in order to help children practise and apply their knowledge in different contexts?

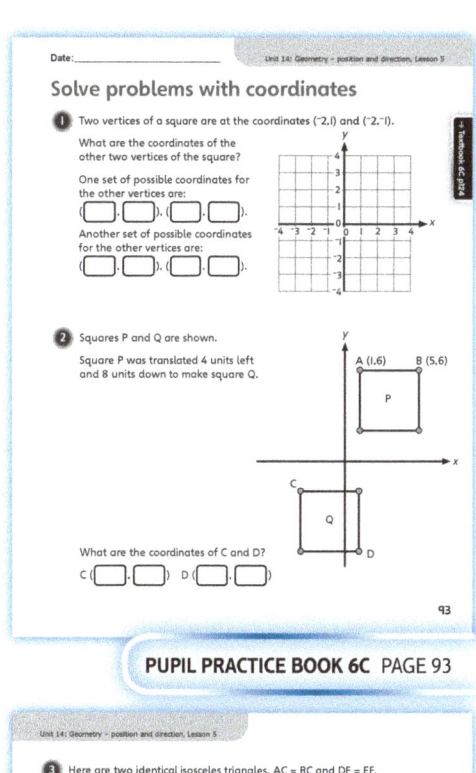

PUPIL PRACTICE BOOK 6C PAGE 93

PUPIL PRACTICE BOOK 6C PAGE 94

PUPIL PRACTICE BOOK 6C PAGE 95

163

# Unit 14: Geometry – position and direction

# End of unit check

**Don't forget the unit assessment grid in the *Power Maths* online subscription.**

**WAYS OF WORKING** Group work adult led

**IN FOCUS**
- This **End of unit check** will allow you to focus on children's understanding of geometry: the position and direction of coordinates plotted in coordinate grids and relating this to their understanding of the properties of shapes.
- Question 5 is presented in the style of a SATs question.

**ANSWERS AND COMMENTARY**

Children who have mastered this unit will be able to:
- plot and read coordinates in all four quadrants
- identify coordinates that form the vertices of a range of common shapes
- solve increasingly complex problems involving shapes in all four quadrants, including working out the positions of vertices and the lengths of the sides of shapes based on the coordinate information given
- translate shapes on a coordinate grid when given a description of the translation, or describe a translation that has occurred when given the original shape and the translated shape
- reflect points and shapes on a coordinate grid in the *x*- and *y*-axes as well as on simple diagonal lines, and carry out multi-step translations
- extend these skills to problems where they are given the values of coordinates only, but not a coordinate grid.

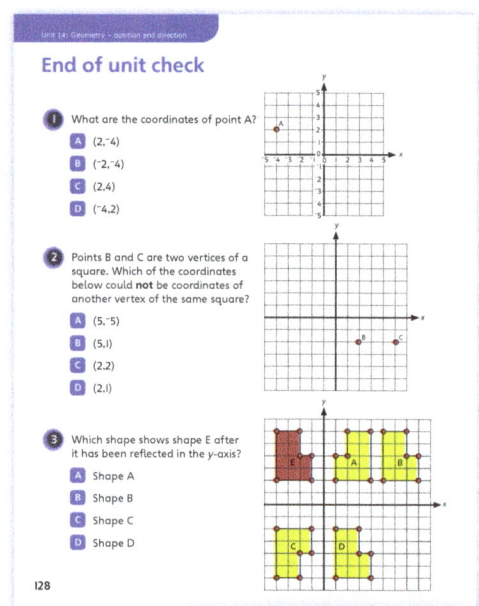

**PUPIL TEXTBOOK 6C** PAGE 128

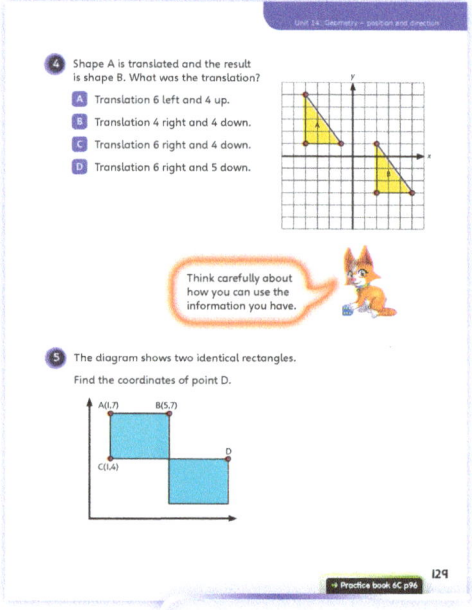

**PUPIL TEXTBOOK 6C** PAGE 129

| Q | A | WRONG ANSWERS AND MISCONCEPTIONS | STRENGTHENING UNDERSTANDING |
|---|---|---|---|
| 1 | D | A suggests children have transposed the coordinates and have recorded the *y*-axis value first. B suggests that children are not confident using negative coordinates. | Encourage children to create the known side of the shape out of matchsticks, and to then manipulate this side from the given vertices in order to check the possible locations of the other two vertices of the shape.  Encourage children to check the results of the reflection using a mirror. |
| 2 | C | D suggests that children have not considered that the square could be completed above the given vertices. A or B suggest that children have miscalculated the side of the square. | |
| 3 | A | C suggests children have confused the *x*- and *y*-axes. D suggests that children have confused translation with reflection. | |
| 4 | C | Wrong answers suggest incorrect counting or counting in the wrong direction. | |
| 5 | (9,4) | As there are no coordinates for the rectangle containing D, or a marked grid, children might think they cannot find D. | |

Unit 14: Geometry – position and direction

# My journal

**WAYS OF WORKING** Independent thinking

**ANSWERS AND COMMENTARY**

Question 1: Children should identify that Kate's statement is incorrect. Children should first identify that, given the two coordinates that are provided, they can work out that the coordinates of the missing vertices are (1,1) and (3,⁻1). They should then be able to see that the x-coordinates are the same distance away from the y-axis on both sides of the reflection. They should use this fact to give the values of the vertices of the reflected points as (⁻1,⁻1), (⁻3,⁻1), (⁻3,1), (⁻1,1).

Question 2: Children should identify that there are eight different possible rectangles that could be drawn which meet the given criteria. They should be encouraged to work systematically, drawing one side length in one orientation (for example, 5 units to the right of point A forms one possible side) and then completing the other sides of the rectangle based on this. They should be encouraged to consider rectangles that are both vertically and horizontally aligned (for example, 3 units from point A to the left and right would both form acceptable sides of the rectangle).

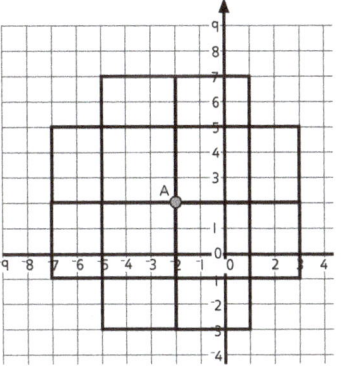

# Power check

**WAYS OF WORKING** Independent thinking

**ASK**

- What do you know now that you did not know at the start of this unit?
- How confident do you feel about solving problems involving coordinates in all four quadrants?

# Power play

**WAYS OF WORKING** Pair work

**IN FOCUS** Use this **Power play** to identify whether children can apply their knowledge of the properties of squares (that all side lengths are the same) and their skill in plotting coordinates in all four quadrants to a game-based situation.

**ANSWERS AND COMMENTARY** Exact answers for this **Power play** depend on the squares that have been drawn by the child and their partner. Assess if children are making connections between given coordinates and possible side lengths in order to then make more informed choices regarding the possible locations of the other vertices of their partner's squares.

# After the unit

- How can you continue to expose children to coordinates in other areas of the curriculum so that this learning is used in different contexts, such as Geography, Science, Computing or PE?
- Will you create a classroom display, so children can reflect back on this unit when necessary?

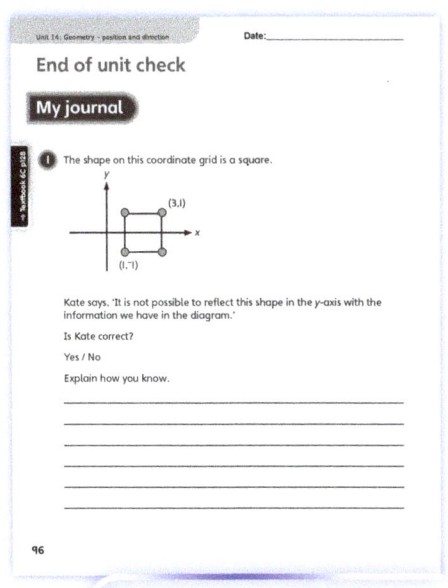

PUPIL PRACTICE BOOK 6C PAGE 96

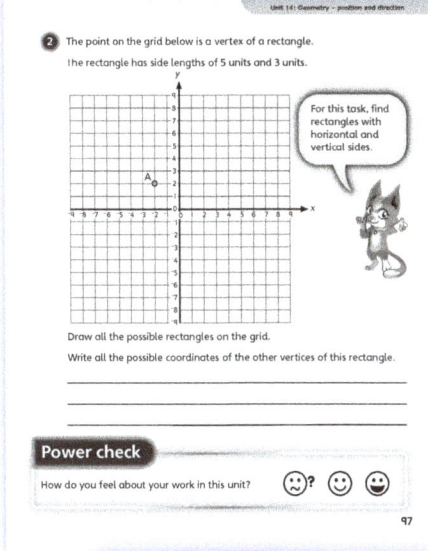

PUPIL PRACTICE BOOK 6C PAGE 97

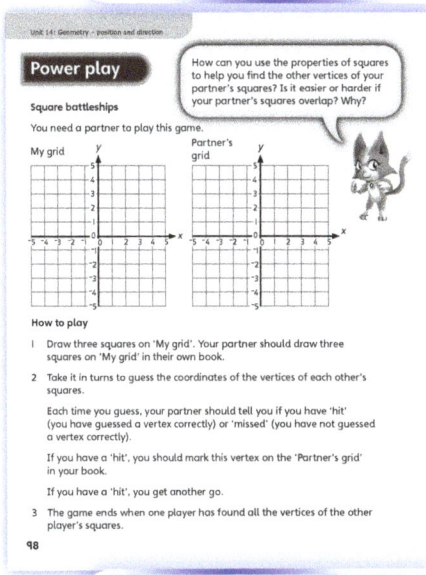

PUPIL PRACTICE BOOK 6C PAGE 98

**Strengthen** and **Deepen** activities for this unit can be found in the *Power Maths* online subscription.

# Unit 15
# Problem solving

**Mastery Expert tip!** 'I found that representing problems using bar models and number lines helped children to develop an understanding of how to approach problems. Annotating their diagrams with information that they were given or found out, helped them to work their way through the steps and ensured that they answered the question.'

**Don't forget to watch the Unit 15 video!**

## WHY THIS UNIT IS IMPORTANT

This unit draws on the extensive range of skills and knowledge acquired by children during Year 6, as well as building on learning from previous years, to solve problems about numbers, measurement and geometry. The emphasis is on reasoning and selecting appropriate methods, and it provides appropriate revision for key stage assessments. The unit will allow teachers to assess children's confidence and ability to apply their understanding in different ways, using both mental and written methods. It will also allow teachers to assess children's ability to use the relationships between numbers to consider more flexible or creative approaches.

## WHERE THIS UNIT FITS

→ Unit 14: Geometry – position and direction

→ **Unit 15: Problem solving**

This unit builds on children's work in previous units. Children apply their knowledge and skills in problems with and without context, some of which may appear less familiar because the problem is non-routine. They are asked to represent problems using bar models to help make sense of the relationships being explored and to make clear the operations needed.

Before they start this unit, it is expected that children:
- can identify the value of each digit in numbers up to 10,000,000
- can apply mental and written strategies for the four operations
- can represent a problem or the steps in a problem using bar models
- can draw on knowledge including that relating to unit conversions, equivalence, coordinates and the properties of shapes.

## ASSESSING MASTERY

Children can reason about and solve a range of mathematical problems with and without a context. They can recognise which operations are required and in which order. They should also be able to explain when calculations should be done in a different order because the relationships between the numbers make it easier. Children can apply learning in different areas of mathematics and can represent problems using bar models to support their thinking.

| COMMON MISCONCEPTIONS | STRENGTHENING UNDERSTANDING | GOING DEEPER |
| --- | --- | --- |
| Children may think that problems can only be solved in the order in which the information is presented. | Explore different types of question where the starting place is not always the first piece of information given, to encourage children to look at the problem as a whole. | Explore more flexible calculating as children use the relationships between the numbers to decide which operation to carry out first. |
| Children may make assumptions about what the question is asking them to find out, possibly relating it to other questions they have answered recently. | Encourage children to use bar models to represent problems, showing clearly what is known and what needs to be found out – and to check at the end that they have answered the actual question. | Ask children to compile a set of 'Helpful tips' that can be used to solve problems. Discuss the roles of estimating and of using the inverse to check answers. |

# Unit 15: Problem solving

## UNIT STARTER PAGES
Use these pages to introduce the unit focus to children. You can use the characters to explore different ways of working.

## STRUCTURES AND REPRESENTATIONS

**Number line:** This model helps children to work with positive and negative numbers, to order numbers (including fractions) and to calculate time intervals. It will also support their understanding of scales for both measurement and statistics.

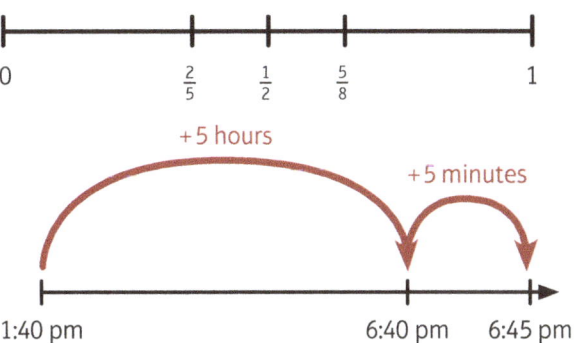

**Bar model:** Bar models help children to represent problems in a range of contexts, including fractions, percentages and ratios, to show what each part represents and to understand what needs to be found.

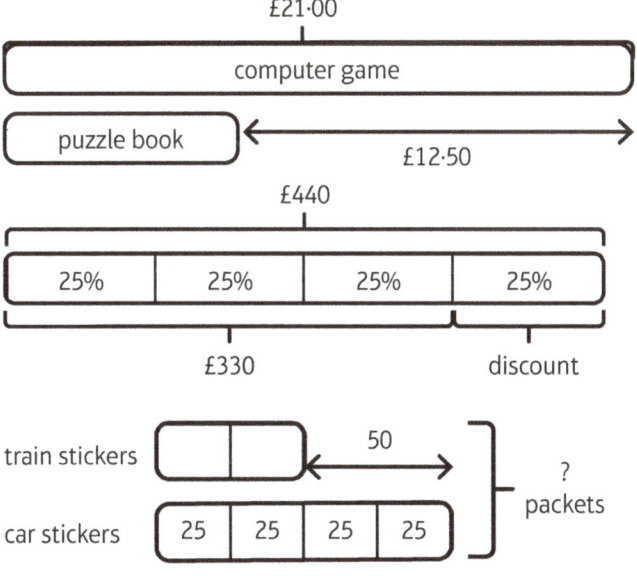

PUPIL TEXTBOOK 6C PAGE 130

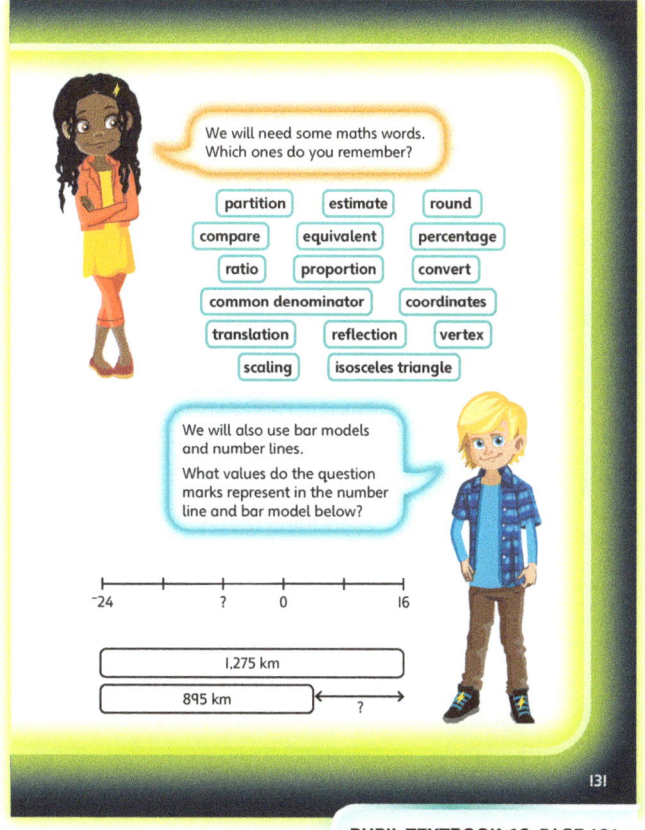

PUPIL TEXTBOOK 6C PAGE 131

## KEY LANGUAGE

There is some key language that children will need to know as part of the learning in this unit:

→ partition
→ estimate, round, compare
→ equivalent, common denominator
→ percentage, ratio, proportion, convert, scaling
→ coordinates, vertex (vertices), reflection, translation
→ sum of interior angles, isosceles triangle

167

Unit 15: Problem solving, Lesson 1

# Problem solving – place value

### Learning focus
In this lesson, children will use their understanding of place value to solve problems involving rounding, estimating and the positional values of digits.

### Before you teach
- Can children identify the value of each digit in numbers up to 10,000,000?
- Can they explain the rules for rounding?
- Can children identify the values represented by intervals on a number line or scale?

#### NATIONAL CURRICULUM LINKS

**Year 6 Number – number and place value**

Solve number and practical problems that involve number and place value.

#### ASSESSING MASTERY

Children can apply their understanding of place value to a range of problems, including those set in the contexts of measurement and statistics.

#### COMMON MISCONCEPTIONS

When identifying the intervals on a number line (or scale), children may divide the amount by the number of intermediate marks on the scale (all marks, excluding the start and end mark) rather than the number of intervals (for example, dividing by 3 rather than 4 when there are 3 intermediate marks showing 4 intervals). Draw a number line on the board with 10 intervals (that is, with 9 intermediate marks). Label the start and end points 5,000 and 6,000 respectively. Ask:
- *How many equal parts between 5,000 and 6,000 does this number line show? What do you have to divide 1,000 by to work out what the number at each mark is?*

#### STRENGTHENING UNDERSTANDING

To develop children's confidence when working with number lines for large numbers, explore a range of number lines and scales with different intervals. Look at how the position of a number may change as it appears on different scales: for example, the number 2,500 on a number line with intervals of 1,000 and another number line with intervals of 500. Practise rounding and ordering different sets of numbers, placing them on number lines with different scales.

#### GOING DEEPER

Ask children to select five digit cards and to make a number using their cards. They can then give clues to help a partner to find the number using the cards. Remind them that they need to be sure that combining all the clues only gives one possible answer.

#### KEY LANGUAGE

**In lesson:** digit, round, estimate, approximate, interval, scale, less than (<)

**Other language to be used by the teacher:** place value, greater than (>)

#### STRUCTURES AND REPRESENTATIONS

Number line, sorting circles

#### RESOURCES

**Optional:** place value counters

 In the eTextbook of this lesson, you will find interactive links to a selection of teaching tools.

### Quick recap

Ask: *What do we mean by a 4-digit number?* Ask children to provide you with examples of 4-digit numbers by writing them on mini-whiteboards or the class whiteboard.

# Unit 15: Problem solving, Lesson 1

## Discover

**WAYS OF WORKING** Pair work

**ASK**

- Question 1 a): *What does the digit 6 represent each time in the number 6,068?*
- Question 1 a): *How can you work out the missing values on the number line?*
- Question 1 a): *What number is half-way between 5,000 and 6,000? Where will it appear on this number line?*
- Question 1 b): *What digit do you need to look at when rounding to the nearest 1,000?*

**IN FOCUS** Question 1 a) requires children to position a set of numbers on a given number line. The number line is only labelled at each 1,000, so children need to work out the value each interval represents. In question 1 b), children need to apply the rules for rounding to reason about distances that round to the same multiple of 1,000 km.

**PRACTICAL TIPS** Create a place value table in which to record all the distances. Then make each distance using place value counters. Children can then compare the value of each distance with the number line.

**ANSWERS**

Question 1 a):

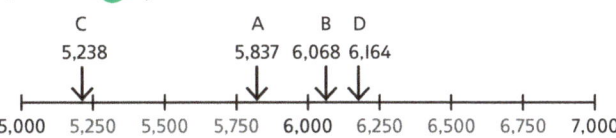

Question 1 b): City A: 5,837 rounds up to 6,000.
City B: 6,068 rounds down to 6,000.
City C: 5,238 rounds down to 5,000.
City D: 6,164 rounds down to 6,000.
The distance from Paris to cities A, B and D rounds to 6,000 km.

## Share

**WAYS OF WORKING** Whole class teacher led

**ASK**

- Question 1 a): *Why is Dexter looking at the four intervals to work out the scale on the number line, rather than looking at the three intermediate marks?*
- Question 1 a): *Is 6,164 closer to 6,000 or 7,000 on the number line? How do you know? How do you know that 6,068 is closer to 6,000 than 6,164 is to 6,000?*
- Question 1 b): *Why do you check the hundreds digit when rounding to the nearest 1,000? Why not the thousands digit?*
- Question 1 b): *What other numbers do you know that round to the same multiple of 1,000?*

**IN FOCUS** In question 1 a), suggest that children could imagine each interval of 250 split into 5 equal intervals of 50; this may help them to position the numbers on the line. In question 1 b), although Ash's method works, it is an informal method and children should be confident with Flo's method. The numbers have been chosen so that one rounds up and the others round down to the same 1,000.

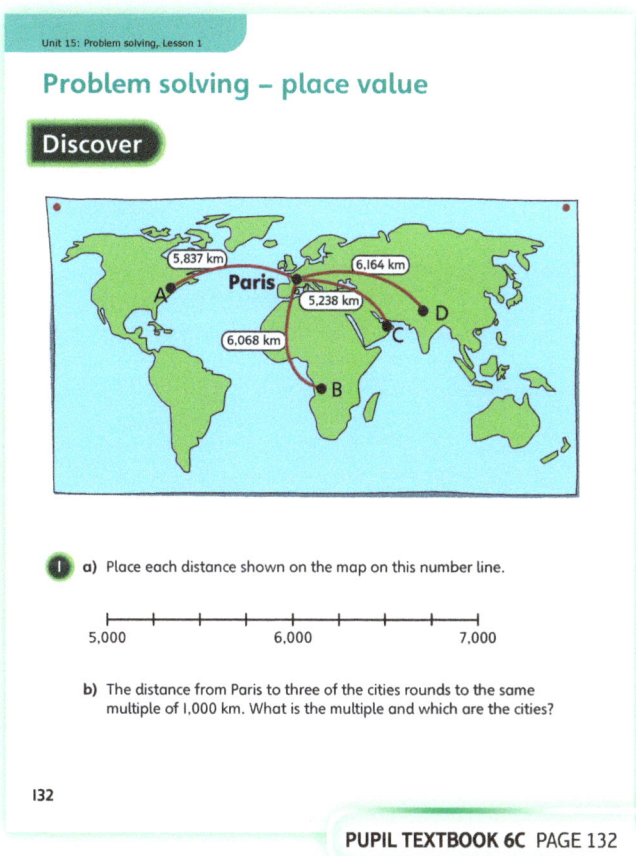

PUPIL TEXTBOOK 6C PAGE 132

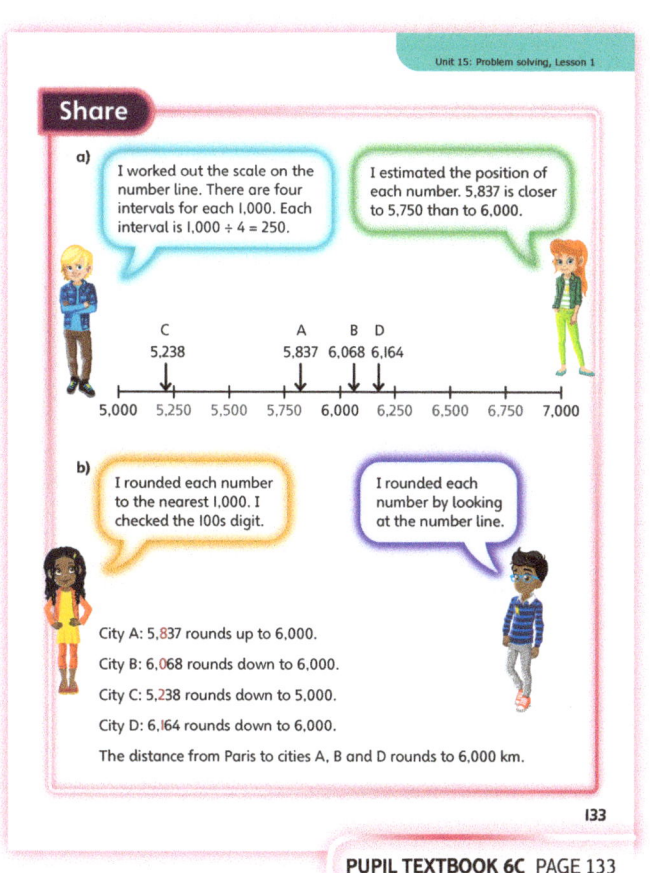

PUPIL TEXTBOOK 6C PAGE 133

# Think together

**WAYS OF WORKING** Whole class teacher led (I do, We do, You do)

**ASK**
- Question ❶: How can you work out the value of each interval on the number line?
- Question ❷: What are the properties of the numbers in the overlapping section of the sorting circles? Why does 10,001 sit outside both sorting circles?
- Question ❸: How do you know that a number is odd? Which digit position is important?

**IN FOCUS** Question ❷ uses a sorting circle, which is a statistical representation; children need to apply their knowledge of numbers and their properties, recognising when a number possesses one, both or neither of these properties. In question ❸, children are required to think about which digit in a number determines a property of the number: for example, the ones digit determines whether a number is odd or even.

**STRENGTHEN** In question ❶, once the interval value has been determined, ask children to label the number line and talk about other numbers that could or could not appear in each interval.

**DEEPEN** For question ❸, ask children to think about another set of criteria that Luis can use to make a different set of numbers for his number line.

**ASSESSMENT CHECKPOINT** Use question ❶ to assess whether children can determine the intervals on a scale and estimate the positions of numbers on a number line. Use question ❷ to assess whether they can sort numbers by their properties.

**ANSWERS**

Question ❶ a):

D B  A  C
900,000  1,000,000  1,100,000  1,200,000

Question ❶ b): 924,500   942,000   1,025,000   1,150,000

Question ❷:   Multiple of 5     Less than 10,000

12,750     6,551
   500
   4,000
20,615

10,001

Question ❸: Section A: a number between 3,000 and 4,000 is not possible with these digits.
Section B: 4,605 is the only possible number.
Section C: 5,406 or 5,460.
Section D: 6,540

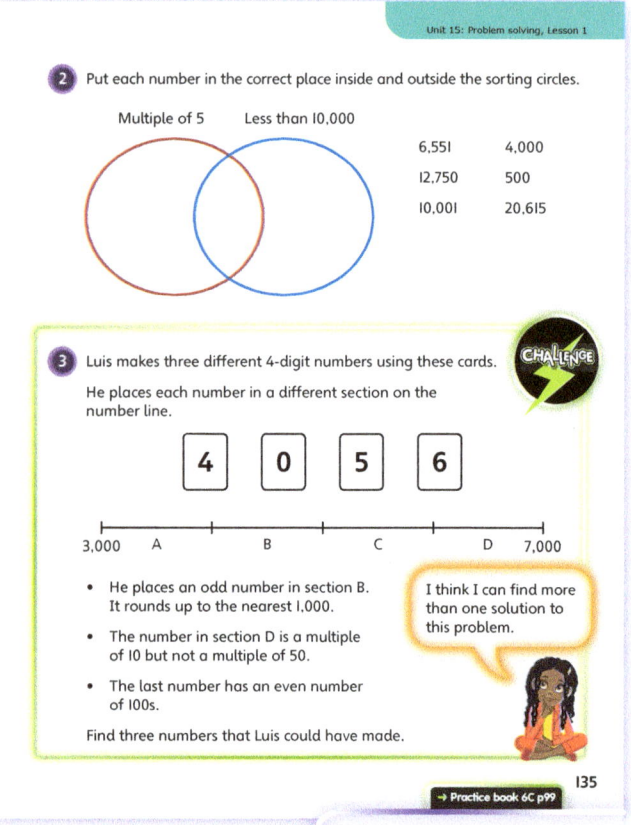

PUPIL TEXTBOOK 6C PAGE 134

PUPIL TEXTBOOK 6C PAGE 135

170

Unit 15: Problem solving, Lesson 1

# Practice

**WAYS OF WORKING** Independent thinking

**IN FOCUS** Question ③ requires children to reason about a possible number that meets all the criteria. There is more than one solution to this problem, so children need to think about making one number and altering single digits, rather than starting from scratch each time. Encourage children to work systematically, perhaps recording their results in a table or ordered list. Question ⑤ provides an opportunity for children to explain their reasoning. Children should think carefully about the language they use, and whether to provide any drawings, to support their explanations. A good strategy here is to encourage children to think about the smallest and greatest numbers that round to 483,000 to the nearest 1,000 and 480,000 to the nearest 10,000.

**STRENGTHEN** For question ④, discuss different interval values for the scale first, then reason about which ones could or could not be possible. This will give children a sense of the size of the scale before they find the actual interval values. You can then talk them through the method of dividing 1,800 by 9 to get the value of 1 interval.

**DEEPEN** Tell children that the line graph used in question ④ now represents a different set of data. Give the value for Monday as 3,600 and ask children to explain what the other values are. Then ask them to suggest alternative values for Monday that would give a sensible scale.

**THINK DIFFERENTLY** In question ④, children apply their knowledge of place value to a new context. They need to realise that the vertical scale is like a number line and divide to get the value of one interval.

**ASSESSMENT CHECKPOINT** Use question ① to assess whether children can compare and order a set of numbers in context. Look to see whether they use a number line or can compare the numbers directly using place value. Use question ④ to assess whether children can transfer their knowledge of working out intervals on a number line to the scale on a graph. Use question ⑤ to check that children understand the effect of rounding to different degrees of accuracy and the possible ranges each time.

**ANSWERS** Answers for the **Practice** part of the lesson can be found in the *Power Maths* online subscription.

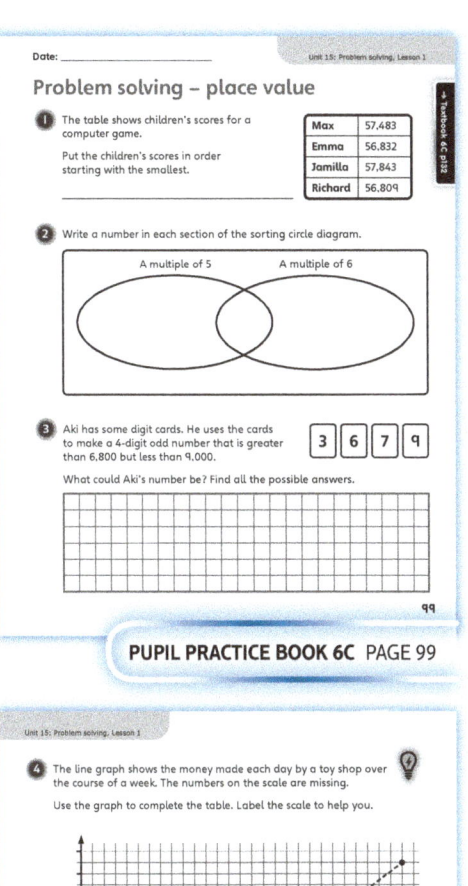

PUPIL PRACTICE BOOK 6C PAGE 99

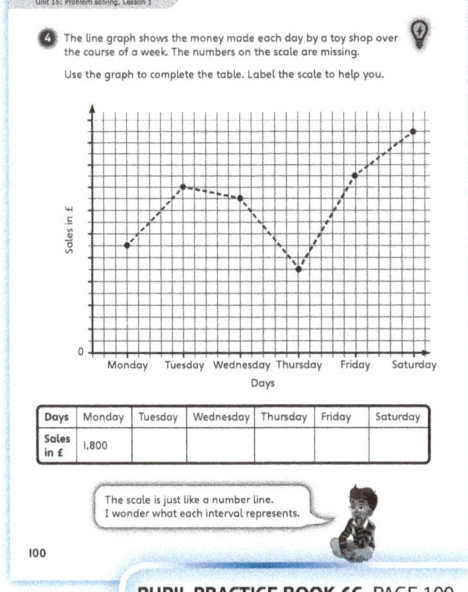

PUPIL PRACTICE BOOK 6C PAGE 100

# Reflect

**WAYS OF WORKING** Independent thinking followed by pair work

**IN FOCUS** Children use their knowledge of number properties to find numbers that would be placed in each section of the sorting circles. They need to know both how to round numbers and how to compare numbers. Children could work individually to complete the task, and then team up with a partner to check one another's work.

**ASSESSMENT CHECKPOINT** Check that children can explain why some numbers belong in both circles and why other numbers belong in none of the circles.

**ANSWERS** Answers for the **Reflect** part of the lesson can be found in the *Power Maths* online subscription.

## After the lesson
- Can children apply their understanding of place value and number to a range of different contexts?
- Can they interpret scales and use known points to identify the value of each interval?

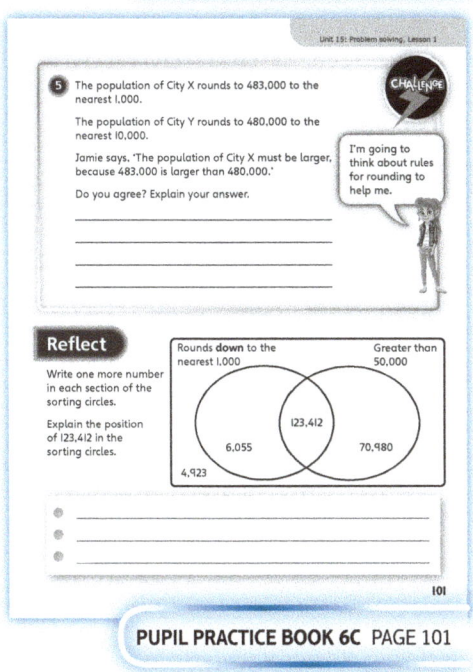

PUPIL PRACTICE BOOK 6C PAGE 101

171

Unit 15: Problem solving, Lesson 2

# Problem solving – negative numbers

## Learning focus
In this lesson, children will use what they have learnt about positive and negative numbers to help solve problems with and without a context. They will build on the previous lesson as they identify the intervals on different scales.

## Before you teach
- Can children count on and back across 0?
- Can they explain why ⁻1 is greater than ⁻10?
- Can they identify the value of the intervals on a number line or scale?

### NATIONAL CURRICULUM LINKS

**Year 6 Number – number and place value**

Solve number and practical problems that involve negative numbers.

### ASSESSING MASTERY

Children can use their knowledge of scales and the number system to solve problems that involve counting on across 0, counting back across 0 and calculating a difference. They can apply their understanding in the context of temperature.

### COMMON MISCONCEPTIONS

When ordering negative numbers, children may reason that a number such as ⁻20 must be greater than ⁻5 because 20 is greater than 5. Practise counting on and back over 0 looking at the symmetry of positive and negative numbers as they move away from 0. Ask:
- *When you move to the right on the number line, do the numbers become greater or smaller? In which direction do you move to go from ⁻20 to ⁻5?*

### STRENGTHENING UNDERSTANDING

Explore differences between pairs of positive and negative numbers, drawing on number bonds to partition differences across 0. For example, ask: *What number is 5 more than 0? What number is 5 less than 0?* Ask children to explain why the difference between these two numbers must be 10.

### GOING DEEPER

Give children a difference: for example, 13. Ask them to find pairs of positive and negative numbers, or two negative numbers, separated by this difference. Challenge children to make up problems, possibly in the context of temperature, related to a difference of 13.

### KEY LANGUAGE

**In lesson:** negative, positive, sequence, difference, half-way

**Other language to be used by the teacher:** scale

### STRUCTURES AND REPRESENTATIONS

Number line, bar model, line graph

In the eTextbook of this lesson, you will find interactive links to a selection of teaching tools.

### Quick recap

Ask children to draw a simple number line showing the following numbers in the correct positions:

4    0    ⁻2    ⁻3

# Discover

**WAYS OF WORKING** Pair work

**ASK**

- Question 1 a): *Zero is given as a value on the number line. What does this tell you about A and B?*
- Question 1 a): *How can you work out the value of A and B? What should you do first?*
- Question 1 a): *How is this problem similar to the number line problems you solved in the previous lesson?*
- Question 1 b): *Where will the half-way point be? Is it before or after 0?*

**IN FOCUS** Question 1 a) requires children to interpret a scale involving positive and negative numbers and to find the value of two points with a given difference. It builds on the number line work in the previous lesson, but this time children are given the difference between two points, rather than working it out.

Question 1 b) has been chosen so that children revisit finding the half-way point between two values. This skill is vital when reading scales for measurements and statistics.

**PRACTICAL TIPS** Practise counting in different intervals across 0. Ask questions such as: *I'm counting on in intervals of 5 from ⁻21. How do you know that I won't say 0 in my count?*

**ANSWERS**

Question 1 a): The value of point A is ⁻100.
The value of point B is 60.

Question 1 b): The value of the half-way point between A and B is ⁻20.

PUPIL TEXTBOOK 6C PAGE 136

# Share

**WAYS OF WORKING** Whole class teacher led

**ASK**

- Question 1 a): *Why can't Astrid's interval value of 10 be correct? What does this tell you about the interval value?*
- Question 1 a): *What is the relationship between a difference of 80 and a difference of 160? Can you use this relationship to explain why the interval must be 20?*
- Question 1 b): *What is the same and what is different about Flo's two strategies?*

**IN FOCUS** In question 1 a), ensure that children recognise why 160 is divided by 8 to find the value of each interval on the number line. In question 1 b), children often halve the difference when finding the half-way point, but forget to add this value to the lowest number; for example, they might say that the half-way point is 80 because this is half of the difference (160). Ensure they remember to add 80 to ⁻100, to find the answer of ⁻20.

**STRENGTHEN** Once the the value of the intervals has been identified, count on and back in intervals of 20 from 0. Use this count to agree the values of A and B, relating A to 5 intervals of 20 less than 0 and B to 3 intervals of 20 greater than 0.

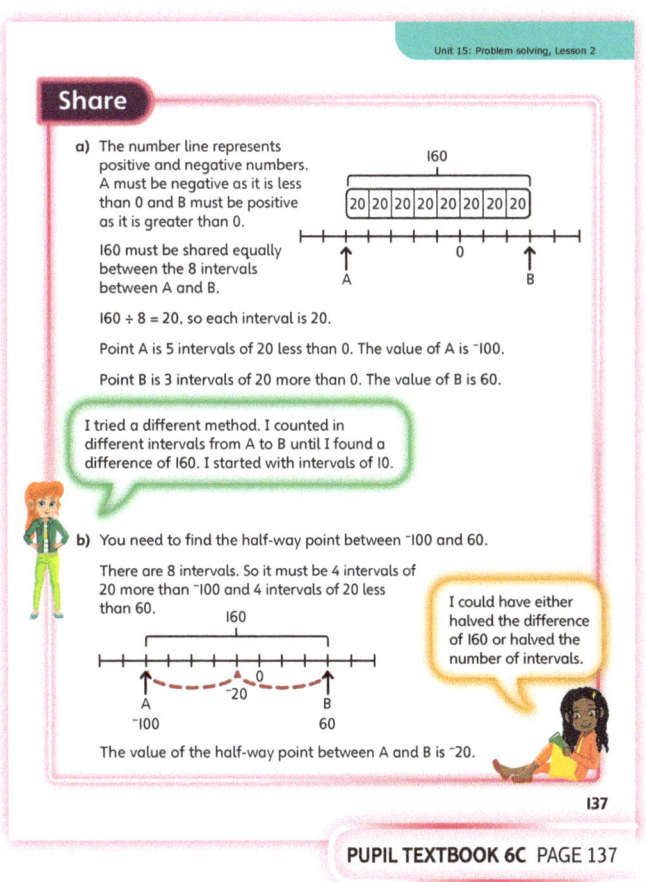

PUPIL TEXTBOOK 6C PAGE 137

# Unit 15: Problem solving, Lesson 2

## Think together

**WAYS OF WORKING** Whole class teacher led (I do, We do, You do)

**ASK**

- Question ❶: *How do you know that one of the temperatures must be negative and the other positive?*
- Question ❷: *What is the same and what is different about finding missing numbers in a sequence and finding missing numbers on a scale?*
- Question ❷: *What will the next number in the sequence be? What is the difference between this number and ⁻22?*
- Question ❸: *How do you know that the temperature at 7 pm must be below 0?*
- Question ❹: *There are no intervals on this number line. How can you find the half-way point?*

**IN FOCUS** Questions ❶ and ❷ provide opportunities for children to apply the same skills but now in the context of temperature or as part of a linear sequence. In question ❶, they need to make a connection between intervals on number lines and scales. In both questions, children have to calculate across 0.

In question ❹, no intervals are shown on the number line but children should recognise that the half-way point can be found by applying the same strategies used in **Share**.

**STRENGTHEN** For question ❹, model using 0 as a stopping point to calculate the difference between two points, for example ⁻24 and 6. Children can then attempt to answer question ❹ using the same strategy.

**DEEPEN** Ask children to explain how they can quickly work out the values of the 8th and 10th terms in the sequence in question ❷. Ask them to investigate whether ⁻181 is in the sequence. Encourage them to reason rather than working out the values up to ⁻190.

**ASSESSMENT CHECKPOINT** Use questions ❶ and ❷ to assess whether children can apply strategies to interpret scales and intervals in other contexts. Check that they can use the number of intervals and the difference to find the interval value. Use question ❸ to assess whether children can find the difference between positive and negative values and find a drop or rise in temperature. Check that children can interpret data presented on a graph.

**ANSWERS**

Question ❶ a): The inside temperature is 30 °C.

Question ❶ b): The outside temperature is ⁻15 °C.

Question ❷: 26, 14, 2, ⁻10, ⁻22, ⁻34

Question ❸ a): It was 12 degrees warmer.

Question ❸ b): The temperature at 7 pm was ⁻1 °C.

Question ❹: ⁻6 is half-way between ⁻30 and 18.

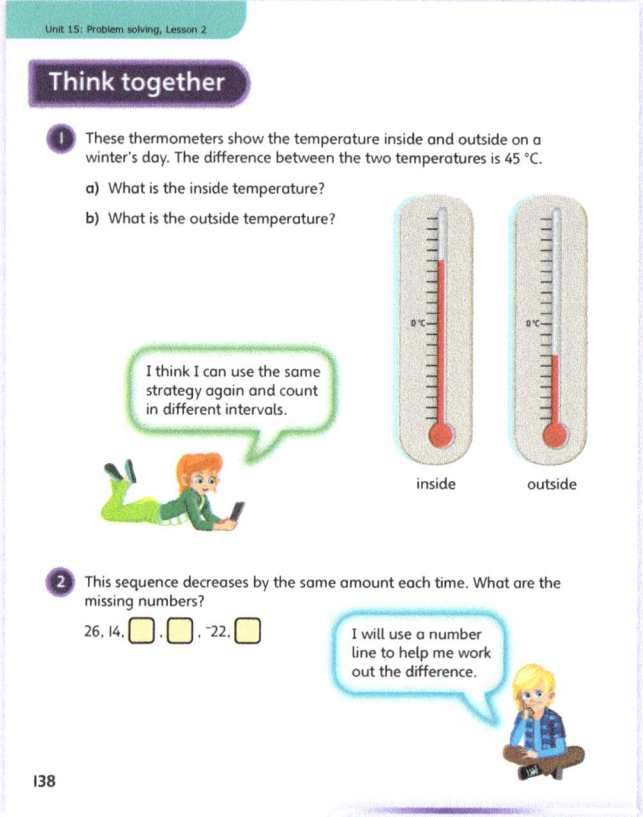

PUPIL TEXTBOOK 6C PAGE 138

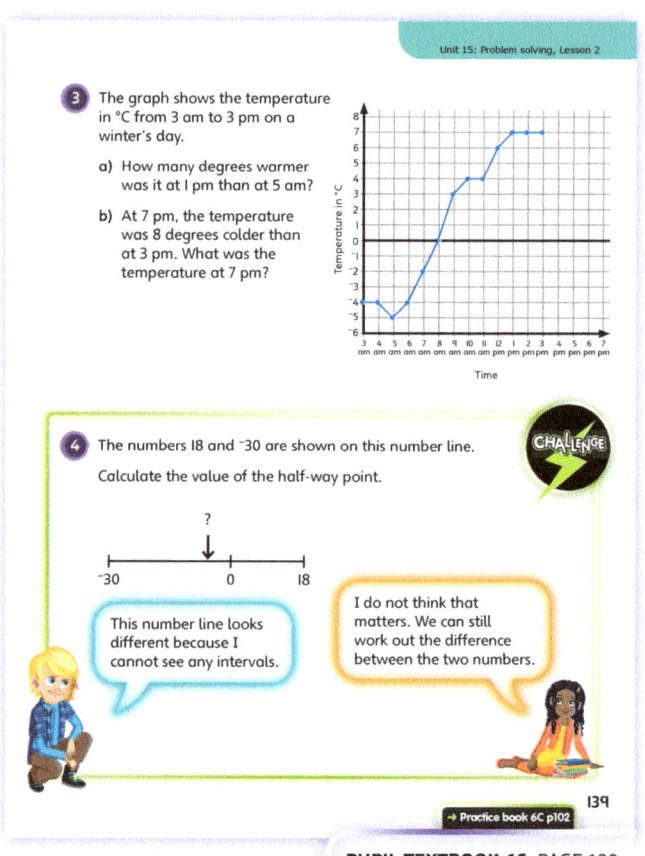

PUPIL TEXTBOOK 6C PAGE 139

# Unit 15: Problem solving, Lesson 2

## Practice

**WAYS OF WORKING** Independent thinking and pair work

**IN FOCUS** Question ❶ requires children to identify the biggest difference between pairs of positive and negative numbers. They should reason about each pair first before calculating the difference. The numbers have been chosen so that two of the differences involve counting across 0 and the third pair involves the difference between two negative numbers.

In question ❷, children work with increasing and decreasing sequences. In part b), the interval value is not given, so they need to calculate this first by adapting the strategies developed in the lesson.

In question ❻, children solve a puzzle as they reason about differences between positive and negative numbers. They may find it useful to write each value on a small piece of paper so they can be easily rearranged on the diagram.

**STRENGTHEN** For question ❸, encourage children to label intermediate points on the vertical scale to help them to make sense of values that lie within intervals on the bar chart.

**DEEPEN** Ask children to make up linear sequence problems for a partner to solve. Ensure their sequences cross 0. Encourage children to use both increasing and decreasing sequences.

**ASSESSMENT CHECKPOINT** Use questions ❶ and ❻ to assess whether children can reason about and calculate the difference between positive and negative numbers. Check whether they can apply reasoning or whether they use a number line to work out the differences.

Use questions ❸ and ❹ to assess whether children can apply their understanding of positive and negative numbers in the context of measurements and statistical representations (that is, when they are used on a bar chart). In question ❹, check that children can work out the interval size from the given difference.

**ANSWERS** Answers for the **Practice** part of the lesson can be found in the *Power Maths* online subscription.

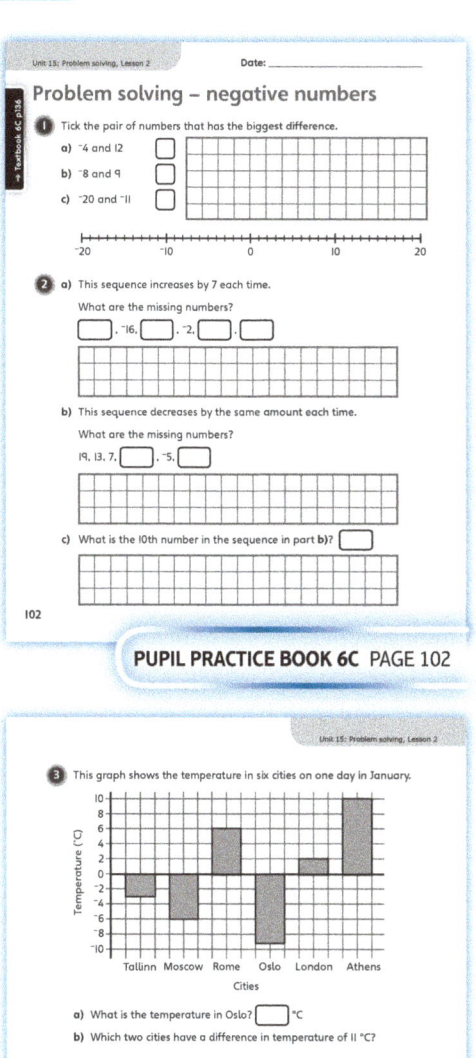

**PUPIL PRACTICE BOOK 6C** PAGE 102

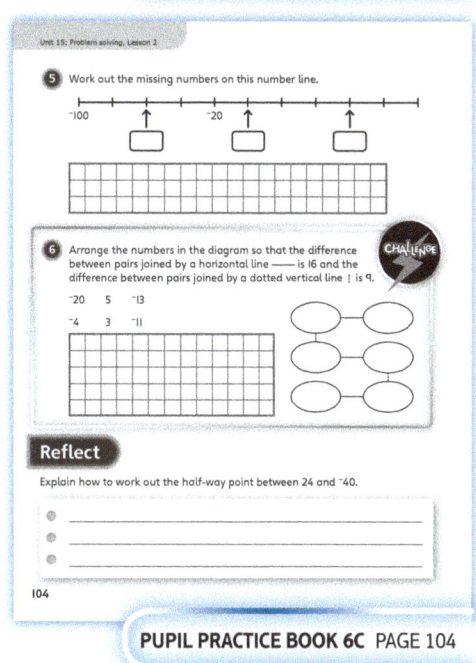

**PUPIL PRACTICE BOOK 6C** PAGE 103

## Reflect

**WAYS OF WORKING** Independent thinking

**IN FOCUS** This **Reflect** question requires children to explain the steps in their strategy to find a point half-way between given positive and negative numbers. They should recognise that the same strategy can be used to find the point half-way between any two numbers.

**ASSESSMENT CHECKPOINT** Check that children remember to add half the difference to ⁻40 (or subtract half the difference from 24) rather than incorrectly giving the half-way point as 32.

**ANSWERS** Answers for the **Reflect** part of the lesson can be found in the *Power Maths* online subscription.

**PUPIL PRACTICE BOOK 6C** PAGE 104

## After the lesson

- Can children calculate the differences between pairs of positive and negative numbers, applying this to problems with or without a context?
- Can they interpret scales that include both positive and negative numbers, including finding a half-way point?

175

Unit 15: Problem solving, Lesson 3

# Problem solving – addition and subtraction

## Learning focus
In this lesson, children will flexibly apply their understanding of addition and subtraction to a range of problems. They will have the opportunity to consider different strategies dependent on the numbers and operations. They will use estimation to check answers.

## Before you teach
- Can children explain why a problem requires them to add and/or subtract?
- Can they use rounding appropriately to make estimations?
- Do they recognise different contexts where addition and subtraction are used, for example in statistics?

### NATIONAL CURRICULUM LINKS

**Year 6 Number – addition, subtraction, multiplication and division**

Use estimation to check answers to calculations and determine, in the context of a problem, an appropriate degree of accuracy.

Solve addition and subtraction multi-step problems in contexts, deciding which operations and methods to use and why.

### ASSESSING MASTERY

Children can work flexibly with addition and subtraction to solve a range of problems, with or without a context. They can recognise and explain why it may be easier to calculate in a different order than the order in which the steps are given in a problem, drawing on their understanding of the order of operations.

### COMMON MISCONCEPTIONS

Most children recognise that addition can be carried out in any order but that subtraction cannot. Although 3,250 – 1,925 – 250 cannot be carried out in any order (for example, 1,925 – 250 – 3,250), children may not recognise that they can reorder the numbers to be subtracted (for example, 3,250 – 250 – 1,925). Similarly, 3,250 + 895 – 250 gives the same result as 3,250 – 250 + 895, but the latter is easier to work out. Ask:
- *For 3,250 + 895 – 250, why might it be easier to subtract 250 from 3,250 first and then add 895?*

### STRENGTHENING UNDERSTANDING

Explore test questions involving both addition and subtraction. Sort the questions into examples where the calculation is best carried out in the order given and examples where the calculation is made easier by reordering the values.

### GOING DEEPER

Ask children to make up calculations or problems where reordering the numbers to be added and subtracted makes the calculations simpler. They should be able to explain their reasoning for the choice of numbers.

### KEY LANGUAGE

**In lesson:** add, subtract, estimate, total, difference

**Other language to be used by the teacher:** order

### STRUCTURES AND REPRESENTATIONS

Column method, bar chart, number line

### RESOURCES

**Optional:** sticky notes

 In the eTextbook of this lesson, you will find interactive links to a selection of teaching tools.

## Quick recap
Ask children to describe a method that they would use to solve each of these calculations:

50 + 990    34,512 – 3,651    2,000 – 3

Unit 15: Problem solving, Lesson 3

# Discover

**WAYS OF WORKING** Pair work

**ASK**

- Question 1 a): *Has Kate given you the whole method, or just one step? How do Max and Kate's methods differ? Will you use a mental or a written method?*
- Question 1 b): *What has Max noticed about the numbers involved? Does it matter whether you subtract 875 from 2,692 first or from 1,975 first? What is the second step in each of these methods? Can you explain why they give the same answer?*

**IN FOCUS** The numbers in this two-step problem have been chosen to encourage children to consider the order in which they carry out a calculation. In this example, it is easier to find the answer by working through the steps in a different order from that given in the problem. In question 1 a), Kate works through the steps in the order in which the numbers are given. In question 1 b), Max recognises that subtracting 875 from 1,975 first makes the calculation easier.

**PRACTICAL TIPS** Write the numbers to be added and subtracted on separate sticky notes so they can be reordered easily to match the different methods.

**ANSWERS**

Question 1 a):

| Th | H | T | O |
|---|---|---|---|
| ¹2 | ⁶6 | ⁸9̸ | ¹2 |
| − | 8 | 7 | 5 |
| 1 | 8 | 1 | 7 |

| Th | H | T | O |
|---|---|---|---|
| 1 | 8 | 1 | 7 |
| + | 1 | 9 | 7 | 5 |
| 3 | 7 | 9 | 2 |
| | 1 | 1 | |

There are 3,792 trees in the forest now.

Question 1 b): 1,975 − 875 = 1,100
2,692 + 1,100 = 3,792
There are 3,792 trees in the forest now.
The numbers are suitable for Max to work it out mentally with the aid of a number line.

# Share

**WAYS OF WORKING** Whole class teacher led

**ASK**

- Question 1 a): *How has Dexter rounded the numbers 2,692 and 875 to estimate that there were 1,800 trees left in the forest before more trees were planted? How would you round the numbers 1,817 and 1,975 to estimate the addition?*
- Question 1 b): *Why has Astrid chosen a mental method? Why will Flo's method give the same answer even though she is adding first?*

**IN FOCUS** Question 1 a) revisits the use of a written method for subtraction and addition. It also demonstrates the use of estimation to check an answer. Question 1 b) requires children to think about why Max has chosen to subtract 875 from 1,975, rather than from 2,692.

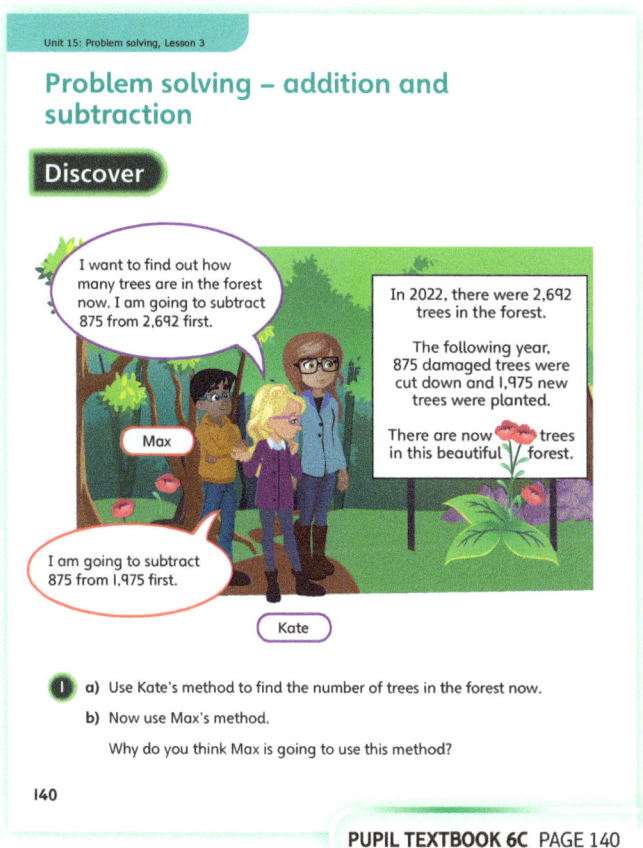

PUPIL TEXTBOOK 6C PAGE 140

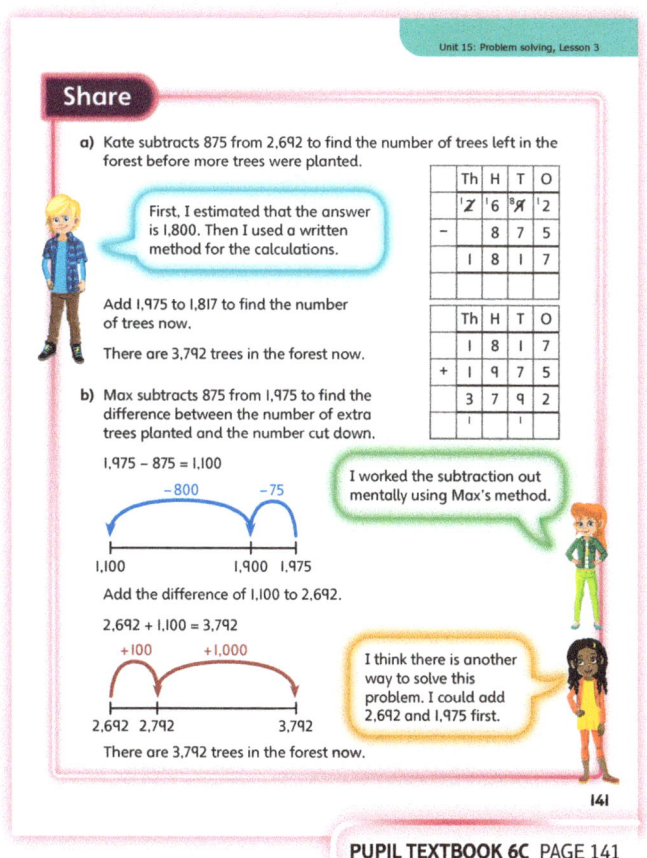

PUPIL TEXTBOOK 6C PAGE 141

# Think together

**WAYS OF WORKING** Whole class teacher led (I do, We do, You do)

**ASK**
- Question ❶: *What can you tell me about the scale? What is the value of each interval? How do you know?*
- Question ❷: *Why might Ash choose to complete the calculations in a different order? What has he noticed?*
- Question ❸ b): *How do you know that the hundredths digit must be less than 6?*
- Question ❹: *What bar model should Astrid draw? How will this help her to solve the problem? Will you add or subtract first? Why?*

**IN FOCUS** Question ❶ has been chosen to help children recognise the application of addition and subtraction to statistics. The questions can be solved in more than one way so children can demonstrate their flexibility with calculation. Question ❷ provides a decontextualised example, so children recognise that similar strategies can be applied and that the numbers involved may determine what part of the calculation they carry out first. In question ❸, children reason about missing values in an addition and a subtraction using the column method. They are required to think about the effect of any place value exchanges made.

**STRENGTHEN** For question ❹, look together at the difference between the items that Mo and Ambika bought. Encourage children to draw a bar model to illustrate their purchases.

**DEEPEN** For question ❶, ask children to describe different strategies to complete the calculations. For example, in part a) they could find the total for each year and then compare, or they could see that £700 more was raised by fun runs in 2023 and £500 more was raised by singing competitions in 2023, giving a total of £1,200 more. Challenge them to make up a similar question for a partner to solve.

**ASSESSMENT CHECKPOINT** Use questions ❶ and ❷ to assess whether children can choose a strategy and an appropriate order for operations depending on the numbers involved. Check that they can explain their strategy. Use question ❸ to assess whether children can use the structure of a column method to help them reason about missing digits.

**ANSWERS**

Question ❶ a): £3,100 in 2023 − £1,800 in 2021 = £1,300 more was raised in 2023 than in 2021.

Question ❶ b): Fun run total is £4,100.
Singing total is £3,400.
The difference in the totals is £700.

Question ❷: Triangle = 2,000
Square = 299

Question ❸ a):

| TTh | Th | H | T | O |
|---|---|---|---|---|
|  | 5 | 3 | 6 | 4 |
| + | 6 | 5 | 3 | 9 |
| 1 | 1 | 9 | 0 | 3 |

b):

| T | O | •Tth | Hth |
|---|---|---|---|
| 6 | 9 | 8 | 5 |
| − 2 | 3 | 5 | 6 |
| 4 | 6 | 2 | 9 |

Question ❹: Pen = 65p   Rubber = 45p

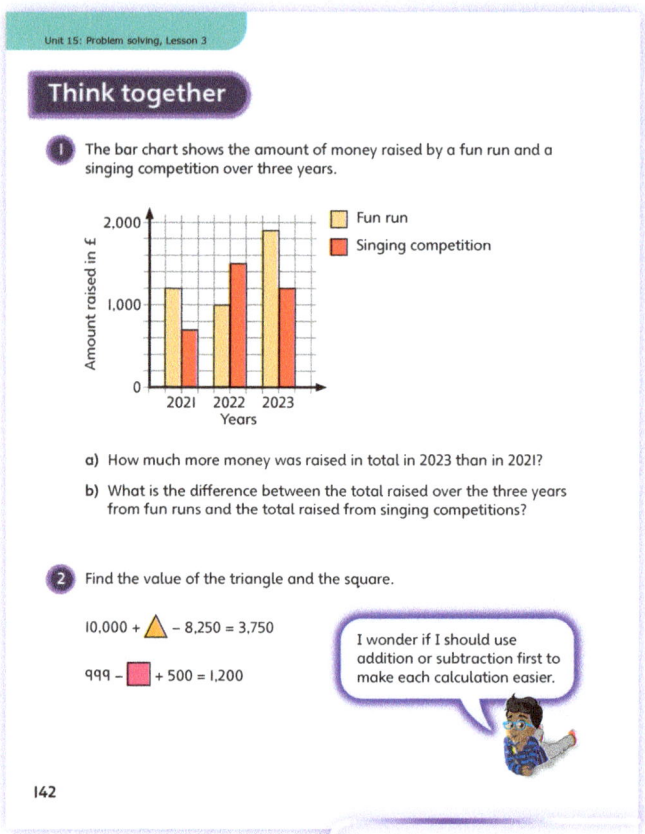

PUPIL TEXTBOOK 6C PAGE 142

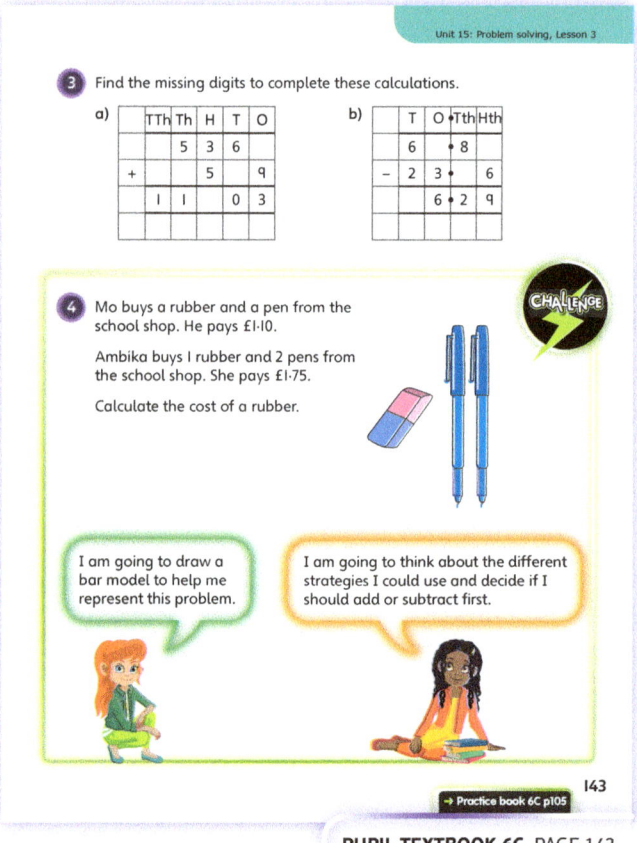

PUPIL TEXTBOOK 6C PAGE 143

Unit 15: Problem solving, Lesson 3

# Practice

**WAYS OF WORKING** Independent thinking

**IN FOCUS** Question ① requires children to think about the order in which they will carry out an addition and a subtraction, making decisions based on the numbers involved. Question ③ has been designed to be slightly more complex than **Think together** question ① in the Textbook: the bar chart is shown in a horizontal orientation and each set of data comprises three bars. Question ④ is a multi-step problem, so children must be careful to complete all steps. In question ⑥, children need to reason about which statement provides the best starting place to help find the unknown values.

**STRENGTHEN** Encourage children to make estimates first and then check their answers against those estimates.

**DEEPEN** Give children algebraic problems similar to question ⑥, where unknown values have to be determined. For example:

$$4{,}599 - \triangle + 401 = 3{,}500 + \square$$
$$\square + \triangle - 975 = 525$$
$$\triangle + \triangle - 545 = 655$$

**ASSESSMENT CHECKPOINT** Use questions ① to ③ to assess whether children can apply strategies of addition and subtraction fluently in different contexts, including statistics. Look to see what strategy they choose each time. Use question ④ to assess whether children can complete a multi-step problem. Check whether children make estimates and then check their answers against these.

**ANSWERS** Answers for the **Practice** part of the lesson can be found in the *Power Maths* online subscription.

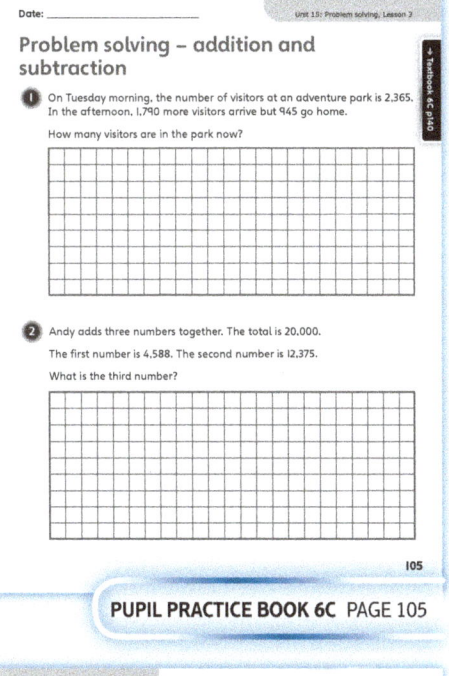

PUPIL PRACTICE BOOK 6C PAGE 105

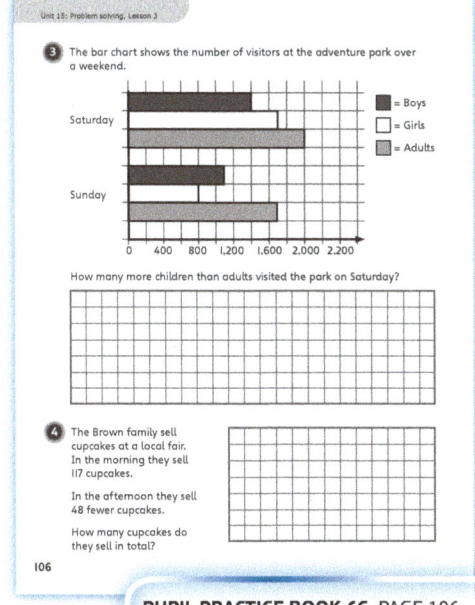

PUPIL PRACTICE BOOK 6C PAGE 106

# Reflect

**WAYS OF WORKING** Pair work

**IN FOCUS** Drawing out a particular question that children find difficult will enable them to consider misconceptions and errors and then formulate possible strategies for dealing with them.

**ASSESSMENT CHECKPOINT** Check that children can explain why they find a particular type of question challenging and what they might do to address this challenge.

**ANSWERS** Answers for the **Reflect** part of the lesson can be found in the *Power Maths* online subscription.

## After the lesson

- Can children flexibly work with addition and subtraction, explaining the order in which they choose to do the calculation?
- Can children solve a range of problems, recognising when they need to add or subtract?

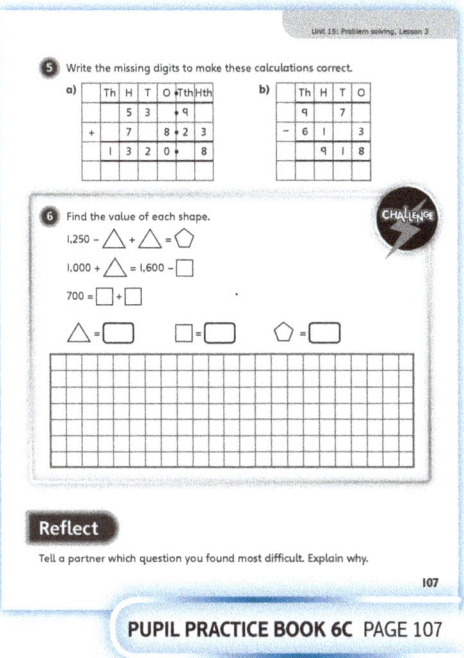

PUPIL PRACTICE BOOK 6C PAGE 107

Unit 15: Problem solving, Lesson 4

# Problem solving – four operations

### Learning focus
In this lesson, children will use the four operations to solve a range of problems. They will make decisions about which operation to use first, and recognise when and why a calculation can be carried out in a different order.

### Before you teach
- Can children explain what a problem is asking them to do?
- Can they explain what steps are required and the operations needed?
- Can they represent the problem with a diagram?

### NATIONAL CURRICULUM LINKS

**Year 6 Number – addition, subtraction, multiplication and division**

Solve problems involving addition, subtraction, multiplication and division.

Use their knowledge of the order of operations to carry out calculations involving the four operations.

### ASSESSING MASTERY

Children can use representations to help make sense of problems and use them to determine the operations required. They can apply mental and written strategies to two- and multi-step problems. Children who have mastered this unit will also be able to draw on their knowledge of algebra from Unit 8 to help them form equations to model a real-life scenario, and then solve them to answer the question.

### COMMON MISCONCEPTIONS

Children may choose the wrong operations to answer problem-solving questions. This is principally due to either a failure to comprehend the text or insecurity in their understanding of the effect of the operations. Encourage children to always draw a diagram to represent the problem. Ask:
- *What information are you given? How can you represent this in a diagram?*
- *What operation does the diagram suggest you should use?*

### STRENGTHENING UNDERSTANDING

Revisit the effect of the four operations, discussing examples of contexts and the language related to them. Give a range of contextualised problems to groups of four children to reinforce the steps required for problem solving. Each child within each group should take one of these roles: making sense of the problem and explaining; making an estimate, explaining any rounding; calculating, explaining and justifying the strategies used; checking the calculated answer, comparing it with the estimate and ensuring the actual question has been answered.

### GOING DEEPER

Look at problems involving two operations with the same order of priority: for example, multiplication and division. Discuss why we may choose to complete a division before a multiplication (or vice versa) even when this is not the order suggested by the problem. Children should recognise that this will depend on the numbers involved. For example, when solving a problem using $45 \times 12 \div 15$, work out $45 \div 15$ first and then multiply the result, 3, by 12. Some children may also see this as $45 \times \frac{4}{5}$ by expressing $12 \div 15$ as a fraction first.

### KEY LANGUAGE

**In lesson:** divide, subtract

**Other language to be used by the teacher:** add, multiply, estimate, order

### STRUCTURES AND REPRESENTATIONS

Bar model

### RESOURCES

**Optional:** pictures of puzzle books, computer games, boxes of colouring pencils

 In the eTextbook of this lesson, you will find interactive links to a selection of teaching tools.

### Quick recap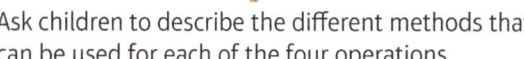

Ask children to describe the different methods that can be used for each of the four operations.

# Discover

**WAYS OF WORKING** Pair work

**ASK**

- Question 1 a): *If the computer game is £15, how much is the puzzle book? If the puzzle book is £15, how much is the computer game?*
- Question 1 a): *How can the problem be represented? You don't know the price of either item – what could you do?*
- Question 1 b): *Using the information given in part a), how do you know that at least 2 boxes of pencils can be purchased for £35 before doing any calculations?*
- Question 1 b): *How can this problem be represented? What operation will you need to use?*

**IN FOCUS** Questions 1 a) and b) both require children to draw on a range of information and to use the relationships between prices to solve the problems. They need to be able to think through each problem systematically.

**PRACTICAL TIPS** Use pictures of puzzle books, computer games and boxes of colouring pencils so children can role-play the scenario with different prices for the items. Look at other possible prices for the puzzle book and the computer game that have a difference of £12·50, agreeing that although this could be used to help solve the problem, it is a less efficient method.

**ANSWERS**

Question 1 a): A puzzle book costs £7·50.
A computer game costs £7·50 + £12·50 = £20.

Question 1 b): Isla can buy 3 boxes of pencils for £35.
She will have £5 left over.

PUPIL TEXTBOOK 6C PAGE 144

# Share

**WAYS OF WORKING** Whole class teacher led

**ASK**

- Question 1 a): *What does the first bar model represent?*
- Question 1 a): *You are told that 2 puzzle books and a computer game cost £35. Why does the second bar model show 3 puzzle books and an additional £12·50?*
- Question 1 b): *Why will both of Flo's strategies work?*
- Question 1 b): *35 divided by 10 is 3·5, so why is the answer to the problem 3, not 3·5?*

**IN FOCUS** Question 1 a) requires children to think flexibly as they use more than one bar model to represent different aspects of the problem. In question 1 b), they need to round after division, using the context of the question to decide whether to round up or down. They can also be asked to calculate how much more money Isla would need to buy a fourth box of pencils.

**STRENGTHEN** Work through the problems in question 1 a), step-by-step, so children understand the order in which calculations must be done. Ask children to check that the solution is correct by working out £7·50 × 2 and then adding £20.

**DEEPEN** Ask children to think of a different question for question 1 b) that would require 3·5 to be rounded up to 4 rather than keeping 3 with a remainder.

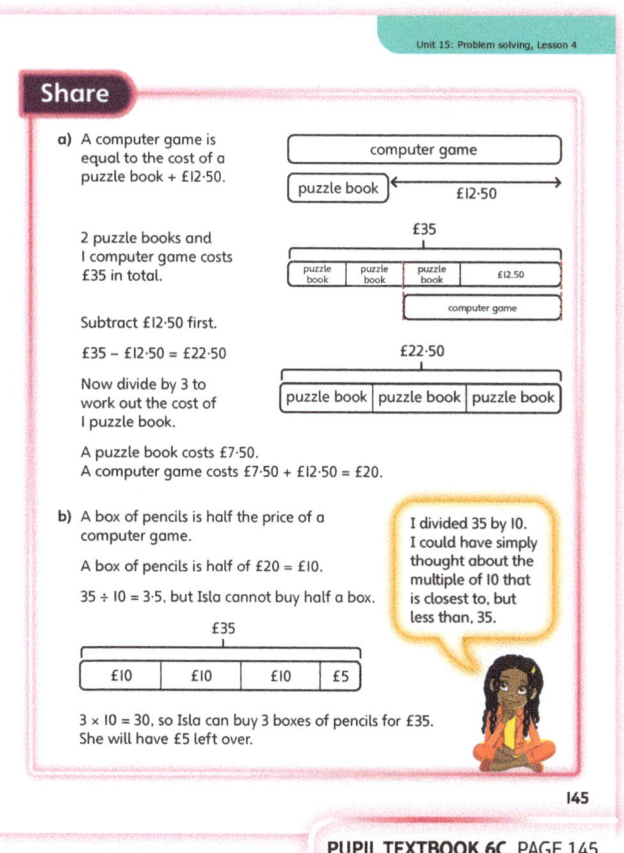

PUPIL TEXTBOOK 6C PAGE 145

# Think together

**WAYS OF WORKING** Whole class teacher led (I do, We do, You do)

**ASK**

- Question ❶: *How can you work out the value of the toy car using what you know about the cost of a whistle?*
- Question ❷: *How could you use algebra to help you write down what the question is telling you, in a simpler form?*
- Question ❸: *What information do you already know? How can you represent this using bar models?*
- Question ❹: *How can you work out the perimeter of the square? What do you need to do next?*

**IN FOCUS** Question ❶ requires children to recognise that although the language is slightly different to that used in question ❶ a) in **Share** ('less than' instead of 'more than'), the same strategy can be used. In question ❷, the numbers are large so you might want to encourage children to revisit what they learnt about algebra in Unit 8. You will need to scaffold this learning. If you let $s$ be the mass of 1 small bag, then $75s = 300$ kg. Children should realise that they need to divide 300 by 75 to find $s$. Similarly, if $l$ is the mass of 1 large bag, guide children to write $60l = 600$ kg. Question ❸ requires children to round to the nearest pound and to reason about the result. Question ❹ is a multi-step problem written in the context of shape and measurement, so children are required to check carefully that they have answered the question and not missed any steps.

**STRENGTHEN** Encourage children to use bar models to represent the problems, looking carefully at the language of the question to help them. They should remember to estimate before calculating and to check their answers against their estimates.

**DEEPEN** Look at different strategies to solve question ❷. Similarly, encourage children to explain the alternative strategies for question ❹.

**ASSESSMENT CHECKPOINT** Use questions ❷ and ❸ to assess whether children can solve multi-step problems, checking that they recognise what operations need to be carried out. Use question ❹ to assess whether children can apply the four operations to problems relating to shape and measurement.

**ANSWERS**

Question ❶: Whistle = £1·10    Car = £1·95

Question ❷: The large bag is 6 kg more than the small bag.
75 small = 600 kg     60 large = 600 kg
1 small = 4 kg         1 large = 10 kg

Question ❸ a): Children pay £27·75, £13 for the coach and £14·75 for the ticket.

Question ❸ b): They do not pay enough because the actual cost is £13·45 which rounds down to £13. They pay 45p less per person than the actual cost of the coach.

Question ❹: $x = 50$ cm
Perimeter of the square is 120 cm × 4 = 480 cm.
Perimeter of the rectangle is 480 ÷ 3 = 160 cm.
Two sides are 30 cm, two sides are $x$ cm.
160 − (2 × 30) = 100 cm
$x = 100$ cm ÷ 2 = 50 cm

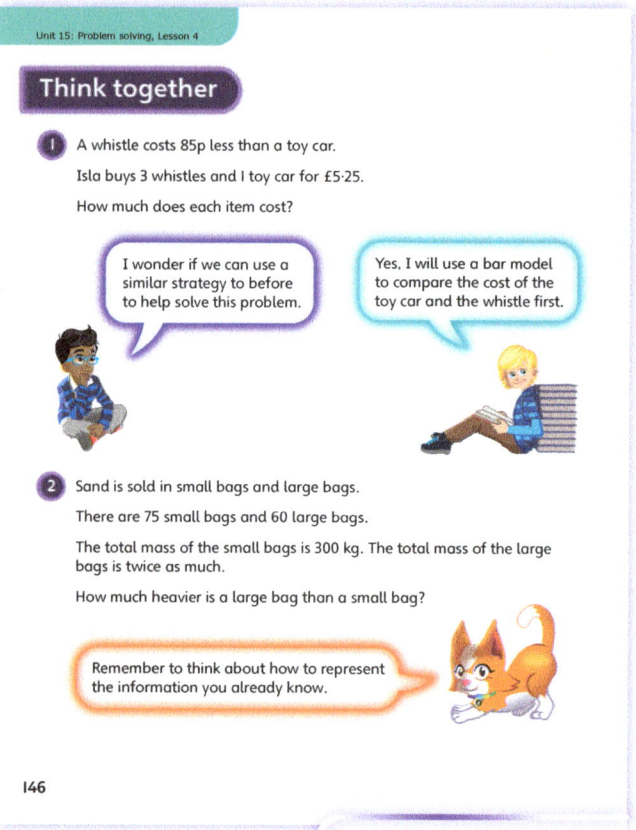

PUPIL TEXTBOOK 6C PAGE 146

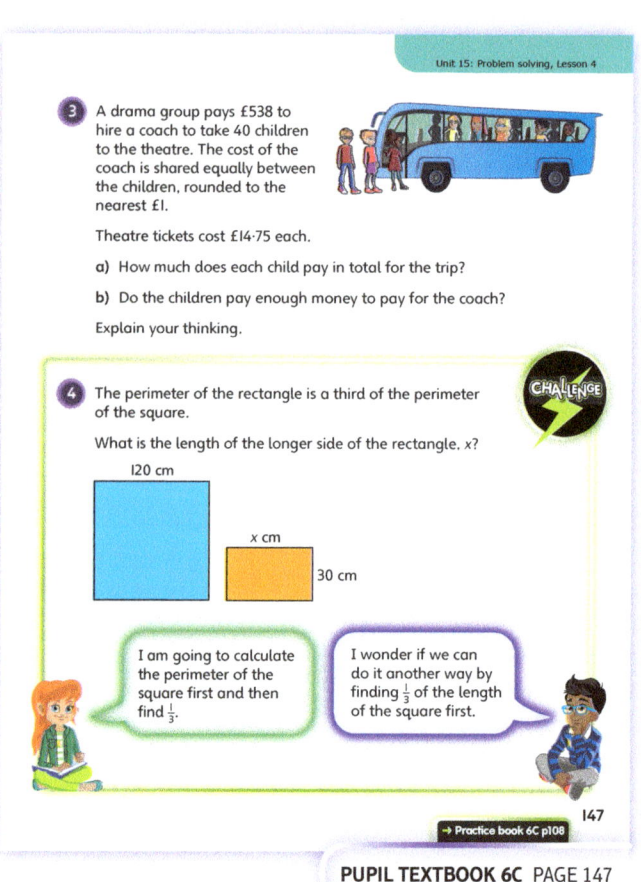

PUPIL TEXTBOOK 6C PAGE 147

Unit 15: Problem solving, Lesson 4

# Practice

**WAYS OF WORKING** Independent thinking

**IN FOCUS** In question ②, children must round up after the division to solve the problem. They can use what they know about the number of 25s in 100 to solve the calculation mentally. Question ③ requires children to recognise that they need to do two separate divisions, rather than simply dividing the total number of fruits by 10. In contrast to question ②, they need to round both numbers down. Question ④ has been chosen so that children can think about possible strategies. Encourage them to think carefully about how the capacities of the cup and the mug are given in different units, so they will need to convert one before they can calculate the total.

**STRENGTHEN** For question ⑥, encourage children to draw bar models to represent the problem first. Focus on the relationship between the number of litres in a tin of red paint compared to a tin of blue, and the total number of litres of red paint compared to the number of litres of blue paint (half).

**DEEPEN** Ask children to look together at question ⑤. Ask them to explain whether Reena's statement is still true if a number is divided by 3 and then multiplied by 6, or multiplied by 3 and then divided by 6.

**THINK DIFFERENTLY** Question ⑤ considers the replacement of two calculations by a single calculation, rather than simply looking at the order in which calculations are carried out. Children need to reason about the effect of multiplying by 6 and dividing by 3.

**ASSESSMENT CHECKPOINT** Use question ① to assess whether children can represent problems using bar models. Check that they recognise when one value can be replaced and represented using its relationship with another. Use questions ② and ③ to assess whether they understand when to round up or down in the context of the problem.

**ANSWERS** Answers for the **Practice** part of the lesson can be found in the *Power Maths* online subscription.

# Reflect

**WAYS OF WORKING** Pair work

**IN FOCUS** Children discuss strategies for problem solving, thinking about the steps they should take to make sense of a problem and to check that they have answered the question posed. Some things that children may include are:
- representing the problem using a bar model or other diagram
- using the diagram to work out what steps they need to take to solve the problem
- identifying which operation they need to use at each step
- checking that their answer makes sense in the context of the problem.

**ASSESSMENT CHECKPOINT** Check that children consider estimates when solving problems.

**ANSWERS** Answers for the **Reflect** part of a lesson can be found in the *Power Maths* online subscription.

## After the lesson
- Can children make sense of a problem and represent it using bar models?
- Can they use a range of strategies for calculations, both written and mental?
- Can children explain which operations they should use and what language within a given question tells them this?

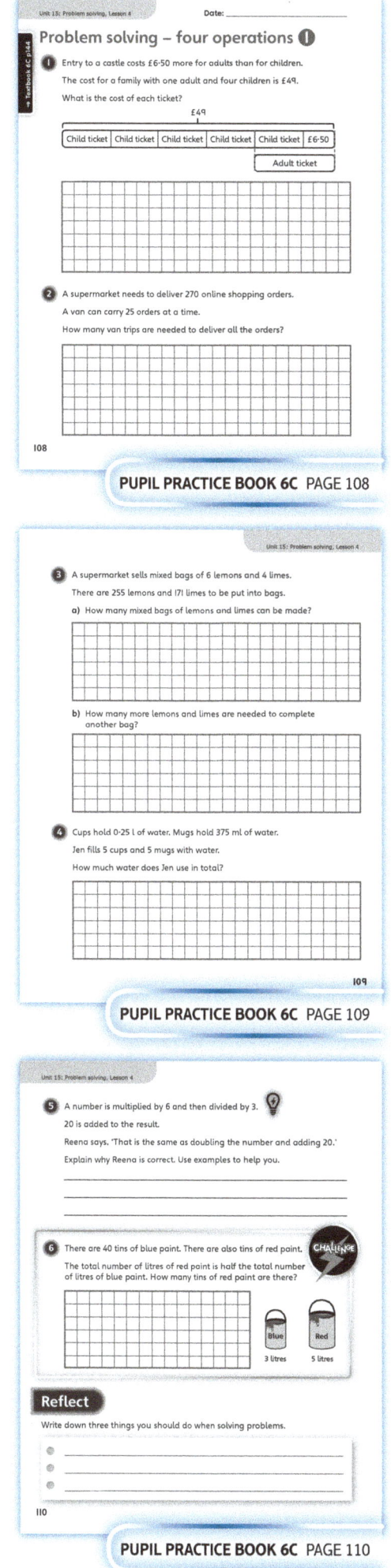

183

Unit 15: Problem solving, Lesson 5

# Problem solving – four operations ❷

## Learning focus
In this lesson, children will use the four operations to solve a range of non-routine problems involving missing numbers and unknown values, and also problems set in the context of measurements. They will reason about the given information and decide the best starting point.

## Before you teach
- Can children explain what a problem is asking them to do?
- Can they explain what steps are required and the operations needed?
- Can they reason about a useful starting point and explain their thinking?

### NATIONAL CURRICULUM LINKS
**Year 6 Number – addition, subtraction, multiplication and division**
Solve problems involving addition, subtraction, multiplication and division.

### ASSESSING MASTERY
Children can explain what a problem requires them to do and which operations they will need to use. They can reason about the most useful starting point and justify their decision.

### COMMON MISCONCEPTIONS
Children often think that the first piece of information they are given is the one they should use first. Remind them that they need to look at the whole problem. In the case of diagrammatic problems, tell children to make annotations to help them make sense of the information they already know; annotating diagrams will also help children to keep track of the stages of the problem, so they do not miss anything out. Ask:
- *What do you need to find? What information do you already know? Can you write it on your diagram? How does this help you decide what to do next?*

### STRENGTHENING UNDERSTANDING
Encourage children to label diagrams with information that they are given in the problem and to discuss how this can be used to solve the problem posed. Discuss problems where the first piece of information given is not the most important, so that children develop the ability to look at a problem in its entirety before deciding what to do.

### GOING DEEPER
Give children a range of algebraic problems with unknown values. Ask them to explain the similarities between these problems and the problems they have been solving in this lesson. Challenge children to express some of the problems from this lesson in algebraic form.

### KEY LANGUAGE
**In lesson:** adding, base, multiplication
**Other language to be used by the teacher:** multiply, divide, multiple, diameter, subtract, equivalent

### STRUCTURES AND REPRESENTATIONS
Column methods for addition, subtraction and multiplication

### RESOURCES
**Optional:** copies of diagrams for children to annotate

 In the eTextbook of this lesson, you will find interactive links to a selection of teaching tools.

## Quick recap
Ask children to write a calculation that they would solve mentally. Then ask them to write a calculation that they would solve using a written method. Finally ask them to write a calculation where they could choose to use either method.

# Discover

**WAYS OF WORKING** Pair work

**ASK**

- Question 1 a): *What is the total of the column? What is the total of the row? What can you tell me about the value of the triangle compared to the hexagon? How do you know?*
- Question 1 b): *Why does Lexi think this? What do you think? What if the totals are halved to 60? What might Lexi say now?*

**IN FOCUS** Question 1 a) exposes children to a non-routine problem as they reason about the value of unknown shapes. Question 1 b) requires them to reason about the relationship between the totals of the row and column and the values of the individual shapes, using Lexi's statement as a starting point.

**PRACTICAL TIPS** Give children copies of the puzzle so they can annotate them with the information they find.

**ANSWERS**

Question 1 a): 120 − (35 × 2)

120 − 70 = 50, so ⬡ = 50.

2△ = 120 − 70 = 50

△ is half of 50, so △ = 25.

Question 1 b):

Row: 70 + 100 + 70 = 240
Column: 70 + 50 + 50 + 70 = 240
Lexi is correct, because doubling the totals is the same as adding the values in the row or column twice.

# Share

**WAYS OF WORKING** Whole class teacher led

**ASK**

- Question 1 a): *Why has Dexter chosen to look at the row first? How do you know that the value of the triangle must be half the value of the hexagon? Many people give the value of the triangle as 50. What mistake have they made?*
- Question 1 b): *What is doubling the same as? Is there another strategy you could use to find the values?*

**IN FOCUS** In question 1 a), children may forget the last step of the problem when finding the value of the triangle (giving the answer as 50 and not halving it to give the value of one triangle). Check the values are correct using the calculations 25 × 2 + 35 × 2 = 50 + 70 = 120 for the column and 35 × 2 + 50 = 120 for the row.

**STRENGTHEN** For question 1 b), write the doubled values in a copy of the diagram so children can check the totals. Agree with the children that this is the same as adding the original values twice.

**DEEPEN** Ask children to think about halving the totals and to explain why the value of each shape must also be halved. Ask them to consider what they could say about the value of the shapes if the totals were 10 times smaller.

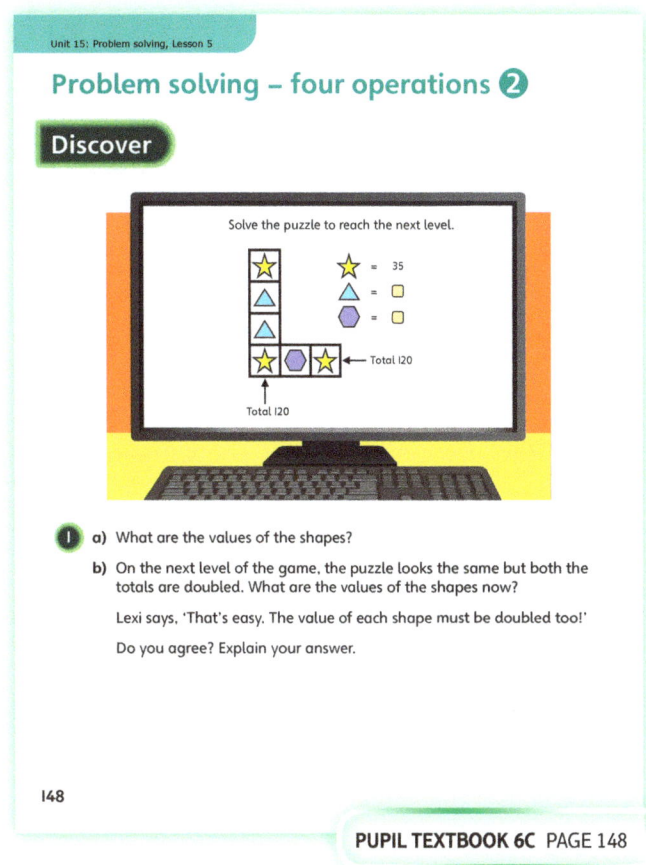

PUPIL TEXTBOOK 6C PAGE 148

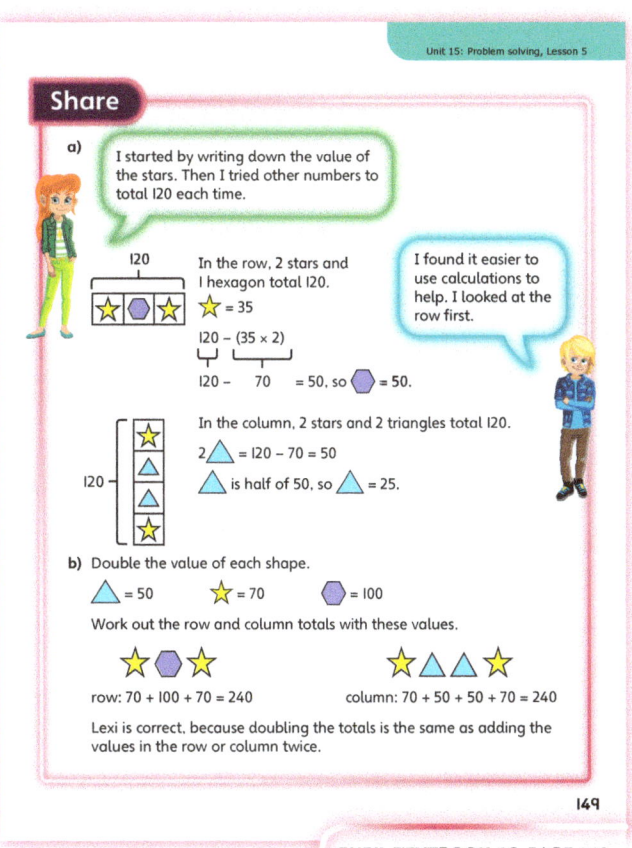

PUPIL TEXTBOOK 6C PAGE 149

185

Unit 15: Problem solving, Lesson 5

# Think together

**WAYS OF WORKING** Whole class teacher led (I do, We do, You do)

**ASK**

- Question ①: *What information do you already know? What operations will you need to use?*
- Question ②: *What measurements can you add to the diagram? How does this help? What calculations do you need to do to solve the problem?*
- Question ③: *How do you know what the last digit (the 1s digit) will be?*
- Question ④: *What is the same and what is different about each side of the balance? How can you show this information in a number sentence? Why should you multiply 448 by 5 instead of 6?*

**IN FOCUS** Questions ① and ② require children to find missing dimensions. In each case, they need to decide what they should do first.

Question ④ gives children an opportunity to explore equivalence and a balancing equation. The question has been chosen because there is also a box on the side with the tins, so the 7 tins must balance 5 boxes. The calculation provides an opportunity to look at strategies to multiply by 5, or to decide on the order of the calculation: for example, 448 × 5 ÷ 7 or 448 ÷ 7 × 5, where 448 can easily be partitioned as two multiples of 7 (420 + 28). Encourage children to make estimates before calculating.

**STRENGTHEN** For question ①, model the question using a bar model, drawing attention to the similarity between the bar model and the diagram in the question. Suggest that children draw their own bar model for question ④. Encourage children to use the inverse to check calculations.

**DEEPEN** Look at the order of the calculation in question ①. The answer can be found using the calculation 90 × 4 ÷ 3. Ask children to explain why the calculation could also be completed as 90 ÷ 3 × 4, and why someone might choose to do this.

**ASSESSMENT CHECKPOINT** Use questions ① and ② to assess whether children can apply reasoning to different contexts. Check that they can select the operation(s) required. Use question ③ to assess whether children can reason about the characteristics of numbers and their behaviours when they are added or multiplied. For example, any multiple of 5 will end in 5 or 10, and any multiple of 10 will end in 0, so neither 1,235 × 4 or 450 × 4 will be correct.

**ANSWERS**

Question ①: 120 mm

Question ②: 108 mm
538 − (2 × 90) − (2 × 120) = 108 mm

Question ③: A, D or E

Question ④: 1 tin = 320 g
Mass of both sides is 6 × 448 = 2,688 g.
The right hand balance is 1 box + 7 tins.
The mass of 7 tins is 2,688 − 448 = 2,240 g.
1 tin = 2,240 ÷ 7 = 320 g

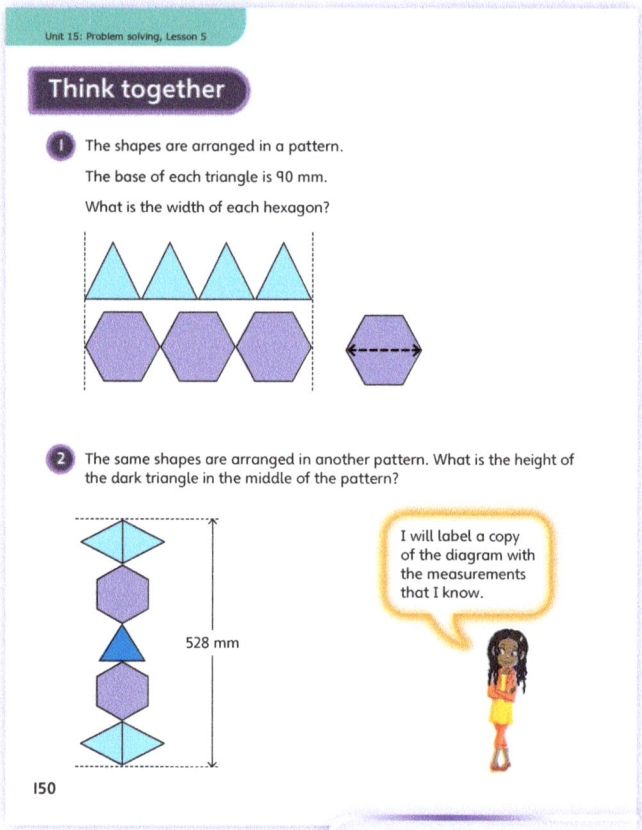

PUPIL TEXTBOOK 6C PAGE 150

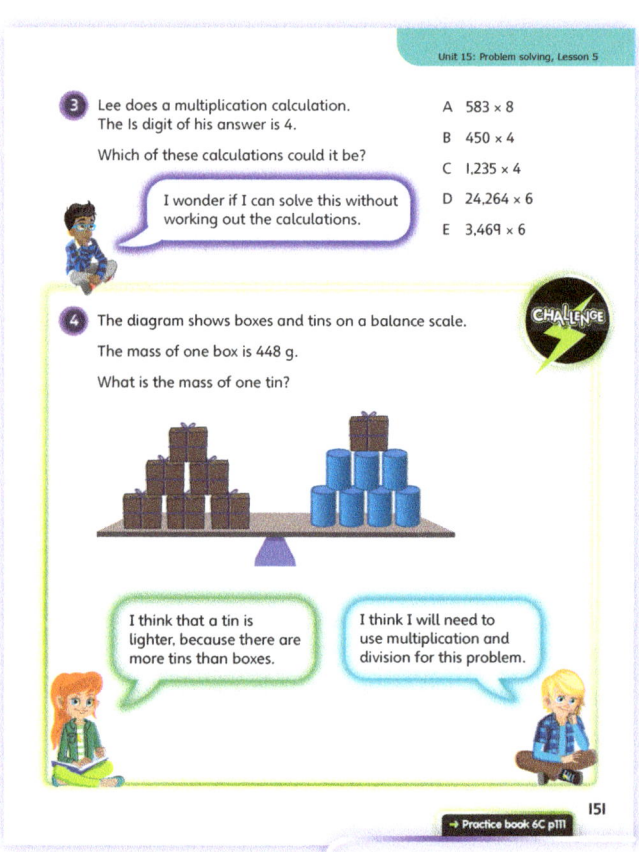

PUPIL TEXTBOOK 6C PAGE 151

Unit 15: Problem solving, Lesson 5

# Practice

**WAYS OF WORKING** Independent thinking

**IN FOCUS** Question ① requires children to apply the strategies used in the lesson to the context of money. They should think carefully about the information they know and decide what to do first. Children may forget to include the price of the lace. Encourage children to annotate the diagram in question ② to aid their thinking.

**STRENGTHEN** Model the answer to question ①, emphasising the importance of working systematically and writing down every step clearly:

lace + 2 plain beads + 3 spotty beads = £1·30
25p + (18p × 2) + 3 spotty beads = £1·30
3 spotty beads = £1·30 − 25p − 36p = 69p
1 spotty bead = 69p ÷ 3 = 23p

**DEEPEN** Ask children to reason about the diameters of the circles in question ⑤ if the measurement given for the two circles on the first row is doubled to 48 cm. Ask them to explain whether the diameter of every circle will double.

**THINK DIFFERENTLY** Question ④ requires children to reason about the results of addition and multiplication, drawing on knowledge of odds, evens and number bonds to achieve an answer with 5 ones: for example, 2 + 3, 7 + 8, etc.

**ASSESSMENT CHECKPOINT** Use questions ① to ③ to assess whether children can complete multi-step problems. Check that they can keep track of the calculations already completed and that they can recognise when the answer has/has not been reached. Use question ④ to assess whether children can predict the 1s digit in the product of a multiplication, recognising that the whole calculation need not be completed.

**ANSWERS** Answers for the **Practice** part of the lesson can be found in the *Power Maths* online subscription.

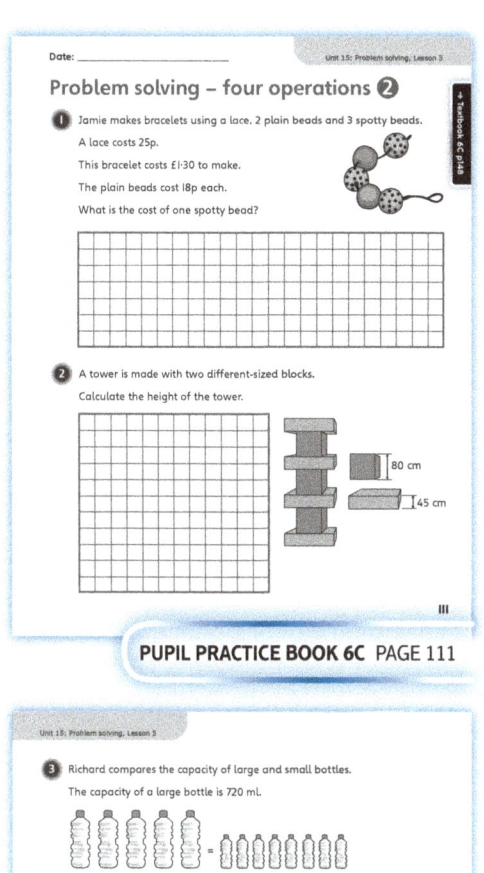

PUPIL PRACTICE BOOK 6C PAGE 111

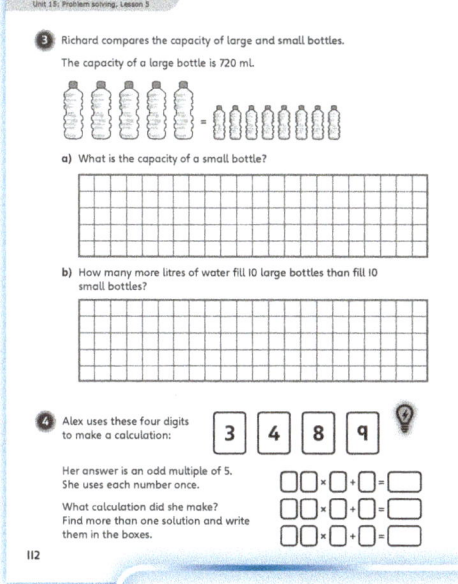

PUPIL PRACTICE BOOK 6C PAGE 112

# Reflect

**WAYS OF WORKING** Pair work

**IN FOCUS** In discussing the strategies used to solve **Practice** question ③ b) in **Practice**, children should draw on previous lessons and think about different ways to find the difference: for example, (720 × 10) − (450 × 10) or simply (720 − 450) × 10.

**ASSESSMENT CHECKPOINT** Check that children understand why different strategies can be used and why the second strategy above would *not* work if they had been asked to find the difference between 10 large bottles and 9 small bottles.

**ANSWERS** Answers for the **Reflect** part of the lesson can be found in the *Power Maths* online subscription.

PUPIL PRACTICE BOOK 6C PAGE 113

## After the lesson

- Are children growing in their ability to make sense of a problem and interpret what steps are needed to solve it?
- Can they use a range of strategies for calculations, both written and mental?
- Are children gaining confidence in deciding which operations to use and how they might reorder a calculation to make it easier?

187

Unit 15: Problem solving, Lesson 6

# Problem solving – fractions

## Learning focus
In this lesson, children will apply their understanding of fractions to help them identify, compare and calculate. They will draw on their knowledge of equivalent fractions to help solve problems and use reasoning skills to make decisions.

## Before you teach
- Can children explain whether a fraction is smaller or greater than $\frac{1}{2}$?
- Can they explain when fractions are equivalent and when they are not?
- Can they order a set of fractions that share the same denominator?

### NATIONAL CURRICULUM LINKS

**Year 6 Number – fractions (including decimals and percentages)**

Recall and use equivalences between simple fractions, decimals and percentages, including in different contexts.

### ASSESSING MASTERY

Children can solve a range of problems about fractions by drawing on their understanding of equivalence and their knowledge of the number line. They can find fractions of amounts and apply this in the context of money and measurements.

### COMMON MISCONCEPTIONS

When asked to compare and order fractions, children may not consider the characteristics of the fractions before converting them to a common denominator. Ask:
- *What can you tell me about these fractions? Do any fractions have the same denominator? … the same numerator? How can you tell which fraction is greater?*
- *Which fractions are more than $\frac{1}{2}$? … less than $\frac{1}{2}$?*

### STRENGTHENING UNDERSTANDING

Look together at different representations of fractions of shapes, agreeing on which are equivalent and which are not – for example, comparing a shape with 8 out of 20 equal pieces shaded and a shape with 6 out of 15 equal pieces shaded. Revisit comparing fractions, focusing on shared numerators and denominators.

### GOING DEEPER

Give children a range of problems or calculations that require them to make use of equivalent fractions. Ask them to sort problems into groups, such as calculations that are easier to solve using equivalent fractions and those that are not: for example, solving $\frac{5}{8} \div 2$ using $\frac{10}{16} \div 2$.

### KEY LANGUAGE

**In lesson:** fraction, numerator, denominator

**Other language to be used by the teacher:** equivalent

### STRUCTURES AND REPRESENTATIONS

Number line, bar model, fraction strip

### RESOURCES

**Optional:** multiplication grid, digit cards

 In the eTextbook of this lesson, you will find interactive links to a selection of teaching tools.

## Quick recap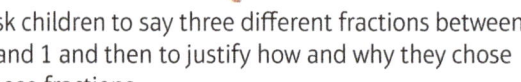

Ask children to say three different fractions between $\frac{1}{2}$ and 1 and then to justify how and why they chose those fractions.

Unit 15: Problem solving, Lesson 6

# Discover

**WAYS OF WORKING** Pair work

**ASK**

- Question ❶ a): *How do you know that none of the children have completely filled their buckets with water?*
- Question ❶ a): *What will you do to help order the fractions? Which fraction do you think is largest? Why?*
- Question ❶ b): *How do you know that Olivia and Bella did not collect 10 litres or more of water together?*
- Question ❶ b): *What do you need to do to solve this problem?*

**IN FOCUS** The fractions in question ❶ a) have been chosen so that children can reason about them rather than simply converting them to a common denominator.

**PRACTICAL TIPS** Draw a number line on the board and ask children to estimate the position of each fraction. This will encourage them to think about a fraction's proximity to other fractions they know.

**ANSWERS**

Question ❶ a): Bella won the race because $\frac{5}{6} > \frac{5}{8} > \frac{2}{5} > \frac{3}{8}$.

Question ❶ b): Olivia and Bella collected 5,800 ml of water in total.

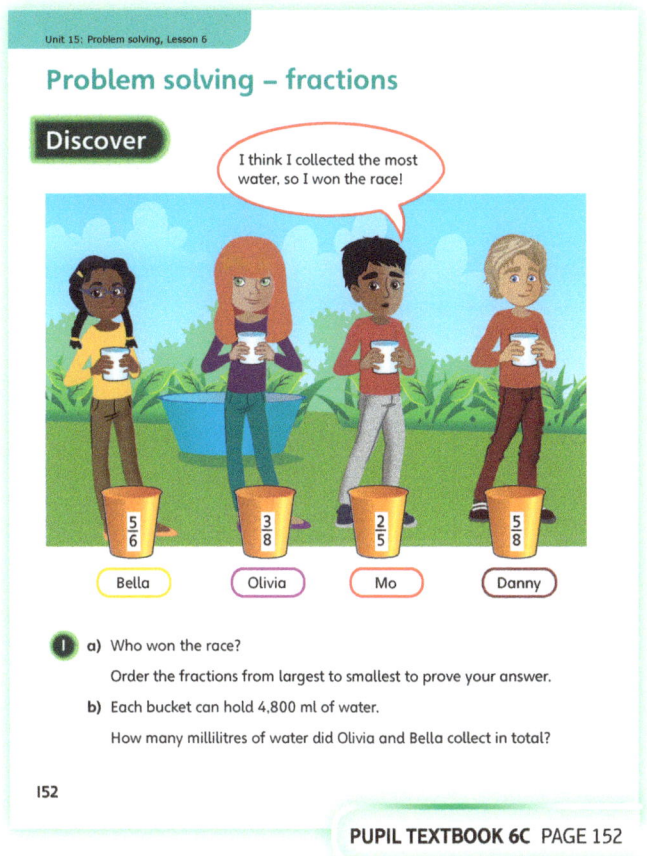

PUPIL TEXTBOOK 6C PAGE 152

# Share

**WAYS OF WORKING** Whole class teacher led

**ASK**

- Question ❶ a): *What has Astrid noticed about the fractions? How does this help?*
- Question ❶ a): *What do you notice about each of the five parts when comparing $\frac{5}{6}$ and $\frac{5}{8}$?*
- Question ❶ a): *How can you prove that $\frac{2}{5}$ is less than $\frac{1}{2}$ and $\frac{5}{8}$ is more than $\frac{1}{2}$?*
- Question ❶ b): *Why do both the methods work? Which do you prefer? Why?*

**IN FOCUS** In question ❶ a), the fraction strips help children to visually compare fractions that share the same numerator by showing that when a whole is split into more equal parts, each part is smaller. Question ❶ b) encourages children to think about different strategies to solve the same problem.

**STRENGTHEN** For question ❶ a), use equivalent fractions to prove $\frac{5}{8}$ is more than $\frac{1}{2}$. For example, use $\frac{4}{8}$ for $\frac{1}{2}$ so that children can clearly see that $\frac{5}{8}$ is $\frac{1}{8}$ more. Similarly, use $\frac{5}{10}$ for $\frac{1}{2}$ and $\frac{4}{10}$ for $\frac{2}{5}$ to compare $\frac{2}{5}$ and $\frac{1}{2}$. Ask children to reason about the fractions $\frac{7}{12}$ or $\frac{5}{12}$ in the same way.

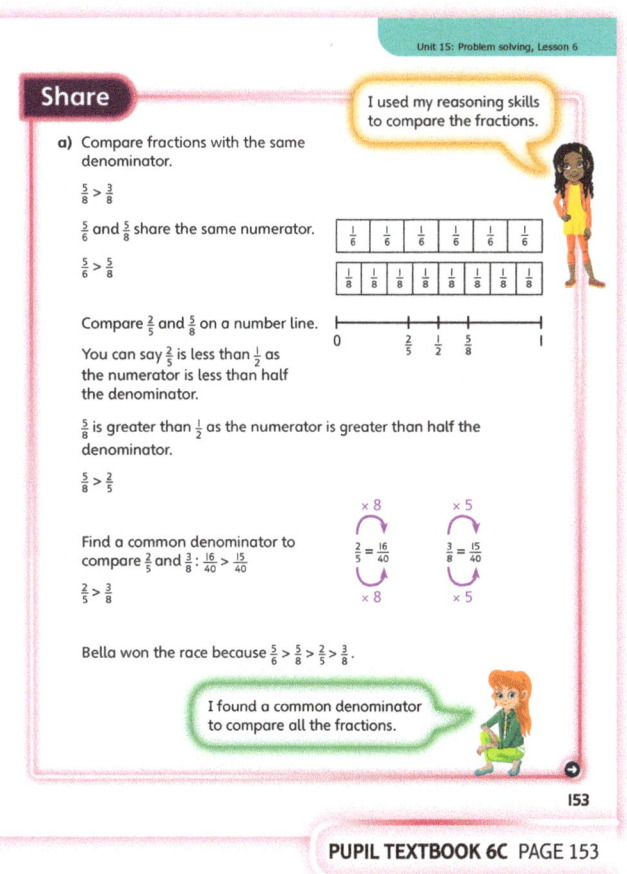

PUPIL TEXTBOOK 6C PAGE 153

Unit 15: Problem solving, Lesson 6

# Think together

**WAYS OF WORKING** Whole class teacher led (I do, We do, You do)

**ASK**
- Question ❶: *What does the question require you to do? What common denominator could you use?*
- Question ❷: *What fraction of a bucket does Mo collect? How can you find half of $\frac{3}{4}$?*
- Question ❸: *How many equal parts is each shape divided into? How can you use equivalent fractions to help?*
- Question ❹: *What fraction of the whole do the lemons and sugar represent altogether? How do you know? How can you represent the problem using a bar model?*

**IN FOCUS** Question ❷ looks at the relationship between dividing by 2 and multiplying by $\frac{1}{2}$. Children can calculate either $\frac{5}{8} \div 2$ or $\frac{5}{8} \times \frac{1}{2}$ ($\frac{1}{2}$ of $\frac{5}{8}$). Look at solving the problem in both ways, to help children make sense of division methods such as 'turn the fraction upside down and multiply'. Question ❸ presents children with different images to represent fractions of a shape. Children must first identify the number of equal parts (which may not look the same in the shape) and then use their knowledge of equivalent fractions to compare. Question ❹ has been designed so children can reason about the information they are given and work out how this relates to the whole: $\frac{3}{5}$ is left so the total of £2·20 plus £2·80 represents $\frac{2}{5}$ of the whole.

**STRENGTHEN** Encourage children to think flexibly about the information they are given each time and about how equivalent fractions might help them to solve the problems in questions ❶ to ❸. Use a multiplication grid to explore strings of equivalent fractions by scaling the numerator and denominator each time as children move from column to column.

**DEEPEN** Look at question ❹. Ask children to explain how their bar model and solution would change if the fraction of the money left was $\frac{2}{5}$.

**ASSESSMENT CHECKPOINT** Use questions ❶ and ❷ to assess whether children can calculate with fractions in a context. Check that they can use equivalent fractions to find a common denominator. Use question ❸ to assess whether children can identify a fraction of a shape, even when the equal parts do not look the same. Use question ❹ to assess whether children can represent a problem and understand how given information relates to the answer.

**ANSWERS**

Question ❶: Bella collected $\frac{13}{30}$ of a bucket more than Mo.
$\frac{5}{6} - \frac{2}{5} = \frac{25}{30} - \frac{12}{30} = \frac{13}{30}$

Question ❷: Danny collected $\frac{3}{8}$ of a bucket.

Question ❸: B has the greatest area shaded.
A and C both have $\frac{2}{5}$ shaded.
$\frac{7}{15} > \frac{2}{5}$ ($\frac{2}{5} = \frac{6}{15}$)

Question ❹: Olivia started with £12·50.
She spent £5 which is $\frac{2}{5}$ of her money.
$\frac{1}{5} =$ £2·50
$5 \times \frac{1}{5} = 5 \times$ £2·50 $=$ £12·50

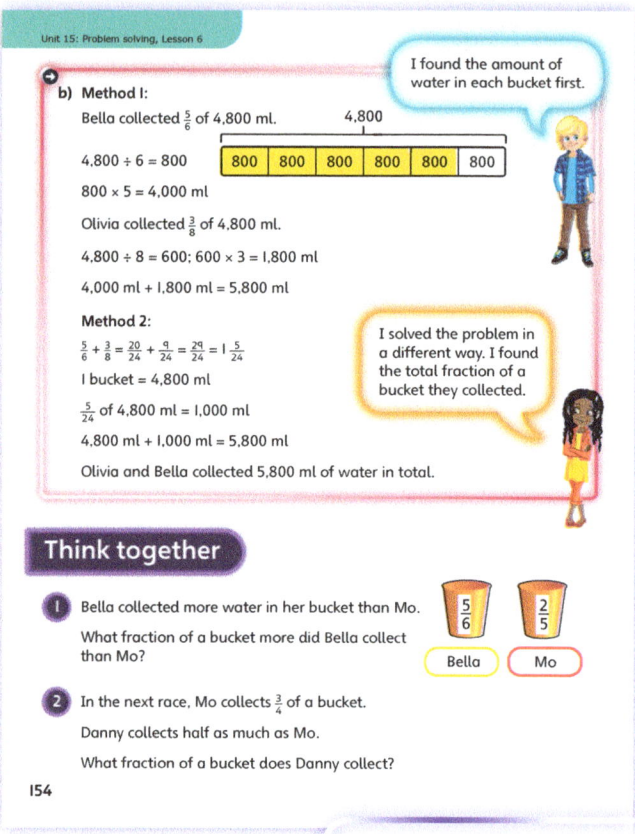

PUPIL TEXTBOOK 6C PAGE 154

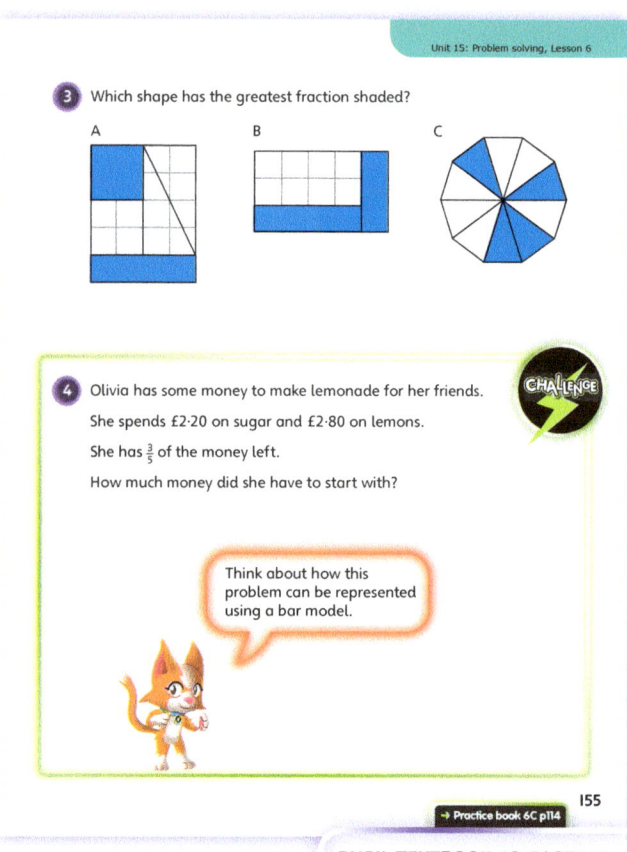

PUPIL TEXTBOOK 6C PAGE 155

# Practice

**WAYS OF WORKING** Independent thinking

**IN FOCUS** Question ❶ has been designed to help children reason about fractions compared to $\frac{1}{2}$. They need to consider equivalent fractions and may also think about using an improper fraction for a solution. Question ❷ b) requires children to think about pairs of fractions that total one whole, recognising that 1 can be written as $\frac{9}{9}$. Question ❻ encourages children to reason about the effect of the *size* of a fraction when carrying out different calculations, and to consider which fractions will give the largest result each time.

**STRENGTHEN** For question ❺, encourage children to sketch a bar model to help make sense of the information they know and to see how this relates to the whole. If necessary, model a similar question and then ask children to apply the same strategy to question ❺.

**DEEPEN** Provide children with the digit cards 2, 4, 6 and 9 and ask them to find a set of answers that will complete the statement $\frac{?}{?} < \frac{1}{4} < \frac{?}{?}$. Then ask children to choose four different digit cards for a partner to solve the problem.

**ASSESSMENT CHECKPOINT** Use question ❷ to assess whether children can confidently add and subtract fractions in context. Check that they recognise the operations needed to solve the problems.

**ANSWERS** Answers for the **Practice** part of the lesson can be found in the *Power Maths* online subscription.

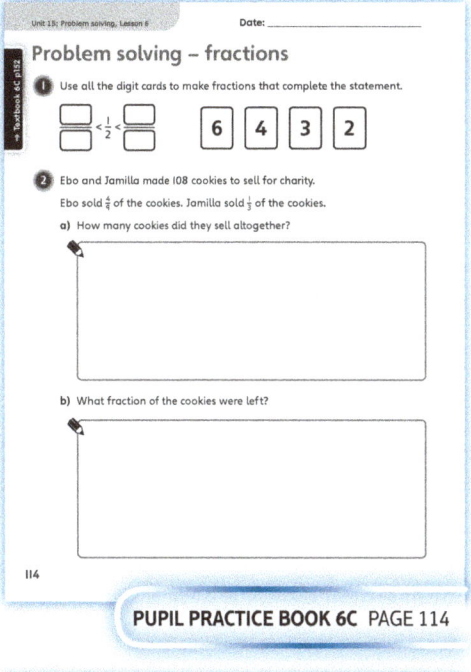

PUPIL PRACTICE BOOK 6C PAGE 114

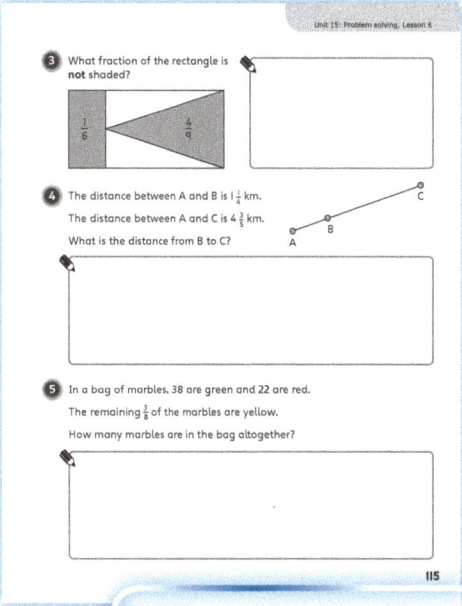

PUPIL PRACTICE BOOK 6C PAGE 115

# Reflect

**WAYS OF WORKING** Pair work

**IN FOCUS** Children work with a partner to reason about a set of fractions, using the learning applied throughout the lesson to help make decisions.

**ASSESSMENT CHECKPOINT** Check that children understand how they can use equivalent fractions to help them compare fractions.

**ANSWERS** Answers for the **Reflect** part of the lesson can be found in the *Power Maths* online subscription.

> ## After the lesson ⏸
> - Can children explain how they have used equivalent fractions to solve problems?
> - Can they confidently calculate with fractions, using equivalence to help find common denominators or to simplify a fraction?
> - Can they represent a problem mathematically (for example, using a fraction strip, number line or number sentence), explaining what they know and what they need to find out?

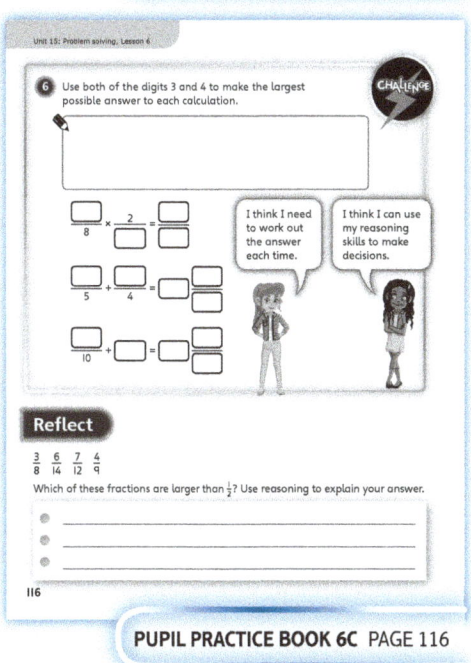

PUPIL PRACTICE BOOK 6C PAGE 116

Unit 15: Problem solving, Lesson 7

# Problem solving – decimals

### Learning focus
In this lesson, children will work with decimals to solve problems with and without a context. They will use representations to help make sense of problems and decide which operations to use.

### Before you teach
- Can children give the value of each digit in numbers up to three decimal places?
- Can they solve a range of two-step and multi-step problems with whole numbers?
- Can they work with decimals in the context of money and measurement?

### NATIONAL CURRICULUM LINKS

**Year 6 Number – fractions (including decimals and percentages)**

Recall and use equivalences between simple fractions, decimals and percentages, including in different contexts.

### ASSESSING MASTERY

Children can confidently work with decimals using knowledge of place values to help them calculate accurately. They can solve a range of problems, applying mental or written strategies to carry out the calculations flexibly.

### COMMON MISCONCEPTIONS

Children may incorrectly apply their knowledge of writing 1·2 for measurements (for example, 1·2 kg or 1·2 m) to write 1·2 in the context of money as £1·2. Show children prices written to two decimal places and ask:
- *How many decimal places do you use to write an amount in pounds and pence? How can you write 1·2 as a decimal to two decimal places? What equivalent fractions can you use to help?* [$\frac{2}{10}$ and $\frac{20}{100}$]

### STRENGTHENING UNDERSTANDING

Use place value counters to support work with decimals, using arrays to work with multiplication as required. Represent each problem using a bar model to help children decide what calculations are needed.

### GOING DEEPER

Explore the effect of a multiplication followed by a division: for example, × 2 and then ÷ 3, relating this to finding $\frac{2}{3}$. Ask: *How does this differ when the calculation is × 3 and then ÷ 2?*

### KEY LANGUAGE

**In lesson:** convert

**Other language to be used by the teacher:** decimal, equivalent

### STRUCTURES AND REPRESENTATIONS

Number line, bar model

### RESOURCES

**Optional:** place value counters, toy coins

 In the eTextbook of this lesson, you will find interactive links to a selection of teaching tools.

### Quick recap

Ask children to solve each of these calculations:

8 + 0·4   8 × 0·4   8 − 0·4   0·4 ÷ 8

# Discover

**WAYS OF WORKING** Pair work

**ASK**

• Question 1 a): *How can you find the price of a child ticket when you only know the price of an adult ticket?*
• Question 1 a): *What method will you use to find the cost of two adult tickets? Is this the same as doubling £6·45?*
• Question 1 b): *What would be a good estimate for the cost of 48 adult tickets? Will the actual amount be more or less than this?*
• Question 1 b): *I think the problem can be solved in more than one way. How could you solve the problem?*

**IN FOCUS** Question 1 a) requires children to recognise that the cost of 3 child tickets is equal to the cost of 2 adult tickets. Look for children using a written method to multiply by 2 rather than simply doubling.

**PRACTICAL TIPS** Use place value counters or toy coins to model the problem. Use these to support doubling £6·45 and dividing £12·90 by 3.

**ANSWERS**

Question 1 a): The price of one child ticket is £4·30.

Question 1 b): The cinema takes £103·20 more when the front row is filled with adults.

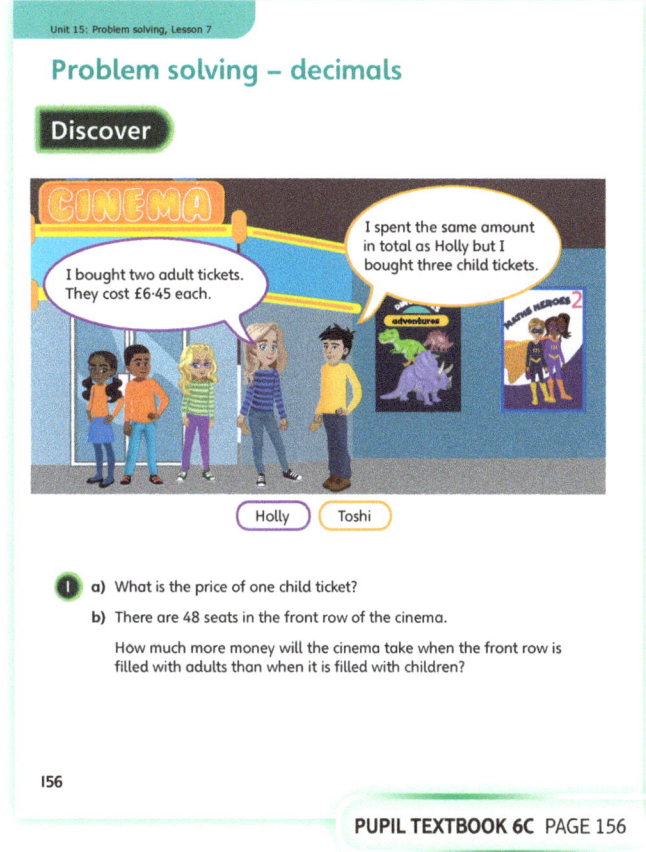

PUPIL TEXTBOOK 6C PAGE 156

# Share

**WAYS OF WORKING** Whole class teacher led

**ASK**

• Question 1 a): *How do you know that the bar model matches the problem?*
• Question 1 a): *What method can you use to divide £12·90 by 3? Why have you chosen this method?*
• Question 1 b): *What method can you use to multiply by 48? Why might you choose to round and adjust?*
• Question 1 b): *Will Flo's method give the correct answer? Which method do you prefer? Why?*

**IN FOCUS** Question 1 a) uses a bar model to represent the relationship between the adult and child tickets. Make sure children recognise that they need to multiply by 2 and then divide by 3. In question 1 b), children could look at mental strategies of rounding and adjusting to multiply by 48 (multiply by 50 and subtract 2 × the number).

**STRENGTHEN** Use toy coins to represent decimals in the context of money: for example, 4·3 as £4·30 and not £4·3.

**DEEPEN** For question 1 a), ask children to explore and explain why the answer £4·30 can also be found by carrying out the calculation $\frac{2}{3}$ of £6·45 (or $\frac{2}{3}$ × £6·45).

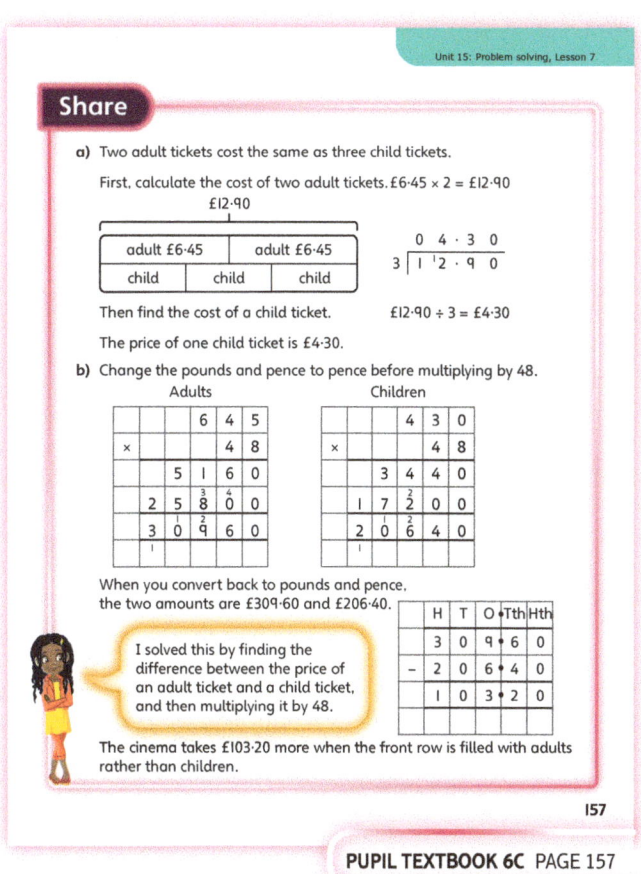

PUPIL TEXTBOOK 6C PAGE 157

193

Unit 15: Problem solving, Lesson 7

# Think together

**WAYS OF WORKING** Whole class teacher led (I do, We do, You do)

**ASK**
- Question ❶: *What do you need to do first? Why?*
- Question ❷: *Why is the answer not simply the product of 48 × 0·6 m?*
- Question ❸: *Where should you position each number on the number line? How do you know?*
- Question ❸: *Do you think that 0·48 is furthest from 0·4 because 48 is much greater than 4? Is that correct?*
- Question ❹: *How do you know that the two numbers cannot be whole numbers?*

**IN FOCUS** Question ❶ is a two-step problem that requires subtraction first; this is different from question ❶ b) in **Share**. Question ❷ provides an opportunity for children to interpret a diagram to help make sense of the problem. Children often forget to complete all the steps in a problem, so encourage them to check that they have answered the question fully.

Question ❸ requires children to apply their understanding of place value to find the number closest to 0·4. They may make an error by relating these decimal numbers to whole numbers, thinking that 0·48 is much greater than 0·4 because 48 is much greater than 4.

Question ❹ has been chosen so that the numbers are required to meet two criteria. With this type of problem, many children will find a solution to suit one criterion but not the other. The answers will be to two decimal places even though the difference is only to one decimal place.

**STRENGTHEN** Encourage children to draw bar models to support problem solving and to explain what each step of the problem requires.

**DEEPEN** For question ❷, ask children to reason about the length of the front row if each seat was 5 cm wider. Ask them whether they need to calculate 48 × 0·65 etc. or whether they can start with their existing answer.

**ASSESSMENT CHECKPOINT** Use questions ❶ and ❷ to assess whether children can use decimal numbers in context and can carry out all steps of the problem. Use question ❸ to assess whether children can apply an understanding of decimal place value. Use question ❹ to assess whether children can work with more than one criterion when solving problems.

**ANSWERS**

Question ❶: The mass of one carton is 0·78 kg.
6·65 kg – 0·41 kg = 6·24 kg is the mass of 8 cartons.
The mass of 1 carton is 6·24 kg ÷ 8 = 0·78 kg.

Question ❷: The row is 30·05 m long.
48 × 0·6 + 1·25 = 30·05 m

Question ❸: 0·35 is the closest to 0·4.

Question ❹: 3·15 and 3·85

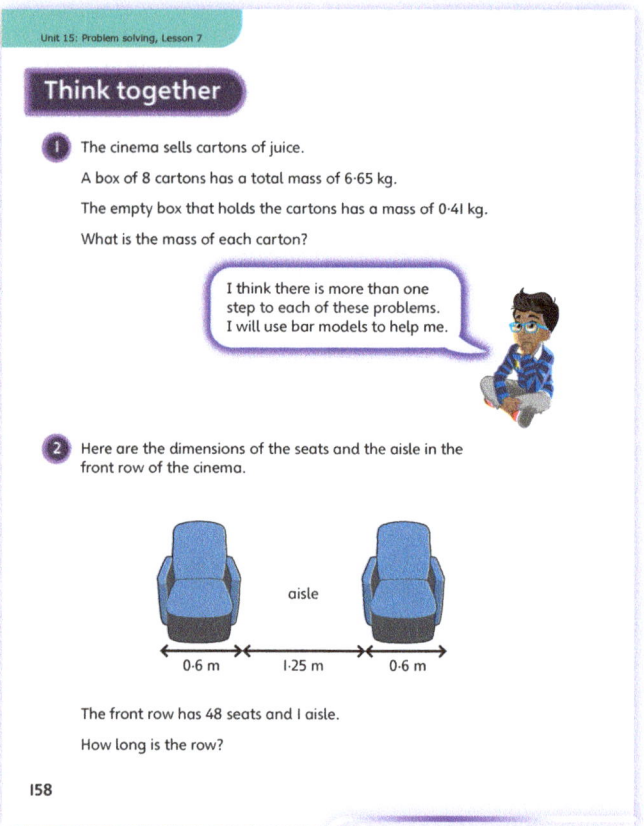

PUPIL TEXTBOOK 6C PAGE 158

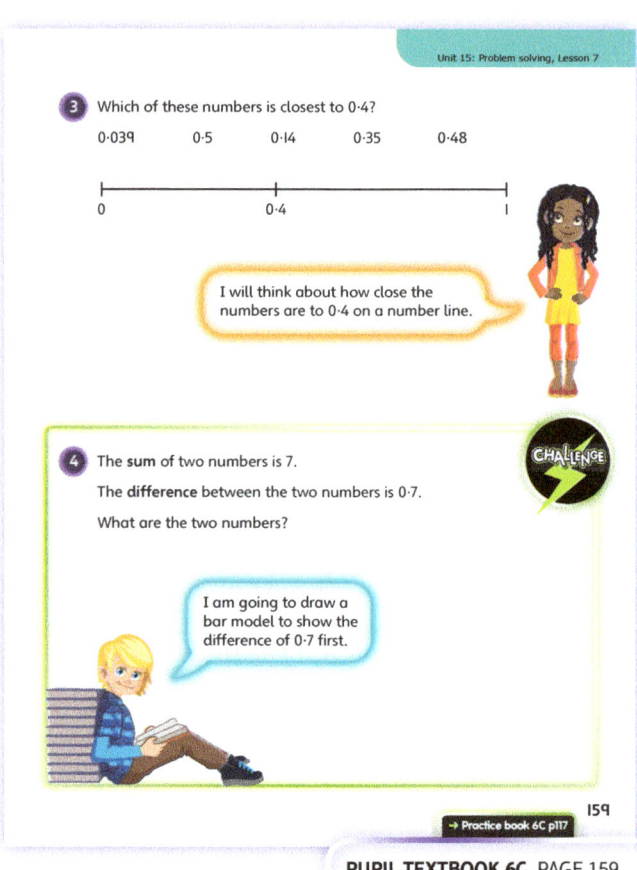

PUPIL TEXTBOOK 6C PAGE 159

# Unit 15: Problem solving, Lesson 7

## Practice

**WAYS OF WORKING** Independent thinking

**IN FOCUS** Question 2 b) provides an opportunity to try different strategies: for example, finding the cost of 8 bags of popcorn by doubling the cost of 4 bags and then finding the cost of 8 cartons before finding the difference; or finding the difference between the cost of one carton and one bag of popcorn before multiplying by 8.

Question 3 has been chosen as a decontextualised problem where children must first identify the scale that has been used. Children may incorrectly give 3·9 as the missing number in the first box, using the pattern 3·9, 4 and 4·1 from the scale.

Question 4 requires children to interpret a balanced scale, recognising that 9 chocolate bars are equal in mass to 6 tins of nuts. Children should be encouraged to first find the total mass of the 9 chocolate bars, and then divide this by 6 to find the mass of 1 tin of nuts.

Question 5 requires children to think flexibly about adding three decimal numbers. They can use estimation to quickly discard combinations and look at the tenths digit to reason about number bonds. Some children may realise that the total for each column/row is equal to the sum of all the numbers divided by 3.

**STRENGTHEN** For question 5, encourage children to look at the whole numbers first and find sets of these numbers where the whole numbers add to the same value. They can then swap the numbers as needed to find sets of three decimals that sum to the same value.

**DEEPEN** For question 4, ask children to look at a method of rounding and adjusting to multiply by 0·2. For example, 10 × 0·2 = 2, so 9 × 0·2 = 2 − 0·2 = 1·8.

**ASSESSMENT CHECKPOINT** Use questions 1 and 2 to assess whether children can solve multi-step problems involving decimals. Check that they can use calculation methods accurately. Use question 3 to assess whether children can apply an understanding of place value to interpret the scale on a number line. Use question 4 to assess whether they can make sense of a balancing problem and interpret a diagram correctly.

**ANSWERS** Answers for the **Practice** part of the lesson can be found in the *Power Maths* online subscription.

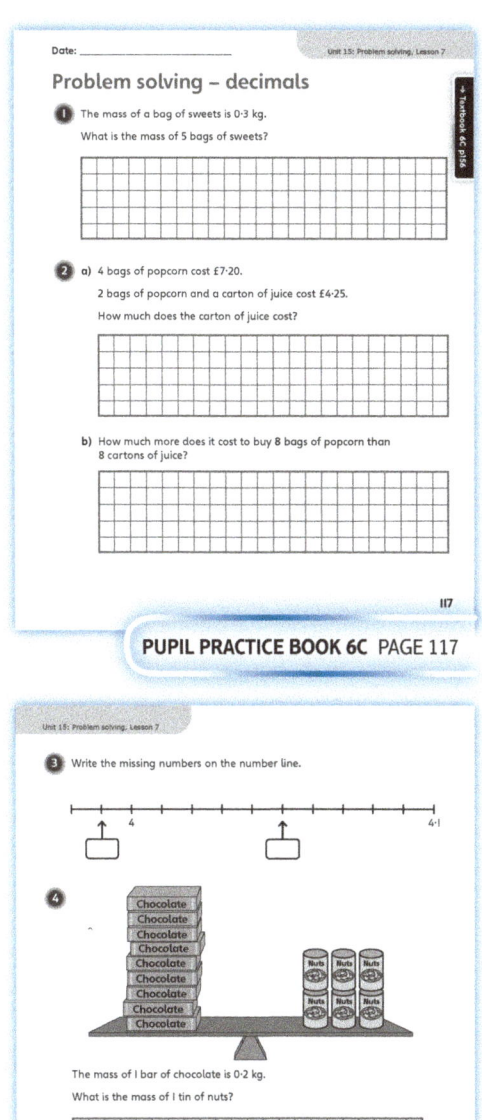

PUPIL PRACTICE BOOK 6C PAGE 117

PUPIL PRACTICE BOOK 6C PAGE 118

## Reflect

**WAYS OF WORKING** Independent thinking

**IN FOCUS** Children are required to use their knowledge of place value to explain which number is closest to 0·9. They may also find it useful to draw a number line.

**ASSESSMENT CHECKPOINT** Check that children understand and can explain why 0·87 is closer to 0·9 than 0·95 is.

**ANSWERS** Answers for the **Reflect** part of the lesson can be found in the *Power Maths* online subscription.

### After the lesson
- Can children confidently calculate with decimals, using place values accurately?
- Can they solve a range of problems, representing them as necessary, and explain what calculations need to be carried out?

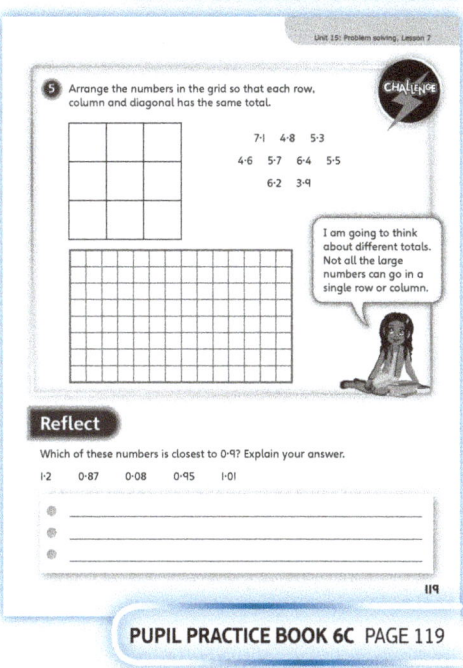

PUPIL PRACTICE BOOK 6C PAGE 119

Unit 15: Problem solving, Lesson 8

# Problem solving – percentages

## Learning focus

In this lesson, children will work with percentages to solve a range of problems. They will use what they know about percentage and fraction equivalence to make decisions about calculating and to help them recognise representations.

## Before you teach

- Can children find 10% of a quantity by finding $\frac{1}{10}$?
- Can they write a percentage as a fraction with the denominator 100?
- Can they use a bar model to represent a problem involving percentages?

### NATIONAL CURRICULUM LINKS

**Year 6 Number – fractions (including decimals and percentages)**

Recall and use equivalences between simple fractions, decimals and percentages, including in different contexts.

### ASSESSING MASTERY

Children can calculate a percentage of a quantity or amount using what they know about fractions to help them. They can also find the value of the whole when given the percentage discount and the discounted price.

### COMMON MISCONCEPTIONS

Children may take what they know about the equivalence of 10% and $\frac{1}{10}$ and assume that 20% is $\frac{1}{20}$ or 5% is $\frac{1}{5}$. Ask:
- *What is 20% as a fraction with the denominator 100? What is the simplest form of this fraction? What is the simplest form of the fraction for 5%?*
- *What is 20% relative to 10%? Think about the calculation $2 \times \frac{1}{10} = \frac{2}{10}$: what is $\frac{2}{10}$ in its simplest form?*

### STRENGTHENING UNDERSTANDING

Revisit fraction and percentage equivalents. Practise finding 10% by dividing by 10, using a place value grid for support.

### GOING DEEPER

Explore finding different percentages of amounts in different ways, for example:
- finding 75% by subtracting 25% from the whole or finding the total of 50% and 25% of the whole
- finding 95% by subtracting 5% from the whole.

Ask children to draw a table to summarise the various ways they can find different percentages.

### KEY LANGUAGE

**In lesson:** percentage, equivalent, fraction

**Other language to be used by the teacher:** denominator

### STRUCTURES AND REPRESENTATIONS

Bar model

### RESOURCES

**Optional:** examples of products, prices and discounts

 In the eTextbook of this lesson, you will find interactive links to a selection of teaching tools.

## Quick recap

Ask children to list all the fraction, decimal and percentage equivalents that they can think of.

Unit 15: Problem solving, Lesson 8

# Discover

**WAYS OF WORKING** Pair work

**ASK**

- Question 1 a): *How can you find 20% of an amount? How can finding 10% help?*
- Question 1 a): *How does place value help you to find 10%? What fraction is the same as 10%?*
- Question 1 b): *How does this problem differ from part a)?*
- Question 1 b): *What is 25% as a fraction? How does this help?*
- Question 1 b): *What fraction or percentage of the whole price does £330 represent?*

**IN FOCUS** These questions require children to use percentages in different ways and to apply knowledge of equivalence to help them. In question 1 a), children find a percentage of an amount, whereas, in question 1 b), they are given a percentage of an amount and must calculate the whole.

**PRACTICAL TIPS** Role play the scenario by setting up a 'shop' using cards to show products with prices and discounts.

**ANSWERS**

Question 1 a): Jen pays £360 for her computer.

Question 1 b): The full price of Amal's television is £440.

PUPIL TEXTBOOK 6C PAGE 160

# Share

**WAYS OF WORKING** Whole class teacher led

**ASK**

- Question 1 a): *Where can you see the 20% discount in the bar model? What percentage of the full price does Jen have to pay?*
- Question 1 a): *20% is equivalent to 0·2 or $\frac{1}{5}$. How can you find $\frac{1}{5}$ of £450?*
- Question 1 a): *Can you explain how Flo's method works?*
- Question 1 b): *Why does £330 only represent three parts on the bar model?*
- Question 1 b): *What discount in pounds did Amal receive?*

**IN FOCUS** Children are required to work flexibly, recognising how bar models can represent the problems, but with the information used differently to solve each one. In question 1 a), children may give the answer as £90, forgetting that this is the discount and so must be subtracted from the full amount. In question 1 b), children may find 25% of £330 because a value and a percentage have been given, without recognising that £330 does not represent the full price.

**STRENGTHEN** Explore Flo's idea for question 1 a). Refer to the bar model to agree that Jen only pays 80%, which can be calculated using 8 × £45 (since 10% of £450 is £45) rather than finding 20% and subtracting this from the whole.

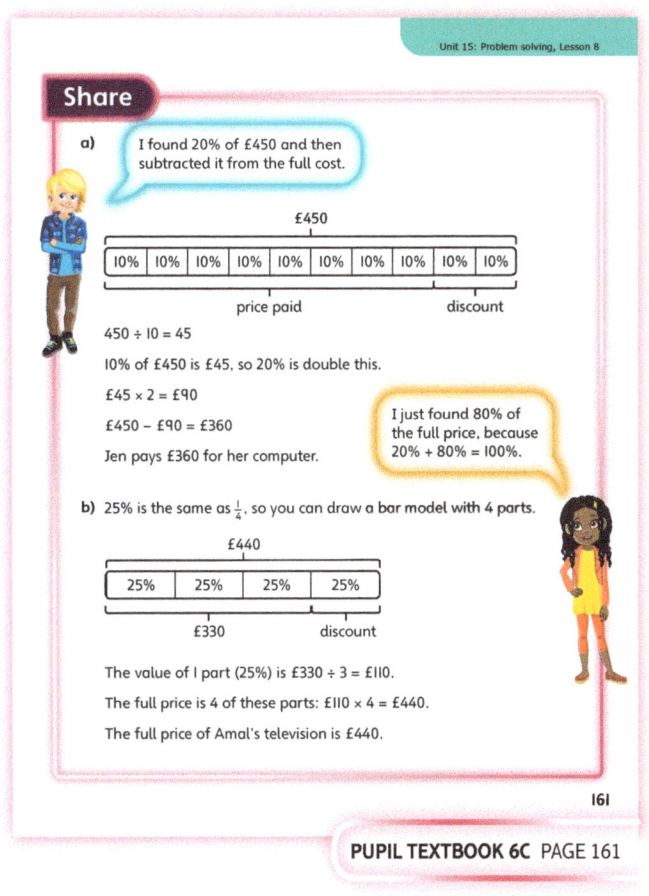

PUPIL TEXTBOOK 6C PAGE 161

197

Unit 15: Problem solving, Lesson 8

# Think together

**WAYS OF WORKING** Whole class teacher led (I do, We do, You do)

**ASK**

- Question ❶: *What percentage of the full price does £42 represent? How do you know?*
- Question ❷: *What percentage of the whole do the children represent? How do you know?*
- Question ❷: *How can you calculate the number of adults?*
- Question ❸: *How many equal parts is each grid divided into? How does this help?*
- Question ❹: *What is $\frac{1}{5}$ as a percentage? What is $\frac{2}{5}$ as a percentage?*

**IN FOCUS** Question ❷ provides an opportunity for children to reason about the information they are given in a table and to use this to find missing information. Question ❸ shows pictorial representations of percentages, so children are first required to interpret the fraction of the whole that each pattern represents. They must then use fraction and percentage equivalents to solve the problem. Similarly, question ❹ requires knowledge of fraction and percentage equivalents. Look for children who incorrectly identify that $\frac{1}{5}$ is 20%, so $\frac{2}{5}$ is 40%.

**STRENGTHEN** For question ❷, ensure children recognise that the whole is 100% and that the children represent 40% of the customers because adults represent 60%. Provide tables with different numbers and percentages for children to practise this skill.

**DEEPEN** Ask children to make up their own percentage problems where the answer is £200. Challenge them to create questions where £200 is the discounted price and where £200 is the full price.

**ASSESSMENT CHECKPOINT** Use questions ❶ and ❷ to assess whether children can solve percentage problems where they need to work out the whole. Check they can interpret a table and recognise that 60% + 40% is equal to the whole 100%. Use questions ❸ and ❹ to assess whether children can use fraction and percentage equivalents to solve problems.

**ANSWERS**

Question ❶: The full price of the monitor stand is £60.
£42 is 70%     £42 ÷ 7 = £6 = 10%
£6 × 10 = £60 = 100% = the full price

Question ❷: The percentage of total children customers is 40%.
The number of adult customers is 1,050.
40% = 700, so 10% = 175
60% = 6 × 10% = 6 × 175 = 1,050

Question ❸ a): B matches all the fractions and percentages.

Question ❸ b): 25% of B is unfilled.

Question ❹: Alex was the winner with 40% of the votes.
$\frac{2}{5}$ = 40%
Luis got 100% – 40% – 35% = 25% of the votes.

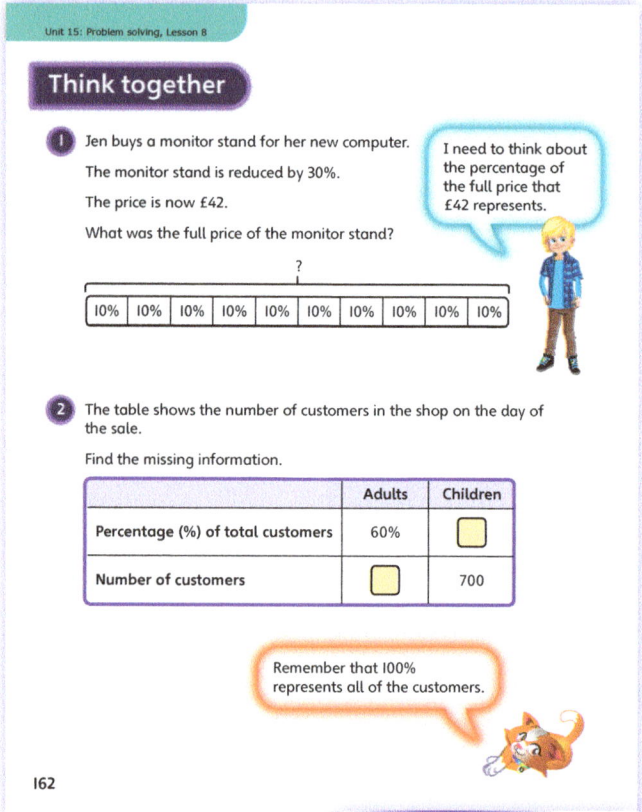

PUPIL TEXTBOOK 6C PAGE 162

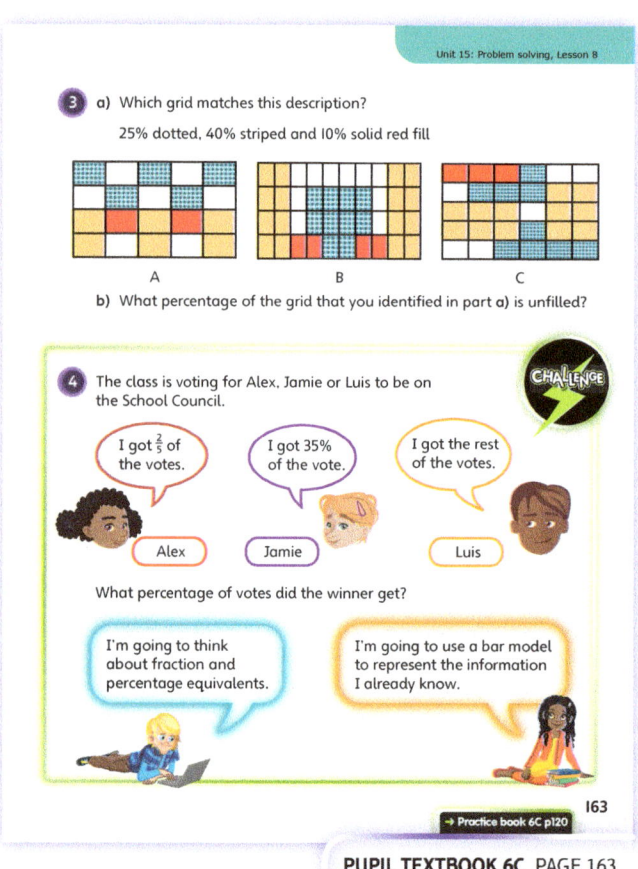

PUPIL TEXTBOOK 6C PAGE 163

# Unit 15: Problem solving, Lesson 8

## Practice

**WAYS OF WORKING** Independent thinking

**IN FOCUS** Question 2 has been chosen so that children can explore different strategies to solve the problem. For example, they can work out how many children cycle to school and how many come by car and subtract the total from 120, or they can recognise that the percentage who walk must be 45% and so calculate 45% of 120. Question 3 requires children to interpret information given in a table, and then apply their knowledge that the whole is 100% to calculate what percentage of the whole a value represents.

**STRENGTHEN** For question 2, encourage children to think through what they need to do to find how many children walk to school. Ask them what 30% of 120 is and what 25% of 120 is. Then ask what they need to do with these numbers.

**DEEPEN** Ask children to work in pairs to make up a problem similar to question 3. They can then swap problems with another pair.

**ASSESSMENT CHECKPOINT** Use questions 1 to 3 to assess whether children can work flexibly with percentages, knowing how to use the given information to solve the problem. Check that children understand when they are given the whole and need to work out a percentage, and when they are given a percentage and need to find the whole.

**ANSWERS** Answers for the **Practice** part of the lesson can be found in the *Power Maths* online subscription.

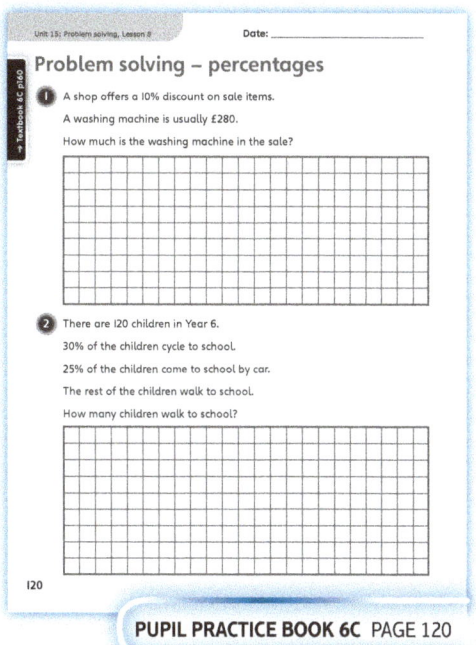

**PUPIL PRACTICE BOOK 6C** PAGE 120

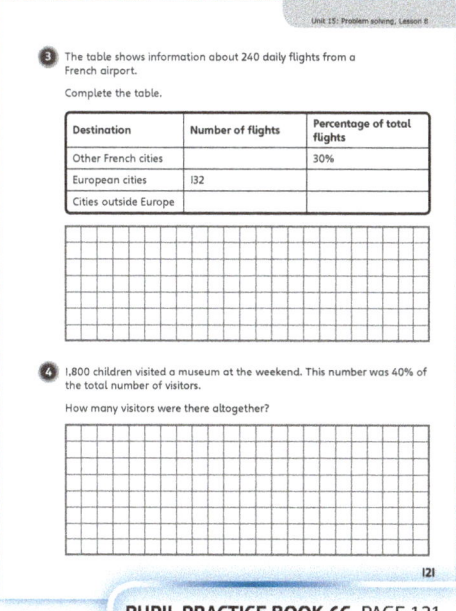

**PUPIL PRACTICE BOOK 6C** PAGE 121

## Reflect

**WAYS OF WORKING** Independent thinking

**IN FOCUS** The shapes have been chosen so they are less familiar and not all equal parts are immediately obvious.

**ASSESSMENT CHECKPOINT** Check that children can use their knowledge of equivalent fractions and percentages to explain why the shaded part of each shape is 60%.

**ANSWERS** Answers for the **Reflect** part of the lesson can be found in the *Power Maths* online subscription.

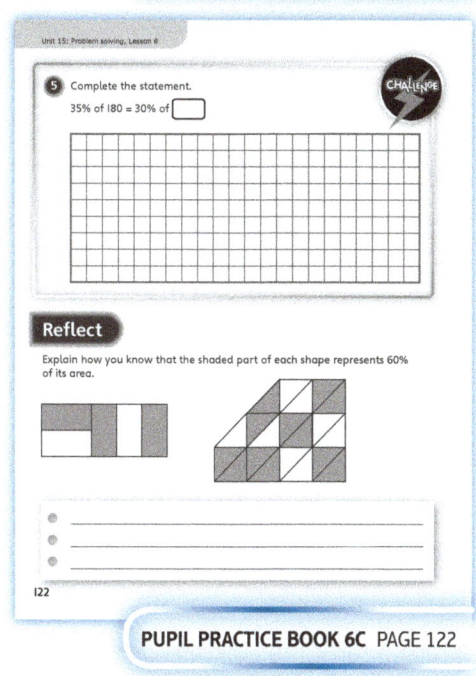

**PUPIL PRACTICE BOOK 6C** PAGE 122

## After the lesson

- Can children explain when they are required to find a percentage of a whole and when they are required to find the whole?
- Can they solve a range of problems, representing them as necessary, and explain what calculations need to be carried out?

199

Unit 15: Problem solving, Lesson 9

# Problem solving – ratio and proportion

## Learning focus
In this lesson, children will further explore ratio as a relationship between parts to help solve problems in different contexts. They will use representations to show a ratio and make use of multiplication facts to help scale quantities.

## Before you teach
- Can children recall and use multiplication and division facts?
- Can they solve simple ratio problems using multiplication as scaling?
- Can they explain how many parts in total for a given ratio?

### NATIONAL CURRICULUM LINKS

**Year 6 Ratio and proportion**

Solve problems involving unequal sharing and grouping using knowledge of fractions and multiples.

Solve problems involving the relative sizes of two quantities where missing values can be found by using integer multiplication and division facts.

### ASSESSING MASTERY

Children can use the language of 'for every' to talk about ratio and can use the colon notation. They can use bar models to solve problems involving ratio and proportion, explaining what each part represents.

### COMMON MISCONCEPTIONS

When dealing with the number of parts in a problem, children may forget to find the total number of parts. For example, in the question, 'In a class of 32 children, there are 5 girls for every 3 boys. How many girls are there?' children may divide 32 by 5 rather than 8. Use bar models to support this concept. Ask:
- *How can you show the number of girls on the bar model? … the number of boys? How many parts in total? What is each part worth?*

### STRENGTHENING UNDERSTANDING

To work with ratio, children need to be secure in their understanding of multiplication as scaling. They also need to be confident with the idea of equivalence – for example, recognising that '2 oranges for every 3 apples' can be scaled up to '4 oranges for every 6 apples' and so on, remembering that the relationship between the number of oranges and apples remains the same. Represent the scaling up of simple ratios with counters or cubes. Look at the relationship between the values each time as the numbers are scaled twice, three times, four times, and so on.

### GOING DEEPER

Look in greater depth at the difference between a ratio and a proportion. Ask children to use sticks of cubes to represent a given ratio or proportion. Ask them to describe the stick using ratio, then proportion. Encourage children to reason about other lengths of sticks with the same ratio. Ask: *What patterns do you notice?*

### KEY LANGUAGE

**In lesson:** ratio, scaling, relationship

**Other language to be used by the teacher:** fraction, similar, proportion

### STRUCTURES AND REPRESENTATIONS

Bar model

### RESOURCES

**Optional:** counters, cubes

 In the eTextbook of this lesson, you will find interactive links to a selection of teaching tools.

## Quick recap

Ask children to list as many ratios equivalent to 2 : 6 as they can.

# Unit 15: Problem solving, Lesson 9

## Discover

**WAYS OF WORKING** Pair work

**ASK**

- Question 1 a): *What do you notice about the number of car stickers compared to the number of train stickers each time?*
- Question 1 a): *How can you describe the relationship between the number of car stickers and train stickers as a ratio?*
- Question 1 a): *What can you tell me about the number of each type of sticker and the total number of stickers in two packets?*
- Question 1 b): *What diagram can you draw to represent this problem?*
- Question 1 b): *How many more car stickers than train stickers are there in each packet? … in two packets? … in ten packets?*

**IN FOCUS** These questions require children to solve ratio problems by reasoning. The ratio of 4 car stickers to every 2 train stickers is not given in its simplest form. Children should notice that this is the same relationship as 2 car stickers for every 1 train sticker, so the number of car stickers is always double the number of train stickers.

**PRACTICAL TIPS** Use counters or cubes to represent the ratio, building these in rows to show the scaling for one packet, two packets, and so on.

**ANSWERS**

Question 1 a): Andy has 48 stickers in total.

Question 1 b): There are 25 packets of stickers in the box.

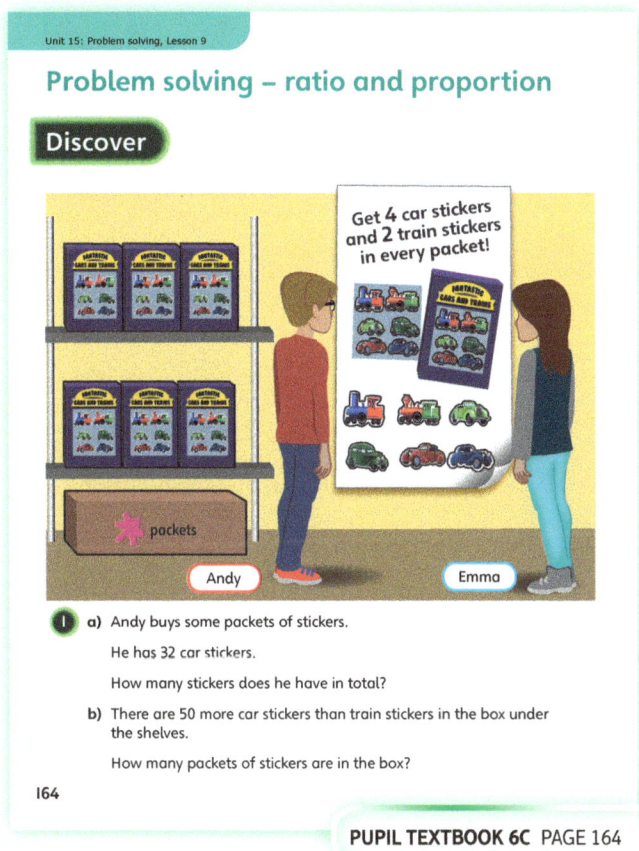

PUPIL TEXTBOOK 6C PAGE 164

## Share

**WAYS OF WORKING** Whole class teacher led

**ASK**

- Question 1 a): *Can you explain how the bar model represents the problem?*
- Question 1 a): *Why does the scaling show 1 packet, 2 packets, 4 packets and 8 packets, but not the other numbers of packets in between (for example, 3 packets)?*
- Question 1 b): *Can you explain how the bar model represents the problem this time?*
- Question 1 b): *Why do you do the calculation 150 ÷ 6 to find the answer?*

**IN FOCUS** Question 1 a) has been chosen to encourage children to explore the ratio between the car stickers and train stickers and to consider how this relates to the total amount. Look for children who recognise that, because there are 6 stickers (or parts) in each packet (2 + 4), the total number of stickers will always be a multiple of 6. Question 1 b) has been chosen to explore the difference between the number of car stickers and train stickers rather than the total number of stickers. Look for children who mistake 50 for the number of car/train stickers rather than the difference between them.

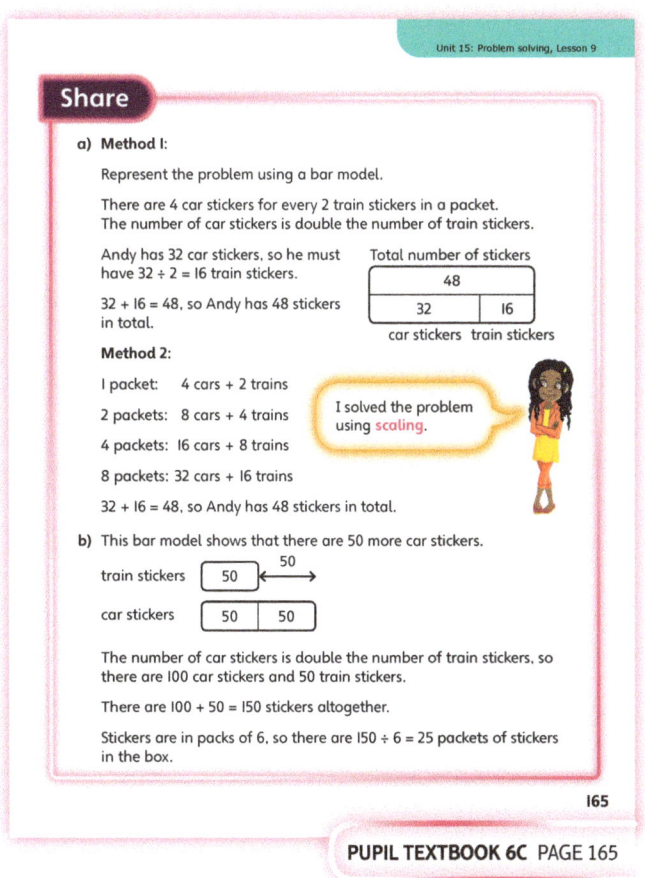

PUPIL TEXTBOOK 6C PAGE 165

201

Unit 15: Problem solving, Lesson 9

# Think together

**WAYS OF WORKING** Whole class teacher led (I do, We do, You do)

**ASK**

• Question ① a): *You know that 1 cm on the sticker represents 2·5 m. How does this help?*
• Question ① b): *Which operation will you need to use?*
• Question ②: *How many grams of fruit are needed for 1 spoon of honey? … 2 spoons? … 8 spoons?*
• Question ③: *How many squares is the diameter of the large circle compared to the diameter of the small circle? How can you describe this as a ratio?*
• Question ④: *What is 4·8 m in centimetres? How many times will the 160 cm pattern be repeated in 480 cm? How can you find out?*

**IN FOCUS** These questions are designed to show ratio in different contexts: scales, recipes, measurements and geometry. For each part of question ①, children need to work out whether they should multiply or divide. In question ②, children may notice that double 240 g is 480 g and only another 120 g (half of 240 g) is needed to make 600 g. Therefore, the amount of honey needed is 8 spoons (double 4 spoons) plus 2 spoons (half of 4 spoons), which is 10 spoons. Alternatively, some children may choose to find the unitary value (1 spoon for 60 g) and then divide 600 g by 60. In question ④, make sure children understand that when the pattern repeats, there will be 2 large square slabs next to each other.

**STRENGTHEN** For question ①, look at scaling the length of the train on the sticker to its real measurement, for example:
1 cm     2·5 m
2 cm     5 m
4 cm     10 m

**DEEPEN** For question ③, discuss how the relationship can also be described as 'the diameter of the small circle is $\frac{2}{5}$ of the diameter of the large circle' or 'the large circle is $\frac{5}{2}$ or $2\frac{1}{2}$ times the diameter of the small circle'.

For question ④, ask children to work out the number of each size of slab needed for different lengths of path: for example, a 9·6 m path. Then ask questions based on the number of slabs. For example: *The same pattern is used for another path. Toshi and Sofia use 56 small slabs. How long is the path? How many large slabs do they use?*

**ASSESSMENT CHECKPOINT** Use question ① to assess whether children recognise when they need to multiply and when they need to divide to solve a ratio problem. Use questions ①, ② and ④ to assess whether children can use what they know about ratio to solve problems involving units of measurement. Use question ④ to assess whether they can solve ratio problems that involve more than one step.

**ANSWERS**

Question ① a): The train is 15 m long in real life.

Question ① b): The sticker is 8 cm long.

Question ②: 10 spoons of honey.

Question ③: The ratio a : b = 2 : 5

Question ④ a): 24 small slabs

Question ④ b): 9 large slabs

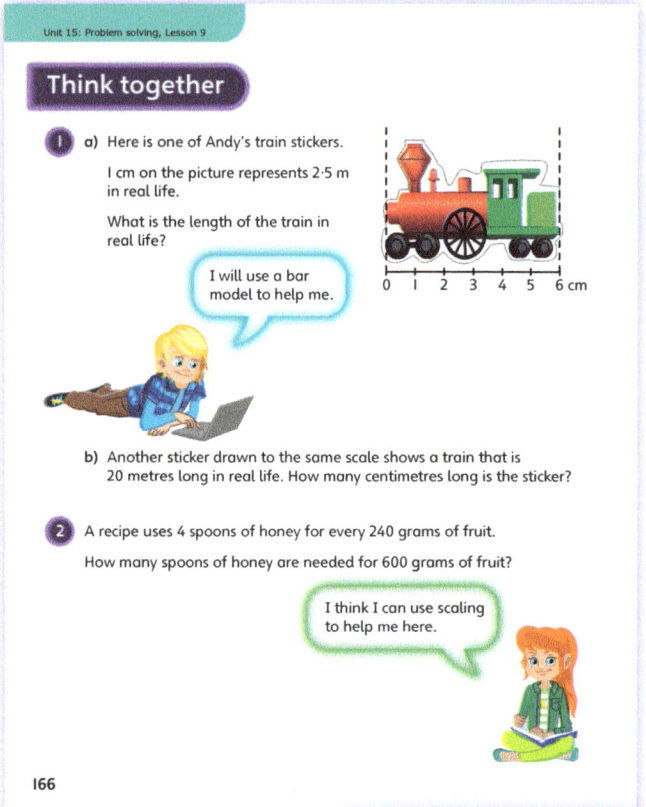

PUPIL TEXTBOOK 6C PAGE 166

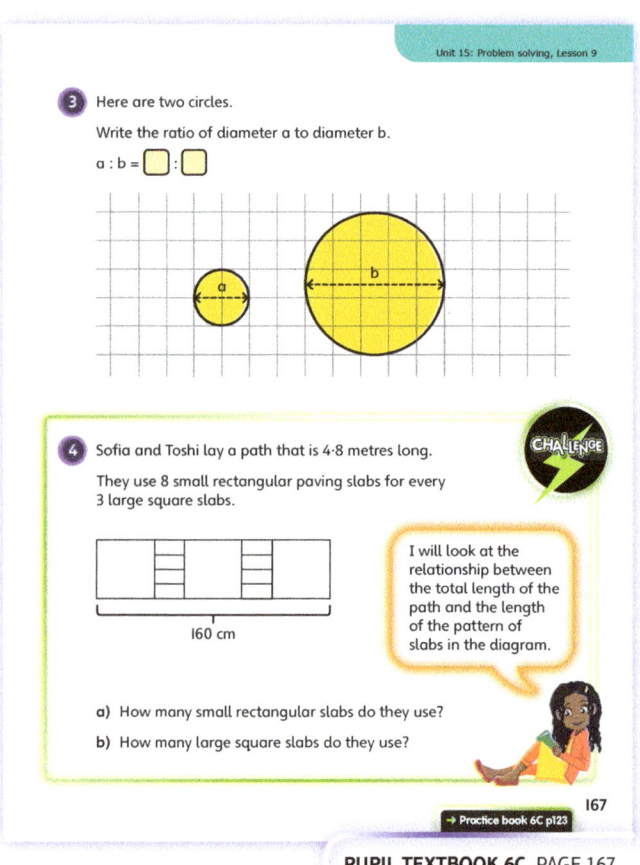

PUPIL TEXTBOOK 6C PAGE 167

# Unit 15: Problem solving, Lesson 9

## Practice

**WAYS OF WORKING** Independent thinking

**IN FOCUS** Question ❶ has been chosen to explore proportion. Children should notice that proportions are written as fractions and show a part compared to the whole: for example, 3 out of 8, so $\frac{3}{8}$.

Question ❷ requires children to scale a recipe for 6 cakes. In part b) they need to scale the recipe for 15 cakes; 15 is not a multiple of 6, so they could think about 15 as 12 + 3 (a multiple of 6 plus half of 6).

In question ❺, children must express a proportion as a ratio. Look for children who show the ratio as 3 boys to every 8 girls because they have incorrectly interpreted the meaning of the fraction. There are 8 parts in the whole, so if boys represent 3 parts, girls must represent 5 parts.

**STRENGTHEN** For question ❺, use a stick of 8 cubes to represent the fraction of boys, for example 3 yellow cubes and 5 red. Discuss what the stick is showing: 8 equal parts and 3 of them represent the boys. Ask children to explain what the other 5 cubes represent. Agree that the stick shows that there are 3 boys for every 5 girls.

**DEEPEN** Look at different strategies for solving question ❷ b): for example, finding the ingredients for 1 cake (unitary value) and then multiplying by 15; finding the ingredients for 3 cakes by halving the ingredients for 6 cakes and then multiplying by 5, as 5 × 3 = 15; using doubling for 12 cakes and halving for 3, then adding.

**ASSESSMENT CHECKPOINT** Use questions ❶ and ❷ to check whether children can use scaling to solve ratio problems. Use questions ❶ and ❹ to assess whether children can interpret a proportion. Use question ❸ to assess whether children can interpret a ratio shown in the context of geometry, and represent it using the colon notation (a : b). Check whether children recognise when a ratio can be shown in its simplest form: for example, 3 : 1 rather than 9 : 3.

**ANSWERS** Answers for the **Practice** part of the lesson can be found in the *Power Maths* online subscription.

## Reflect

**WAYS OF WORKING** Independent thinking

**IN FOCUS** Children are required to show that they understand how to solve problems involving ratio. Encourage them to show the correct way to write a ratio using a colon and explain what it means.

**ASSESSMENT CHECKPOINT** Check that children can clearly explain the steps they need to take to solve the problem. If they can do this, it is likely they have mastered the topic.

**ANSWERS** Answers for the **Reflect** part of the lesson can be found in the *Power Maths* online subscription.

## After the lesson

- Can children solve a range of different ratio problems, applying multiplication or division facts as required?
- Can they explain how scaling can be used to solve ratio problems, explaining how the relationship stays the same?
- Can children interpret a fraction as a proportion, recognising that the denominator describes the total number of equal parts? Can they describe it as a ratio?

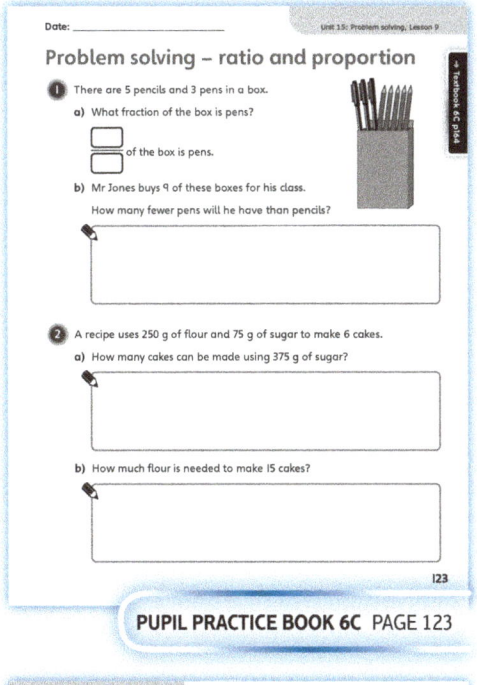

**PUPIL PRACTICE BOOK 6C** PAGE 123

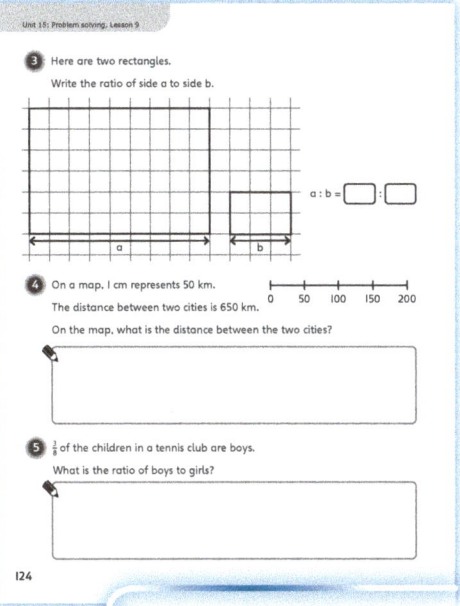

**PUPIL PRACTICE BOOK 6C** PAGE 124

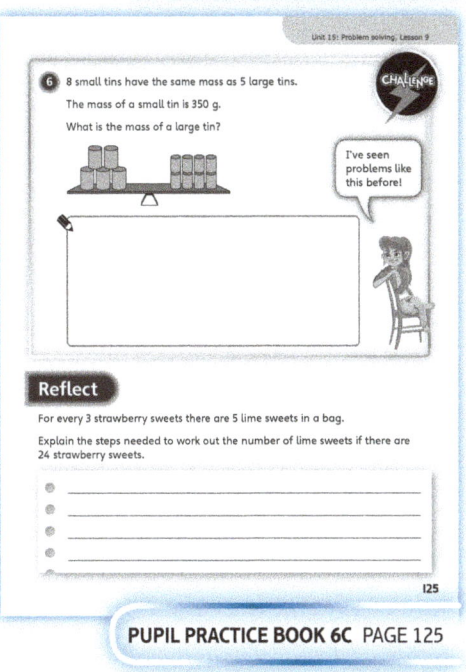

**PUPIL PRACTICE BOOK 6C** PAGE 125

203

Unit 15: Problem solving, Lesson 10

# Problem solving – time

### Learning focus
In this lesson, children will calculate time intervals and convert between units of time to solve problems. They will interpret and make use of number lines as time lines.

### Before you teach
- Can children convert between hours and minutes?
- Can they represent or calculate an interval using a number line?
- Can they convert between the 12-hour and 24-hour clock?

#### NATIONAL CURRICULUM LINKS

**Year 6 Measurement**

Use, read, write and convert between standard units, converting measurements of length, mass, volume and time from a smaller unit of measure to a larger unit, and vice versa, using decimal notation to up to three decimal places.

#### ASSESSING MASTERY

Children can solve a range of problems using time conversions. They can calculate an interval or use a given interval to identify a specific time.

#### COMMON MISCONCEPTIONS

When calculating time intervals, children may revert to familiar methods of adding and subtracting quantities, which are incorrect when working with time. Look together at a range of time lines, counting on in hours and minutes and counting up or back to the next or previous hour. Ask:
- *What is the time now? How many minutes have passed? What was the time 40 minutes ago?*

#### STRENGTHENING UNDERSTANDING

Use a geared clock with a time line to show the jumps moving from one time to the next on the time line. Model a problem that involves times on a 24-hour clock.

#### GOING DEEPER

Look at calculating time intervals as part of line graphs. Ask children to explain why the processes are the same as those used within this lesson.

#### KEY LANGUAGE

**In lesson:** hour, minute, day, week, month, am, pm, time line

**Other language to be used by the teacher:** second, 24-hour clock, 12-hour clock

#### STRUCTURES AND REPRESENTATIONS

Number line, time line, calendar

#### RESOURCES

**Optional:** geared clock, calendar

 In the eTextbook of this lesson, you will find interactive links to a selection of teaching tools.

### Quick recap

Ask children to answer the following time questions: *How many seconds are in one minute? How many minutes are in one hour? How many hours are in one day? How many days are in one week?* If children are feeling confident, ask them if they can work out how many hours are in one week.

Unit 15: Problem solving, Lesson 10

# Discover

**WAYS OF WORKING** Pair work

**ASK**

- Question ❶ a): *What do you need to do first?*
- Question ❶ a): *Why do you need to know about the dentist's 20-minute breaks in the morning and afternoon?*
- Question ❶ b): *How many weeks are the same as 28 days?*
- Question ❶ b): *Why do you need to know the number of days in April?*

**IN FOCUS** Question ❶ a) requires children to reason about the number of 15-minute appointments in the morning and afternoon sessions. They need to calculate time intervals and make allowances for the dentist's 20-minute breaks. Question ❶ b) has been chosen as children will need to apply several known facts and skills: the number of days in a week, the number of days in April, and counting backwards over a month boundary.

**PRACTICAL TIPS** Use a calendar to explore counting over month boundaries and showing the same count of weeks or days on a number line.

**ANSWERS**

Question ❶ a): 3 more appointments can be made in the afternoon than in the morning.

Question ❶ b): The date of the previous dentist clinic was 14 April.

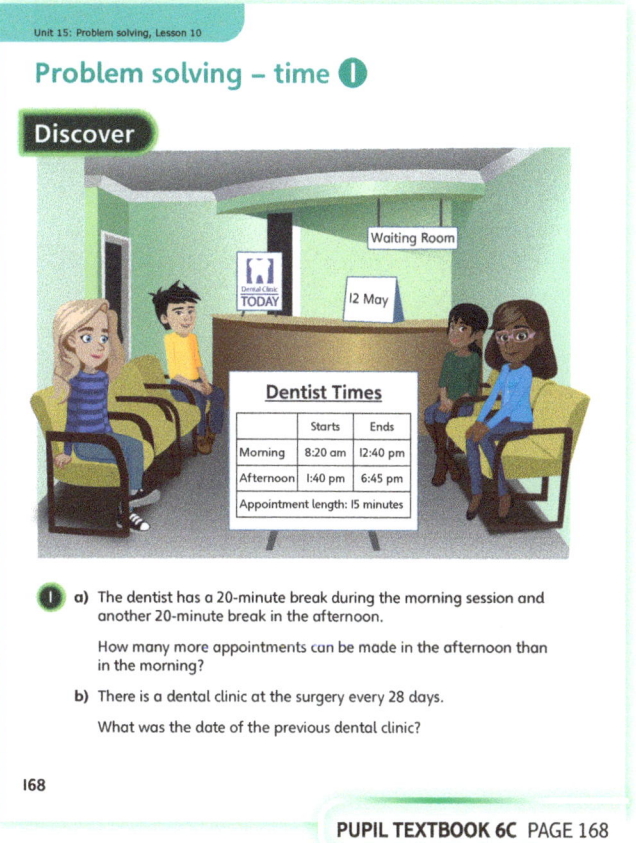

PUPIL TEXTBOOK 6C PAGE 168

# Share

**WAYS OF WORKING** Whole class teacher led

**ASK**

- Question ❶ a): *How has the time line been used to calculate time intervals? What jumps can you see? Could you have made different jumps and still calculated the intervals as 4 hours 20 minutes and 5 hours 5 minutes?*
- Question ❶ a): *Can you tell me a different way to solve the problem?*
- Question ❶ b): *How do you know that 14 April and 12 May are both on the same day of the week?*

**IN FOCUS** Number lines (referred to as time lines here) have been used to solve both problems. In question ❶ a), children are given the start and end times and must calculate a time interval. In question ❶ b), children are given an end date and a time interval, and must calculate a start date. Use a calendar to support children counting back in weeks from May into April.

**STRENGTHEN** For question ❶ a), discuss why children do not need to work out the number of 15-minute sessions in 4 hours and again in 4 hours 45 minutes to find the difference. Although this is a credible method, it takes much longer.

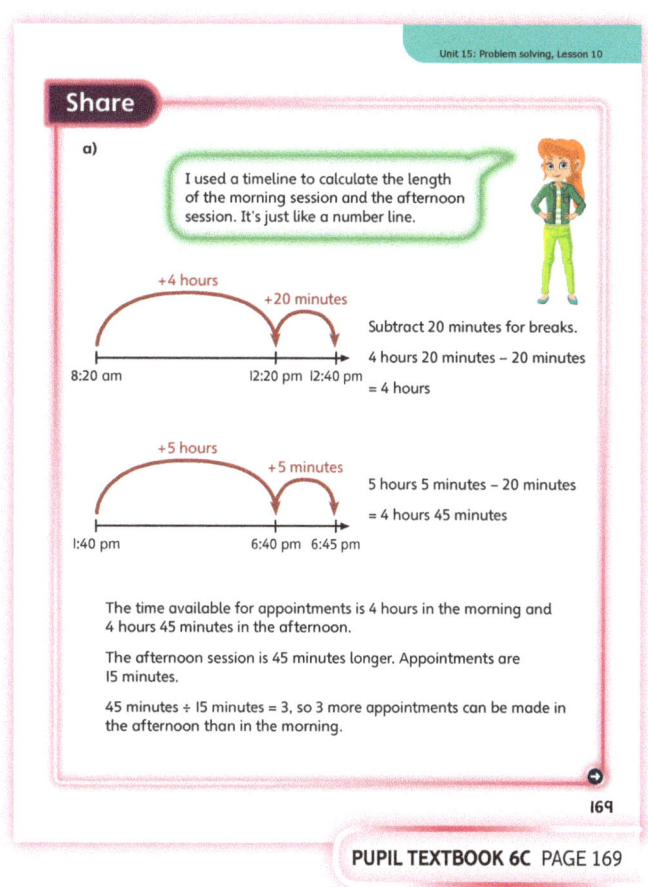

PUPIL TEXTBOOK 6C PAGE 169

205

# Think together

**WAYS OF WORKING** Whole class teacher led (I do, We do, You do)

**ASK**
- Question ① a): *What time is Mr Nash's appointment? When does Miss Ana's appointment end? How can you use this information?*
- Question ②: *How long did Jamilla take to run her laps?*
- Question ②: *What do you notice about the number of laps completed by Max compared with Jamilla?*
- Question ③: *How can you use a number line to help?*
- Question ④: *Why might it be useful to make a timetable for each bus?*

**IN FOCUS** In question ①, children need to interpret a time line to answer two different problems relating to intervals of time. Not all of the information is given on the time line so they will need to use what they know about the length of each appointment.

Question ③ requires children to calculate a time interval in months and then multiply this by the cost of electricity per month. Children may forget to carry out the second step.

Question ④ has been chosen so that children work with two different sets of information to find the next time when the bus departures coincide.

**STRENGTHEN** Remind children to use time lines to help solve the problems. Explore the effect of using different jumps on the time line, encouraging children to work with jumps that are manageable for them, breaking numbers across hour boundaries as appropriate to avoid errors.

**DEEPEN** For question ④, ask children to reason about other times in the day when the buses depart at the same time. Challenge them to identify any patterns that could help.

**ASSESSMENT CHECKPOINT** Use question ① to assess whether children can interpret and use a time line. Use question ② to assess whether children look for relationships within the given information to help them. Check that they can work with the 24-hour clock notation and that they can convert between hours and minutes. Use question ③ to assess whether children can work with units of months and years, recognising that there are 12 months in each year.

**ANSWERS**

Question ① a): 55 minutes

Question ① b): 11:50 am

Question ②: Jamilla runs faster.
Max runs 15 laps in 45 minutes, so 3 minutes per lap.
Jamilla does 30 laps in 86 minutes, which is less than 3 minutes per lap (2·867 minutes).

Question ③: The company spent £10,780 in total.
(3 × 12) + 8 months = 44 months
44 × £245 = £10,780

Question ④: The next time they will both depart together is at 11:45.
There are 3 hours 45 minutes between each time the buses depart together, so 15:30 then 19:15.

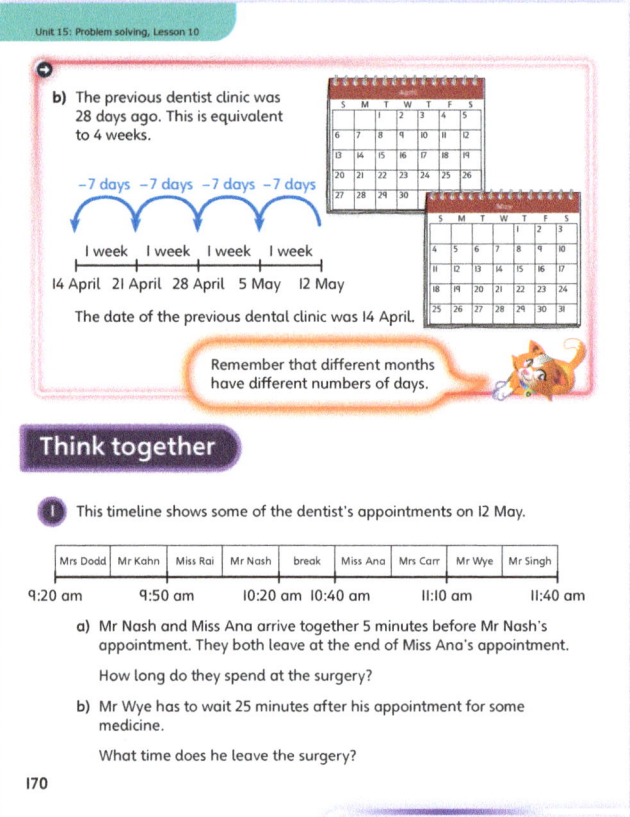

PUPIL TEXTBOOK 6C PAGE 170

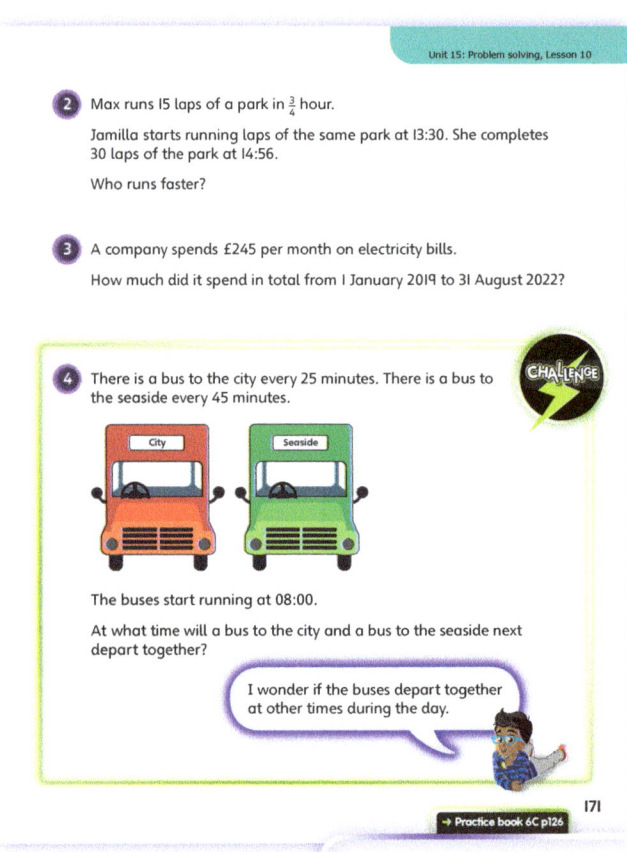

PUPIL TEXTBOOK 6C PAGE 171

# Practice

**WAYS OF WORKING** Independent thinking

**IN FOCUS** Question ❶ a) requires children to convert between 12-hour and 24-hour notation. Children may mistakenly record the answer as 4 hours 25 minutes by misinterpreting 18:45 as 8:45 pm. Question ❸ is a two-step problem: children must first find the length of time for which Olivia walked and then calculate the amount of money raised.

Question ❹ has been designed to allow children to use different strategies to find 12 intervals of 45 minutes. For example, they can: multiply 45 by 12 and then divide by 60 to find the number of hours; round 45 minutes to 1 hour and then subtract 12 lots of 15 minutes from 12 hours; or look at 6 lots of $1\frac{1}{2}$ hours or 3 lots of 3 hours. Question ❺ requires another conversion, but this time from hours to days. Children will also need to use their knowledge of the calendar to find when the puppy was born.

**STRENGTHEN** For question ❷, encourage children to use a number line as a time line and to mark the different appointments and breaks for Tuesday. They can then add this to the number of appointments on Wednesday to work out the total.

**DEEPEN** Ask children to calculate how many weeks/minutes/seconds the puppy in question ❺ has been alive for. Then ask them to work out how old it will be on the upcoming New Year's Eve.

**ASSESSMENT CHECKPOINT** Use questions ❶ and ❷ to assess whether children can calculate and work flexibly with time intervals. Use questions ❹ and ❺ to assess whether children can accurately convert between units of time. Use question ❹ to check that children understand how to compare a duration of minutes with a fraction of a day.

**ANSWERS** Answers for the **Practice** part of the lesson can be found in the *Power Maths* online subscription.

# Reflect

**WAYS OF WORKING** Independent thinking

**IN FOCUS** Children first need to work out a time, given the starting time and a time interval. They then need to write this answer in three ways: using the 12-hour and 24-hour clocks and in words. They should notice that the time is in the evening rather than the morning.

**ASSESSMENT CHECKPOINT** Check that children can add a time interval to a given time, crossing the hour boundary correctly. Check that they can write the time using the 12-hour and 24-hour clock notation, and that they can explain how to convert from one to the other. Check that they correctly use pm to show an evening time in 12-hour clock notation.

**ANSWERS** Answers for the **Reflect** part of the lesson can be found in the *Power Maths* online subscription.

## After the lesson

- Can children interpret time lines to help them work with and calculate time intervals?
- Can they convert between different units of time, including between 12-hour and 24-hour clock notations?
- Can they work with time to solve a range of problems?

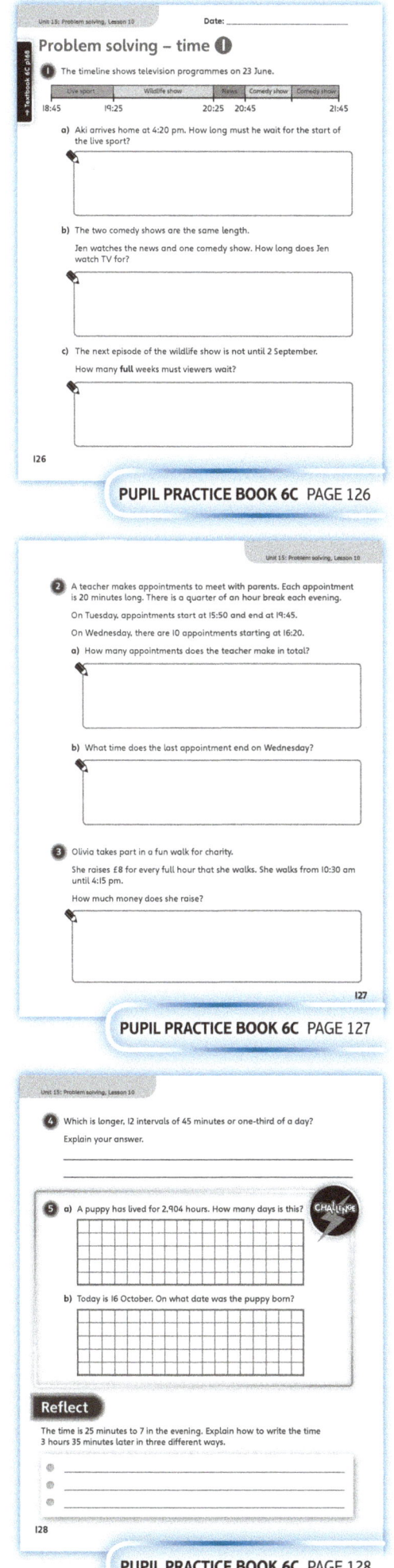

Unit 15: Problem solving, Lesson 11

# Problem solving – time 2

## Learning focus
In this lesson, children will solve more complex problems about time involving two or more steps. They will convert between units of time to calculate and compare. They will also draw on their understanding of timetables, the number line, measurement and statistics.

## Before you teach
- Can children convert between 12- and 24-hour times?
- Can they represent or calculate a time interval using a number line?
- Can they explain why timetables usually use the 24-hour clock?

### NATIONAL CURRICULUM LINKS

**Year 6 Measurement**

Use, read, write and convert between standard units, converting measurements of length, mass, volume and time from a smaller unit of measure to a larger unit, and vice versa, using decimal notation to up to three decimal places.

### ASSESSING MASTERY

Children can solve a set of contextualised problems that involve several steps. They can draw on time conversions to interpret and work with timetables, line graphs and other representations.

### COMMON MISCONCEPTIONS

Children may fail to check the notation (12-hour or 24-hour) that has been used to represent a time. They should recognise that timetables usually use 24-hour notation, and understand why this is the case. Similarly, they may not check units before comparing. Ask:
- *Do these times include am/pm? What does that tell you?*
- *What do you need to do before comparing these times?*

### STRENGTHENING UNDERSTANDING

Model the use of a number line to calculate a time interval. Discuss how the axis on a time graph can be seen as a number line and interpreted in the same way.

### GOING DEEPER

Look at a range of problems involving time. Ask children to sort them into those that require a time conversion and those that do not. Include some that require conversion between 12- and 24-hour times, but not between units of time.

### KEY LANGUAGE

**In lesson:** hour, minute, 24-hour time, pm

**Other language to be used by the teacher:** second, 12-hour time, am

### STRUCTURES AND REPRESENTATIONS

Number line, timetable, line graph

 In the eTextbook of this lesson, you will find interactive links to a selection of teaching tools.

## Quick recap

Ask: *What is the time now? How many minutes will it be until* [for example] *lunchtime, home time or 9 pm?*

# Unit 15: Problem solving, Lesson 11

## Discover

**WAYS OF WORKING** Pair work

**ASK**

- Question 1 a): *Sofia has just missed a train. How many minutes before 11:43 did this train depart?*
- Question 1 a): *What time train must she catch now? How do you know that she will arrive in Stanton in time?*
- Question 1 b): *What steps do you need to take to solve this problem?*
- Question 1 b): *How do you know that the length of the train journey from Winbeech to Stanton is always the same?*
- Question 1 b): *How many minutes earlier does the bus arrive in Stanton than the train?*

**IN FOCUS** Children are required to interpret a train timetable, using given information to help them make decisions and calculate answers. Both questions involve times after midday, so children may wish to convert the times to the 12-hour clock to make sense of the problem, particularly as Sofia uses this notation to give the time she needs to be in Stanton. In question 1 b), children may forget to complete the final step, giving the answer as 2 hours 16 minutes; alternatively, they may calculate the departure time based on the arrival time of the train, rather than the bus.

**PRACTICAL TIPS** Draw number lines to help children to work with time intervals. Remind them that they can use number lines to count on or to count back. Model the first train in the timetable on a time line.

**ANSWERS**

Question 1 a): Sofia will have to wait 22 minutes for her train.

Question 1 b): The bus leaves Winbeech at 10:54.

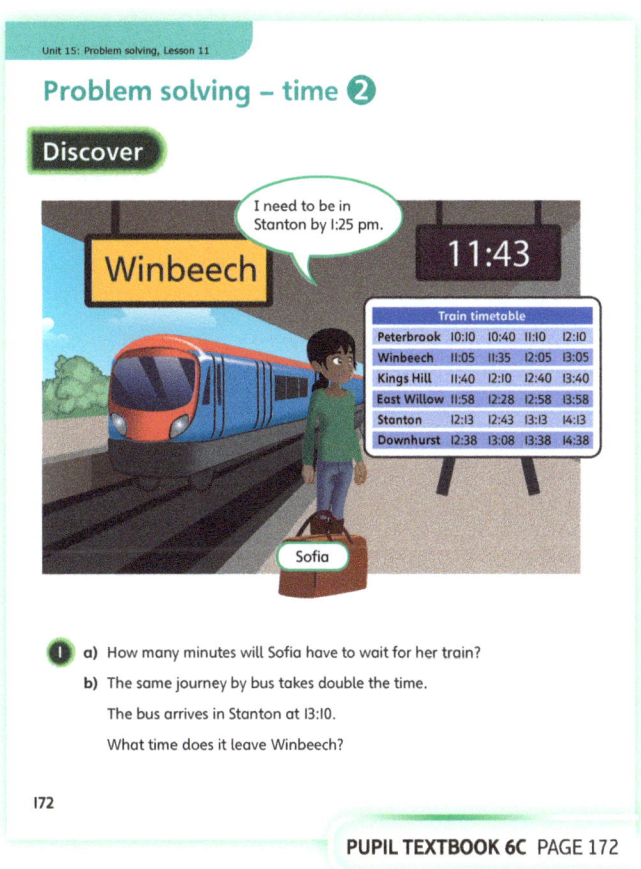

PUPIL TEXTBOOK 6C PAGE 172

## Share

**WAYS OF WORKING** Whole class teacher led

**ASK**

- Question 1 a): *Is 13:25 the same as 3:25 pm? Why not?*
- Question 1 a): *Why is the first jump on the time line only 17 minutes?*
- Question 1 b): *On the time line, why has 16 minutes been partitioned into 10-minute and 6-minute jumps?*

**IN FOCUS** Question 1 a) has been chosen so children first carry out a straightforward time conversion and calculation of a time interval. Question 1 b) is more complex as it requires several steps. Both parts have been approached using time lines, partitioning time intervals as necessary to count across an hour boundary.

**STRENGTHEN** Look together at partitioning across hour boundaries to ensure that calculations are done accurately. Discuss how partitioning can be used to count on or back over a boundary.

**DEEPEN** Ask children to explain how much earlier Sofia would have needed to arrive at Winbeech in order to catch the 10:54 bus.

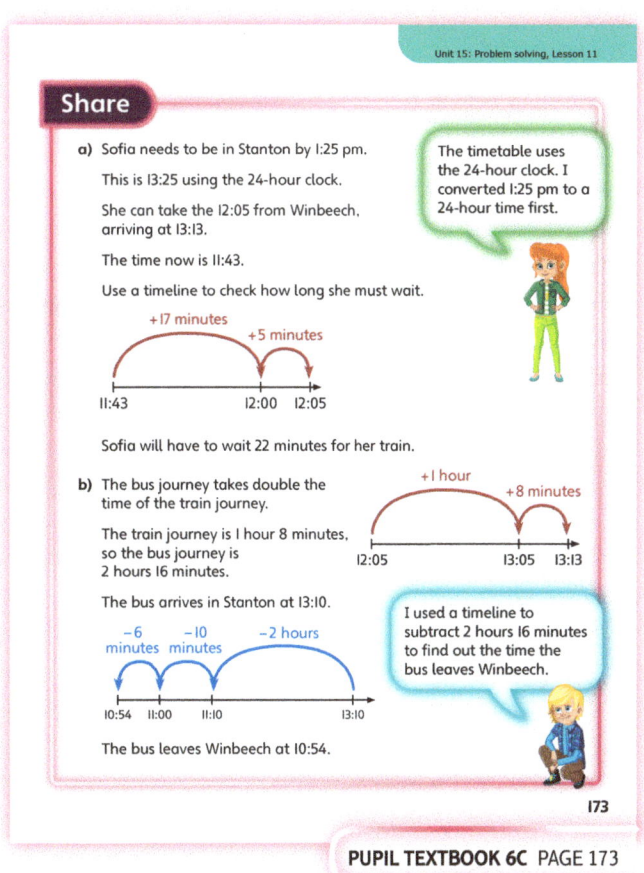

PUPIL TEXTBOOK 6C PAGE 173

209

# Think together

**WAYS OF WORKING** Whole class teacher led (I do, We do, You do)

**ASK**
- Question ❶: *There is a lot of information here. What do you need to find out first? Why?*
- Question ❷ a): *Why do you need to check the length of each lesson before calculating? How can you calculate this?*
- Question ❸ b): *At what time did the number of visitors reach 1,000? At what time did the number of visitors drop again to under 1,000? How does this help?*
- Question ❹: *What do you notice about the relationship between Holly and Toshi's times?*

**IN FOCUS** Question ❷ features a different structure for a timetable. For part b), children can consider different strategies for their calculations. For example, they can: find the total time available for hire each day and work out the difference; or compare the time available each day by looking at what is the same and what is different.

For question ❹, children may think that Toshi was faster because he swam for longer or that Holly was faster because she swam lengths. Children need to work out how far they each swam in 45 minutes.

**STRENGTHEN** For question ❶, consider strategies for calculating 5 × £2·95. For example, children can round to £3 and then adjust, or they can multiply by 10 and then halve the result.

**DEEPEN** For question ❹, ask children to look at different strategies. For example, children can compare how far Holly and Toshi swam in the same amount of time, or they can compare the time it took each of child to swim a given number of metres.

**ASSESSMENT CHECKPOINT** Use questions ❶ and ❹ to assess whether children can solve more complex multi-step problems. Use questions ❷ and ❹ to assess whether children look for relationships within the given information to help them. Use question ❸ to assess whether children can interpret a scale showing measurement and can identify a specific time or calculate a time interval using the scale.

**ANSWERS**

Question ❶: They pay £19·95 in total.
1 hour 40 mins = 5 twenty minute sessions:
5 × £2·95 = £14·75
2 rackets: 2 × £2·60 = £5·20

Question ❷ a): 6 hours 45 minutes

Question ❷ b): 3 hours longer on a Saturday than on a Sunday.

Question ❸ a): 08:30

Question ❸ b): 2 hours 15 minutes

Question ❹: Toshi swims faster.
Holly swims 630 m in 45 minutes = 1,260 m in 90 minutes.
Toshi swims 1,280 m in 90 minutes.
Holly: 630 ÷ 45 = 14 m per minute
Toshi: 1,280 ÷ 90 = 14·22 m per minute
Holly: 630 ÷ 3 × 4 = 840 m per hour
Toshi: 1,280 ÷ 3 × 2 = 853·33 m per hour

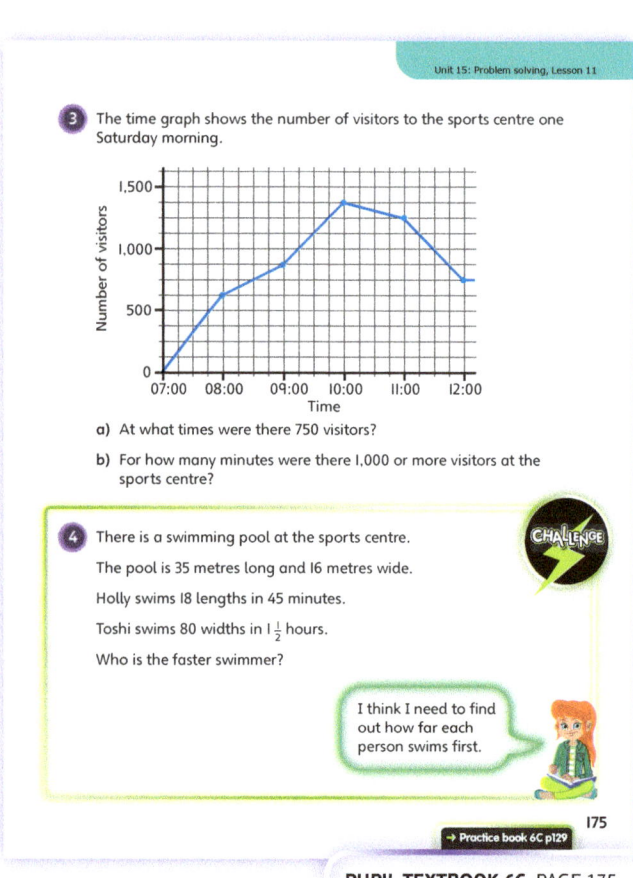

PUPIL TEXTBOOK 6C PAGE 174

PUPIL TEXTBOOK 6C PAGE 175

Unit 15: Problem solving, Lesson 11

# Practice

**WAYS OF WORKING** Independent thinking

**IN FOCUS** Question ❶ provides an opportunity for children to work independently and interpret a timetable. The buses do not always stop at all of the stations so children should think carefully before calculating each time. For part a), some children may notice that both buses leave at 12 minutes past the hour but that the 15:12 bus arrives 45 minutes after the hour, compared with 42 minutes past for the 16:12.

Question ❸ has been designed to provide another opportunity for children to interpret scales on a line graph. They must reason about the 'story' of the graph to find when Mrs Dean stopped for lunch.

**STRENGTHEN** For question ❸, encourage children to tell the story of the graph to a partner, explaining what was happening at different intervals and how they know.

**DEEPEN** For question ❸, ask children to describe Mrs Dean's journey home and show this on a line graph. Remind them that the line will go down again as she gets nearer home.

**ASSESSMENT CHECKPOINT** Use questions ❶ and ❷ to assess whether children can complete multi-step problems with time intervals. Use question ❸ to assess whether children can work with two different scales on a line graph.

**ANSWERS** Answers for the **Practice** part of the lesson can be found in the *Power Maths* online subscription.

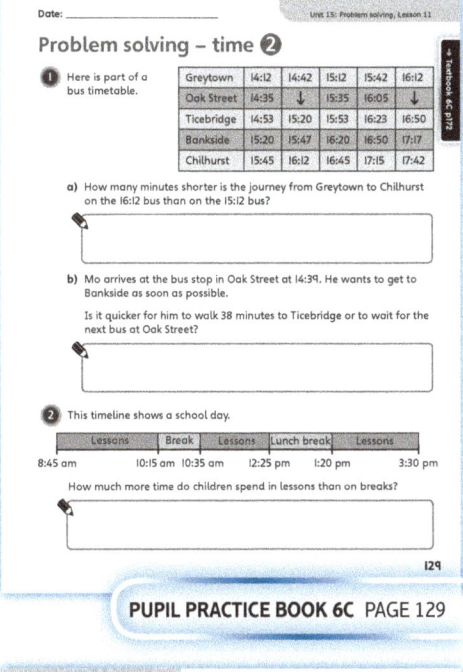

PUPIL PRACTICE BOOK 6C PAGE 129

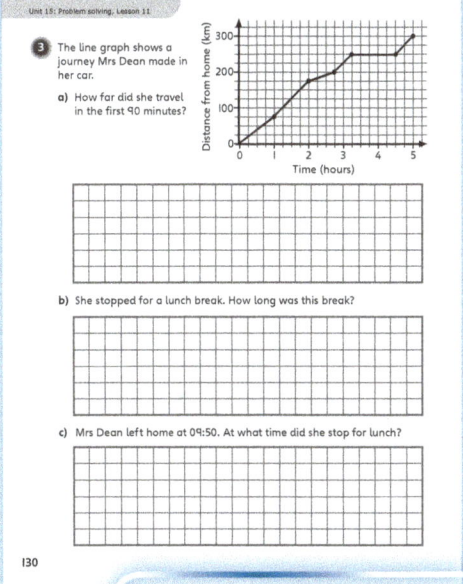

PUPIL PRACTICE BOOK 6C PAGE 130

# Reflect

**WAYS OF WORKING** Pair work

**IN FOCUS** Children are required to explain the mistake Lexi has made when calculating what time it will be in 1 hour 55 minutes. They should notice that she has not added 55 minutes to 45 minutes correctly. 55 minutes is only 5 minutes less than an hour, so the time will be nearly 2 hours later.

**ASSESSMENT CHECKPOINT** Check that children understand the 24-hour clock; and that 12.45 is quarter to 1.

**ANSWERS** Answers for the **Reflect** part of the lesson can be found in the *Power Maths* online subscription.

## After the lesson

- Can children work with time and other aspects of measurement to solve a range of multi-step problems?
- Can they interpret time lines as part of a line graph, reading the scale accurately and calculating intervals?
- Can they explain the relationships they may find between given numbers or measurements and how this can be used to help solve the problem?

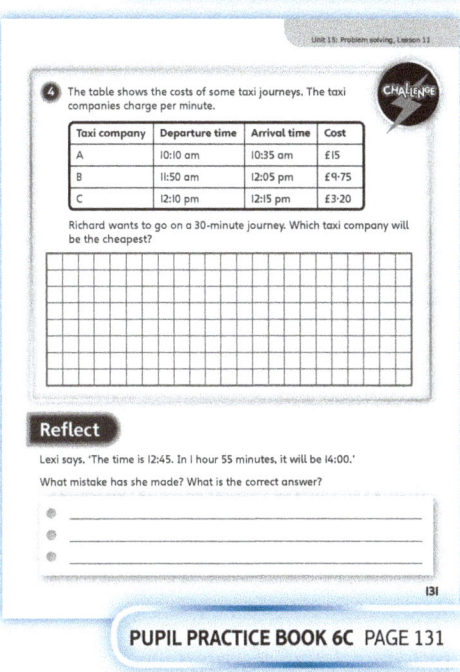

PUPIL PRACTICE BOOK 6C PAGE 131

Unit 15: Problem solving, Lesson 12

# Problem solving – position and direction

## Learning focus
In this lesson, children will solve problems using coordinates in all four quadrants. They will apply their knowledge of the properties of shapes to reason about the coordinates of an unlabelled or unknown vertex, including following a translation or reflection. They will also find half-way points, using the structure of the grid.

## Before you teach
- Can children plot or identify coordinates in all four quadrants?
- Can they explain what is the same and what is different about a shape following a reflection?
- Can they explain what is the same and what is different about a shape following a translation?

### NATIONAL CURRICULUM LINKS
**Year 6 Geometry – position and direction**
Describe positions on the full coordinate grid (all four quadrants).

### ASSESSING MASTERY
Children can identify and use coordinates in all four quadrants. They can use the structure of the grid to reason about plotted sequences or vertices of shapes. They can use reflections and translations.

### COMMON MISCONCEPTIONS
Children may not make the link between the axes and the number line as it crosses 0. They may not recognise the position of negative values in relation to 0 (for example, ⁻20 is smaller than ⁻2 so it is further away from 0). Ask:
- *Can you count back along the x-axis from 5? What happens when you reach 0? What is the next number?*

### STRENGTHENING UNDERSTANDING
Children often find it difficult to identify coordinates on a blank grid with few or no labels on the axes. Draw axes and a shape on the board, labelling the vertices. Ask children to take turns to add labels to the axes; at the same time, they should explain how they know these values.

### GOING DEEPER
Give children a range of questions that require them to think flexibly about the properties of shapes so that they have to reason at a deeper level about the coordinates of vertices following a transformation – for example: a shape shown in a more unusual orientation; or a reflection where the mirror line goes through the shape.

### KEY LANGUAGE
**In lesson:** coordinates, *x*-axis, *y*-axis, reflected, translated, mirror line, vertex, vertices, square, rectangle, parallelogram, isosceles

**Other language to be used by the teacher:** axes, rhombus, trapezium, half-way

### STRUCTURES AND REPRESENTATIONS
Coordinate grid

### RESOURCES
**Optional:** squared paper, set squares or protractors, tracing paper

 In the eTextbook of this lesson, you will find interactive links to a selection of teaching tools.

## Quick recap
Ask: *What does (3,4) mean on a coordinate grid? What mistake might someone make when they are interpreting this coordinate? What does (⁻3,4) mean on a coordinate grid? Which quadrant would you find these coordinates in?*

# Discover

**WAYS OF WORKING** Pair work

**ASK**

- Question ① a): *How can you use what you know about the coordinates (4,15) to help you find the x-coordinate for vertex A?*
- Question ① a): *Which coordinate can you use to help you find out about the y-coordinate for vertex A? Why?*
- Question ① b): *What can you tell me about reflecting a shape? What stays the same and what changes?*
- Question ① b): *What is the length and width of the original rectangle? How does this help?*

**IN FOCUS** Children must reason about the coordinates of the vertices of a rectangle before and after a reflection. In question ① b), children need to use the fact that the reflected rectangle is the same size as the original rectangle.

**PRACTICAL TIPS** Draw the diagram on the board and annotate the coordinate grid. Use the given coordinates to add labels on the axes: for example, 4, 10 and 18 on the x-axis.

**ANSWERS**

Question ① a): Vertex A is (4,5).
Vertex B is (10,15).

Question ① b): (24,15), (18,5), (24,5)

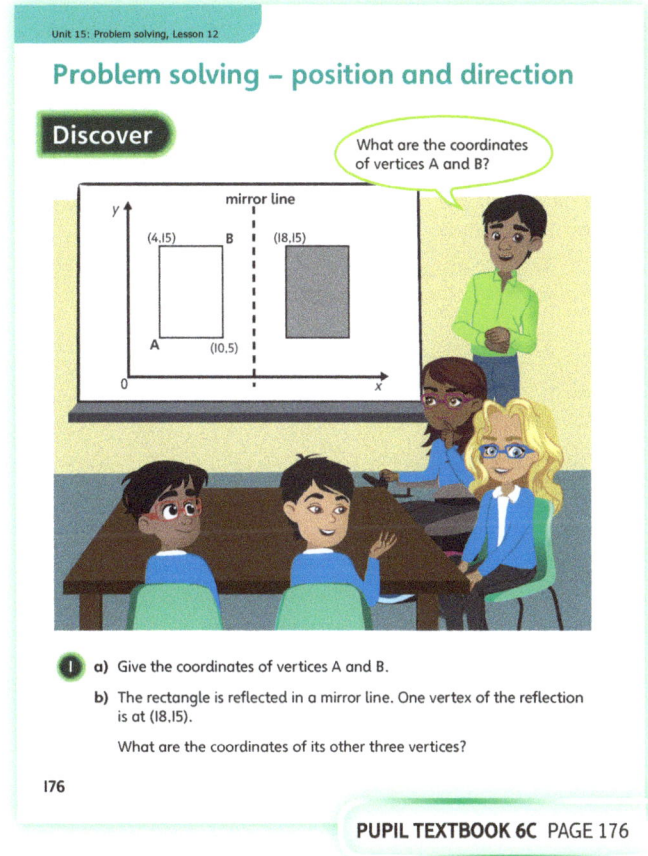

# Share

**WAYS OF WORKING** Whole class teacher led

**ASK**

- Question ① a): *Why is it important to know about the properties of a rectangle here?*
- Question ① a): *Why has the grid been annotated with lines that pass through the x- and y-axes?*
- Question ① b): *How do you know that the y-coordinates must stay the same for the reflected vertices?*
- Question ① b): *Is there another way you could find the vertices of the reflected rectangle?*

**IN FOCUS** Question ① a) has been chosen so that children can see how coordinate problems can be solved even when the grid and labels are missing, by using the structure of the grid. Question ① b) shows how to apply understanding of the properties of a rectangle and of a reflection. Some children may suggest an alternative strategy of reflecting each vertex of the rectangle in the mirror line. They need to remember that the reflection is the same distance from the mirror line as the original shape.

**STRENGTHEN** Revisit reflections, reminding children that the reflection is the same size and shape as the original but is 'flipped' – this is not obvious here so it is useful to label the reflected vertices A and B as $A^1$ (24,5) and $B^1$ (18,15) to show this. Model reflections of scalene triangles to emphasise the properties of reflection. Ensure children understand that the reflection is the same distance from the mirror line as the original shape.

**DEEPEN** Ask children to explain where the mirror line passes through the x-axis, using the grid to help them.

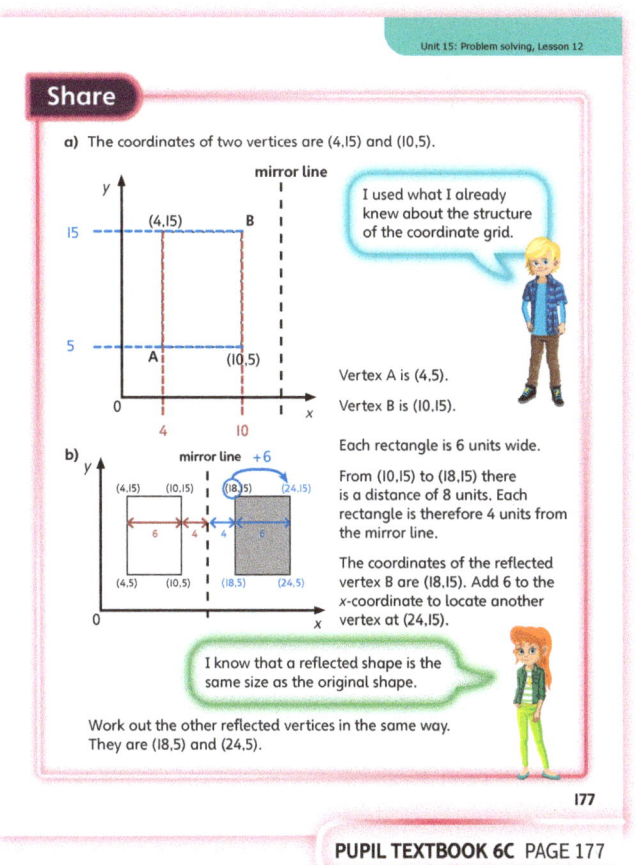

213

# Think together

**WAYS OF WORKING** Whole class teacher led (I do, We do, You do)

**ASK**
- Question 1 a): *What do you know about the properties of an isosceles triangle? How does this help?*
- Question 2: *How can you work out the x-coordinate for point P by using what you know about the x-coordinates for N and S?*
- Question 3 b): *What do you know about a shape following a translation?*

**IN FOCUS** Question 2 has been chosen to allow children to reason about given information, spotting patterns in the linear sequence. This includes recognising that point N must have the coordinates (0,0) even though it is not labelled. Question 3 b) uses a translation, requiring children to know that the translated parallelogram will be the same size, shape and orientation as the original.

**STRENGTHEN** Provide children with squared paper so they can draw diagrams to check their solutions. For question 3 a), discuss why it is important to know the length of the horizontal sides to find the coordinate of the fourth vertex.

**DEEPEN** For question 3 b), ask children to find the new coordinates of all four vertices of the translated parallelogram.

**ASSESSMENT CHECKPOINT** Use questions 1 and 3 to assess whether children can reason about shapes following a reflection or translation. Use questions 1 and 3 to assess whether they can apply their knowledge of the properties of shapes to reason about coordinates. Use question 2 to assess whether they look for relationships within the information provided.

**ANSWERS**

Question 1 a): (⁻14,9), (⁻10,9)

Question 1 b): A (6,9), B (10,19), C (14,9)

Question 2: P (20,12), T (60,36)

Question 3 a): (6,⁻6)

Question 3 b): (⁻4,⁻1)

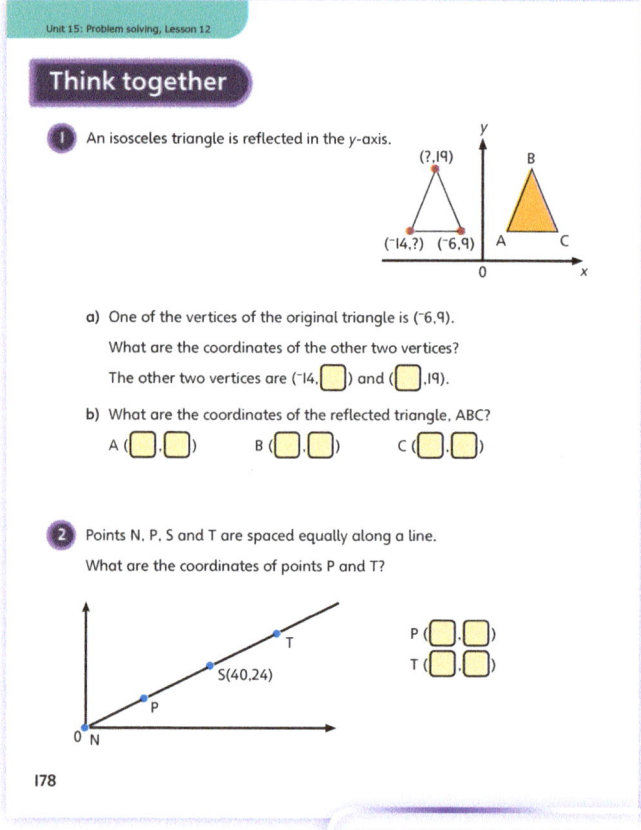

PUPIL TEXTBOOK 6C PAGE 178

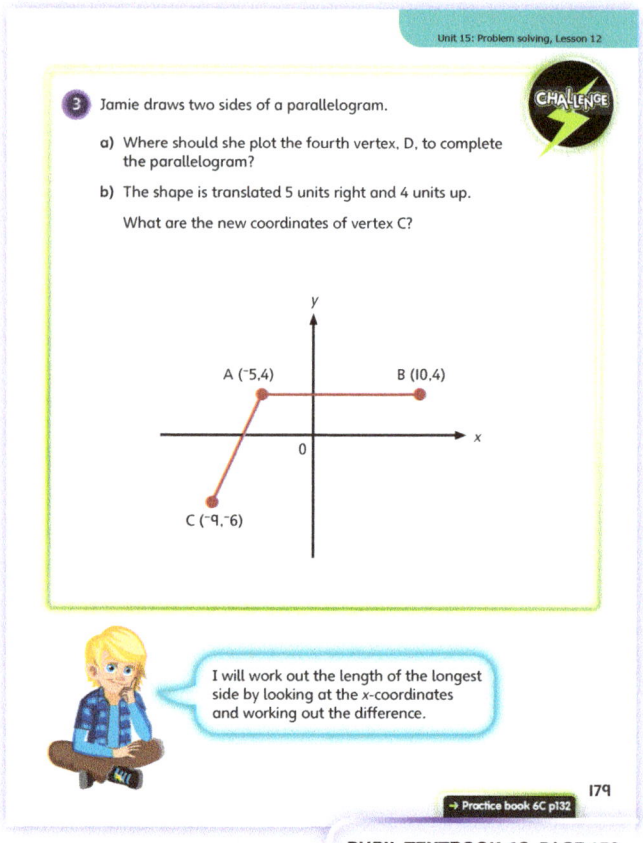

PUPIL TEXTBOOK 6C PAGE 179

Unit 15: Problem solving, Lesson 12

# Practice

**WAYS OF WORKING** Independent thinking

**IN FOCUS** The line in question ❶ has been chosen so that children need to think about positive and negative values for the *x*-coordinates. In question ❸, the point where the mirror line passes through the *y*-axis is not labelled, so children must look at the information given and use it to make decisions. For example, the reflection of vertex (32,22) is at (32,14); since the mirror line is half-way between the *y*-coordinates 22 and 14, it must have the *y*-value 18.

Question ❹ requires children to reason about four possibilities for a missing vertex, drawing on their understanding of right-angled triangles. They may find it useful to use a set square, a protractor or tracing paper to reason about the triangles that are not immediately obvious. For example, children could trace one of these triangles and reposition it on the grid.

**STRENGTHEN** For question ❸ c), encourage children to estimate and draw the position of each of the coordinates to find the pair that is inside the shape. Then discuss how they can reason about this. Children should think about how far along each axis the vertices of the reflected shape are, and how this can help them to discard coordinates that do not fit in these ranges. Encourage children to reason about any other coordinates that will be inside the shape.

**DEEPEN** For question ❹, ask children to investigate the different positions of the third vertex for an isosceles triangle.

**ASSESSMENT CHECKPOINT** Use question ❶ to assess whether children can use the structure of the coordinate grid to reason about points on a straight line. Use question ❷ to assess whether they can complete a reflection and give the new coordinates. Use questions ❸ and ❹ to assess whether children can use their knowledge of the properties of shapes to solve problems.

**ANSWERS** Answers for the **Practice** part of the lesson can be found in the *Power Maths* online subscription.

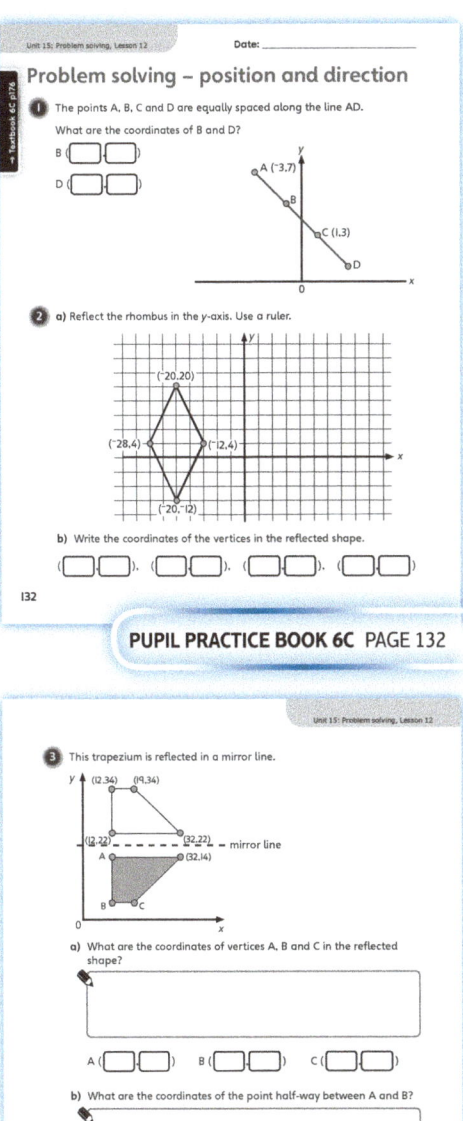

PUPIL PRACTICE BOOK 6C PAGE 132

PUPIL PRACTICE BOOK 6C PAGE 133

# Reflect

**WAYS OF WORKING** Independent thinking

**IN FOCUS** Children are required to explain how to find the half-way point between two coordinates. Some children may choose to draw the points on a coordinate grid, while others may sketch the axes and points.

**ASSESSMENT CHECKPOINT** Ensure children notice that the two given points have the same *x*-coordinate, so the half-way point must also have the same *x*-value.

**ANSWERS** Answers for the **Reflect** part of the lesson can be found in the *Power Maths* online subscription.

## After the lesson ⏸

- Can children explain why the properties of shapes help them to solve problems on a coordinate grid involving an unknown vertex or a transformation?
- Can they confidently plot or identify a given coordinate given information and the structure of the grid?
- Can children find half-way points between two given coordinates?

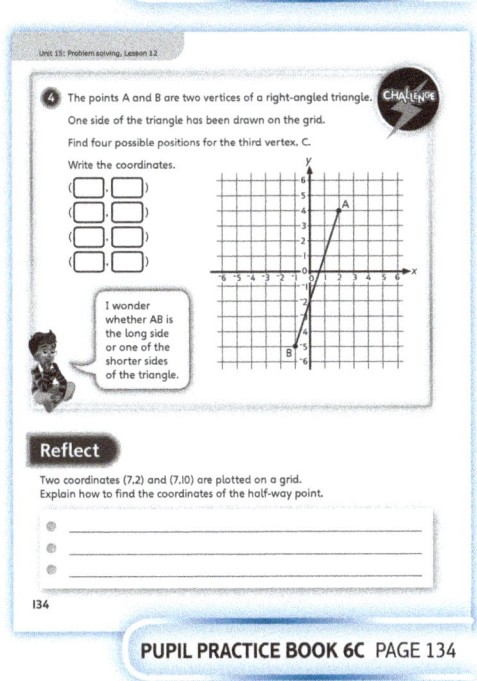

PUPIL PRACTICE BOOK 6C PAGE 134

215

Unit 15: Problem solving, Lesson 13

# Problem solving – properties of shapes ❶

### Learning focus
In this lesson, children will solve problems using the angle sum of triangles and quadrilaterals, angles on a straight line or at a point, and vertically opposite angles. They will use standard mathematical notation and will reason about the sizes of missing angles.

### Before you teach
- Can children recall the sum of the interior angles in a triangle or quadrilateral?
- Can they find the missing angle on a straight line when they know the other angles?
- Can they use the properties of shapes to reason about the size of angles?

#### NATIONAL CURRICULUM LINKS
**Year 6 Geometry – properties of shapes**

Recognise angles where they meet at a point, are on a straight line, or are vertically opposite, and find missing angles.

Compare and classify geometric shapes based on their properties and sizes and find unknown angles in any triangles, quadrilaterals and regular polygons.

#### ASSESSING MASTERY
Children can flexibly apply what they know about interior angles in shapes to help them find missing values. They can explain and use what they know about the sum of angles on a straight line or at a point to solve problems.

#### COMMON MISCONCEPTIONS
Children may think that they always need to use a protractor to solve missing angle problems. Remind them that diagrams are not always drawn to scale. Ask:
- *What does 'Not drawn to scale' mean? What information does the diagram show? What angle facts do you know about triangles/ quadrilaterals/straight lines/etc.?*

You could also look at some examples where there is not sufficient information and a protractor must be used.

#### STRENGTHENING UNDERSTANDING
Look together at angles that meet at a point or on a straight line. Relate this to two right angles on a straight line and to four right angles meeting at a point. Label each of the right angles. Discuss how to use the right angles to prove the angle sum on a straight line and at a point.

#### GOING DEEPER
Encourage children to reason about and explore different quadrilaterals. Ask them to draw a quadrilateral with:
- three obtuse angles and one acute angle
- two obtuse angles and two acute angles
- three acute angles and one obtuse angle.

Ask them to explain why a quadrilateral cannot have four obtuse angles or four acute angles.

#### KEY LANGUAGE
**In lesson:** angle, right angle, straight line, point, obtuse, acute, isosceles, scalene

**Other language to be used by the teacher:** sum of interior angles, vertically opposite

#### RESOURCES
**Optional:** protractors

 In the eTextbook of this lesson, you will find interactive links to a selection of teaching tools.

### Quick recap
Challenge children to tell you all the angle facts they can remember.

# Unit 15: Problem solving, Lesson 13

## Discover

**WAYS OF WORKING** Pair work

**ASK**

• Question 1 a): *You know that the triangle is isosceles. How does this help?*
• Question 1 a): *How do you know that one of the angles in the shaded triangle makes a right angle with angle a? How can you use this information to calculate the size of angle a?*
• Question 1 b): *How can you estimate the size of angle b? Is it acute or obtuse?*
• Question 1 b): *You don't know the size of any of the angles on the straight line with angle b. How can you find out their sizes?*

**IN FOCUS** Children are required to draw on their knowledge of the sum of the interior angles in a triangle and to use what they know about right angles or angles that meet on a straight line. Children should recognise that the two unlabelled angles in the isosceles triangle must be equal. Some children may forget that the triangle is drawn inside a rectangle, whose interior angles are all 90°.

**PRACTICAL TIPS** Encourage children to annotate diagrams with information they know and to add angles as they work them out. This will help them to work towards the solution.

**ANSWERS**

Question 1 a): Angle a is 58°.
(180 – 116) ÷ 2 = 32°, 90° – 32° = 58°

Question 1 b): Angle b is 116°.
**Share** uses angle facts for triangles and straight lines.
Children could also use facts involving parallel lines:
Angle b is an alternate angle to the one marked 116°, so is also 116°.

## Share

**WAYS OF WORKING** Whole class teacher led

**ASK**

• Question 1 a): *How do Dexter's annotations help you to reason about the size of angle a?*
• Question 1 a): *Why is the calculation 180° – 116° written in brackets? Why do you need to divide by 2?*
• Question 1 b): *How do Dexter's annotations help you to reason about the size of angle b?*

**IN FOCUS** Both of the problems require several steps, emphasising the need for a systematic approach. Question 1 a) starts by demonstrating what is known about angle a, establishing that children must first find the missing angles in the isosceles triangle. Question 1 b) requires children to recognise that another triangle has been formed when the shaded triangle was drawn inside the rectangle.

**STRENGTHEN** For question 1 b), ask children to explain why the third angle in the right-angled triangle could have been calculated simply by finding 90° – 58° rather than 180° – 90° – 58°. Discuss why this method is possible when finding the third angle in right-angled triangles, but is not possible otherwise.

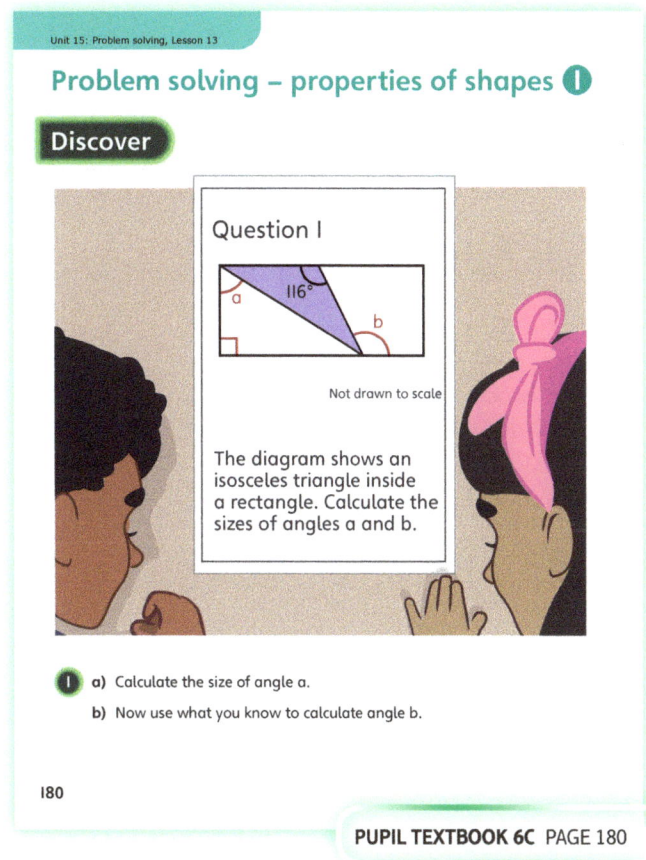

PUPIL TEXTBOOK 6C PAGE 180

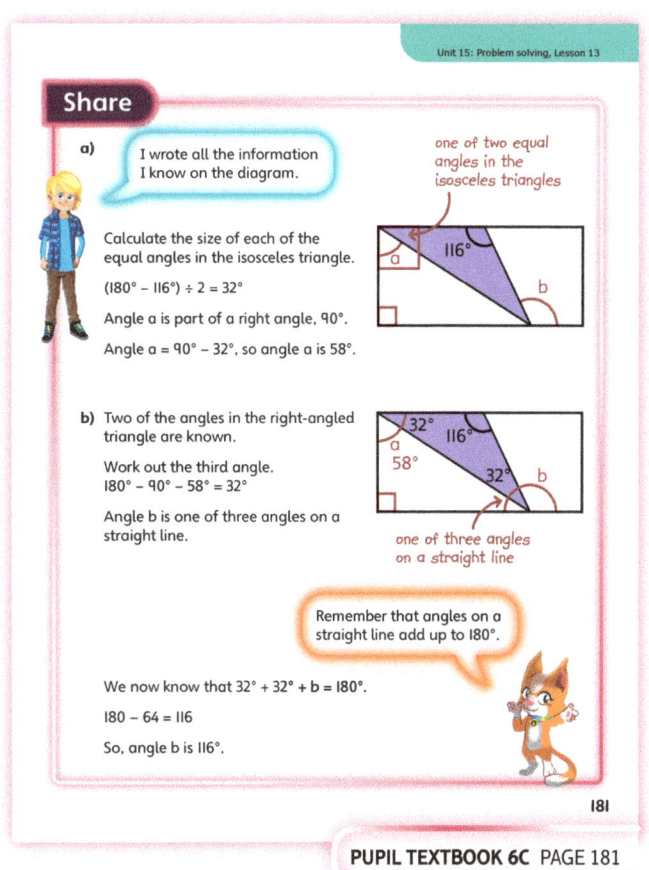

PUPIL TEXTBOOK 6C PAGE 181

Unit 15: Problem solving, Lesson 13

# Think together

**WAYS OF WORKING** Whole class teacher led (I do, We do, You do)

**ASK**
- Question ❶: *None of the angles in the isosceles triangle are known. Can you use what you know about vertically opposite angles?*
- Question ❷: *You only know the size of one angle in the triangle so you can't use the sum of the internal angles. What else do you know?*
- Question ❷: *What type of angle is n? How do you know?*
- Question ❸: *What do you know about obtuse angles? So what do you know about angle a? What is the range of possible sizes for angle b? How do you know?*
- Question ❹: *The two lines are the diagonals in the rectangle. How does this help?*

**IN FOCUS** These questions encourage children to use a chain of reasoning, establishing what they need to find out before finding the angle asked for.

Question ❶ requires children to reason about both vertically opposite angles and the properties of an isosceles triangle. Check that they can explain why angles c and d are equal. Question ❷ involves a reflex angle, n. Children may try to subtract from 180° rather than 360° – assuming that, because the angle is connected to the triangle, they must still use what they know about the sum of angles in a triangle. Question ❸ is an abstract problem that requires children to apply what they know about the sizes of acute and obtuse angles.

For question ❹, children must draw upon other aspects of geometry, recognising that the lines within the rectangle are the diagonals, so creating isosceles triangles.

**STRENGTHEN** For question ❸, discuss which angle children can work out immediately [angle c]. Encourage them to make lists of possible angles for a and b, using what they know about angle c to help them.

**DEEPEN** For question ❸, revisit ratio. Ask children to give the ratio of a to b. Challenge them to use this information to find the solution.

**ASSESSMENT CHECKPOINT** Use questions ❶ to ❹ to assess whether children can use a chain of reasoning to find unknown angles. Use questions ❶, ❷ and ❹ to check that children can apply knowledge of the sum of the interior angles in a triangle. Use questions ❶ and ❹ to check that children recognise that vertically opposite angles are equal.

**ANSWERS**

Question ❶ a): Angles a and b are both 48°.

Question ❶ b): Angles c and d are both 96°.
c and d are opposite angles, so they are equal.

Question ❷: m = 73°   n = 285°
3rd angle in triangle = 180 – 32 – 73 = 75°.
360° – 75° = 285°.

Question ❸: a = 95°   b = 190°   c = 75°

Question ❹: x = 116°   y = 58°   z = 58°

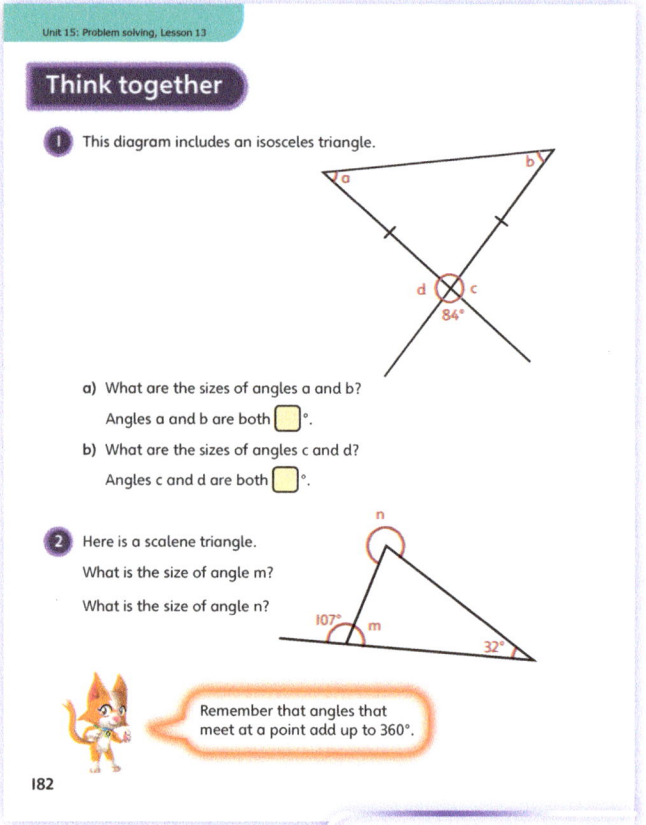

PUPIL TEXTBOOK 6C PAGE 182

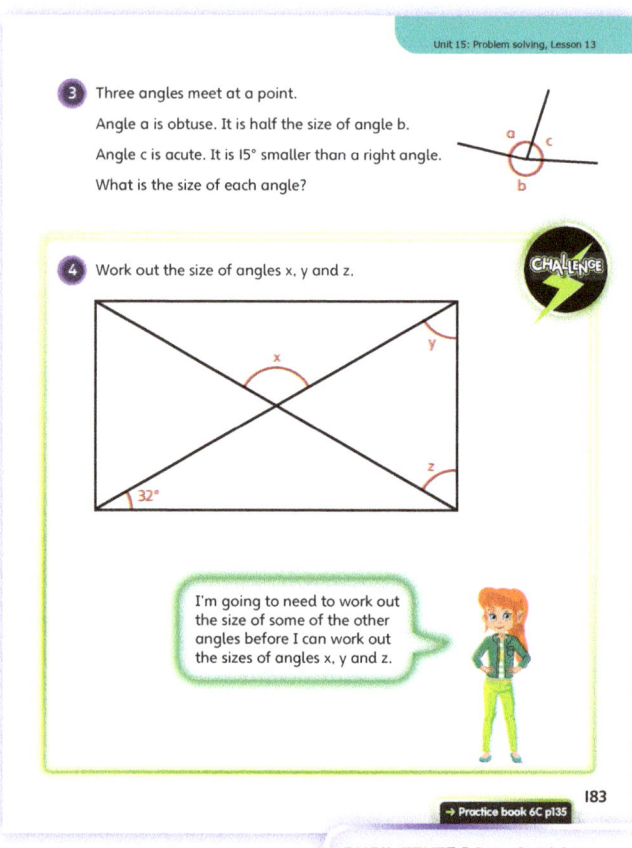

PUPIL TEXTBOOK 6C PAGE 183

Unit 15: Problem solving, Lesson 13

# Practice

**WAYS OF WORKING** Independent thinking

**IN FOCUS** Question ① requires children to interpret the notation used to show a right angle, so that they can take account of this 90° when finding the missing angle. Question ② has been chosen as it requires children to find missing angles in a triangle and a quadrilateral. They must use a chain of reasoning to find the required angles.

In question ③, children need to apply their knowledge about the angles in a square to reason about missing angles. Children may find this question more challenging because the right angles are not labelled. Question ⑤ requires children to follow a chain of reasoning, applying their understanding of right angles in shapes, the sum of interior angles in a quadrilateral, angles on a straight line and vertically opposite angles.

**STRENGTHEN** In question ② b), children need to explain how they will find the size of two angles. Encourage them to annotate the diagram with the information they know from part a) to help them. Look together at the correct terminology (for example: 'vertically opposite', 'angles on a straight line', 'equal', etc.) to help children who may find it difficult to construct an explanation. Write these terms on the board to help children write their explanation.

**DEEPEN** Ask children to make up problems similar to question ④ for a partner to solve. Encourage them to include relationships such as double, one third, half, difference, sum, and so on The problems could be related to angles that are on a straight line or that make a right angle. Children should include terminology such as acute and obtuse.

**THINK DIFFERENTLY** Question ④ is an abstract problem, requiring children to reason about the relationships between the angles. They may find it useful to draw bar models to help them explore the relationships.

**ASSESSMENT CHECKPOINT** Use questions ① to ③ to assess whether children can apply what they know about the sum of the interior angles of a triangle to find missing angles. Use questions ②, ④ and ⑤ to assess whether they can reason about angles that meet at a point or on a straight line. Check that children can interpret standard mathematical notation (such as the right-angle marker, or dashes representing equal-length sides) to help them ascertain information about the sizes of angles in the problem.

**ANSWERS** Answers for the **Practice** part of the lesson can be found in the *Power Maths* online subscription.

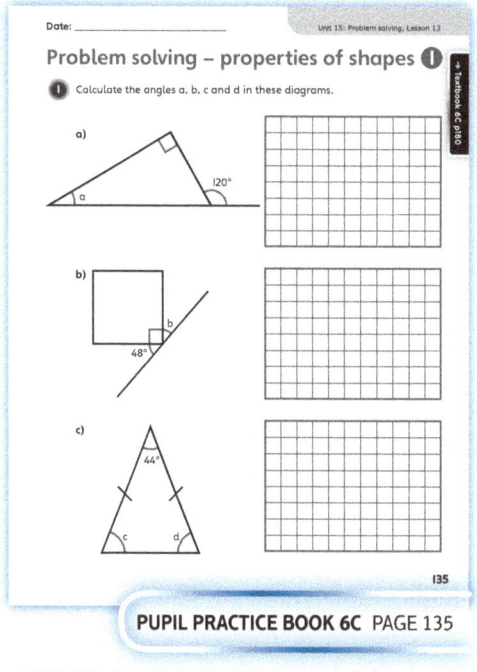

PUPIL PRACTICE BOOK 6C PAGE 135

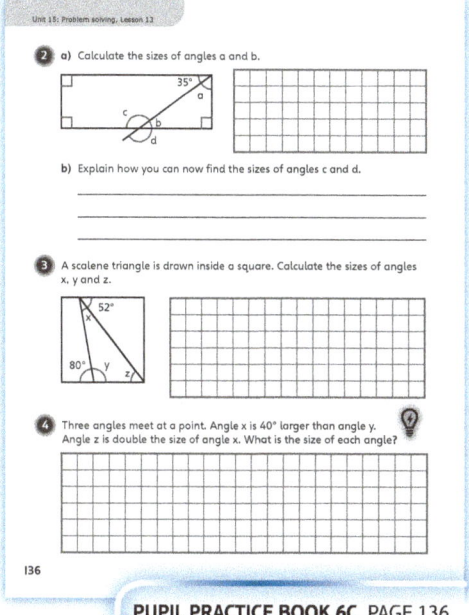

PUPIL PRACTICE BOOK 6C PAGE 136

# Reflect

**WAYS OF WORKING** Independent thinking

**IN FOCUS** This question has been chosen as there is more than one solution to the problem.

**ASSESSMENT CHECKPOINT** Children should recognise that the unknown angles must sum to 92° as this is the difference between the known angle and 180°.

**ANSWERS** Answers for the **Reflect** part of the lesson can be found in the *Power Maths* online subscription.

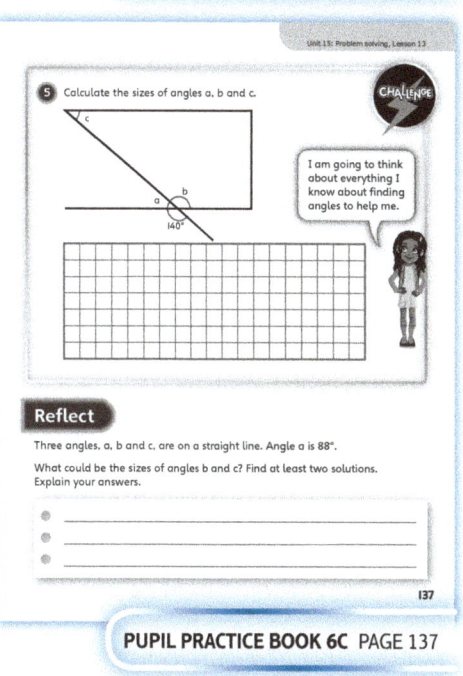

PUPIL PRACTICE BOOK 6C PAGE 137

## After the lesson

- Can children use a chain of reasoning to identify unknown angles?
- Do they make use of notations and of the properties of shapes to help solve problems?
- Can children use the correct terminology to explain and reason about missing angles (for example, 'vertically opposite')?

Unit 15: Problem solving, Lesson 14

# Problem solving – properties of shapes ❷

### Learning focus
In this lesson, children will continue to reason about the sum of interior angles in triangles and quadrilaterals, and angles on a straight line and at a point. They will revisit calculating the sum of the interior angles in regular polygons to identify the size of each angle. They will continue to apply their understanding to find missing angles.

### Before you teach
- Can children recall the size of each angle in an equilateral triangle?
- Can they find a missing angle at a point?
- Can children use the properties of shapes to reason about the sizes of angles?

#### NATIONAL CURRICULUM LINKS

**Year 6 Geometry – properties of shapes**

Recognise angles where they meet at a point, are on a straight line, or are vertically opposite, and find missing angles.

Compare and classify geometric shapes based on their properties and sizes and find unknown angles in any triangles, quadrilaterals and regular polygons.

#### ASSESSING MASTERY

Children can recall and calculate the sum of the interior angles in a polygon and use this to find the size of each angle. They can solve problems that involve a chain of reasoning to find the size of an unknown angle.

#### COMMON MISCONCEPTIONS

Children may think that irregular polygons do not have the same sum of interior angles as regular polygons, because the angles are not all the same size. Use a protractor to check the size of angles in irregular pentagons, hexagons and octagons, finding the sum each time. Ask:
- *What do the angles in a regular pentagon/hexagon/octagon add up to? What do the angles in this irregular pentagon/hexagon/octagon add up to? What is the same and what is different about the shapes?*

#### STRENGTHENING UNDERSTANDING

Give children regular pentagons or hexagons to cut up into triangles. Ask them to measure and label the angles. Reassemble the regular shape and add the angles of the triangles that make up each vertex, agreeing that they sum to 108° for a pentagon and 120° for a hexagon.

#### GOING DEEPER

Give children a set of 2D shapes including regular and irregular polygons. Ask them to arrange the shapes in different ways, reasoning about the size of any angles they make. Ask children to explain when they may need to measure at least one of the angles in a shape to get started, and to identify situations in which they can just calculate the angles.

#### KEY LANGUAGE

**In lesson:** angle, straight line, regular, irregular, polygon, equilateral, quadrilateral, pentagon, hexagon

**Other language to be used by the teacher:** sum of interior angles, point, right angle, octagon

#### RESOURCES

**Optional:** protractors, 2D shapes

 In the eTextbook of this lesson, you will find interactive links to a selection of teaching tools.

### Quick recap
Ask children to draw a quadrilateral that has angles of 45°, 100° and 80°. Ask: *What is the size of the final angle?*

# Unit 15: Problem solving, Lesson 14

## Discover

**WAYS OF WORKING** Pair work

**ASK**

- Question ① a): *What do you know about each angle in a regular shape?*
- Question ① a): *Do you remember the size of each angle in a regular pentagon? How can you work it out?*
- Question ① b): *What do you notice about angle b?*
- Question ① b): *The pentagon is inside a rectangle. How does this help?*

**IN FOCUS** Children need to reason about the sizes of angles that have been formed by placing a regular pentagon inside a rectangle. In question ① a), they are asked to find the size of each angle in the pentagon. In question ① b), children should recognise that each of the unknown angles is on a straight line with an angle in the pentagon.

**PRACTICAL TIPS** Provide paper versions of the image for children to annotate or cut up to help them make sense of the problem.

**ANSWERS**

Question ① a): Each angle in a regular pentagon is 540° ÷ 5 = 108°.

Question ① b): Angle a is 72°.
Angle b is 36°.

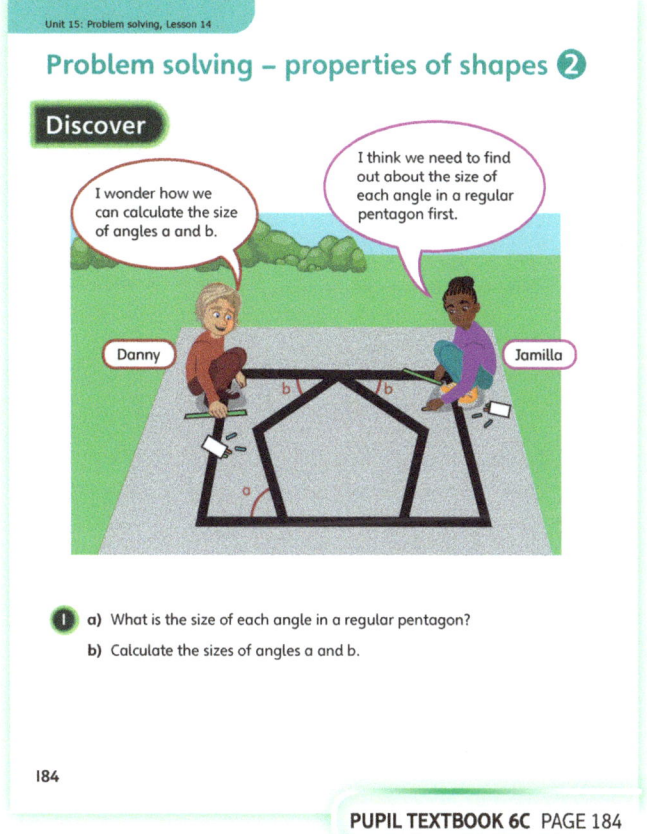

**PUPIL TEXTBOOK 6C** PAGE 184

## Share

**WAYS OF WORKING** Whole class teacher led

**ASK**

- Question ① a): *How does splitting the regular shape into triangles help?*
- Question ① a): *Why do you need to divide 540° by 5 and not 3 to match the number of triangles?*
- Question ① b): *What do you know about angles on a straight line?*
- Question ① b): *Why do you have to divide 72° by 2 to find the size of angle b?*

**IN FOCUS** Question ① a) enables children to revisit a method for finding the sum of the interior angles in a regular polygon and to use this to find the size of each angle. Question ① b) requires children to recognise that the unknown angles are on a straight line with angles within the pentagon. Make sure children understand that angle b is not 72° (180 − 108°) since two equal angles of size b make up this amount.

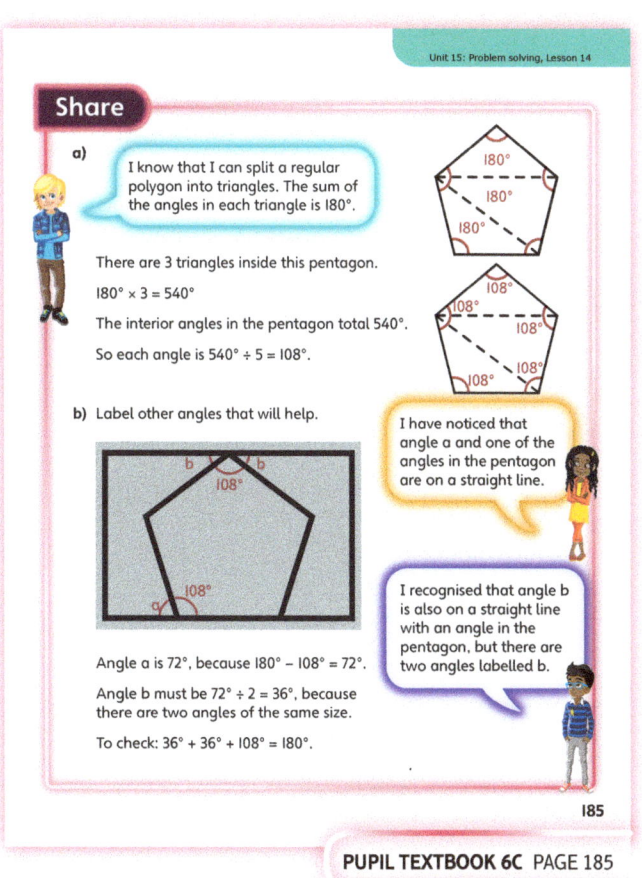

**PUPIL TEXTBOOK 6C** PAGE 185

221

# Think together

**WAYS OF WORKING** Whole class teacher led (I do, We do, You do)

**ASK**
- Question ❶: *What do you need to find first? How can you do this?*
- Question ❷: *Do you agree with Astrid? Why or why not?*
- Question ❸: *What are the names of the two quadrilaterals? What do you know about their properties?*
- Question ❹: *What is the size of each angle in an equilateral triangle? How can you check?*

**IN FOCUS** Question ❶ has been chosen because it requires children to recall or calculate the size of each interior angle in a regular hexagon. Children may divide the sum of the interior angles by 5 rather than 6 as this was the calculation used in **Share**.

Question ❷ helps children to reason about the similarities and differences between a regular pentagon and an irregular pentagon, recognising that the sum of the interior angles is the same for both (although the angles in an irregular shape are not equal).

**STRENGTHEN** For question ❶, begin to formulate a rule to help children calculate the size of each interior angle in a regular polygon: they have to divide the sum each time by the number of equal angles.

**DEEPEN** For question ❶, children could further develop the rule for finding the size of angles in a regular polygon by looking at the number of triangles that can be made each time in relation to the number of sides in the shape: the number of triangles is two less than the number of sides. They could explore heptagons, nonagons and decagons to check this.

**ASSESSMENT CHECKPOINT** Use questions ❶ to ❹ to assess whether children can use their knowledge of angles in polygons and of angles on a straight line. Use question ❶ to assess whether they can calculate the size of each angle in a regular polygon. Use questions ❷ and ❸ to assess whether they can apply this understanding of the sum of interior angles to irregular shapes, recognising that the total is the same as for regular shapes.

**ANSWERS**

Question ❶: Each angle in a regular hexagon is
$720° ÷ 6 = 120°$.
Angle $x = 180° − 120° = 60°$.
Angle $y = 180° − 60° − 90° = 30°$.

Question ❷: Angle $a = 26°$ ($540°$ − sum of all the other angles)

Question ❸: For quadrilaterals the angle sum is $360°$.
Parallelogram: angle $a = (360° − 260°) ÷ 2 = 50°$.
Trapezium: angle $a = 360° − 180° − 130° = 50°$.

Question ❹: Angle $a = 180° − 108° − 60° = 12°$.

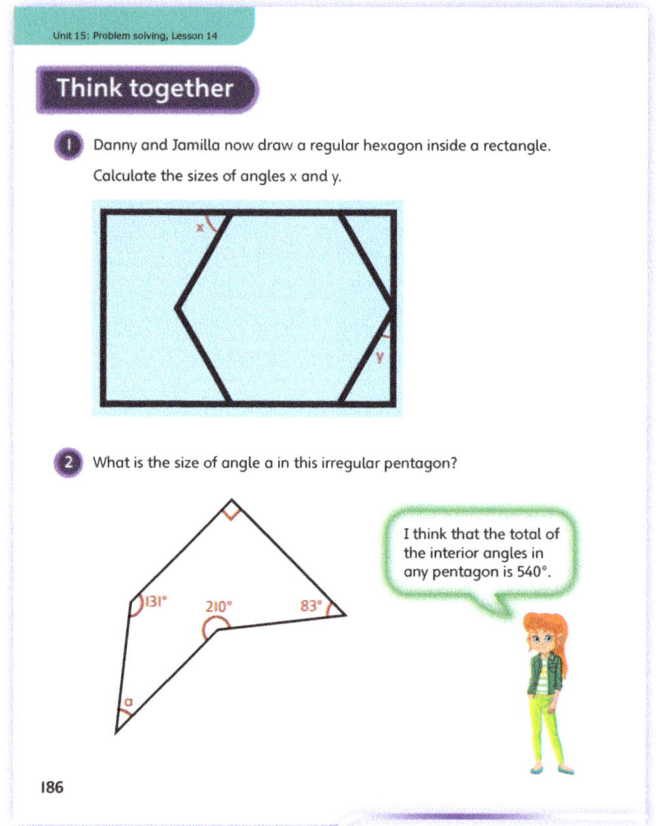

PUPIL TEXTBOOK 6C PAGE 186

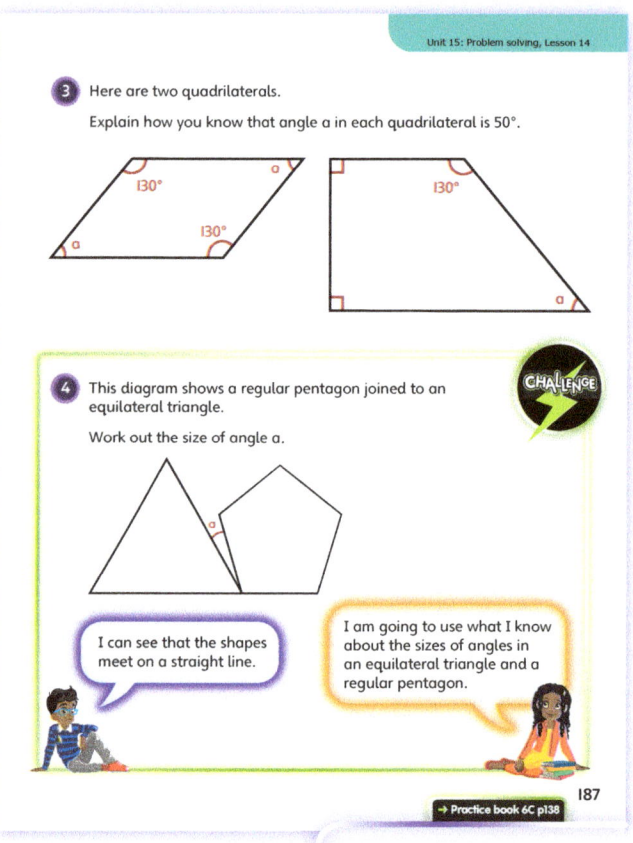

PUPIL TEXTBOOK 6C PAGE 187

# Unit 15: Problem solving, Lesson 14

## Practice

**WAYS OF WORKING** Independent thinking

**IN FOCUS** Question ❷ has been chosen as it requires children to reason about a range of different polygons. One of the criteria focuses on the sum of the interior angles, hence the inclusion of different quadrilaterals.

Questions ❸ and ❹ both combine angles meeting at a point and the sum of interior angles in a regular polygon. Question ❹ also includes the properties of a parallelogram (equal diagonally opposite angles). Children may also notice that the missing angle a sums to 180° with 60°.

**STRENGTHEN** For question ❺, discuss with children how they could represent the problem using bar models. Ensure children understand that the sum of the interior angles in an irregular hexagon is the same as in a regular hexagon.

**DEEPEN** Ask children to reason about other sets of regular shapes that will meet at a point like the hexagons in question ❸. Ask them to look at tessellations of squares and equilateral triangles and explain why these also meet at a point (all have angles that are factors of 360°). Challenge children to make a pattern of more than one regular shape meeting at a point (for example, two octagons and a square).

**ASSESSMENT CHECKPOINT** Use question ❶ to assess whether children can calculate the size of each interior angle in a regular polygon. Use question ❷ to assess whether they can apply knowledge of the properties of different shapes to categorise them accurately. Use questions ❹ and ❺ to assess whether children can use known and derived information flexibly to reason about missing angles.

**ANSWERS** Answers for the **Practice** part of the lesson can be found in the *Power Maths* online subscription.

## Reflect

**WAYS OF WORKING** Independent thinking

**IN FOCUS** This question has been chosen so that children make decisions about which method to use to prove that three angles in a regular pentagon cannot add up to 330°. Although the question does not state that the three angles are equal, children can make this assumption as otherwise the pentagon would obviously not be regular. So they can either compare one interior angle of a regular pentagon with 110°, or multiply the interior angle by 3 to compare with 330°.

**ASSESSMENT CHECKPOINT** Check that children understand how to find the interior angle in a regular pentagon.

**ANSWERS** Answers for the **Reflect** part of the lesson can be found in the *Power Maths* online subscription.

## After the lesson ⏸

- Can children recall or calculate the size of each angle and the sum of angles in a regular polygon?
- Do they make use of notations and the properties of shapes to help solve problems?
- Can children reason about angles that meet at a point or on a straight line to help find missing angles?

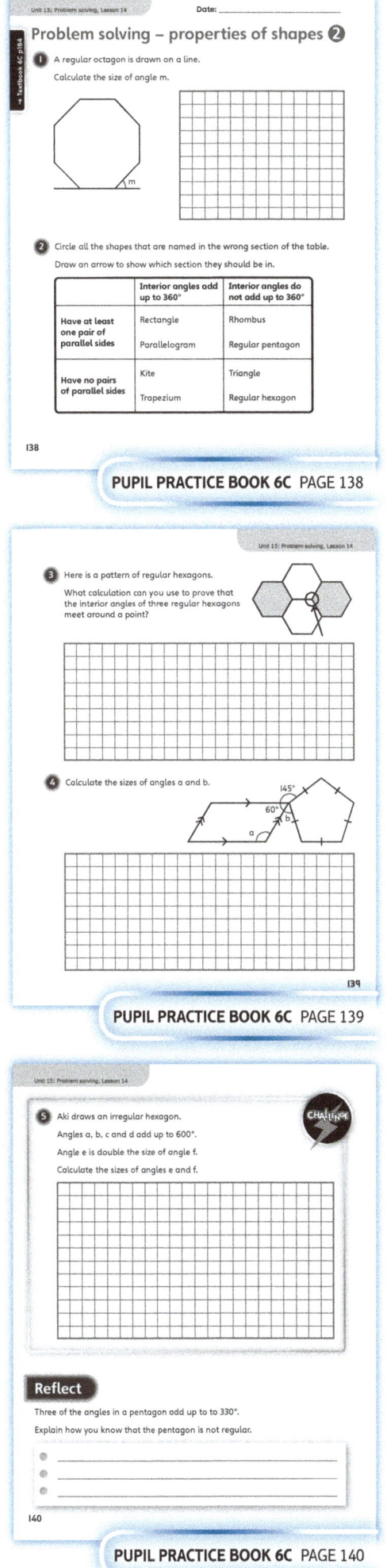

PUPIL PRACTICE BOOK 6C PAGE 138

PUPIL PRACTICE BOOK 6C PAGE 139

PUPIL PRACTICE BOOK 6C PAGE 140

# Unit 15: Problem solving

# End of unit check

> Don't forget the unit assessment grid in the *Power Maths* online subscription.

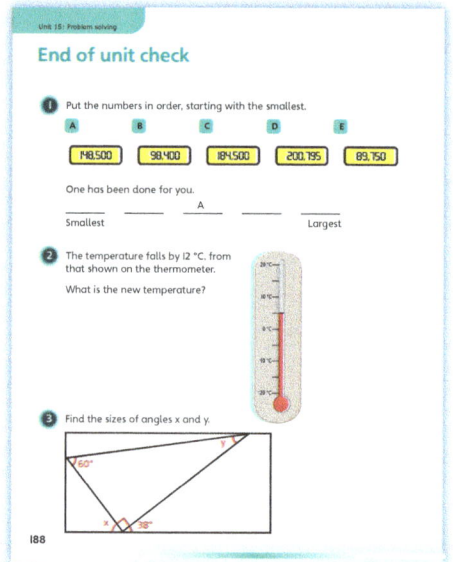

**PUPIL TEXTBOOK 6C** PAGE 188

**WAYS OF WORKING**  Group work adult led

**IN FOCUS**  All the questions are SATs-style questions to draw out the range of skills taught across the unit. There are more questions than in other *Power Maths* textbooks.
- Many of the problems can be represented using bar models (questions 4 to 9) or solved using number lines (questions 1, 2, 10), although children may choose to use different approaches.
- Questions 4, 7 and 8 have been written using numbers that will give children opportunities to think flexibly about the order in which they approach the calculations.
- Question 5 is set in the structure of a bar model. Children need to notice that the two given fractions and the unknown value can be added to give a total of 1. Children should use their knowledge of equivalent fractions to add the given fractions.

**ANSWERS AND COMMENTARY**  Children who have mastered this unit will apply their understanding of numbers, measurements and geometry to a range of problems. They will reason about the relationships between known and unknown information, representing this as required. They will calculate flexibly, choosing a mental or written method depending on the numbers involved.

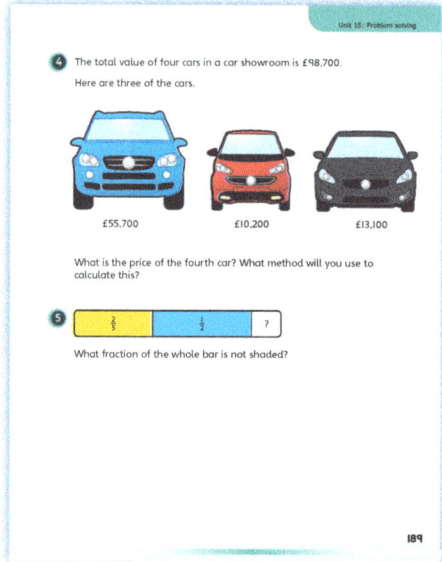

**PUPIL TEXTBOOK 6C** PAGE 189

| Q | A | WRONG ANSWERS AND MISCONCEPTIONS | STRENGTHENING UNDERSTANDING |
|---|---|---|---|
| 1 | E, B, A, C, D | Children may think that, for example, 89,750 is greater than 148,500 because it starts with the digit 8. | Suggest that children use a place value grid to help order the numbers. |
| 2 | ⁻7 °C | Children may add rather than subtract 12 or they may miscalculate as they cross 0. | Encourage children to stop at 0, partitioning the number to help complete the calculation. |
| 3 | x = 52°, y = 30° | Children may overlook the notation for the right angle and conclude that they have insufficient information. | Encourage children to annotate diagrams with any known information, including labelling right angles as 90°. |
| 4 | £19,700 | Children may not complete all steps. For example, they may find the total of the known values, but not subtract this from £98,700. | Revisit the use of a bar model to represent problems so children are secure with the number of steps required. |
| 5 | $\frac{1}{10}$ | Children may find $\frac{1}{2} + \frac{2}{5}$, but not complete the last step. As 5 is not a multiple of 2, they may struggle to find a common denominator. | Look at other calculations involving fractions where one denominator is not a multiple of the other, and remind children how to find equivalent fractions in these cases. |

# Unit 15: Problem solving

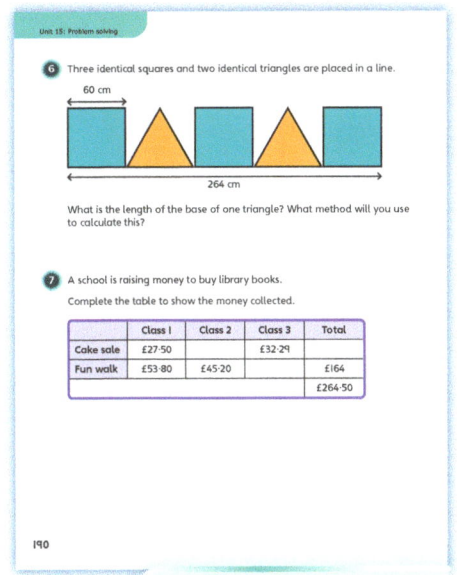

**PUPIL TEXTBOOK 6C** PAGE 190

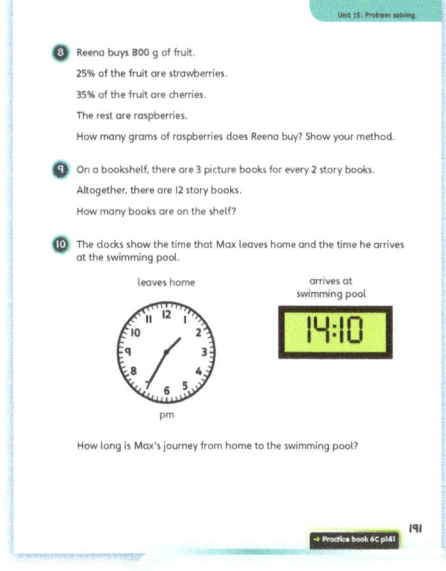

**PUPIL TEXTBOOK 6C** PAGE 191

| Q | A | WRONG ANSWERS AND MISCONCEPTIONS | STRENGTHENING UNDERSTANDING |
|---|---|---|---|
| 6 | 42 cm | Children may give the total length of the bases for the two triangles as the answer, rather than dividing by 2. | Encourage children to check their answers, summing the values to check that they total 264 cm. |
| 7 | top row: £40·71, £100·50; bottom row: £65 | Some children may struggle to interpret the relationships between the pieces of information in the table. | Explore retrieving information and finding missing information in a range of tables and charts. |
| 8 | 320 g | Children may find the total mass of strawberries and cherries but not use this to find the mass of raspberries. | Explore different strategies to solve this problem. For example, use bar models to make relationships explicit. |
| 9 | 30 | Children may not recognise that, as the number of story books has been scaled by 6, so the total number of books must also be scaled by 6. | Use bar models or counters to explore ratios, emphasising the relationship between the parts and the whole. |
| 10 | 35 minutes | Children may misread 14:10 as 4:10 pm rather than correctly interpreting the 24-hour clock notation. | Practise converting between the 12-hour and 24-hour clock notation. |

# Unit 15: Problem solving

## My journal

**WAYS OF WORKING** Independent thinking

**ANSWERS AND COMMENTARY**

Toshi will save £7,776 in 3 years.

This problem draws on children's knowledge of money, percentages, fractions, ratio and proportion. Encourage children to read the question carefully and to approach it one step at a time. Ask:
- *What is the first thing you need to do? How will you find 25% of £1,200?*

For the next step, ensure children understand that they need to find $\frac{3}{10}$ of the original amount (£1,200), not $\frac{3}{10}$ of the amount they just calculated. Ask:
- *How will you find $\frac{3}{10}$ of £1,200? What is $\frac{3}{10}$ as a percentage?*

If children get stuck, encourage the use of a bar model at this stage. It should help them to understand that Toshi spends 25% of his monthly income on rent and 30% on food and entertainment, so he has 45% left for bills and savings.

Children then need to determine the proportion of £540 (45% of £1,200) Toshi saves each month. Ask:
- *How can you express the amount Toshi saves per month as a ratio? What is this as a fraction? As a percentage?*

Ensure children then complete the question by calculating how much Toshi saves over 3 years, not just over 1 month.

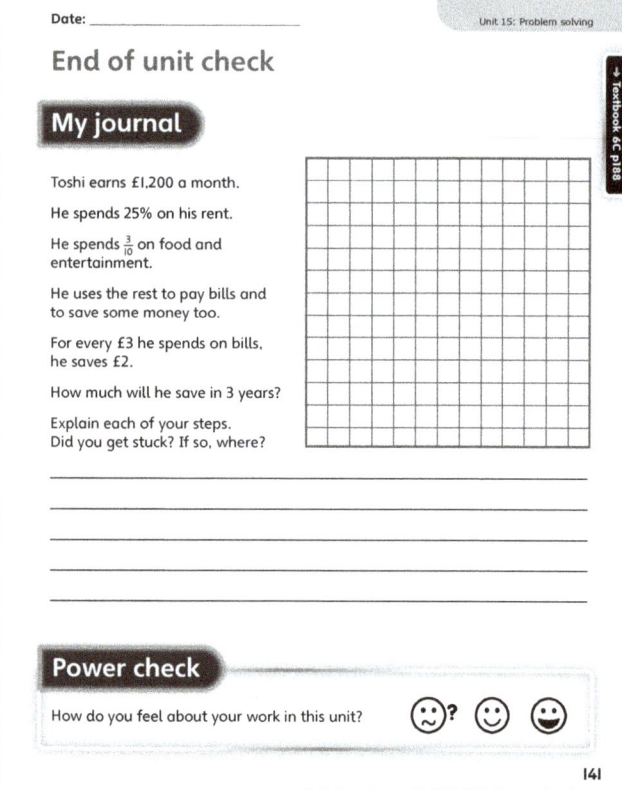

**PUPIL PRACTICE BOOK 6C** PAGE 141

## Power check

**WAYS OF WORKING** Independent thinking

**ASK**
- *In what different ways have you used bar models and number lines? How have they helped?*
- *How confident are you about identifying the calculation(s) needed to solve a word problem?*
- *What is the same and what is different about finding fractions of amounts and percentages of amounts?*
- *What can you tell me about the sum of the interior angles in different shapes?*

# Power puzzle

**WAYS OF WORKING** Pair work

**IN FOCUS** This **Power puzzle** draws on aspects of multiplication, fractions, money and time. Children need to make use of and draw on the relationships between the given information to decide what is being asked and what they need to do first. The information they may need to use first is not given until the end of the problem, so they need to look at the problem as a whole. They are required to represent their solutions in a table so they must decide what goes where.

**ANSWERS AND COMMENTARY**

|  | Money spent | Arrival time | Departure time |
| --- | --- | --- | --- |
| Jamie | £7·50 | 13:00 | 14:15 |
| Max | £2·50 | 10:30 | 13:00 |
| Zac | £10 | 11:15 | 13:15 |

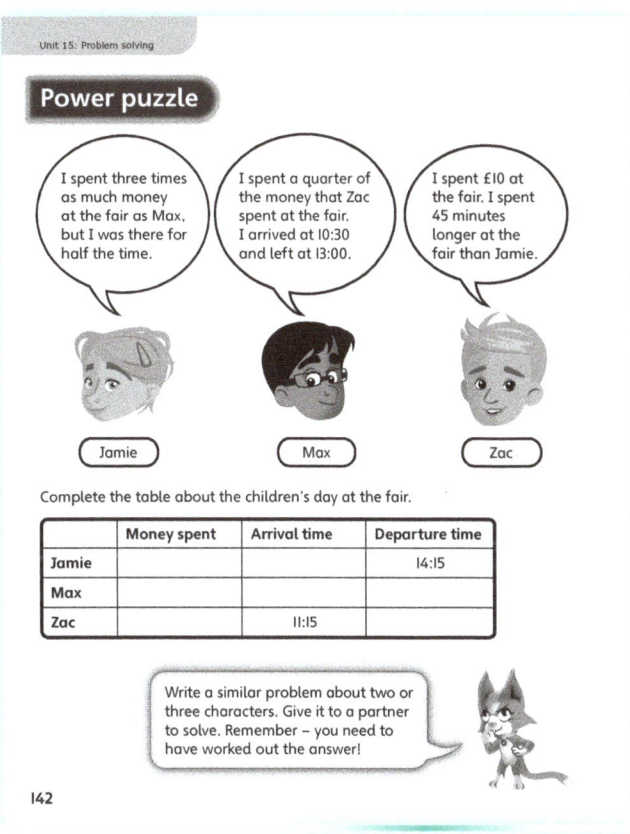

PUPIL PRACTICE BOOK 6C PAGE 142

# After the unit

- How well did the prompts and questions promote learning and what were children's responses to them?
- Are children ready to move on with their learning? Following on from the end of unit assessment, how confident are they in representing and solving a range of problems in different contexts?

**Strengthen** and **Deepen** activities for this unit can be found in the *Power Maths* online subscription.

Published by Pearson Education Limited, 80 Strand, London, WC2R 0RL.

www.pearsonschools.co.uk

Text © Pearson Education Limited 2018, 2023
Edited by Pearson and Florence Production Ltd
First edition edited by Pearson, Little Grey Cells Publishing Services and Haremi Ltd
Designed and typeset by Pearson and PDQ Digital Media Solutions Ltd
First edition designed and typeset by Kamae Design
Original illustrations © Pearson Education Limited 2018, 2023
Illustrated by Diego Diaz, Adam Linley and Nadene Naude at Beehive Illustration;
and Kamae Design
Images: The Royal Mint, 1971, 1982, 1990, 1997, 1998: 87, 123
Cover design by Pearson Education Ltd
Back cover illustration Diego Diaz and Nadene Naude at Beehive Illustration

Series editor: Tony Staneff; Lead author: Josh Lury
Authors (first edition): Liu Jian, Josh Lury, Catherine Casey, Zhou Da, Zhang Dan, Zhu Dejiang, Emily Fox, Tim Handley, Wei Huinv, Hou Huiying, Zhang Jing, Steph King, Huang Lihua, Yin Lili, Liu Qimeng and Zhu Yuhong
Consultants (first edition): Professor Liu Jian and Professor Zhang Dan

The rights of Tony Staneff and Josh Lury to be identified as authors of this work have been asserted by them in accordance with the Copyright, Designs and Patents Act 1988.

This publication is protected by copyright, and permission should be obtained from the publisher prior to any prohibited reproduction, storage in a retrieval system, or transmission in any form or by any means, electronic, mechanical, photocopying, recording, or otherwise. For information regarding permissions, request forms and the appropriate contacts, please visit https://www.pearson.com/us/contact-us/permissions.html Pearson Education Limited Rights and Permissions Department.

First published 2018
This edition first published 2023

27 26 25 24 23
10 9 8 7 6 5 4 3 2 1

**British Library Cataloguing in Publication Data**
A catalogue record for this book is available from the British Library

ISBN 978 1 292 45064 3

**Copyright notice**
All rights reserved. No part of this publication may be reproduced in any form or by any means (including photocopying or storing it in any medium by electronic means and whether or not transiently or incidentally to some other use of this publication) without the written permission of the copyright owner, except in accordance with the provisions of the Copyright, Designs and Patents Act 1988 or under the terms of a licence issued by the Copyright Licensing Agency, Barnards Inn, 86 Fetter Lane, London EC4A 1EN (http://www.cla.co.uk). Applications for the copyright owner's written permission should be addressed to the publisher.

Printed in the UK by Ashford Press Ltd

For Power Maths online resources, go to:
www.activelearnprimary.co.uk

**Note from the publisher**
Pearson has robust editorial processes, including answer and fact checks, to ensure the accuracy of the content in this publication, and every effort is made to ensure this publication is free of errors. We are, however, only human, and occasionally errors do occur. Pearson is not liable for any misunderstandings that arise as a result of errors in this publication, but it is our priority to ensure that the content is accurate. If you spot an error, please do contact us at resourcescorrections@pearson.com so we can make sure it is corrected.